Controversies in Crime and Justice
series editor Victor E. Kappeler Eastern Kentucky University

D0082478

Controversies in

White-Collar Crime

edited by Gary W. Potter
Eastern Kentucky University

anderson publishing co.
2035 Reading Road
Cincinnati, OH 45202
800-582-7295

Controversies in White-Collar Crime

Copyright © 2002
Anderson Publishing Co.
2035 Reading Rd.
Cincinnati, OH 45202

Phone 800.582.7295 or 513.421.4142
Web Site www.andersonpublishing.com

Library of Congress Cataloging-in-Publication Data

Controversies in white-collar crime / edited by Gary W. Potter.
    p. cm. -- (Controversies in crime and justice)
  Includes bibliographical references and index.
  ISBN 1-58360-514-2 (pbk.)
  1. Commercial crimes. 2. White collar crimes. 3. Globalization. I. Potter, Gary W. II. Series.

HV6768 .C66 2001
364. 16'8--dc21

00-048543

Cover design by Tin Box Studio, Inc.

EDITOR Gail Eccleston
ASSISTANT EDITOR Genevieve McGuire
ACQUISITIONS EDITOR Michael C. Braswell

Acknowledgments

Compiling an edited volume of original works from the best scholars in the field is a more prodigious task than it might at first seem. Simply deciding on the organization for the book and themes to be addressed while surveying the body of empirical work on white-collar crime was probably the hardest part. The task was made much easier and very pleasant by the excellent work done by the contributors for this volume, and the high degree of collegiality and cooperation they showed toward me. In that I was imposing on their already ambitious scholarly endeavors and their valuable time, I will be forever grateful for their generosity and enthusiasm.

In addition to the those who did the writing for this volume, many others helped out as well, including, I suspect, some who didn't even know they were helping. Vic Kappeler, who is the series editor, is someone I have worked with many, many times. He allowed me to proceed in my quirky way, and removed the obstacles that cropped up from time to time. He also, as always, overlooked my idiosyncrasies and various personality disorders as the work progressed. We work well together and I hope we will continue to do so for the rest of my academic career. I also need to thank an unwitting accomplice in this task, Helen Eigenberg of the University of Tennessee at Chattanooga. Whether she knows it or not, Helen was largely responsible for how the theme of this work came together. A couple of years ago, sitting in the bar, at an ASC meeting in Washington, Helen lectured me (or as she might put it, engaged in a consensus-building discourse with me) on the fact that I had consistently failed to embed basic elements of feminist theory in my work. She was particularly irked by a chapter, of which I had been the primary author, in *The Mythology of Crime and Criminal Justice*. I've never forgotten her admonitions, and have tried to do better in subsequent work. But, it was largely her suggestions that led me to try to highlight themes of gender, race, and class in the present volume. In addition to Vic and Helen, some other people also played a role in helping me put this book together through their advice and suggestions were Marjorie Zatz at Arizona State University, Laureen Snider at Queens College, Kitty Calavita at the University of California – Irvine and Mickey Braswell at East Tennessee.

I also want to thank to thank my wife, Karen Miller, who worked with me on this project. In that our research interests often diverge and in that working with me on any writing project is often, politely put, trying, we usually go our own ways in scholarly endeavors. But this time I was able to persuade her to work with me on a chapter and to help me tidy up after my very untidy practices with regard to endnotes and references. She made the project much easier and more fun than it otherwise would have been. I hope we will work together again in the near future.

Finally, I need to thank everyone at Anderson Publishing who always makes getting a manuscript from paper to the the finished book easy.

Preface

Controversies in White-Collar Crime introduces the topic of white-collar crime in the tradition of Edwin Sutherland, as "crime committed by a person of respectability and high status in the course of his occupation." The chapters written for this volume tackle all the major controversies related to white-collar crime: issues of definition, questions of harm and cost, conflicts of interest in enforcement and control, and questions of public policy. But the chapters written for this volume go far beyond the normal discourses of criminology, law and political science. They situate white-collar crime in a political-economic and social reality that captures its true scope and true threat. White-collar crime is not a pathology, not an aberration, not a dysfunction, but a normative exercise in doing business and making law in contemporary society. White-collar crime, in all its ramifications, from workplace crime, to graft and bribery, to corporate crime, and to political crimes by the state, is simply the way the we produce and sell products, the way we make law and adopt policy, the way we manage the lives of billions of people around the world.

The enormity of the issue is what this volume has tried to capture. At the turn of millennium, white-collar crime has gone global, impoverishing, subjugating, defrauding, maiming, killing, and disenfranchising those without "respectability and high status" in every corner of the world. It is ironic, but little discussed, that those most victimized by white-collar crime are also those most victimized by "street crime" and, not coincidentally, by those policies enacted by the state to control street crime. Women, who bear the brunt of violent victimization in a most personal and intimate way around the world, despite the pandering state and media portrayals of "stranger violence" and "random violence," also bear the brunt of white-collar victimization. From corporate violence, to the political use of rape, to economic deprivation, to sexual harassment, it is women who are the special targets of those criminals of "respectability and high status." Just as they are the primary victims of violent street crime, and just as they are the primary victims of the criminal justice system, racial, and ethnic minorities are selected for special carnage and degradation by white-collar criminals. From environmental racism, to the dumping of unsafe products, to the economic slavery perpetuated by international debts and the global reach of corporate enterprise, ethnic and racial minorities, from Nazi Germany of the 1930s to the African famines of the 1990s, face white-collar genocide. And finally, as

Sutherland so clearly implied, it is those without "respectability and high status," who die in the factories, who eat the poisoned food, who are subjected to the dangerous and fraudulently tested drugs, who die in the nursing homes and are turned away by the hospitals. Objectively white-collar crime is defined by class; objectively white-collar crime denies economic, political, social, and human dignity to the overwhelming majority of people in this world who work at dangerous and alienating jobs and who give their lives to make others rich, respectable, and of high status. The articles in this volume seek to embed race, class, and gender as fundamental to any explication of white-collar crime.

The volume opens with a general introduction to many of the issues related to white-collar crime, in "Thinking About White-Collar Crime," by Gary Potter and Karen Miller. Discussions of cost and harm, legality, and the rending asunder of the social fabric of contemporary society are addressed.

In Chapter 2, "White-Collar Crime," Gil Geis, no doubt the preeminent American scholar on this topic, discusses the evolution and development of theory and research on white-collar crime. Geis addresses the role of individualism, capitalism, and power in the etiology of white-collar crime. He then traces the development of theory and research from Sutherland's classic writings on the topic to work by Clinard, Merton, and Bell. The chapter provides a compelling critique of the Yale white-collar crime research, as well as a critique of subsequent work by Gottfredson and Hirschi. Geis concludes the chapter with a look at recent research and new directions in scholarship.

In Chapter 3, "State-Corporate Crime in a Globalized World: Myth or Major Challenge?," David Friedrichs, the author of the very important text on white-collar crime, *Trusted Criminals*, expounds on one of the new avenues of research discussed by Geis, state-corporate crime. Friedrichs carefully elucidates the origins of the concept and disposes of socially constructed neutralizations proposed by the state and corporations to excuse their criminality. He then discusses important examples of state-corporate crime, including a compelling summary of his work on the role of state-corporate crime in the development of the Nazi state in Germany. The chapter concludes with a terse and parsimonious theory of state-corporate crime and with a discussion of mechanisms of control.

In Chapter 4, "Toward an Understanding of Academic Deviance," the eminent legal scholar, Bankole Thompson, tackles a little-discussed and definitionally difficult aspect of white-collar crime, white-collar deviance in academic settings. Thompson presents both legal and conceptual conundrums and then provides a model for understanding academic deviance in the reified world of scholarship and academic integrity.

Chapter 5, "A Critical Model for the Study of Resource Coloniziation and Native Resistance," begins the exploration of gender, race, and class as defining elements of white-collar crime. Linda Robyn's compelling case study of the struggles of indigenous peoples against the power of multinational corporations provides a breathtaking panorama of the sweep of white-collar crime and the complexity of trying to resist that sweep. Focusing on the Chippewa people of Wisconsin, Robyn details the cultural conflicts inherent in centuries of colonization and victimization by white Europeans. She clearly explicates the spiritual harms inflicted on an indigenous people by the imposition of cultures of greed and exploitation on a society defined by cooperation, harmony, and environmental respect. She then turns to a discussion of the social, economic, and political conflicts between the Chippewa and state-corporate criminal actors, including one of the major criminal recidivists of the twentieth century, the Exxon corporation. Robyn portrays in detail the many and varied harms that state-corporate crime inflicts and the extreme difficulties and frustrations of attempts to resist that harm. This case study is one of the most important pieces of empirical research produced in the last decade on corporate crime. It is classic in both its detail and clarity.

Chapter 6, "Toxic Crimes and Environmental Justice: Examining the Hidden Dangers of Hazardous Waste," builds upon this theme with a compelling discussion of environmental justice by Mike Lynch, Paul Stretesky, and Danielle McGurrin. The authors present a definition of toxic crime and then delineate its social organization. They follow with an in-depth discussion of environmental justice, both detailing case study research on Hillsborough County, Florida, and reviewing the full-range of scholarly studies on environmental justice and toxic crime. They close with five additional case studies. This chapter defines an important new area of research in white-collar crime and explicitly ties corporate violence and toxic crime to issues of race and class. The chapter presents groundbreaking research into little explored areas of respectable criminality and constructs a theoretical approach that clearly demonstrates that those most exploited by society will also be those targeted as corporate victims of toxic crime.

David Simon, the author of the highly regarded text *Elite Deviance*, tackles yet another area of white-collar crime in Chapter 7, "The Scandalization of America: Political Corruption in the Postmodern Era." Simon looks at the world of political crime, profiling cases ranging from the Kennedy assassination, to FBI and CIA repression of dissent, to Watergate through Iran-Contra and Iraqgate. Simon's description of political crime demonstrates how normative criminality is to the operation of the state in the late twentieth century and strongly suggests that, as we enter the postmodern era, we face government by scandalization as the last pretenses of a democratic state are wiped away by rampant state criminality.

In Chapter 8, "Downsized by Law, Ideology, and Pragmatics – Policing White-Collar Crime," Anne Alvesalo of the Finnish Police College takes on the issue of controlling, regulating, and policing white-collar crime. She asks the compelling question of why non-enforcement is the policy for white-collar crime while over-enforcement is the policy for the crimes of the poor. In answering this question, Alvesalo explicates the difficulties of definitions in white-collar crime, particularly as those definitions relate to the law. She strongly suggests that obfuscation and legal constructions in this area are reflections of power in society and then reflects on the difficulties caused by those legal anomalies and problems of definition. She concludes with a clear and concise discussion of the role and limitations of the criminal law in regulating white-collar crime and the constraints on policing produced by the vagaries of definition and law. The chapter concludes with a strong analysis of the complexity of white-collar crime enforcement and the social processes that hamper it.

In Chapter 9, "Globalization, State-Corporate Crime, and Women: The Strategic Role of Women's NGOs in the New World Order," Nancy Wonders and Mona Danner expand the dimensions of our discussion by introducing the impacts of globalization and by clearly defining gender as a cornerstone of any discussion of white-collar crime. Wonders and Danner make a compelling case that it is the hyper-exploitation of women that is a major factor driving the globalization of state-corporate crime. They contend that "old" crimes and outrages, no longer tolerated in western industrial nations, are now being replicated with increased ferocity in less-developed nations. This hyper-exploitation is driven by the enormous economic and political power possessed by transnational corporations and subsequent weakening of the state in an era of globalization. That the burden of these developments is borne by women is made obvious in their discussion of the impact of economic displacement, unfair and unsafe work practices, environmental harms, and increased militarism. Finally, the authors suggest the futility of state legal apparatuses as means of controlling these crimes and ameliorating these harms, suggesting that the burden of controlling state-corporate victimization rests with women's nongovernmental international organizations. They discuss the development these organizations and the limitations of international law and conclude by pointing to the history of women's organizing efforts around the world as models for resisting state-corporate victimization.

This volume concludes in Chapter 10, "States, Corporations, and the 'New' World Order," by Frank Pearce and Steve Tombs, with a detailed theoretical and empirical discussion of globalization. Building upon Pearce's classic and seminal work *Crimes of the Powerful: Marxism, Crime and Deviance*, published in 1976, Pearce and Tombs observe the workings not just of transnational capitalist enterprises, but the also of the state, in creating a new hegemony, which will take state and corporate crime international in the new millennium. The development of "neoliberalism," particularly in the United States and the United Kingdom is explored in detail, with the strong suggestion that this is the ideological banner under which global impoverishment and exploitation will be advanced. Pearce and Tombs look in detail at the impact of globalization on the distribution of wealth and income, and the impact of mega-mergers and increasing corporate economic concentration. They make clear that the ideological response to the need for regulating corporate crime is in fact to deregulate it under global-ization as a new hegemonic order, thus allowing the "market" to select its own victims and its own crimes. The authors explore the role of the state in this process and challenge the notion that state sovereignty has given way to cor-porate globalization. Ultimately Pearce and Tombs argue, as Pearce did 25 years ago, that politics must be brought back into the discussion of white-col-lar crime, and even more importantly that the concepts of class and resistance must be brought back into both political and criminological analyses. Pearce and Tombs have set the stage for the next level of discourse on white-collar crime and for discussions of both legal and extralegals controls.

The discussions presented in this volume are staggering in their expli-cations of the enormity of the white-collar crime problem. They are also encouraging in that they situate this issue clearly where it should be, raising issues of race, class and gender, and challenging the hegemony of the "new world order." The work done by these authors will revitalize and regenerate the debate. Speaking only for myself, as the editor, that is a most encourag-ing development. It is a development that will be played out in the conflicts between and among powerful economic actors, between and among those actors and the various governments they will try to dominate, played out in the struggles of the women's movement, the labor movement and struggles of ethnic and racial minorities for basic dignity and justice. The issues pre-sented here will be the subject of argument in corporate boardrooms, the edifices of governmental injustice, and, perhaps most importantly, in the streets. The demonstrations that disrupted the World Trade Organization meetings in Seattle in the Spring of 2000, the demonstrations that disrupt-ed the Republican and Democratic conventions in Philadelphia and Los Angeles in the summer of 2000, and the mass protests at G-8 Meetings in Geneva in July 2001, may be among the most optimistic developments of all.

Gary Potter
Volume Editor

Table of Contents

Chapter 7

**The Scandalization of America: Political Corruption
in the Postmodern Era   137**

David R. Simon

Chapter 8

**Downsized by Law, Ideology and Pragmatics - Policing
White-Collar Crime   149**

Anne Alvesalo

CHAPTER 1

Thinking About White-Collar Crime

Gary W. Potter
Karen S. MIller

In his much-read and debated paean to orthodox, conservative crime ideology, *Thinking About Crime*, Professor James Q. Wilson dismisses the importance of white-collar crime in American society by arguing that the essence of "real" crime is (1) the arousal of fear and the occurrence of injury; (2) a rending asunder of the "social contract"; (3) the commission of acts that are not merely dangerous but more importantly "immoral"; and (4) the commission of acts that are clear violations of criminal statutes.[1] To Professor Wilson's way of thinking, crimes committed by those with economic and social power are really ambivalent acts for which condemnation is apparently a matter of personal taste. He says:

> By contrast, while some nations punish businessmen who form industrial trusts, others elevate such men to peerage. Some nations think the quality of the environment or the safety of cars or the corruption of political life are largely private matters; others think they are public ones. But all nations punish, in the name of the state, theft and unjustified violence.[2]

So, price-fixing, anti-trust violations, pollution, dangerous working conditions, bribery, and unsafe consumer products could be, in Professor Wilson's view of the world, both private affairs and even honorary acts. In fact, Professor Wilson gets somewhat indignant about the whole topic, arguing:

> To me, and I suspect most citizens, all this seems obvious, and thus one should not have to apologize for writing a book about predatory crime and leaving to others the important task of writing about "white-collar" crime. But some leftist intellectuals are so preoccupied with turning all discussions of social problems into an attack on the prevailing economic and political order that their customary response to the public's concern with street crime is to change the subject.[3]

1

Not wanting to incur Professor Wilson's wrath, let's not change the subject. No one disputes that "street crime" is a serious problem with serious consequences, despite an unbroken, 27-year pattern of declining victimization.[4] But, like many conservative intellectuals so preoccupied with justifying repressive crime control policies and so insistent upon apologizing for the immoral behavior of the powerful that makes a mockery of the social contract, Professor Wilson protests too much. The facts of "white-collar crime" are simple. In any given year, it causes exponentially more economic damage than all street crimes put together. In any given year, it kills, maims, and injures exponentially more innocent people than all street crimes combined. It makes the social contract a social joke by violating obligations to consumers, employees, and the state. In the words of C. Wright Mills, it mocks social and political order by creating a "higher immorality."[5] And, as Clinard and Yeager point out, it reveals what Professor Wilson feels to be ambivalence, as what it really is, social hypocrisy of the most despicable kind:

> Corporate crime provides an indication of the degree of hypocrisy in society. It is hypocritical to regard theft and fraud among the lower classes with distaste and to punish such acts while countenancing upper-class deception and calling it "shrewd business practice." A review of corporate violations and how they are prosecuted and punished shows who controls what in law enforcement in American society and the extent to which this control is effective. Even in the broad area of legal proceedings, corporate crime is generally surrounded by an aura of politeness and respectability rarely if ever present in cases of ordinary crime. Corporations are seldom referred to as lawbreakers and rarely as criminals in enforcement proceedings. Even if violations of the criminal law, as well as other laws, are involved, enforcement attorneys and corporation counsels often refer to the corporation as "having a problem": one does not speak of the robber or the burglar as having a problem.[6]

So, let us begin thinking about white-collar crime by addressing the issue of heinousness, both economic and predatory.

White-Collar Crime, the Arousal of Fear and the Occurrence of Injury

The Cost of White-Collar Crime

In simple calculations of economic loss it is clear that losses from white-collar crime exceed losses from "street crimes" by an enormous margin in any given year. The economic losses resulting from street crimes are generally estimated by the FBI's *Uniform Crime Reports* to be between $10 billion and $13.5 billion a year.[7] The total economic damage from white-collar crime exceeds this total in every category. For example, Clinard and Yeager estimated the annual cost of corporate crimes to be between $174 billion and $231 billion a year.[8] A 1982 analysis of the costs of corporate crime by *U.S. News & World Report* estimated that price fixing, false advertising, corporate tax evasion, and corporate fraud cost $200 billion a year.[9] The General Accounting Office established the annual loss from healthcare fraud at $70 billion a year.[10] Researchers estimate that employee theft, pilferage, and embezzlement cost about $200 billion a year.[11] Medicaid and Medicare fraud cost us about $61 billion a year.[12] Unnecessary surgery costs the public about $4 billion a year.[13] The costs of pollution, occupationally generated disease, adverse patient reactions to unsafe drugs, and the like are impossible to calculate with any degree of accuracy. So the total, very conservative estimate, of economic costs from white-collar crime would be between $509 billion and $566 billion a year, or roughly 38 to 57 times the cost of street crime, and none of this takes into account personal tax evasion by those who are involved in white-collar crime, which is safely estimated to be about an additional $100 billion.

The Occurrence of Injury

Some critics, like Professor Wilson, would tell us that these losses, while significant are spread across 217 million or so consumers, taxpayers, and workers. Being somewhat diffuse these losses are said to be less traumatic and upsetting to the victims than a robbery or burglary. Nonetheless, the loss is still about $2,608 per person, far in excess of the average loss of less than $62 from street crimes. But conservative critics would also aver that street crimes cause injury and death, thereby inculcating fear and trauma in potential victims. But even here, the claim of injury and death as an index of the severity of street crime is far too facile. White-collar criminals kill and maim in numbers that are truly staggering. As Steven Barkan points out, conservative estimates of the carnage from white-collar crime would include 55,000 annual deaths resulting from injuries or illnesses occurring at work; 30,000 annual deaths from the sale of unsafe consumer products; 20,000 deaths from various forms of environmental pollution; and 12,000 annual deaths from unnecessary surgery.[14] In addition, about 100,000 workers die each year in the United States from work-related diseases, and an additional 11,000 die from work-related accidents.[15] Somewhere between 12,000 and 16,000 people die each year from unnecessary surgeries.[16] There is no way to determine how many people die from the inappropriate prescribing of prescription drugs; or inadequate nursing home care, or the denial of medical care in order to maximize insurance company profits. Nonetheless, again a very conservative estimate would be that at least 240,000 people die each year as a result of white-collar crime, compared to an annual homicide total of about 23,000, or a ratio of corporate carnage to street crime of about 10 to 1. And these numbers do not reflect the two million workers injured each year on the job because of dangerous working conditions maintained by their employers in violation of prevailing safety standards; or the 380,000 workers who contract new cases of job-related illnesses; or the 20 million serious injuries caused each year by unsafe and defective merchandise produced by corporation and sold to consumers.[17] These 22 million corporate assaults are 26 times the total number of simple and aggravated assaults committed every year in the United States.

The Arousal of Fear

"Fear of crime" is a highly subjective criteria. As we know, many of the public's perceived "fears" are based not on facts but on incorrect perceptions. For example, the public believes violent crime is constantly increasing, but in reality victimizations have been on a steady three-decade decline. The public fears crimes committed by strangers, but in reality they are in far greater danger from friends, acquaintances, and relatives. These social perceptions of crime are largely based on media accounts and official government pronouncements designed to raise levels of public support for Draconian anti-crime initiatives. While the reality may be different, the fear itself is often quite real, but so, too, is the fear of white-collar crime. The fear of white-collar crime has a much more disturbing element. When people walk down the streets they may fear strangers, but they have no trust relationship with those strangers, no contractual agreement with those strangers, no expectation that those strangers will act in their best interests. Such is not the case with white-collar crime. When we go to work we do so as a matter of trust in our employers. We trust they will pay us, we trust they will provide us with a safe environment to carry out our occupational tasks. When we buy a car, or baby food, or tires, or meat, we trust that we are getting what we pay for and that the product will not injure or kill us. When we go to the doctor we trust that this professional, with so much more knowledge and education about the human body, will treat us with proven drugs and proven methods, will refer us to the best specialists, and will not subject us to unnecessary tests or surgeries. When we fill the prescription from these doctors, we trust that the pharmaceutical company has not falsified test results or withheld evidence of dangerous reactions, and that we trust that the medicine will work. When we invest our money we trust that brokerage house or bank to act in our best interests, not in the interests of its brokers or in the interests of other, larger institutional investors. When we elect politicians to office or use tax money to hire police, we trust they will act lawfully and in the interests of society at-large. The problem with white-collar crime is that we trust too much. The most basic agreements that bind

society together are willfully violated by white-collar criminals. The fear produced from such violations of trust causes much more than momentary
alarm, it erodes basic confidence in the social order. And the crimes and predations of criminals who violate that trust are every bit as hideous and hor-
rifying, if not more so, than the predations of street criminals. Consider just
a few examples of situations arousing public fear.

Many people face the difficult and heart-rending decision to place elderly parents, who are either too ill or too frail to care for themselves, in the
care of professionals. Entering into a trust relationship with a nursing home
or elder care facility is an anguished decision. But imagine the anguish
when that trust relationship is violated. Imagine the fear aroused by a situation in which an elderly nursing home resident is allowed to wander out of
a facility, unattended, fall into drainage ditch, and drown. Imagine the
anguish when an Alzheimer's patient simply disappears from a nursing
home never to be found again. Consider the family guilt to be endured when
a nursing home patient's foot develops a bedsore which goes untreated and
develops gangrene and maggot infestation. What about a situation in which
an 89-year-old nursing home patient's hands, face, and vagina swells uncon-
trollably over a 16-day period and the staff fails to notify a physician? Even
when a nurse found that patient with mucus around her mouth, the patient's
vital signs were not checked. The patient died 25 minutes later. What fear
is aroused when a 65-year-old man, suffering from diabetes and crippled by
arthritis, is placed in a nursing home because he can no longer give himself
insulin injections? In that nursing home, the staff administered the wrong
dosage of insulin for seven consecutive days and failed to feed that patient
for hours after his injections, a situation which lowered his blood sugar to
dangerous levels. Upon lapsing into diabetic shock, a nurse forced a feeding
tube through his nose and pumped orange juice into him. Rather than raising his blood sugar levels, the procedure killed him because the tube had
been improperly placed and the orange juice was being forced into his
lungs. Care often lapses into neglect and cruelty in these settings. How
much fear is generated when an 81-year-old Alzheimer's patient is placed in
a nursing home in Alabama and then breaks his hip when slipping in a pud-
dle of his own urine? That patient is then heavily sedated and restrained in
a bed, subsequently developing bedsores. Two months after entering the
nursing home at 182 pounds, he dies, weighing only 94 pounds. In one nursing home, staff members slapped, pinched, and forced a bar of soap into the
mouth of an elderly woman who they felt complained too much about her
care. In another case, an Alzheimer's patient was strangled by a restraining
device used to keep her in bed.[18]

Fear when one is walking on a dark street in the early morning hours is
one thing. But what about fear of death and injury when one is going to
work on a daily basis? The contract between employees and companies is
clear. Employees perform tasks during hours of accumulated work which
result in the production of products from which the company profits. For

these hours worked and tasks performed, companies provide workers with salaries and safe working environments. That, after all, is one of the fundamental principles of a capitalist economy. It is a relationship built on a trust agreement between workers and employers. But what level of fear is generated when a worker arrives at his or her job at the Imperial Food Products plant in Hamlet, North Carolina, and dies in a fire? On September 3, 1992, a fire started in one of the grease vats in the frying room at that plant. Twenty-five employees were killed and 56 more were seriously injured. The plant had no sprinkler system, no fire alarm, and the fire exits had been padlocked by management. There had not been a single safety inspection of the plant in the 11 years it was operating.[19] In another case, Utah Power and Light Company was cited for 34 safety violations at one of its coal mines. Subsequently, a mine fire killed 27 miners. Nine of the uncorrected safety violations were found to be directly responsible for that fire.[20] In yet another case, Costain Coal Inc. pled guilty in 1993 to 23 felony counts and six misdemeanor counts involving violations of Mine Safety Act and making false statements with regard to health and safety standards at their Kentucky mine where a 1989 explosion had killed 10 workers.[21] Rockwell International Corporation pled guilty to three felony counts and paid a $6.5 million fine resulting from a 1994 chemical explosion that killed two of the company's scientists. The explosions resulted from the illegal storage and disposal of hazardous waste, specifically an explosive used as a gun propellant. The explosion occurred when the two men were illegally burning the waste to dispose of it.[22] American Steel was cited by the Occupational Safety and Health Administration for violating safety standards requiring fall prevention devices two weeks after a construction worker fell to his death after being hit by a steel brace that snapped free. The company's fine was $720.[23]

Can we seriously claim that the employees of Decoster Egg Farms, one of the country's largest egg producers, are more fearful of street predators than their employers? At Decoster's plant in Turner, Maine, more than three million chickens produce almost 14 million eggs a week. Workers at the plant worked in shifts of 10 to 15 hours a day. The workers were provided with no safety equipment. They collected and discarded dead chickens with their bare hands. They handled Salmonella-infected manure without wearing gloves. On a daily basis, they were exposed to life-threatening electrical hazards. Workers injured on the job were routinely left untreated. One worker lost three fingers in a machine used to scrape chicken manure from the barns. As many as 12 people lived in one 10' by 60' trailer. Living quarters featured live electrical connections, inoperable smoke alarms, and a septic system so overtaxed that toilet content backed up several inches into shower tubs. In 1997, the company settled Labor Department charges by paying $2 million in penalties and agreeing to pay full restitution and back wages to workers.[24]

Should we be more fearful of the relatively rare murderer in American society (the odds of being murdered are about 12,000 to 1), or more fearful of the omnipresent asbestos industry? As early as 1934, major asbestos manufacturers in the United States were aware, as a result of their own research, that exposure to asbestos caused "white-lung" disease in workers and consumers.[25] Two of the largest asbestos manufacturers in the world, Johns-Manville and Raybestos-Manhattan not only were aware of the danger, but covered up the findings by preventing researchers from publishing their work. A third manufacturer, the Philip Carey Company, fired its own medical consultant when he warned them of the dangers of the disease and its progressive nature (the longer the exposure, the worse the disease becomes). Rather than taking the steps necessary to protect the health of workers, the asbestos companies engaged in a policy of quietly and surreptitiously settling death claims. Johns-Manville, despite a company-required annual medical exam for its employees, refused to notify workers that they had contracted the disease, thereby preventing early treatment. In 1992, Johns-Manville filed for bankruptcy protection, despite sales of $2.2 billion, in an attempt to ward off lawsuits related to asbestosis.[26] In 1994, a Texas court found three asbestos companies, Owens Corning, Pittsburgh Corning, and Fuller-Austin Insulation, liable for causing disease or death in 11 workers.[27] Needless to say, consumers who were studying in schools full of asbestos and who were being treated in hospitals made "fire-safe" with asbestos, and who were working in plants built with asbestos, were not informed of the danger. It strains reason not to equate these actions with criminal manslaughter, it defies logic not to infer criminal intent, and it requires deliberate obfuscation not to recognize the actions of the asbestos industry as an assault upon the social contract.

Are we, as a society, more fearful of the extremely rare stranger murderer of children or of the corporations that produce goods and products for those children? The H.J. Heinz Company produced 12,000 cases of baby food contaminated with pieces of rubber.[28] The Beech-Nut Nutrition Corporation mislabeled its baby food, claiming that a substance which was primarily colored sugar water was apple juice for babies. The company entered guilty pleas to 215 criminal counts charging that it had intentionally defrauded and misled the public.[29] In 1995, manufactures of the "Luv'N'Care" baby pacifier pled guilty to 14 violations of federal law because their products put babies and very young children in danger of suffocation and choking.[30] A 1995 study found traces of pesticides, all either neurotoxins or probable human carcinogens, in 53 percent of all baby food from major national manufacturers.[31] In 1997, Andrew and Williamson Sales Company, a major fruit distributor in the United States, pled guilty to criminal charges in connection with an outbreak of hepatitis that made 198 school children and teachers dangerously ill. The company fraudulently sold Mexican-grown strawberries to the school lunch program.[32] Odwalla, Inc., a company that bases its advertising on the provision of pure, clean, and nutritious juice drinks, pled guilty to criminal charges of selling contaminated apple juice, which killed a 16-month-old girl and made at least 70 others sick.[33] It is hard to imagine assaults upon more innocent victims and it is hard to imagine that the routineness of such crime does not precipitate the arousal of fear.

What happens to a society that becomes fearful of the arcane, the scientific, the specialized areas of knowledge that common citizens do not possess and have no ability to access? When we go to the doctor and seek treatment for a malady, we trust his or her knowledge, and we trust the efficacy and reliability of the treatments prescribed. But we have great reason to fear what we do not know. When we leave the physician's office and fill our prescriptions at the pharmacy we are assured, as a matter of fundamental trust in both the government and the pharmaceutical industry, that the medicines we receive will be safe, tested, reliable, and effective. It is a misplaced trust, as the following examples make clear. Warner-Lambert, a Fortune 500 drug company, pled guilty in 1995 to felony charges related to its production of an anti-epileptic drug named Dilantin. Shipments of the adulterated drug had been distributed and FDA efforts to determine the potency of the drug shipments had been obstructed.[34] Greentech, Inc. was fined $30 million and pled guilty to marketing Protropin, a synthetic growth hormone, to doctors for uses which had not been approved by the Food and Drug Administration. The prescription drug was recommended for a variety of medical conditions even though it had not undergone clinical trials required for prescription drugs.[35] Copley Pharmaceutical pled guilty to conspiracy charges and agreed to pay a fine of $10.65 million after changing FDA mandated manufacturing methods for its prescription drugs; falsifying batch records submitted to the FDA; and submitting false annual reports to the FDA.[36] Abbott Laboratories had to withdraw its anti-infection drug Omniflex from the market after it was directly linked to 50 adverse reactions and three deaths.[37] Ortho Pharmaceutical Corporation paid a $5 million criminal fine for obstructing justice in a government investigation of its advertising claims that Retin-A was an effective agent for treating sun-wrinkled skin. Retin-A is a drug approved for the treatment of acne, not photoaged skin. Ortho Pharmaceutical had ordered its employees to destroy documents related to Retin-A and wrinkled skin.[38] In 1995 three executives of the C.R. Bard, Inc., a manufacturer of balloon tips used in angioplasty, pled guilty to 391 counts of fraud. Bard had concealed from the FDA malfunctions in its products, including balloon ruptures, deflations, and breakages, which caused serious heart injuries resulting in emergency coronary bypass surgery. All told, 22,000 people had used the catheters before they were recalled, at least one of them died, and at least 10 patients had to undergo emergency heart surgery.[39]

If the punishment should fit the heinousness of the crime, then our crime control policies have missed the mark by a wide measure. Professor Wilson's emphasis on "predatory crime," a misleading term at best, in that white-collar crime is every bit as predatory as street crime, is fundamentally misleading. First, it deceives us into thinking that our "fear" of street crime can be translated into action. Virtually every criminologist in America, Professor Wilson's protestations notwithstanding, recognizes that there is very little the police, the courts, and the prisons can do about street crime. At best, we can respond to them, but controlling or preventing them is beyond the purview of criminal justice. The clear linkages of violent crime and theft to the state of economy, the gender of both victim and perpetrator, and the age of the criminal, place solutions to the crime problem squarely at the feet of a system of institutional class, gender, race, and age discrimination in the United States. The only thing the criminal justice system can do about street crime is to reduce its considerable overreach in defining incivility, nuisance, and personal morality as matters of the criminal law. But more importantly, Professor Wilson deflects our attention from another simple fact. As we have seen all of the violent crime, all of the property crime, all of the crime we concentrated the immense resources of the criminal justice to combat is less dangerous and less threatening than white-collar crime. As Bertram Gross would say, Professor Wilson is concealing the criminal justice system's "dirty little secret:"

> We are not letting the public in on our era's dirty little secret: that those who commit the crime which worries citizens most—violent street crime—are, for the most part, products of poverty, unemployment, broken homes, rotten education, drug addiction, alcoholism, and other social and economic ills about which the police can do little if anything. . . . But, all the dirty little secrets fade into insignificance in comparison with one dirty big secret: Law enforcement officials, judges as well as prosecutors and investigators, are soft on corporate crime. . . . The corporation's "mouthpieces" and "fixers" include lawyers, accountants, public relations experts and public officials who negotiate loopholes and special procedures in the laws, prevent most illegal activities from ever being disclosed and undermine or sidetrack "overzealous" law enforcers. In the few cases ever brought to court, they usually negotiate penalties amounting to "gentle taps on the wrist."[40]

If, as Professor Wilson suggests, "the arousal of fear" and the "occurrence of injury" are the hallmarks by which we should judge our crime control policies, we clearly have the wrong people in prison.

Rending the Social Contract Asunder

Perhaps there is something other than carnage that should capture our attention. After all, as Professor Wilson suggests, crime does serious damage to the fabric of the social contract which holds civil society in place. The concept of a social contract implies that society is held together by an agreement between citizens and property owners. The enforcement mechanism for that contract is governmental authority. We, as citizens, are required to surrender some degree of our autonomy and some portion of our individuality so that a government of laws can act in the common good. The social contract, as Professor Wilson implies, regulates and protects society by the rule of law, and makes those who break those rules subject to punishment.[41] Professor Wilson argues that predatory criminals rend asunder the social contract by breaking those rules and defying the law. But white-collar criminals do the same. They defy the law, they break the rules, and they go further. White-collar criminals bring into question the legitimacy of the social contract itself by corrupting the lawfulness of the very government created by that contract.

Hyundai Motor Company pled guilty to violations of the Federal Election Campaign Act in the 1992 elections and paid a criminal fine of $600,000. In that same election, Korean Airlines was fined $250,000, Daewoo International was fined $200,000; and Samsung America was fined $150,000, all for making contributions to political candidates in violation of the criminal law.[42] Sun-Land Products, a major producer of nuts and dried-fruits, paid a $400,000 criminal fine for making illegal contributions to the 1992 Bush-Quayle presidential campaign.[43] Crop Growers Corporation, the second largest seller of crop insurance in the United States, paid a $2 million criminal fine for making illegal campaign contributions in the 1994 elections.[44] Tyson Foods paid $6 million in fines and expenses in a public corruption case involving the distribution of gratuities to the Secretary of Agriculture in relation to USDA regulations that required food processors to place safe handling instructions on their products.[45] Illegal campaign contributions were made to both the Dole and Clinton campaigns in the 1996 presidential election by Empire Sanitary Landfill. The company pled guilty to criminal charges and paid an $8 million fine.[46] These blatant attempts to curry favor with the government established to enforce the "rule of law" are certainly more egregious assaults upon the social contract than the predations of "street criminals."

Influence peddling and corporate bribery are not limited to elected officials and politicians; they find equally fertile ground in foreign policy and defense. Unisys bribed three former high-ranking Navy officials.[47] General Electric pled guilty to defrauding the federal government out of $26.5 million in the sale of military equipment to Israel in 1992. As part of this conspiracy General Electric paid millions of dollars in bribes to a former Israeli Air Force General.[48]

Can it be argued with any degree of seriousness that predatory street crime is more subversive to the social contract than white-collar crime, which seeks to subvert the legitimate role of government in establishing foreign policy and a national defense? How many street crimes pose the potential for a nuclear holocaust? A unit of IBM pled guilty to a 17-count criminal information charge involving the unlawful sale of computers to a Russian nuclear lab. IBM admitted that it sold and exported computers to Arzamas-16, the Russian nuclear lab, "having reason to believe that the computers would be used directly or indirectly in research on or development, design, manufacture, construction, testing or maintenance of nuclear explosive devices."[49] Case Corporation pled guilty to two criminal charges involving its sale of heavy construction equipment to Libya in direct violation of prohibitions against supporting commercial or government projects in that country.[50] Teledyne Industries pled guilty to criminal charges that it had illegally exported cluster bomb components, anti-personnel devices that break apart upon hitting the ground, causing massive human injury and death, to Iraq.[51] Baxter International apparently felt it should have its own private foreign policy when it committed a felony by suppling information to the Arab League about its business dealings with Israel in violation of the federal Anti-Boycott statute.[52]

White-collar criminals cannot even be counted on to fulfill their contractual obligations to the government related to the provision of a national defense. Lucas Western pled guilty to 37 counts of submitting false statements and paid a $18.5 million criminal fine in 1995 for certifying to the Defense Department that gear boxes it had manufactured for the F/A-18 aircraft and the Multiple Launch Rocket System were fully inspected, when in fact the required inspections had not been performed.[53] Teledyne Industries also defrauded the U.S. military, pleading guilty to 35 criminal counts and agreeing to pay a $17.5 million fine in 1992 after falsely certifying to the federal government that their electronic relays met rigorous military testing requirements.[54] Teledyne Industries also pled guilty to three felonies in another case involving making false statements to the government in relation to millions of dollars it was paying to "consultants" in order to obtain military contracts from the government of Taiwan.[55] In 1990, Northrop, one of the largest defense contractors in America, paid a $17 million fine after pleading guilty to 34 counts of submitting false statements over a three-year period with regard to the Air Launched Cruise Missile and the Navy Harrier Jet.[56] Litton Industries, another major defense contractor, pled guilty to felony charges and agreed to pay $16.5 million in criminal fines in a conspiracy to defraud the governments of the United States, Greece, and Taiwan in connection with the sale of military equipment. In addition, Litton pled guilty to conspiracy and mail fraud charges.[57] E-Systems, Inc, defrauded the defense department by falsifying test results on Army field radios.[58] United Technologies Corporation pled guilty to four felony counts related to a Marine Corps radar system and the Navy's F-404 jet engines.[59]

Can it be argued with any degree of seriousness that the predations of a burglar, drug dealer, or thief do more damage to the fabric of the social contract than the wholesale corruption of the criminal justice system itself? Can we seriously contend that when the social control system created to punish the predations of street criminals becomes a criminal enterprise that the social contract is not sullied beyond redemption? Consider the following: Dade County Judge Roy Gelber was convicted of racketeering after taking bribes from drug defendants in 1991. Judge Gelber implicated several other judges as well, who had taken a total of $226,000 in bribes. How much damage to the social contract was done by federal district judge Robert Collins of Louisiana who was convicted of bribery, conspiracy, and obstruction of justice in taking a bribe from a drug dealer in return for a lighter sentence? Zapata County, Texas, Judge Jose Luis Guevara was convicted on six drug felonies in 1993. Guevara was caught on videotape welcoming the pilot of a plane loaded with cocaine that had landed at the local airport. How eroded was the public trust when the police chief of Rochester, New York, was convicted on drug trafficking charges in 1991? In Inglewood, California, 15 officers were disciplined for running an illegal bookmaking operation over police department telephones. Also in California, 26 Los Angeles County deputy sheriffs were convicted of skimming millions of dollars from drug money they had seized. The chief of the Newark police department pled guilty to stealing $30,000 from a police fund. Trust and confidence in the social contract was certainly shaken when the sheriff of Bristol, Virginia, killed himself after being indicted for embezzling $377,000. Sixty thousand dollars in cash was found in the sheriff's desk drawer.[60]

But it was in New York City that public confidence in the viability of social contract really took a beating. Michael Dowd and five other NYPD officers were arrested on drug trafficking charges. Dowd was coordinating the operations of an organized crime group made up of 15 to 20 Brooklyn police officers. Three New York City officers were arrested for stealing cash and drugs from crack houses and then meeting in an abandoned coffin factory to apportion the spoils. Thirteen patrol officers and three sergeants from New York's 48th precinct were charged with thievery, perjury, and brutality. One of the officers had stolen $400 from a man buying a Christmas present for his mother and another had stolen a victim's dog.[61]

Outside of the criminal justice system, white-collar criminals do immense damage to the rule of law when they misuse the trust the public has placed in them by electing them to high political office for personal gain. For example, Governor Guy Hunt of Alabama stole money from his own inauguration funds for personal use. Guy Tucker, the governor of Arkansas, was convicted of fraud and conspiracy in relation to the Savings and Loan scandals. Catalina Vasquez Villapondo, the Treasurer of the United States, in a case full of irony, pled guilty to tax evasion in 1994. Secretary of the Interior James Watts was convicted of attempting to mislead a grand jury investigation of influence peddling in the Reagan administration. U.S. Representative Caroll Hubbard, Jr., from Kentucky, drew a three-year prison sentence in a conspiracy to file false campaign finance reports. Congressman Joseph Kolter of Pennsylvania was convicted of conspiring to defraud taxpayers. The Speaker of the Rhode Island House of Representatives was fined after introducing numerous legislative bills designed solely to enrich himself. The treasurer of Orange County, California, managed to bankrupt one of the richest counties in the United States. He pled guilty to six criminal charges, including misappropriation of public funds and making false material statements. In a double-edged assault upon both the secular and spiritual public trust, Congressman Walter Tucker III, also an ordained minister, was convicted of extorting bribes while serving as the mayor of Compton, California.[62]

Even when we try to abide by the spirit of the social contract and do the most good for the most people, white-collar criminals still defile the social contract. If acts of charity lead to the gates of heaven, they also apparently lead to the gates of prison. William Aramony, the president of the United Way, the largest charitable organization in the United States, was convicted of fraud and money-laundering as a part of a 71-count criminal indictment. Aramony misappropriated $1.5 million in United Way monies, and liberally salted the United Way payroll with relatives and close friends. Dallas evangelist Robert Tillman was fined $80,000 by a judge when he refused to provide information related to healing miracles he claimed he could perform as part of his telem-inistries fund-raising. And California televangelist and minister Tony Alamo was jailed for tax evasion and failing to file personal tax returns.[63]

Crime as a Violation of Criminal Statutes

One of the most effective and nefarious neutralizations used by those who wish to deflect attention from white-collar crime is the claim that mur-der, rape, armed robbery, assault, and the other "street crimes" are clear vio-lations of criminal statutes, while white-collar crimes are simply some kind of aberration in compliance with pesky rules and regulations governing the conduct of business. Professor Wilson suggests exactly this when he asserts that predatory crime should be given precedence because it involves willful violations of the criminal statutes. While there is a very good argument to be made that much corporate and professional behavior which is not covered by the criminal law ought to be as a simple matter of social justice and a simple assessment of social harm, it is not necessary to make that argument in order to suggest that Professor Wilson has grossly misstated the case.

Some confusion over the issue of criminality emanates from the more polite names we give to white-collar robbery, assault, murder, and theft. But politeness aside, we may rest assured that price-fixing; fraud; restraint of trade; false advertising; environmental pollution; and the production of unsafe products for the consumer market, are every bit as criminal as the FBI's Index crimes. A quick review of some of these criminal acts should suf-fice to put aside the canard that white-collar crime isn't really statutory crim-inality after all.

Price-Fixing and Restraint of Trade

There is no serious argument to be made that when corporations engage in price fixing and restraint of trade, they are not engaged in violations of the criminal statutes. In fact, it is impossible to argue that when they engage in these acts they are not doing so in a deliberately premeditated manner, in that it would be impossible to commit these crimes without considerable planning and coordination. It is furthermore impossible to argue that these crimes do not do egregious social harm. International conspiracies to fix prices and limit competition, costing consumers billions of dollars, have recently been prosecuted in several vital industries, including food preservatives and additives, the international vitamin market, the production and sale of milk and dairy products, the thermal fax paper market and the production of graphite electrodes, essential for the steel-making industry.

In the food processing industry, at least four major international conspiracies have resulted in criminal convictions during the 1990s. In the largest and most complex of these, Archer Daniels Midland (ADM), whose advertising tells us that it is the "supermarket to the world," was fined $100 million after pleading guilty to participation in a conspiracy to fix prices and eliminate competition in the food preservative and additive industry. ADM's price-fixing cost consumers at least $500 million in added costs.[64] In the second conspiracy to fix prices of food preservatives, Hoechst AG paid a $36 million criminal fine and pled guilty to charges that it had participated in a 17-year conspiracy to fix prices in the sorbate industry. Sorbates are preservatives used in cheese, dairy products, and baked goods. Also pleading guilty and paying a $21 million fine was Nippon Goshei, a large Japanese chemical processor and Eastman Chemical Company was fined $11 million.[65] In the third international food additive conspiracy, Pfizer, Inc., the fourth largest pharmaceutical company in the United States, pled guilty and was fined $20 million for participating in an international price-fixing conspiracy involving the food additives sodium erythorbate and maltol. Sodium erythorbate is a food preservative used in meat, vegetables, and processed foods. Maltol is a flavoring agent used in fruit, candy, and beverages.[66] Finally, Haarman and Reimer Corporation, a subsidiary of the giant pharmaceutical company, Bayer AG, and Cerestar Biopproducts BV, pled guilty in 1997 and agreed to pay a $50 million fine for participating in an international conspiracy to fix prices in the citric acid market. Citric acid is a flavor additive and preservative used in soft drinks, processed food, pharmaceuticals, cosmetics, and detergents. The Citric Acid industry is a $1.2 billion annual enterprise.[67]

In the vitamin industry, F. Hoffman-LaRoche. Ltd. paid a $500 million criminal fine after entering a guilty plea to charges that it engaged in a worldwide conspiracy to fix prices on vitamins. BASF Aktiengellschaft pled guilty and paid a $225 million criminal fine in the same case. Lonza AG, a Swiss vitamin manufacturer, and five of its U.S. executives pled guilty and paid a $10.5 million fine in the same case.[68]

SGL Carbon Aktiengesellschaft pled guilty to criminal violations of the Sherman Antitrust Act and agreed to pay a $135 million criminal fine in 1998 as part of a conspiracy to fix the prices of graphite electrodes, used in the steel industry. Other companies involved in this international conspiracy were UCAR International, Inc., fined $110 million; Showa Denko Carbon, fined $9 million and Tokai Carbon Limited, fined $6 million.[69]

In another recent criminal prosecution, Southland Corporation and Borden, Inc. rigged bids on contracts on milk and dairy products sold to school lunch programs in Florida and to military installations. These two major dairy corporations rigged school milk bids in Florida from the early 1970s through at least 1988.[70]

Finally, Kanzaki Specialty Papers, Inc. and Mitsubishi Corporation pled guilty to charges that they conspired to fix the price of thermal fax paper, a conspiracy which raised prices by at least 10 percent.[71]

Bank Fraud

Bank fraud is a crime, and it is a crime that fundamentally damages the economic foundations of the American economy. Bank fraud is also a common crime and a crime that puts the work of bank robbers to shame. Between 1980 and 1992, 686 Savings and Loans were forced to shut down, two-thirds of them because of acts of fraud. Losses averaged about $12 million for each of these institutions. Another financial institution, Keating Savings and Loan, cost taxpayers $3.4 billion to pay off its debts after it was seized by bank regulators, roughly 100 times the total value of all bank robberies each year in the United States.[72] Recently, Daiwa Bank pled guilty to 16 federal felonies and paid a $340 million criminal fine in 1996 after covering-up massive securities trading losses and then deceiving and defrauding bank regulators. The company pled guilty to two counts of conspiracy, one count of misprison of a felony, 10 counts of falsifying bank records, two counts of wire fraud, and one count of obstruction of justice.[73] Banker's Trust was fined $60 million and pled guilty to three counts of making false entries in bank books and records in 1999. Three Banker's Trust executives were also indicted in the case.[74]

In the biggest bank fraud of all time, the Bank of Credit and Commerce International pled guilty to 29 counts of laundering illegal drug profits.[75] BCCI was the seventh-largest privately owned bank in the world. It had more than 400 branch offices operating in 73 countries. Among its many criminal activities was the laundering of at least $14 billion for the Colombian cocaine cartels; the facilitating of financial transactions for Panamanian president Manuel Noriega and international arms merchant Adnan Khashoggi; the funneling of cash to the contras for illegal arms deals and contra-backed drug trafficking; and the assisting of Philippine President Ferdinand Marcos in transferring his personal fortune, accrued through corruption and graft, out of the Philippines. Despite the enormity of BCCI's crimes and its vital role in drug trafficking, the U.S. Justice Department was more than reluctant to investigate. In fact, the Justice Department had complete information on BCCI's drug and arms operations and its illegal holdings in the United States for over three years before it even initiated an inquiry. Perhaps the reluctance of American law enforcement to interfere with such a major criminal enterprise can be explained by the proliferation of what some have perceived as BCCI's "friends" in the U.S. government holding high office.[76]

Financial fraud is common in other businesses as well. In 1999, Sears Bankruptcy Recovery Management Services paid a $60 million fine related to a massive 12-year scheme designed to defraud individuals engaged in bankruptcy proceedings who were not represented by an attorney.[77] In yet another recent major prosecution, Ryland Mortgage Company pled guilty on two criminal counts related to defrauding the Resolution Trust Corporation, the entity handling compensation payments in the Savings and Loan scandal.[78]

Financial Fraud in the Medical Industry

Defrauding Medicaid and Medicare, two federally sponsored programs for certain low-income people and the elderly, seems to be a major business enterprise in and of itself. Smith Kline Beecham, one of the world's largest drug companies, paid $300 million in fines because it had defrauded Medicare for unneeded blood tests, and Corning, Inc. paid $6.8 million to settle a federal case involving Medicare billings for blood tests that hadn't been requested by physicians.[79] In 1996, Damon Clinical Laboratories pled guilty to fraud charges related to the Medicare Program. The company was fined $35.2 million for performing unnecessary blood tests on Medicare patients.[80] Kimberly Home Health Care Products and its parent company Olsen Corporation pled guilty and agreed to pay a $10 million criminal fine on conspiracy and mail fraud charged in a scheme to defraud the Medicare program through false billings.[81] In yet another case, Allied Clinical laboratories, paid a $5 million fine after admitting that it routinely submitted false claims for medically unnecessary laboratory tests to federal and state health insurance programs.[82]

In a different kind of medical fraud, Blue Cross/Blue Shield of Illinois pled guilty to eight felony counts and paid a $4 million criminal fine, after admitting it concealed evidence of poor performance in processing Medicare claims and artificially inflating performance results. The company falsified some documents and destroyed others related to contract with the government to insure integrity in the Medicare program.[83] Blue Shield of California also pled guilty to three felony counts in a conspiracy to conceal claim processing errors from federal examiners.[84]

In one of the largest healthcare frauds ever perpetrated, National Medical Enterprises, Inc., a corporation that manages more than 60 substance abuse and psychiatric hospitals, paid $379 million in criminal fines and civil damages for instructing administrators to bring patients in for unnecessary and lengthy treatment, billing insurance companies multiple times for the same services, and billing insurance companies when no services were provided.[85]

But, the true extent and scope of healthcare fraud becomes obvious when we consider the criminal conduct of one of the largest healthcare corporations in the United States. Columbia/HCA controls more than 340 hospitals. Columbia/HCA has a simple business plan for increasing profits: cut costs, cut staff, and cut patient services. One of Columbia/HCA's managers, in an interview with ABC's "20/20" said, "I committed felonies every day . . . Let me tell you this – this company is a ruthless, greedy company – period. Employees are the largest operating expense. Cut that to the bone. Cut nursing to the bone. I mean, cut it to as low as your conscience will allow." In the "20/20" interviews, one telemetry technician said she had to watch 72 monitors of heart patients at once. Other employees told the story of a homeless man who was brought to the hospital by paramedics. Because the man had no health insurance: "No tests were run. No blood tests. No X-rays. Nothing. He was given a glass of juice and dismissed, discharged." The man died 30 feet outside the hospital's door. Federal officials raided Columbia hospitals in Tennessee, Georgia, Texas, and Florida, charging that the company was involved in a systematic effort to defraud federal health programs.[86]

Consumer Fraud

Consumer fraud is clearly a crime and in the business world is equally clearly not an uncommon crime. In 1992 California officials accused Sears, Roebuck department stores of fraud in auto repairs by both overcharging customers and making unnecessary repairs. Sears paid auto repair personnel a commission on work they did thereby accelerating the fraud. In the end, Sears agreed to pay $50 million to about 900,000 defrauded customers.[87] ConAgra, Inc., one of the largest food companies in the United States, pled guilty to criminal charges after defrauding farmers and customers. ConAgra fraudulently mis-graded grain, thereby allowing smaller payments to the farmers selling the grain. They then added water to the grain to increase its weight, thereby defrauding the grain buyers purchasing from them.[88]

Tax Fraud

Tax fraud is not just a crime, it is a crime that victimizes every citizen of the United States, it is a crime directed against the very government granted the authority to uphold the social contract. Northern Brand International, a subsidiary of R.J. Reynolds Tobacco, pled guilty to criminal charges that it evaded more than $2.5 million in U.S. excise taxes. The company told U.S. Customs that 26 loads of Canadian cigarettes were being exported to Estonia and Russia, instead the company moved the cigarettes into the United States for sale, obviously without paying federal taxes.[89] Georgia Pacific

Corporation found another inventive way to engage in tax evasion. The company simply made a false claim of $24 million in charitable contributions on its tax returns, a violation of criminal law by any standard.[90]

Environmental Pollution

Sometimes the devastating effects of white-collar crime are harder to quantify and even more difficult to see. In the 1980s one out of every five public water systems in the United States was found to be contaminated to one degree or another.[91] Other research indicates that there are about 30,000 waste sites in the United States that pose a significant threat of water pollution.[92] Violation of clean water laws, often over long periods of time and with obvious criminal intent is a discernible pattern of conduct in several industries, such as the petroleum industry, wood and paper products, the pharmaceuticals and chemical industry, meat packing, and most ironically, the pleasure cruise ship industry, which of course, is totally dependent on water.

In the petroleum industry, Exxon is a career criminal. In 1991, Exxon Corporation and Exxon Shipping pled guilty to criminal violations of federal environmental laws and paid a $125 million fine related to the 11 million gallons of crude oil spilled from the *Valdez* oil tanker, which polluted 700 miles of Alaska shoreline, killed birds and fish, and destroyed the means of making of a living for thousands of Native Americans.[93] Exxon also pled guilty to federal charges related to a 567,000 gallon spill of home heating oil in the narrow waterway which separates New York City from New Jersey.[94]

Other petroleum companies fouling our waterways include the following: Iroquois Pipeline Operating Company and four of its corporate officers pled guilty to violations of the Clean Water Act in 1996 as a result of damage done to nearly 200 streams and wetlands during the construction of a natural gas pipeline. The company agreed to pay criminal fines of $15 million.[95] Colonial Pipeline Company pled guilty to criminal charges in connection with a one million gallon oil dump into the Reedy River in South Carolina. The spill impacted a 23-mile long stretch of the river, killing fish, beavers, muskrats, and turtles.[96] Chevron pled guilty to 65 separate violations of the Clean Water Act in relation to the discharge of oil and grease into the Santa Barbara Channel. Chevron also admitted that it had falsified waste water samples prior to testing by the EPA and lied about the amount of oil and grease it was discharging into the water.[97] Saybolt, Inc., pled guilty to falsifying reports to the EPA and violations of the Foreign Corrupt Practices Act after lying about the oxygen content of reformulated gasoline. Saybolt's business is to be a watchdog corporation testing petrochemicals to ensure that they meet legal standards.[98] Unocal Corporation pled no contest to three felony charges resulting from the discharge of 8.5 million gallons of petroleum and petroleum thinner into the ocean and into groundwater at its Guadalupe, California, oil field over a 40-year period.[99] Doyon Drilling Company, an oil drilling firm in Alaska, pled guilty to 15 criminal charges for illegally discharging oil and other hazardous substances off of the northern coast of Alaska.[100] Marathon Oil pled guilty to criminal charges in relation to a two-year investigation by the FBI of an explosion and house fire. The house, located downstream from the Marathon refinery, was destroyed in a mysterious explosion. Subsequent tests at the discharge point of the refinery's sewage system showed 100 percent levels of explosivity, thus explaining the house fire. The company illegally had been discharging explosive pollutants from its Indianapolis refinery.[101]

Wood and paper products companies were no more careful with water quality in the United States. For example, Ketchilkan Pulp Company, a subsidiary of Louisiana Pacific, pled guilty to dumping sludge and waste water into Alaska's Ward Cove in an intentional dumping act that lasted for five straight days.[102] Dexter Corporation, a Connecticut-based paper company, pled guilty to eight felony counts after purposely disposing of the dangerous chemical carbon disulfate by dumping it into waterways.[103]

The pharmaceutical and chemical industries, in addition to producing unsafe and often fraudulently tested products, also makes a considerable contribution to water pollution. Warner-Lambert, the major pharmaceutical company, pled guilty to criminal charges after routinely releasing excessive levels of pollutants, violating the law at least 347 times, into the Cibuco River in Vega Baja, Puerto Rico.[104] Arizona Chemical Company operates chemical manufacturing plants in Gulfport and Picayune, Mississippi. The company pled guilty to felony violation of the Clean Water Act for manipulating the plant's wastewater treatment system on days the water was to be sampled so that it could meet environmental regulations. In addition, that company also accumulated and illegally stored drums of hazardous waste that it simply mislabeled on inventory sheets as "cleaning oil."[105] Bristol-Myers Squib, a pharmaceutical industry giant, pled guilty to illegally discharging pollutants into the waters near Syracuse, New York. The company conveniently simply discharged its chemical pollutants into the local sewage system.[106]

The meat packing and slaughter industry has also been a prime violator of water pollution laws. John Morrell and Company pled guilty to criminal charges related to the dumping of slaughterhouse waste in the Big Sioux River, in South Dakota and then submitting falsified test data to hide the crime. These illegal discharges occurred over an eight-year period.[107] Also, in 1997, federal judge Rebecca Beech Smith, fined Smithfield Foods and two of it's subsidiary companies $12.6 million for discharging illegal pollutants into the Pagan River in Virginia. Smithfield's subsidiaries operate two hog slaughtering and meat processing plants in Smithfield, Virginia. The ruling found that Smithfield had committed more than 5,000 violations of permit limits for phosphorous, fecal coliform, ammonia, cyanide, oil, and grease. Fecal coliform is an organism found in animal and human waste that is associated with bacteria known to cause serious illness in humans. These violations occurred over a five-year period and seriously degraded the Pagan

River, the James River, and the Chesapeake Bay. In addition, the judge's ruling found that Smithfield has routinely falsified documents and destroyed water quality records.[108]

Among the most egregious polluters of the 1990s were several cruise lines that promised pleasant vacations while dumping waste into the oceans. In 1999, Royal Caribbean Cruises pled guilty to 21 felony counts and agreed to pay a $18 million criminal fine for dumping old and hazardous chemicals in U.S. harbors and along U.S. coastlines, all the time claiming in its paid advertising that it was an environmentally responsible company. Also, in 1999, Palm Beach Cruises and Princess Cruises, Inc., pled guilty to criminal charges for discharging waste oil and dumping garbage off the Florida coast. Regency Cruises pled guilty to criminal charges for illegally dumping plastic garbage into the Gulf of Mexico. Previously, in 1998, Royal Caribbean pled guilty to a conspiracy involving dumping oil into the ocean and then lying to the Coast Guard about their activities. Also in 1998, the company that operates Holland American Line cruise ships, HAL Beheer BV, pled guilty to felony violations involving the discharge of oily mixtures into coastal waters.[109]

Other industries managing to make major contributions to our water pollution problems include mining, shipbuilding and repair, railroad transportation, medical waste disposal and brewing. In 1996, Summitville Consolidated Mining pled guilty to 40 criminal violations of the Clean Water Act, conspiracy charges, and charges of making false statements, and agreed to pay a $20 million fine as the result of a cynanide leak that killed 16 miles of the Alamosa River in Colorado.[110] In shipbuilding and repair, Eklof Marine Corporation, two affiliated companies, and the company's president pled guilty to a series of environmental crimes related to an 826,000 gallon oil spill off Rhode Island in 1996. The negligence of the companies involved caused extensive environmental damage, killing marine and bird life.[111] Also, the Bethship-Sabine Yard in Port Arthur, Texas, a division of Bethlehem Steel, illegally discharged pollutants from its dry dock facility in the Sabine Neches Waterway, thereby endangering coastal wetlands and wildlife in the area.[112] Conrail pled guilty to six felony charges as a result of deliberately discharging oil and grease into the Charles River in Allston, Massachusetts, creating an oil slick hundreds of yards long.[113] In a particularly dangerous case of criminal waste disposal, Browning-Ferris, Inc. pled guilty to discharging contaminated wastewater into the Washington, D.C., sewer system from its medical waste facility and then failing to tell anyone that the dangerous discharge had occurred.[114] And finally, a company which markets itself with commercials of bucolic mountainsides and meandering streams, Adolph Coors Company, the major brewer, pled guilty to two criminal charges after illegally discharging hazardous waste into groundwater and a creek near its Golden Colorado facility, ostensibly the source of its clean and pure Rocky Mountain spring water.[115]

Turning our attention from water to air, consider the current crisis with regard to air pollution. Estimates by the EPA and the Harvard School of

Public Health identify 50,000 to 60,000 deaths each year in the United States as the direct result of particle pollution from manufacturing plants. Particularly at risk are children and the elderly with respiratory diseases and workers living near those plants.[116] In 1990 EPA identified 149 manufacturing plants in 33 states where the air pollution levels in the surrounding communities were considered dangerous.[117] There can be no doubt that criminal violation of air pollution laws endangers the public far more than the predations of all street criminals put together. Recently, Louisiana-Pacific Corporation was fined $37 million and pled guilty to 18 felonies in 1998 for violations of the Clean Air Act. On 12 different occasions Louisiana-Pacific tampered with its mill's air pollution monitor, submitted false reports and samples of its plywood products for testing, and lied to consumers about the quality of its products.[118] American Cynamid pled guilty to building an unauthorized power plant in violation of air quality laws in Rockland County.[119]

Corporations in the United States create 280 million tons of dangerous garbage each year and 10.3 billion pounds of toxic chemicals.[120] The law requires that this waste be disposed of in safe, proper, and careful ways. Failure to do so is a crime that endangers and victimizes everyone. But failing to properly dispose of this waste seems to be more the rule than the exception. For example, ALCOA, the huge aluminum company, pled guilty to environmental crimes, illegally disposing of hazardous waste at its Massena, New York, facility.[121] United States Sugar Corporation pled guilty to eight felony charges involving illegal disposal and transportation of hazardous wastes. The crimes occurred at the company's plant near Lake Okeechobee in south Florida, where the company illegally disposed of highly dangerous lead-based wastes.[122] Chemical Waste Management, a subsidiary of the notorious company Waste Management, Inc., pled guilty to six felony charges when it decided to speed up the clean-up of a dangerous dump site near Scranton, Pennsylvania. Instead of removing and properly disposing of drums containing hazardous substances, the company simply crushed them on site.[123] United Technologies Corporation pled guilty to six felony charges as a result of illegally dumping hazardous waste into the ground at its Stratford, Connecticut, Sirkosky Aircraft Division. International Paper pled guilty to five felony counts for illegally storing and treating hazardous wastes at its mill in Jay, Maine. In addition, the company gave false material statements to regulators concerning the hazardous waste.[124] Consolidated Edison Company pled guilty to four counts of environmental crime when it released 200 pounds of asbestos in the Gramercy Park section of Manhattan. The company not only did not report the release of the asbestos but subsequently denied that it was a result of their operations.[125] And, Eastman Kodak pled guilty to criminal charges related to a 5,100-gallon spill of methylene chloride, a dangerous chemical, and the company's failure to notify governmental authorities of the spill.[126]

More than Criminal, the Immorality of White-Collar Crime

Finally, Professor Wilson argues that predatory street crime is more egregious than predatory white-collar crime because it is immoral. Morality is a complex philosophical topic that far exceeds the provenance of this exposition. Obviously morality is subject to serious issues of interpretation. Questions such as whose morality are valid, particularly when powerful interest groups seek to impose their version of morality on others. Morality is also subject to continual and sometimes rapacious change. Thankfully society's "morality"—for example, related to the role of women—has changed dramatically over the years. But, nonetheless, morality, as it is used by Professor Wilson, had been the subject of criminological discussion and discourse. Without implying endorsement and foregoing the debate for a different time and place, the issue of morality and crime can be defined in the words of Victoria Swigert in this manner: "Shared morals and ethics bind individuals to one another. Without these bonds, society would disintegrate. A legally enforced morality, therefore, is a necessary cost of human association."[127]

But how do we measure immorality? Surely it can be argued that murderers, rapists, armed robbers, burglars, and thieves impair society's bonds. Perhaps it could be argued that the deliberateness of predatory street crimes, the criminal intent to do harm, elevates them to a higher level of immorality. After all, while white-collar crime causes immense economic damage and human suffering, it does so without the cold-bloodedness of a robber's gun in your stomach. In fact, let us recall Professor Wilson's reference to the ambivalence surrounding white-collar crime, whereby in some nations, knighthood would be conferred on the villains. Surely there is a different quality in these acts. In fact, might we not excuse them altogether if they were simply the result of excessive enthusiasm for the social contract itself. After all, if white-collar criminals are merely reacting to the market pressures inherent in a capitalist economy; or to oversights resulting from the zealousness of competition; or to negligence emanating from a desire to move all of society forward with new discoveries and wonders, then we might not just excuse the perpetrators, we might indeed name libraries, universities, and museums after them (the American version of being elevated to peerage). Is it criminal intent that rends the social contract asunder? If so, we might conclude that even if the acts are dirty, the soul is pure.

Well, we might reach such a conclusion if we conveniently omitted any discussion of the facts of white-collar crime. But the illusion that white-collar criminals lack criminal intent is simply that, illusion. For example, we know that the thousands of injuries and deaths that occur each year in factories, mines, and construction sites are not simple matters of carelessness or neglect brought about by the pressures of the marketplace, they are willful criminal acts. Messerschmidt finds that between 35 and 57 percent of on-the-job "accidents" are the result of violations of safety codes and regulations by employers.[128] Schraeger and Short found that 30 percent of all industrial accidents were the result of safety code violations and that another 20 percent were the result of unsafe working conditions.[129] When Chrysler Corporation was fined $1.5 million for exposing its workers to lead and arsenic and 800 other health and safety violations,[130] it simply strains credulity to assume more than 800 concurrent oversights. When 90 percent of the 88 billion pounds of toxic waste produced by American industry is disposed of in violation of the law every year it is hard to imagine how "negligence" and "oversights" can be used as an excuse.[131] When, as we have seen, corporations are convicted of elaborate conspiracies to control markets by fixing prices; deliberate misrepresentation of test results related to pharmaceutical production; tampering with air pollution test equipment, falsifying records about water pollution, and lying about hazardous waste; engaging in massive financial and medical frauds, it is difficult to see how criminal intent, and indeed, extensive criminal planning, was not inherent in the act.

So, if it is not the quality of the act that determines morality, perhaps it is its frequency and prevalence. Perhaps Professor Wilson and others would argue that it is the normalcy of crime for some robbers, thieves, and burglars that troubles morality. Perhaps that argument could be made if it were not more true for white-collar criminals. In the 1990s, alone, Exxon, Royal Caribbean, Rockwell International, Warner-Lambert, Teledyne, and United Technologies were all adjudged to be guilty of more than one serious crime. They were all criminal recidivists. And there is something about their criminal careers that is more chilling, more damaging to our "shared morals and ethics "than the predations of street criminals. Few of us would think of engaging in daily social intercourse with armed robbers. Few of us would find ourselves dependent on armed robbers for medication, fuel to operate our cars, food for our tables, papers for our books, or healthcare for our loved ones. But the reality is that we are dependent on white-collar criminals. We are, by the nature of American society, forced into daily dealings with career criminals who control the necessities of life. Unlike armed robbers, thieves, burglars, rapists, and murderers, we are dependent on criminals for our very survival in the case of white-collar crime. How sinister an immorality is that extortionate relationship?

But before we move on in this discussion, let us point out one obvious fact. Professor Wilson and others who make much of the repeat criminality of few "bad apples" among street predators have really missed the big picture when it comes to white-collar crime. The research shows clearly that crime is a way of life for those respectable citizens who form the ranks of white-collar citizens. It is so much a way of life that it would be not be an overstatement to suggest that crime is the norm rather than the deviation among these high-status offenders. How odd it is to refer to the "immorality" of robbers as deviant and to the "immorality" of white-collar criminals as normative. Consider the facts.

Consider Edwin Sutherland's[132] findings in his ground-breaking research on white-collar crime conducted a half-century ago. Sutherland searched the records of regulatory agencies and commissions, and federal, state, and local courts looking for adverse decisions handed down against the 70 largest corporations in America over a 20-year period:

> Each of the 70 large corporations has 1 or more decisions against it, with a maximum of 50. The total number of decisions is 980, and the average per corporation is 14.0. Sixty corporations have decisions against them for restraint of trade, 53 for infringement, 44 for unfair labor practices, 43 for miscellaneous offenses, 28 for misrepresentation in advertising, and 26 for rebates.[133]

Sutherland found that major corporations engaged in widespread criminality, and they were recidivists, committing their crimes both frequently and on a continual basis (97.1% of the corporations in his study were recidivists). These numbers are even more compelling when one considers that little effort is put into discovering and prosecuting corporate violations; therefore, adverse decisions represent only a tiny portion of the actual crime committed. Later studies have confirmed Sutherland's conclusions.

In 1980, Marshall Clinard and Peter Yeager's findings with regard to crimes committed by the 477 largest manufacturing corporations and the 105 largest wholesale, retail, and service corporations in the United States in 1975 and 1976 are equally disturbing. In that two-year period, these 582 corporations were the subjects of 1,553 federal cases initiated against them. Because these numbers include only cases brought against the corporations, they once again represent a major underestimate of the total amount of crime committed by these corporations. Clinard and Yeager suggest they had uncovered only "the tip of the iceberg of total violations."[134] They found that in just two years, 60 percent of the corporations had at least one action initiated against them, 42 percent of the corporations had two or more actions initiated against them, and the most frequent violators were averaging 23.5 violations per corporation.[135] In the face of these numbers, it is extremely difficult to argue that corporate criminality is random, isolated, and lacking intent.

An investigation of white-collar crime by *U.S. News & World Report* found that during the 1970s, almost 2,700 corporations were convicted of federal criminal charges.[136] The cost to the public from price fixing, pollution, corruption of public officials, and tax evasion was $200 billion a year. Sociologist Amatai Etzioni found that 62 percent of the Fortune 500 companies were involved in at least one act of bribery, price fixing, tax fraud, or environmental crime between 1975 and 1984. A similar study by the *Multinational Monitor* found that the 25 largest Fortune 500 corporations had all been convicted of a criminal act or fined and required to make civil restitution between 1977 and 1990.[137]

So, if it is not the intent of the criminal or the normalcy of the crime that defines "immorality," what other factors can be considered? What might one conclude about the "morality" of defining the very crimes for which one is prosecuted?

When legislators write laws outlawing rape, burglary, armed robbery, larceny, and theft, they do not consult with, negotiate with, or solicit the concerns of the criminals involved. But when legislators enact criminal laws regulating white-collar crime, they actively seek input and advice from those they are ostensibly setting out to criminalize. How immoral is a system of criminal law that is enacted only with the consent of the criminals? How much does such a solicitous concern for the well-being of criminals weaken the social bonds of human association? The history of government regulation of white-collar crime is one of white-collar criminals regulating themselves for their own benefit. The earliest white-collar crime laws were the antitrust acts of the late 1800s. These laws were in fact initiated and supported by the very businesses they ostensibly regulated.[138] Legal prohibitions against monopolies and price-fixing were used by the robber barons to stabilize the market and to make the economy more predictable. Concurrently, these laws were also useful for driving smaller competitors out of business by denying them the use of the same unethical and illegal tactics that the large corporations had used in creating their dominant economic positions. The 1906 Meat Inspection Act is but one case in point. Ostensibly, the Act was passed to protect consumers from spoiled, contaminated meat products. In fact, the meat-packing laws had the full support of the large meat-packing companies because they kept imported meat off the United States market at government expense, and they hindered smaller meat-packing companies by making it hard for them to survive and to compete with the major corporations.[139] The contemporary situation is no different. The automobile industry, for example, has successfully, for at least 30 years, blocked legislation that would criminalize knowing and willful violations of federal automobile safety laws. It is simply impossible to reconcile a law-making process that criminalizes controls on foreign imports, that enacts massive government bailouts, and that provides government assistance to "beleaguered" corporations, with the "morality" of law.

And the "immorality" of the law-making process is clearly reflected in the "immorality" of the marketplace, where free enterprise and competition have become anachronistic slogans. Corporations in the United States have made the most of their ability to define the criminality of their own crimes. They have used the law to create "shared monopolies," entire markets controlled by four or fewer firms.[140] Shared monopolies can now be found in the tire industry, aluminum industry, soap industry, tobacco industry, cereals, bread and flour, milk and dairy products, processed meats, canned goods, sugar, soups, and light bulbs. One hundred corporations, out of the approximately 200,000 operating in the United States, control 55 percent of all industrial assets in the United States. The largest 500 industrial corporations control 75 percent of all manufacturing assets.[141] In the transportation and utilities industries 50 of the 67,000 corporations control two-thirds of the assets in the airline, railroad, communications, electricity, and gas industries.[142] Only 50 of the 14,763 banks in the United States control 64 percent of all banking assets.[143] And in the insurance industry, 50 of 2,048 companies control 80 percent of all insurance assets.[144]

Not only do a few corporations control most of the manufacturing capacity and wealth in America, but they have interlocked their managements, in clear violation of the intent of the anti-trust statutes, in a manner that guarantees they can work in relative harmony with each other in pursuing both market objectives and government protections. Chief executive officers of 233 of the 250 largest U.S. corporations sit on the board on at least one of those 250 largest corporations, many of them sitting on the boards of ostensibly competing corporations, a clear criminal violation of the Clayton Antitrust Act of 1914.[145]

In addition, white-collar criminals enjoy enormous benefits from the laws that do exist. Corporate welfare programs are just one example. Corporate welfare, consisting of tax deductions, tax exemptions, and tax-free investments, amounts to about $448 billion a year, almost four times as much as the United States spends on social programs for the poor.[146] The queen of corporate welfare is the price-fixing, trust creating, Archer Daniels Midland Corporation. As a result of federal protections provided to the sugar industry, ethanol subsidies, and subsidized grain exports, ADM has cost U.S. taxpayers $40 billion between 1980 and 1995. For every dollar in profits made on ethanol sales, ADM costs taxpayers $30. For every dollar in profits made on corn sweetener, ADM costs consumers $10.[147]

It is also important to note that these corporate welfare benefits have not led to over-taxation. During the Roosevelt administration in the 1940s, corporate income taxes made up one-third of all federal tax revenues; by 1996 corporate income taxes made up only 15 percent. In fact, about 90,000 corporations pay absolutely no taxes each year.[148] In the 1991-1992 tax year, Chase Manhattan, one of the largest banking conglomerates in the world, paid a tax rate of 1.7 percent on its $1.5 billion in income. Texaco paid only 8.8 percent of its $2.7 billion in income in taxes.[149]

And it is not just the "morality" of white-collar criminals actively defining the laws under which they are governed that is troubling, but the "morality" of white-collar criminals choosing those who enforce those laws that adds a final insult to the bonds of human association. Imagine the outrage if heroin syndicates were allowed to select the head of the DEA, or the public outcry if burglars were given the task of setting patrol patterns for local police departments. Well, that is precisely the case with white-collar crime. Not only do white-collar criminals write their own laws, they choose their own to enforce those laws.

The law enforcement agents whom the government employ to enforce laws against white-collar criminals are hardly in an adversarial relationship with those they monitor. The white-collar police come to government service from the same industries and corporations they are supposed to be regulating. The enforcement of laws against white-collar crime involve at the very least, cordial relations between enforcers and criminals, and quite frequently involve collaborative relations. Regulators who have come to the government from private enterprise are often more concerned with the needs of the corporations they are regulating than with the safety or economic health of the public. Many of these regulators not only come to white-collar crime enforcement from those against whom they ostensibly will enforce the law, but they also return to those very entities after ending their government careers to work for the companies they regulated.[150] This conflict of interest has been apparent in several cases, but the most blatant example can be found in the Environmental Protection Agency during the Reagan administration. Rita Lavelle was appointed by the president to oversee the government's "superfund" program, designed to clean up the most threatening cases of corporate pollution resulting from improper disposal of toxic waste. She had previously been employed at Aerojet-General Corporation in California. During her tenure at the EPA, she participated in decisions relating to her former employer (a clear conflict of interest), entered into "sweetheart deals" with major polluters, and used the superfund allocations for political purposes. In 1983, Lavelle was convicted on four felony counts.[151]

The law and its enforcement can even be criminogenic in the case of white-collar crime. Probably the best example is the Savings and Loan scandal. The Reagan administration deregulated the savings and loan industry in order to stimulate growth in the banking industry. In addition, they increased insurance protection for depositor's accounts at these institutions from $40,000 to $100,000. The administration argued that deregulation would make S & Ls more competitive. What it did was make them more criminal. Following deregulation, S & L executives began using institutional funds for their private expenses, thereby robbing their own banks.[152] In addition, the new federal regulations allowed the S & L to engage in such practices as accepting deposits contingent upon loans being made to the depositors. The depositors then defaulted on the loans. Not only did those depositors essentially obtain interest-free money to invest in high-risk speculations, but go-betweens were paid very generous "finder's fees" for arranging the loans. The S & Ls profited because the deposits artificially inflated the assets of the bank, which resulted in higher dividends being paid to stockholders and extravagant bonuses being paid to S & L executives.[153] In the end neither the business people who got the phony loans nor the S & L owners and executives (with a handful of exceptions) were held accountable for the billions of dollars in missing cash. The bill was presented to the taxpayers.

Professor Wilson and other "law and order" advocates are quick to argue, albeit incorrectly, that crime can be controlled by "sure, swift, and severe punishment." But in the case of white-collar crime, the opposite is true. The ability to define their own crimes and select their own enforcers makes the risk of apprehension for white-collar criminals very low. The Federal Trade Commission (FTC) offers an excellent example.[154] On an annual basis, the FTC receives about 9,000 complaints. Of those 9,000 complaints, one is referred for criminal prosecution. Of those referred for criminal prosecution, some have been delayed as long as 20 years in going to trial by the corporations involved. The FTC only rarely uses its power to conduct hearings and has been extremely reluctant to use any of the enforcement mechanisms granted to it by law. This laxity in enforcement is not unique to the FTC but has been documented for other agencies as well.[155]

In order to make a successful case against a corporation, defendant cooperation is almost always necessary.[156] Unmotivated, understaffed, underfunded enforcement agencies are not able to litigate even those few cases of corporate crime that actually come to their attention. The result is one of the most bizarre remedial measures found in law, the consent decree. Under the terms of a consent decree, a defendant corporation negotiates with the government over the violations the corporation has committed. It agrees to alter its pattern of conduct. In return, the government agrees that the company will not have to admit guilt. The company does not have to admit its culpability with regard to a crime, but it does have to promise to stop committing the crime, thereby ending the prosecution. The irony of this "sanction" is made clear by Peter Wickman and Phillip Whitten:

> Corporations that have been involved in polluting the environment sign consent decrees with the EPA and announce that they are working on the problem. Imagine the public reaction if a common street criminal were to be dealt with in this fashion. Here's the scene: Joe Thug is apprehended by an alert patrolman after mugging an 85-year-old woman in broad daylight on the streets of Paterson, New Jersey. Brought down to police headquarters, he holds a press conference with the assistant police chief. While not admitting his guilt, he promises not to commit any future muggings and announces that he is working on the problem of crime in the streets.[157]

No matter how serious the crime or how flagrant the violation, the fact is that severe sanctions are rarely applied in the case of white-collar criminals. In their study, Clinard and Yeager found that the sanctions applied to corporate criminals were weak at best.[158] The most common sanction was a warning which was issued in 44 percent of the cases. Following warnings, corporate criminals were assessed fines 23 percent of the time, although those fines were negligible. In 80 percent of the cases, they were for $5,000 or less – hardly a significant sanction to corporations earning billions of dollars a year. The Senate Governmental Affairs Subcommittee noted an even more disturbing fact.[159] Over a 30-month period, 32,000 fines levied against white-collar crime offenders had gone uncollected by the government. In only one and one-half percent of the cases was a corporate officer convicted of a crime, and in only 4 percent of those convictions did the offender go to jail. Even so, their terms of incarceration were very light – averaging 37 days.[160] This pattern appears to be consistent throughout United States history. Albert McCormick Jr. studied antitrust cases brought by the Department of Justice from 1890-1969 and found that only two percent of the violators served any prison time at all.[161]

Sexism, Racism, and U.S. Corporations

Finally, how seriously impacted are those "shared morals and ethics which bind us together" when white-collar criminals advance racism and sexism as their version of "morality." The demeaning and brutalizing impact of sexism and racism is very much a part of America's work environment. Consider how it would feel to go to work at Mitsubishi everyday if you happened to be a woman. In 1996, the Equal Employment Opportunity Commission filed a sexual harassment lawsuit against Mitsubishi Motor Manufacturing of America. The EEOC suit charged that hundreds of female workers had been victimized, and those who had complained had been forced to quit. Among the specific actions cited by the EEOC were (1) a practice by male employees of grabbing female employees' breasts, buttocks, and genitals, including one instance where a male worker put a gun between a female co-worker's legs and pulled the trigger; (2) drawings of various acts of sexual intercourse with female employees' names that were placed all along the assembly line; (3) a practice of supervisors calling female employees sluts, whores, bitches, and other names; and (4) routine questioning of female employees about their sexual habits and preferences.[162]

American corporations also export their sexism. Consider the case of Nike and its practice of subcontracting its shoe production. Nike came under scrutiny in 1996, when CBS News' "48 Hours" ran an exposé on working conditions at its Vietnam plant. Nike workers in Vietnam were being paid 20 cents an hour. Fifteen of the women who worked at the plant were struck on the head by their supervisor as a means of discipline and 45 women were made to kneel on the ground with hands in the air for 25 minutes in another disciplinary incident. One of the women's supervisors returned home to Korea after he was accused of routinely sexually molesting female workers.[163]

While some corporations keep the glass ceiling very low for women, others keep the curtain of racism drawn equally tightly around their executive offices. In November 1996 the *New York Times* ran a front-page story exposing racist comments and discussions by the highest-ranking executives of Texaco, the major oil producer. The comments were made at an August, 1994, meeting about minority employees who had brought a discrimination lawsuit against Texaco. Among the more enlightening comments made by Texaco executives at that meeting were: "This diversity thing. You know how black jelly beans agree." "All the black jelly beans seem to be glued to the bottom of the bag." "I'm still having trouble with Hanukkah. Now we have Kwanzaa." The lawsuit had alleged that Texaco fostered a racially hostile environment. The tapes of the meeting, turned over to the *New York Times* by Texaco's former senior coordinator for personnel services in the finance department, certainly proved the case. Additionally, the tape contained comments from executives about the destruction of company records subpoenaed by the plaintiffs' attorneys.[164] So much for the morality that binds us together.

Conclusion

So, with all due respect and consideration to the "harmfulness" of predatory crime proposed by Professor Wilson, allow us to suggest that it is at least arguable that white-collar criminals meet the necessary criteria, with considerable room to spare, when compared to "street" criminals.

Sadly, the best we could do in this chapter is to refute the canard that white-collar crime is somehow less predatory, less damaging, and less deserving of attention than street crime. But the fact of the matter is that the predations of white-collar criminals are given little attention by the news media, politicians, and even academics. Rather than changing the subject, Professor Wilson and other crime control advocates simply ignore these heinous acts committed by "respectable" people. Agencies funding research into crime are far more concerned about dubious data derived from urine tests on arrestees and unproven models attempting to predict career criminality among the poor than they are about the insidious nature of white-collar crime.

But the shortcomings of our attempt to describe white-collar criminality tell us more about the insidious nature of these crimes than the particulars of the criminal acts we described. The fact is that the hundreds of cases of wanton criminality we discussed in this chapter represent only the tiniest tip of the white-collar crime iceberg. For every successful prosecution of a white-collar offender, there are literally thousands of others never caught or even investigated. For every white-collar offender convicted of a crime and heavily fined or even jailed, there are hundreds of others who face only the mildest of reprimands when confronted by the criminal justice system. And even more debilitating to the social order and the social contract is the fact that for every white-collar offender prosecuted and convicted of a criminal act there are thousands of others whose criminality has been "elevated to peerage" and defined as noncriminal as a result of the millions of dollars in political contributions and the millions of dollars spent on legislative lobbying that has so perverted the law-making, crime-defining process. For every white-collar criminal tried and convicted, thousands of others escape prosecution because of the immense resources they can bring to bear in their defense, often overwhelming prosecutors and investigators, not just in the courts, but in the congress and legislatures.

In the end, protestations from conservative crime theologians aside, the facts are simple. We are in the midst of a white-collar and corporate crime epidemic. These crimes are not aberrations, but simply the normal means of doing business in America. These criminals inflict far more economic harm and predatory violence on this society each year than all varieties of street criminals combined can inflict in a decade. And while we spend enormous sums of money in failed attempts to control street crime through the kinds of ineffective and Draconian crime policies advocated by Professor Wilson and others, we give those primarily white, predominantly male, and exclusively well-off criminals a license to commit carnage. The hypocrisy of such a crime control policy shreds the social contract and mocks any definition of morality. And so, we feel no need to apologize for writing about white-collar crime, unlike so many conservative intellectuals who so blatantly distort the nature of crime by contributing to an unwarranted public hysteria over street crime while going to any lengths to excuse the "higher immorality" of elite criminals.

Notes

1   Wilson, 1975:5.

2   Wilson, 1975:5-6.

3   Wilson, 1975:6.

4   Kappeler, Blumberg, and Potter, 2000:chapter 2.

5   Mills, 1952.

6   Clinard and Yeager, 1980:21.

7   Coleman, 1994.

8   Clinard and Yeager, 1980.

9   *U.S. News & World Report*, 1982 (September 6):25.

10   Andrews, 1994.

11   Greenberg, 1997.

12   Jesilow, Pontell, and Geis, 1993:12.

13   Jesilow, Pontell, and Geis, 1993:19.

14   Barkan, 1997:371-172.

15   Freidrichs, 1996.

[16]   Reiman, 1995; Coleman, 1994.

[17]   Coleman, 1994.

[18]   Rosoff, Pontell, and Tillman, 1998:341-342.

[19]   Rosoff, Pontell, and Tillman, 1998:122.

[20]   Eitzen and Zinn, 1992.

[21]   *Corporate Crime Reporter* 9(10), March 1, 1993.

[22]   *Corporate Crime Reporter* 15(4), April 15, 1996.

[23]   Rosoff, Pontell, and Tillman, 1998:114.

[24]   *Multinational Monitor*, 1997.

[25]   Carlson, 1979.

[26]   Rosoff, Pontell, and Tillman, 1998:91.

[27]   Rosoff, Pontell, and Tillman, 109.

[28]   Rosoff, Pontell, and Tillman, 1998:64.

[29]   Eitzen and Zinn, 1992.

[30]   *Multinational Monitor*, 1995.

[31]   Rosoff, Pontell, and Tillman, 1998:63.

[32]   *Corporate Crime Reporter*, 44(4), November, 17, 1997.

[33]   *Corporate Crime Reporter* 30(1), July 27, 1998.

[34]   *Multinational Monitor*, 1995.

[35]   *Corporate Crime Reporter* 16(3), April 19, 1999.

[36]   *Corporate Crime Reporter* 22(1), June 2, 1997.

[37]   Rosoff, Pontell, and Tillman, 1998:362.

[38]   *Corporate Crime Reporter* 2(3), January 16, 1995.

[39]   Simon, 1999:120; *Corporate Crime Reporter* 41(1), October 25, 1993.

[40]   Gross, 1980:113-115.

[41]   Beirne and Messerschmidt, 2000:62-64.

[42]   *Corporate Crime Reporter* 47(1), December 11, 1995; 48(3), December 18, 1995; 6(5), February 12, 1996; 13(3), April 1, 1996.

[43]   *Corporate Crime Reporter* 33(1), August 17, 1998.

[44]   *Corporate Crime Reporter* 4(3), January 27, 1997.

[45]   *Corporate Crime Reporter* 1(1), January 5, 1998.

[46]   *Corporate Crime Reporter* 39(3), October 13, 1997.

[47]   *Corporate Crime Reporter* 35(11), September 16, 1991.

[48]   *Corporate Crime Reporter* 30(7), July 27, 1992.

[49]   *Corporate Crime Reporter* 32(1), August 10, 1998.

[50]   *Corporate Crime Reporter* 22(4), June 3, 1996.

[51]   *Corporate Crime Reporter* 5(3), February 6, 1995.

[52]   *Corporate Crime Reporter* 13(7), March 29. 1993.

[53]   *Corporate Crime Reporter* 4(6), January 30, 1995.

[54]   *Corporate Crime Reporter* 39(9), October 12, 1992.

[55]   *Corporate Crime Reporter* 34(1), September 6, 1993.

[56]   *Corporate Crime Reporter* 9(1), March 5, 1990.

[57]   *Corporate Crime Reporter* 27(1), July 5, 1999.

[58]   *Corporate Crime Reporter* 33(4), September 3, 1990.

[59]   *Corporate Crime Reporter* 34(4), September 7, 1992.

[60]   Rosoff, Pontell, and Tillman, 1998:288; 290; 297; 298.

[61]   Rosoff, Pontell, and Tillman, 1998:305; 306.

[62]   Rosoff, Pontell, and Tillman, 1998:1; 280; 292; 293; 295; 308; 312; 410.

[63]   Rosoff, Pontell, and Tillman, 1998:179; 180; 181.

[64]   *Corporate Crime Reporter* 40(1), October 21, 1996.

[65]   *Corporate Crime Reporter* 19(6), May 10, 1999; *Corporate Crime Reporter* 29(3), July 19, 1999; *Corporate Crime Reporter* 38(5), October 5, 1998.

[66]   *Corporate Crime Reporter* 30(1), July 26, 1999.

[67]   *Corporate Crime Reporter* 5(4), February 3, 1997; *Corporate Crime Reporter* 28(3), June 29, 1998.

[68]   *Corporate Crime Reporter* 21(1), May 24, 1999:12; *Corporate Crime Reporter* 10(1), March 8, 1999.

[69]   *Corporate Crime Reporter* 19(4), May 10, 1999:12; *Corporate Crime Reporter* 15(6). April 13, 1998:12.

[70]   *Corporate Crime Reporter* 11(9), March 19, 1990.

[71]   *Corporate Crime Reporter* 29(4), July 18, 1994.

[72]   Rosoff, Pontell and Tillman, 1998:15; 16.

[73]   *Corporate Crime Reporter* 9(3), March 4, 1996:10.

[74]   *Corporate Crime Reporter* 11(1), March 15, 1999.

[75]   *Corporate Crime Reporter* 3(1), January 22, 1990.

[76]   Kappeler, Blumberg, and Potter, 1993:237-238.

[77]   *Corporate Crime Reporter* 7(1), February 15, 1999.

[78]   *Corporate Crime Reporter* 32(1), August 10, 1998.

[79]   Simon, 1999:120.

[80]   *Corporate Crime Reporter* 39(6), October 14, 1996.

[81]   *Corporate Crime Reporter* 30(6), July 26, 1999.

[82]   *Corporate Crime Reporter* 45(1), November 25, 1996.

[83]   *Corporate Crime Reporter* 29(1), July 20, 1998.

[84]   *Corporate Crime Reporter* 18(3), May 6, 1996).

[85]   Rosoff, Pontell, and Tillman, 1998:324.

[86]   *Multinational Monitor*, 1997.

[87]   Kelly, 1992.

[88]   *Corporate Crime Reporter* 12(1), March 24, 1997.

[89]   *Corporate Crime Reporter* 1(1), January 4, 1999.

[90]   *Corporate Crime Reporter* 38(8), October 7, 1991.

[91]   Shavelson, 1988.

[92]   Rosoff, Pontell, and Tillman, 1998.

[93]   *Corporate Crime Reporter* 11(3), March 18, 1991.

[94]   *Corporate Crime Reporter* 12(1), March 25, 1991.

[95]   *Corporate Crime Reporter* 22(1), June 3, 1996.

[96]   *Corporate Crime Reporter* 9(3), March 1, 1999.

[97]   *Corporate Crime Reporter* 22(1), June 1, 1992.

[98]   *Corporate Crime Reporter* 33(1), August 17, 1998.

[99]   *Corporate Crime Reporter* 12(8), March 21, 1994.

[100]   *Corporate Crime Reporter* 21(1), May 25, 1998.

[101]   *Corporate Crime Reporter* 22(5), June 3, 1991.

[102]   *Corporate Crime Reporter* 13(1), April 13, 1995.

[103]   *Corporate Crime Reporter* 35(6), September 14, 1992.

[104]   *Corporate Crime Reporter* 37(3), September 29, 1997.

[105]   *Corporate Crime Reporter* 39(5), October 14, 1996.

[106]   *Corporate Crime Reporter* 18(3), May 4, 1992.

[107]   *Corporate Crime Reporter* 6(3), February 12, 1996.

[108]   *Multinational Monitor*, 1997.

[109]   *Corporate Crime Reporter* 30(4), July 26, 1999; *Corporate Crime Reporter* 39, (4), October 12, 1998; *Corporate Crime Reporter* 23(3), June 8, 1998.

[110]   *Corporate Crime Reporter* 20(3), May 20, 1996.

[111]   *Corporate Crime Reporter* 37(4), September 29, 1997.

[112]   *Corporate Crime Reporter* 26(4), July 3, 1995.

[113]   *Corporate Crime Reporter* 30(1), July 31, 1995.

[114]   *Corporate Crime Reporter* 23(3), June 8, 1998.

[115]   *Corporate Crime Reporter* 43(3), November 12, 1990.

[116]   Simon, 1999:11.

[117]   Simon, 1999:11.

[118]   *Corporate Crime Reporter* 23(1), June 8, 1998.

[119]   *Corporate Crime Reporter* 46(5), December 3, 1990.

[120]   Seager, 1993:72.

[121]   *Corporate Crime Reporter* 29(6), July 22, 1991.

[122]   *Corporate Crime Reporter* 27(4), December 9, 1991.

[123]   *Corporate Crime Reporter* 40(5), October 19, 1992.

[124]   *Corporate Crime Reporter* 31(7), August 5, 1991.

[125]   *Corporate Crime Reporter* 46(5), November 28, 1994.

[126]   *Corporate Crime Reporter* 14(1), April 9, 1990.

[127]   Swigert, 1984:97.

[128]   Messerschmidt, 1986.

[129]   Schraeger and Short, 1978.

[130]   Eitzen and Zinn, 1992.

[131]   Coleman, 1989.

[132]   Sutherland, 1949.

[133]   Sutherland, 1949:15.

[134]   Clinard and Yeager, 1980:111.

[135]   Clinard and Yeager, 1980.

[136]   *U.S. News & World Report,* 1982.

[137]   Donahue, 1992:14-19.

[138]   Pearce, 1976; Weinstein, 1968.

[139]   Kolko, 1963.

[140]   Green, Monroe, and Wasserstein, 1972.

[141]   Dowd, 1993:113-115.

[142]   Dye, 1986:16-19, 38.

[143]   Simon, 1999:14.

[144]   Dye, 1986:16-19.

[145]   Simon, 1999:15.

[146]   Zepezzaur and Naiman, 1996:6.

[147]   Bovard, 1995.

[148]   Simon, 1999:62.

[149]   Simon, 1999:62.

[150]   Hagan, 1986.

[151]   Hagan, 1986.

[152]   Calavita and Pontell, 1993.

[153]   Calavita and Pontell, 1990.

[154]   Hills, 1971.

[155]   Benekos, 1983; Snider, 1982; Hagan et al., 1980; Clinard and Yeager, 1979.

[156]   Hagan et al., 1980.

[157]   Wickman and Whitten, 1980:367.

[158]   Clinard and Yeager, 1980.

[159]   Senate Permanent Subcommittee on Investigations, Committee on Governmental Affairs, 1983.

[160]   Clinard and Yeager, 1980.

[161]   McCormick, 1977.

[162]   *Multinational Monitor*, 1996.

[163]   *Multinational Monitor*, 1997; Glass, 1997.

[164]   *Multinational Monitor*, 1996.

CHAPTER 2

White-Collar Crime

Gilbert Geis

There is no section of any penal code, federal or state, that includes the words "white-collar crime." Nonetheless, the term is employed widely in legal circles. Prosecutors may be assigned to a "white-collar crime unit" that typically is charged with locating and seeking redress – in forms such as injunctions, restitution, fines, or incarceration – for illegal commercial behaviors that can range from trivial matters to billion-dollar depredations. Judges not uncommonly employ the term white-collar criminal when they sentence certain types of offenders, usually persons who are well-dressed and who have been well-placed in the world of the haves as contrasted to that of the have-nots. Though they know better, the judges are likely to proclaim that their imposition of a 30-day jail term for this or that antitrust conspirator demonstrates that the courts will be no more tolerant of suite criminals than they are of street offenders.

For the media, the term "white-collar criminal" has evocative potential and is widely used in news stories and television investigative reports. The stories include such things as announcements that there will be a crackdown on telemarketing scams, violations of the Environmental Protection Act, manipulations of the prices and quantities recorded on gasoline pumps, welfare cheating by recipients, or bribery and other forms of corruption in the Congress, the state legislature, or the local governing body.

Can each of these highly variant behaviors – and a horde of others – sensibly be labeled white-collar crime and, if so, what use is the term if it embraces almost anything that an onlooker casually declares to be a "white-collar crime"? Organized crime, the other large category of illegal behavior that does not have a place in legal codes, at least can be looked at in terms of an affiliation with a syndicate and with other persons who identify with the aims and take part in the acts of the particular group. There are, in fact, significant similarities between organized and white-collar crime in the corporate world. Both seek monopoly control over a product (be it widgets or cocaine), and both often will use heavy-handed tactics to buy out or push out competitors. Perhaps the major distinction is that businesses eschew violence, which often is a hallmark of organized crime activity.

This said, what is it that should "qualify" a law-breaker to be placed into the white-collar criminal category and what consequences might flow from whether or not one or another yardstick is used to make that judgment? These are two issues that will receive close attention in the following pages. The chapter also will set in place the historical background surrounding the emergence of the term "white-collar crime" and provide details of the biography of the concept in regard to research and proposals for changes in its embrace.

It remains arguable whether the considerable intellectual energy that has gone into attempts to expand or contract the definition of what is to be called white-collar crime is more than a semantic squabble, full of sound and fury but signifying very little. It might be said of white-collar crime, as a Supreme Court justice did of pornography, that he was unable to provide a satisfactory definition, but he knew it when he saw it. The trouble with this position is that it is not notably helpful as a guideline either for courts or for those promulgating or seeking to prohibit what *they* believe is pornography. Somewhat the same can be said of definitions of white-collar crime. While it may not matter to a court or to an offender whether what has been done, say cashing a check with insufficient or no funds in the bank account on which it is drawn, is or is not to be classified as a white-collar offense. But, as we shall see, it can make a significant difference both in regard to theories of crime causation and in the manner that enforcement resources are allocated and used.

Business as Usual

Historically in western societies there always has been one or another crusade to seek to control exploitative behavior on the part of those with power. The biblical prophets foresaw only doom for merchants who cheated; indeed, some could not see any difference between deceit and commercial enterprise. Christ's driving the money lenders from the temple is perhaps the most readily recalled of the crusades to fashion a fiscally decent society.

In the United States, the deeply ingrained concept of individualism, which was carried to these shores from England as part of our common-law heritage, has played a prominent role in determining what kinds of business, political, and professional behavior the law will prohibit. Perhaps the best way to illustrate the powerful position individualism possesses in Anglo-American law is to point out that in England, and in virtually all American jurisdictions, no penalty is attached to a failure to aid a fellow human being in dire straits even if this can be done with little effort. Thus, an Olympic swimmer who is sunbathing and who remains unresponsive to the call for help of a child drowning in the water nearby, will stand no risk of legal involvement, either criminal or civil. In contrast to this policy, almost all European countries provide criminal punishment for such failures to act.[1]

Individualism combines with the ethos of capitalism and is attached to the axioms of *laissez faire* (don't interfere with what business is doing) and *caveat emptor* (let the buyer beware) to often allow big business to determine the rules under which it will operate and to head off any attempt to curtail its freedom. Well-paid lawyers, skillful lobbyists, and probably most important, financial and other contributions to the election campaigns of politicians all have helped the corporate elite to keep their business affairs pretty much out of the reach of the law.

Inevitably, though, ugly abuses have occurred. Lord Acton's memorable phrase, "Power corrupts and absolute power corrupts absolutely," has, over the years, proved to be right on target. In England there was the infamous South Sea Bubble case in the early eighteenth century, involving scandals on the newborn stock exchange. In the United States, there is a considerable roster of episodes of wrongdoing in the halls of power. The list includes such events as the Credit Mobilier outrage in 1867 (when, among other things, railroad entrepreneurs bribed members of Congress in order to secure construction subsidies), the Teapot Dome case in 1922 (corruption in the sale of oil leases by high government officials), the series of commercial outrages pinpointed by the muckrakers during the 1920s (for instance, tainted meat and rigged oil prices), and, more recently, the twin illegal escapades of both the president and vice-president: Richard Nixon's cover-up in the Watergate burglary and Spiro Agnew's acceptance of bribes while he was in the White House, bribes growing out of his earlier position as executive officer in Baltimore County.

Two things are notable in regard to the consequences of these outrages. First, there were reforms that escalated the penalties for such acts or outlawed them if they couldn't be dealt with under existing statutes. Second, the reforms, though ballyhooed as responsive to the public will, had a considerable tendency to be less formidable than they might have been.

Underlying this situation is another pair of axioms. When a legislator is besieged by public outcries, the first person he almost invariably will seek to serve is himself. A politician's overweening priority is to stay in office, and if in order to do so it is necessary to placate the voters at the expense of those who financed his or her political campaigns, then so be it. Second, reform generally will go only so deep as to placate the electorate sufficiently so that it will not turn against the officeholder. Conciliatory concessions will be made to those to whom politicians are beholden for financial support.

This process can be illustrated by the passage of the Sherman Antitrust Act in 1898. Big business had been rapaciously exploiting consumers by forming monopolies that could, without competitive challenge, raise prices to virtually unconscionable levels. The monopolies were particularly prominent in the oil industry and in railroad transportation of farm products and other merchandise. Under great public pressure, Congress prohibited any business or merger that appeared to be "a conspiracy in restraint of trade."

For a law so important, the Sherman Act was surprisingly brief; less than two pages in length in the *Statutes at Large*. It also was "vague," "terse," and "ambiguous" and never clearly defined what it meant by "monopoly" or "restraint of trade."[2] Not surprisingly, during the first decades of the Act's life, its enforcement remained in a near-moribund state. The Department of Justice filed only nine cases during the five years following passage of the Act, and only 16 in the first 12 years.[3] And if the government won a case, its victory was likely to be overturned on appeal. Not a single violator of the Sherman Act would be imprisoned until 1921, more than 30 years after the provision of criminal penalties in the statute. During the first 50 years of the law's existence, only 24 cases led to jail sentences out of 252 prosecutions. Eleven of these cases involved businessmen, the persons the reform measure presumably had targeted. The rest were labor union leaders. Acts of violence, threats, or other forms of intimidation underlay 10 of the 11 business cases; in the remaining one the jail terms were suspended.[4]

What the public had been promised with the passage of the Sherman Act obviously was not delivered. The most recent history of the Act also shows that following a period of tough enforcement, the Department of Justice has retreated from a standard that focused on the potential to exploit a marketplace position to a stance that allows economists to prevail if they can convince the courts that a merger, however monopolistic, might benefit the public by reducing costs and presumably prices as well.[5] Those who track the pricing tactics of such enterprises as cable television companies might be persuaded that it is almost irresistible for an enterprise without competition to milk the consumer for as much as can be gotten, especially if demand for the product is relatively inelastic.

Sometimes the bones legislators throw to their financial supporters can take a curious shape. When the public first began a crusade against advertising by tobacco companies, the courts mandated that those opposed to smoking had to be afforded equal tube time in order to transmit their message. The tobacco lobby quickly got Congress to pass a bill forbidding all advertising of their products, thus allowing legislators to claim credit for a people-serving measure while at the same time protecting the tobacco companies from the devastating drone of counter-advertising that was putting forth the message that their product was a death-dealing commodity.

The same kind of symbolic gestures can take place when corporate giants throw support to remedial measures, such as those related to factory emission standards. They may do so not out of social sensitivity, but because they are aware that their smaller competitors will find it fiscally cumbersome, if not impossible, to meet such standards, while their own budget can readily accommodate the outlay for the more sophisticated equipment that will be required by law.

Sutherland and White-Collar Crime

It is against this background, particularly in terms of the antisocial marauding of the so-called Robber Barons at work in the last half of the nineteenth century, that Edwin H. Sutherland, a sociologist at Indiana University, introduced the term "white-collar crime" into our language. Sutherland employed the words in his 1939 presidential address to the annual meeting of the American Sociological Society in Philadelphia. He hammered home the point that the standard theories of crime seemed ludicrous when they were applied to white-collar law-breakers. In a memorable passage that he later wrote regarding psychiatric postulates about criminal behavior, Sutherland used white-collar crime to observe that General Motors does not have an Oedipus complex, United States Steel does not suffer from an inferiority complex and the DuPonts do not desire to return to the womb.[6]

In his presidential address Sutherland criticized other theories of crime as well: White-collar offenders, with few exceptions, were not reared in poverty, were not members of deteriorated families and were neither feebleminded nor psychopathic.[7] In 1949, Sutherland expanded on these themes and offered more data in his classic monograph, *White Collar Crime*.

Sutherland's writings on white-collar crime have had a profound impact on criminological research and thinking. If nothing else, persons in the field now are keenly aware of the subject matter and often feel compelled to include it within their considerations of other forms of law-breaking. Among hundreds of examples, I might note the observation of sociologist Lonnie Athens, after his analysis of a particularly grisly and brutal assault by a man on a woman, a stranger, who had crudely insulted him when she saw him peering into her unoccupied camper. Criminals who commit such heinous crimes, Athens observes, "are the most dangerous violent criminals in our society."[8] Then he feels constrained to add: "With perhaps the exception of certain white-collar criminals whose actions jeopardize the health or safety of large numbers of people."

Why did Sutherland, then 56 years old and undoubtedly the most distinguished criminologist in the United States, abruptly shift his attention in this presidential address to a subject that lay in a quite different realm from that of all his previous scholarly work? Answers to this question can help to clarify later issues that arose in regard to Sutherland's white-collar crime work.

A personal notation on the typescript of Sutherland's presidential address puzzled me when I first heard of it. It said, to the best of my memory: "To Mary Bess Owen who wrote it, and to Lois Howard who slept through it." Both Owen and Howard were graduate students at Indiana University in 1939. Owen later became an administrator at Hunter College in New York City. During an interview there, many years after Sutherland's presidential address, she told me that the jotting on the typescript was just Sutherland being playful: she had nothing to do with the composition of the paper. But then she added: "Edwin's heart was in the right place, but he was concerned about offending important people if he wrote about white-collar crime. He was a cautious man. I kept pushing him to tackle the subject."

Mary Bess Owen, while in graduate school, married Kenneth Cameron, a professor in the English Department at Indiana University. Cameron was a highly regarded scholar who focused on the nineteenth-century English poet Percy Bysshe Shelley. He also was a dedicated communist who wrote a highly laudatory biography of Josef Stalin; Cameron's wife stood by his side ideologically. In that regard, her efforts to have Sutherland attack the establishment made sense. She was very close to Sutherland at that time, but they went their separate ways when he found her political views unpalatable. Her doctoral dissertation on shoplifting, which later was published as *The Booster and the Snitch*,[9] was written under another faculty member's supervision.

Sutherland's caution is reflected in the fact that, fearful of being sued, he deleted the names of the offending corporations from the manuscript of *White-Collar Crime* before it was published. It was not until 1983 that Yale University Press issued an unexpurgated edition of the monograph, naming names. But *White Collar Crime* remains a puzzling book in many regards. Only in a footnote does Sutherland make a pass at defining his subject. The footnote reads: "The term 'white collar' is used here to refer principally to business managers and executives, in the sense in which it was used by a president of General Motors who wrote *An Autobiography of a White Collar Worker*."[10] The word "principally" renders the boundaries of the definition unclear. Besides, Sutherland, who was a meticulous scholar, uncharacteristically miscites the title of the book by Albert Sloane, the GM president. In addition, the Sloane book sheds no light at all on the traits of white-collar work.

The matters addressed in *White Collar Crime* add further confusion to the question of a proper definition of the term. Sutherland alludes at times to notorious kingpins of fraud. But the numerical data that he analyzes deals exclusively with corporate bodies, not individuals. Beyond that, Sutherland uncritically compares the records of huge businesses, subject to a multitude of laws and often with thousands of employees, with individual offenders and declares that many of the corporations are no different than career criminals. Sutherland also includes an appendix, derived largely from material supplied by his students, that tells stories about "white-collar crimes" committed by non-elite and rather powerless persons such as shoe salesmen.

Nonetheless, despite his failure to impose some definitional order on his material, it seems obvious, to use current language, from where Sutherland was coming. It was people who used positions of prestige and power to violate the law who most concerned him. Sutherland himself, Nebraska-born, had grown up in a family with a strict Baptist heritage. His father was a minister and spent most of his life as a college president at Baptist institutions. Sutherland, in his later life, was a religious backslider – he drank some and was an avid card player, for instance – but he never lost the sense of moral outrage that pervaded both the midwest of his childhood during the progressive era and the religious faith in which he was raised. His work on white-collar crime has deep roots in that soil: it is a fervid denunciation of wrongdoing in the upper echelons of the business and political world. But, given Sutherland's doctoral training at the University of Chicago, where he had changed his major from theology to sociology, the book also had to have a veneer of scientific neutrality. The attempt to blend indignation and objectivity would make the ideas in *White Collar Crime* endlessly controversial as scholarship in the field developed.

Theorizing About White-Collar Crime

For some time Sutherland's theory of differential association dominated not only interpretations of white-collar crime but those of all forms of crime. The theory had nine propositions of highly uneven importance. Simply put (and it was a much too simple theory), Sutherland posited that criminal behavior is learned in association with others and that it takes place when what has been learned inclines one more toward crime than away from it.

Early research on white-collar crime – and there wasn't very much of it – almost invariably forsook Sutherland's explanatory position. Marshall Clinard's 1952 inquiry into black marketing concluded that efforts to understand offenders ought to focus on psychological variables. Donald Cressey's 1953 study of incarcerated embezzlers pointed out that there was precious little that they hadn't known about embezzling, and that what was required was not learning but a situation that prompted them to steal and a set of rationalizations that allowed them to calm their conscience. A decade and a half later, my own study of the General Electric antitrust conspiracy offered some support to Sutherland. It was clear enough that the offenders were instructed in price-fixing tactics by their superiors after they gained executive positions in the company. They also did not necessarily think of the behavior as seriously wrong. Notable, for instance, was the plaint of one offender that while he knew that price-fixing was illegal, he was stunned that it also was criminal. On the other hand, Sutherland's theory of differential association failed to capture many of the key ingredients of this antitrust conspiracy.[11]

Another major theory of crime causation also embraced white-collar crime. Robert Merton's classic statement of anomie theory has a coda that appeared in his later writings, but is often overlooked. Merton maintained that crime in the United States grew out of our overwhelming emphases on money and the barriers that some persons could not surmount to achieve that goal by legitimate means. In regard to white-collar crime, Merton postulated an "anomie of success," which, he said, "arises when progressively higher aspirations are fostered by each temporary success and by the enlarged expectations visited upon [financially successful people] by associates."[12] Daniel Bell has made the same point.[13] "Wants," Bell wrote, "by their nature are unlimited and insatiable." Readers might ponder this point. What will satisfy them? And if they achieve that goal, will they remain content to stop there?

After a few toe-in-the-water movements into white-collar crime research and theory, there ensued a considerable time lapse in regard to work on the subject, perhaps because of the dampening effect of the McCarthy witch-hunting period during which those deemed to be straying from political orthodoxy lost jobs and were ostracized. Not until later, when an icono-clastic, anti-authority mood took root in significant segments of the popu-lation and the academic community was there a renaissance of inquiries into white-collar crime.

Corporate and State Crime

A major subsequent contribution to white-collar crime scholarship was the splitting of the concept into two categories: The first concerned offens-es committed by individuals; the second, those by organizations, most par-ticularly corporate bodies. This two-part division of the subject posed con-siderable analytical problems of its own. There is no question that corporations routinely are prosecuted for violations of criminal law, and on very rare occasions, such as in the *Pinto* case, they even may be charged with homicide.[14] Guilty outcomes or *nolo contendere* (no contest pleas which almost invariably indicate guilt) typically lead to fines; corporations, after all, cannot be imprisoned, though the government's intrusion into corporate boardrooms increased dramatically when the U.S. Sentencing Commission promulgated guidelines that allowed corporations to be placed on probation and to be closely monitored if they are found guilty of a criminal act.[15]

A major question remains unresolved: How can criminological theories be developed in regard to corporate misconduct? Is not such conduct no more than the product of the behavior of individuals or groups of individu-als? The corporation may act in its own name, but it is human beings who decide what that action is to be and carry it out. Donald Cressey, in a notably forceful essay, insisted that criminologists were proceeding up a blind alley when they uncritically assumed that they could locate a causal explanation for corporate crime.[16] Corporations, he maintained, could not feel guilty, learn, or decide. Cressey was answered by John Braithwaite and Brent Fisse, who found his arguments less than persuasive. They argued that what a corporation did and what it stood for often represented the product of innumerable considerations that added up to a stance that was uniquely that of the organization and not of any particular individuals.

Other offshoots of Sutherland's formulation also found a place in the scholarly sun; some of these are represented in this book. Most prominent is a focus on crimes committed by a sovereign state, including such acts as genocide launched against minorities in its midst, unprovoked attacks against dissidents, the muzzling of the media, and failure to provide assistance to citizens and other residents who are unable to care for themselves.

The concept of state crime substitutes a more amorphous, though by no means a lesser, standard of judgment regarding what should be included within its framework than does white-collar or corporate crime, which depend on laws to define their embrace. As with corporate crime, there can be complications involved in separating the state from those who are acting in its name. Was the Vietnam War (or, the American War, as it is called in Vietnam today) a state crime? If so, who are we to designate as the offenders: John Kennedy, Richard Nixon, Lyndon Johnson, Robert McNamara, the members of the Congress, or those citizens who endorsed the military action? Or are we to brand the country itself as criminal? The concept is very important, but it is difficult to formulate and pursue within the usual boundaries of criminological and social scientific work.

The Yale White-Collar Crime Research

Probably the single most important set of contributions to research to white-collar crime after Sutherland were made by a group of scholars – mostly social scientists – based in the law school at Yale University.[17] Their research added dramatically to what is known about white-collar crime, but it, too, has been criticized in the internecine warfare that has characterized scholarship on the subject.

The Yale studies demonstrate the ever-increasing ability of the government to set the agenda for university research. The research was funded during the Presidency of Jimmy Carter when he decided to put white-collar crime high on his domestic policy agenda. The National Institute of Justice thereupon used a significant part of the money allocated to it to launch a long-term study of the phenomenon under the direction of Stanton Wheeler. Wheeler assembled a team of outstanding colleagues, a group of largely young, bright, and energetic investigators.

The immediate issue facing Wheeler's team was to resolve the nagging definitional debate about precisely what is and what is not white-collar crime. The tactic they chose made research sense, since it allowed them to focus on a specific group of violators rather than having to grapple with such hard-to-pin-down identifiers such as positions of power and elite status. They queried federal prosecutors about which offenses they considered to be white-collar crimes, ultimately pinpointing statutes about which there was general agreement. These were: bribery, embezzlement, income tax evasion, false claims, mail fraud, securities violations, antitrust offenses, and credit fraud.

Thereafter, the research group conducted a series of sophisticated inquiries into a variety of matters that characterized these offenders. What they found contradicted many of Sutherland's somewhat off-the-cuff pronouncements about the nature of upperclass offending. They discovered, for instance, that persons convicted of the offenses they had denominated as white-collar crime often committed second and third offenses.[18] This was contrary to the prevailing wisdom in criminology that maintained that once burned white-collar offenders would desist, partly because they had learned their lesson and/or they would not again find themselves in a position where they could violate the law.

The difficulty is that the Yale group was looking at law violators significantly different from those who had received earlier attention in white-collar crime studies. Among the women in the Yale sample, for instance, about one-third were unemployed,[19] while the total sample showed an unemployment rate of eight percent. All told, at least two-thirds of their sample was made up persons who were not in positions of much clout and a not insignificant number who did not even have jobs. These were not the kind of persons and the kind of behavior that Sutherland had in mind.

In a major contribution, David Weisburd and colleagues summarized a good portion of their work under the title *Crimes of the Middle Class*. Their position was that the persons Sutherland and his followers had studied as white-collar criminals were but a small portion of the total. Sutherland's response presumably would have been that, of course, you are obtaining different results because you are looking at a very different group of persons than those I had in mind. He also might have argued that the offenders in the Yale samples were not necessarily middle-class, but persons from all classes who had committed denominated federal crimes. The argument also might have been made that the Yale group, if they had chosen to follow Sutherland's lead, could have siphoned off the elite in their crime categories and focused their attention on them. Failing to do so, they perhaps could have labeled that which they were investigating as something other than white-collar crime.

Fallout from the Yale Studies

There is no easy way to judge whether the revisionist Yale work has advanced or further confounded and confused the study of white-collar crime. But the move away from spotlighting the perversion of positions of power as a distinctive crime category found its way into other work. James Q. Wilson, for instance, wrote that "predatory crime" was far more serious than white-collar crime, as if white-collar crime wasn't often strikingly predatory. Besides, wrote Wilson: "I am rather tolerant of some forms of civil corruption (if a good mayor can stay in office and govern effectively only by making a few deals with contractors and insurance agents, I do not get overly alarmed."[20]) Later, relying upon the highly limited embrace of white-collar crimes in the Uniform Crime Reports, Wilson and Richard Herrnstein, in a widely read book, proclaimed that there was no distinctive category of white-collar crime; besides, they wrote, what is regarded as white-collar crime shows that blacks are overrepresented in its ranks to the same degree that they are in so-called street crimes.[21]

The Yale Studies approach also played a part in the delineation of self-control theory,[22] which at the moment is the theoretical position that draws the largest degree of support from the criminological research community. Put very simply, self-control theory maintains that the key ingredient of law-breaking is the individual's failure to develop self-control. This failure can be traced to inadequate monitoring of a child's early years to make certain that he or she is disciplined satisfactorily to respond to the social demand for law-abiding behavior.

Criminological theories of the past have stumbled badly when it came to interpreting white-collar crime. We noted earlier, for instance, Sutherland's sneering observation that white-collar offenders can hardly be said to suffer from an Oedipus complex. Nor, at least at the time that Sutherland was writing, were they likely to have been raised in broken homes.

Gottfredson and Hirschi's self-control theory met the white-collar crime challenge head-on by maintaining that white-collar criminals were no different from any other kinds of offenders and therefore could readily be understood best in terms of insufficient self-control.[23] They were able to sustain this argument by focusing on the sample employed by the Yale team which, in essence, did not differ dramatically from run-of-the-mill offenders. Their theory was said to embrace *all* criminals: "Our portrait of the burglar applies equally well to the white-collar offender, the dope dealer, and the assaulter," Gottfredson and Hirschi maintain. "They are the same people."[24]

Gottfredson and Hirschi's claim was repudiated in three major articles demonstrating that if they had used the criteria enunciated by Sutherland to denote white-collar offenders, their conclusion would have been much different.[25] As Katherine Jamieson points out: "The complexities behind decisions of corporate executives to engage in illegal behaviors cannot be overestimated."[26] But the self-control theory demonstrated that they can be underestimated.

Note might also be taken of a study of the savings and loan swindles which, depending again on your definition, might or might not be regarded as white-collar crimes. The research concluded that what was learned moved "in exactly the opposite direction to Gottfredson and Hirschi's theoretical position by suggesting that many forms of white-collar crime are not reducible to individuals and their characteristics, but are embedded in large institutional and organizational arrangements."[27]

Trust and Antitrust

The second major revisionist attempt to redraw the boundaries of white-collar crime – to liberate it from Sutherland's shackles – was offered by Susan Shapiro, a member of the original Yale study team. Shapiro maintained that the term ought to refer specifically and only to violations of trust that enable people "to rob without violence and burgle without trespass."[28] Offenders said to deserve the white-collar crime label do things such as manipulate requirements for disclosure and for disinterestedness that apply to the roles they play in commercial and similar kinds of transactions. Their behaviors involve lying, misrepresentation, stealing, misappropriation, self-dealing, corruption, and conflict of interest.

Prosecution of crimes involving abuse of trust is handicapped, Shapiro points out, because victims are often unaware that they are being gulled and by the fact that the suspects tend to have control of the crucial evidence that would inculpate them. Shapiro grants that Sutherland's definitional heritage is not readily cast aside, because the concept of white-collar crime is "polemically powerful" and "palpably self-evident."[29] She also grants that her redesign of the concept may have its own shortcomings – for instance, it excludes antitrust crimes as well as corporate violence that grows out of deliberate decisions or negligence. Nonetheless, Shapiro concluded with a resounding indictment of the usual way that white-collar crime has been looked at, an approach which is said to have

> created an imprisoning framework for contemporary scholarship, impoverishing theory, distorting empirical inquiry, oversimplifying policy analysis, inflaming our muckraking instincts, and obscuring fascinating questions about the relationships between social organization and crime.[30]

It is arguable whether the reformulation that Shapiro offers will find followers. In the decade since its enunciation it does not seem to have gained a great deal of support, though its statement challenges current researchers to defend their own choice of a "proper" white-collar crime definition.

Drifting Into Difficulty

In a notably sophisticated and comprehensive analysis of what went wrong when the spaceship *Challenger* plunged to earth almost immediately after its launching in January, 1986, Diane Vaughan[31] suggests that what happened was a consequence of an innocent but faulty decision-making process that often is at the root of white-collar crimes committed within organizations. There had been a constant slippage of wariness about various safety aspects of the launching program. The slippage was not the result of anything sinister, but merely the product of the need to make program decisions on the basis of information that never was totally conclusive. It occurred in small ways; and at the time of the decision to launch the *Challenger*, prior sensible compromises fed into what would become a lethal operation.

Even then, happenstance played its part in the launching decision. The Thiokol engineers in Utah had recommended against the launch because of unacceptably cold weather conditions. Those at the project headquarters in

Huntsville, Alabama, asked them to reconsider, fully expecting them to remain anchored in their no-go recommendation. But, partly out of weariness, they did not keep the phone line open so that the main decisionmakers were not privy to the debate that followed in Utah. The Thiokol team sensed that headquarters was putting them under great pressure to reverse their recommendation: there was some pressure, but a no-launch decision would have been honored. The engineers in Utah scrupulously reviewed what they knew and decided that there was no conclusive evidence that the flight would not be routine: all the previous ones, inevitably launched with some uncertainty about this or that, had worked out fine. They then changed their recommendation and sent the *Challenger* crew to their deaths.

While few suggested criminal negligence on the part of the *Challenger* decisionmakers, Vaughan believes that the same sort of drifting process can be found in many white-collar crimes that arise in an organizational context. Her stand is backed by work on the *Pinto* case by Matthew Lee and David Ermann,[32] who argue that, contrary to popular opinion, the *Pinto* case was not characterized by a callous conspiracy by people preoccupied with profit maximization. The Pinto's safety profile was comparable to that of other cars in its class and the decision to market it was the result of a conclusion reached by a group of loosely allied managers, none of whom had an evil intent or a risk-taking impulse.

Conclusion

Work on white-collar crime has been driven in recent times by the strong movement of criminological research toward the use of highly sophisticated statistical techniques. The mode is to establish or locate large data sets and to analyze these in terms of pre-established variables in order to correlate these with an outcome. Such enterprises rarely succeed in explaining more than a small fraction of the variance, but the elegance of the mathematical manipulations rather than the importance of the issue or the significance of the results seems to be sufficient unto the day. For academics, dependent on publication in good scholarly outlets, the arguments for performing such work are compelling.

The study of white-collar crime, however, does not readily lend itself to what has become the dominant form of criminological research. White-collar crime research gets a more hospitable reception from book publishers than from journal outlets. But the gestation period for books is long and the book publishing for young scholars involves pinning one's hopes of academic survival on a single product, rather than pumping out (the term of art among academics) a bevy of shorter, number-crunched journal pieces.

There has been important numerical work on some aspects of white-collar crime. Prominent are several studies that have sought to determine whether convicted persons categorized as white-collar offenders get more lenient or tougher sentences in terms of their status and in regard to other criminals.[33] That these studies report contradictory conclusions may be a function of looking at different kinds of offenders or using different definitions of white-collar crime.

In addition, Marshall Clinard and Peter Yeager[34] contributed a book that impressively followed-up on Sutherland's early effort to tabulate and interpret the offenses of corporations. There also has been valuable research that has sought to delineate the characteristics of corporations that are related to offenses against the criminal and the regulatory laws.[35]

There remains, however, a pressing need for intensive field studies of individual white-collar offenders and organizational law violators. This would be demanding work: unlike juvenile delinquents and incarcerated adult offenders, white-collar criminals do not make themselves available for study and, when they do, they are likely to be skillful at avoiding forthcoming responses to the kinds of questions that a criminologist might put to them.

More than a century ago, during the drafting of the India Evidence Act, a commentator noted: "It is far pleasanter to sit comfortably in the shade rubbing pepper into a poor devil's eyes than to go about in the sun hunting clues."[36] This preachment, directed to the Indian police, led to the banning in court of any statement derived from the accused. The idea can be applied to research on white-collar crime as well. I would take issue with the advice of a prominent scholar who has encouraged efforts to understand corporate law-breaking through empirical studies that are "especially attractive because the indicators cited can readily be computed or accessed without gaining entry to the firms themselves."[37] On the basis of such advice, students of white-collar crime increasingly have preferred to park themselves in front of computers in temperature-modulated environs and crunch out correlations between this and that aspect of a corporation and its record for criminal and regulatory act violations.

There is an insufficiency of work in the field that determines first-hand those conditions, both objective and subjective, that trigger white-collar offending. That said, I want to indicate what I personally regard as the best definition of white-collar crime that has been put forward to date. Albert J. Reiss and Albert Biderman believe that its content can be captured in terms of the following delineation:

> White-collar crime violations are those violations of law in which penalties are attached that involve the use of a violator's position of economic power, influence, or trust in the legitimate economic or political institutional order for the purpose of illegal gain or to commit an illegal act for personal or organizational gain.[38]

It seems preferable also to subdivide various forms of white-collar crime into categories with some resemblance to each other and to study these in depth rather than to attempt to formulate explanatory models for so variegated a range of actions as those that come under the white-collar crime heading. Many of these acts have very little in common beyond the fact that they are violations of law. They differ among themselves in terms of the motives and characteristics of the victims, the situations in which they occur, the techniques used, and the damages that result, among other things.

It might be observed, finally, that white-collar crime as a field of study has much to recommend it. A large segment of street crime has to be seen as related in some measure to disadvantages experienced by people who drew a losing hand in the lottery of life. Such people should not be allowed to exploit and hurt others, but it is easy (at least for me) to be sympathetic to their plight. White-collar crime, on the other hand, is much more often committed by those who have lived very well, but nonetheless have felt compelled to gather unto themselves an even greater share of wealth and the things that it will purchase. It is more attractive work (again, at least for me) to try to determine why they behaved as they did and to find ways to stop them from doing so.

Notes

[1]   Geis, 1991.

[2]   Friedman, 1993:117.

[3]   Posner, 1970.

[4]   Claubert and Burton, 1966.

[5]   Geis and Salinger, 1998.

[6]   Sutherland, 1956.

[7]   Sutherland, 1940.

[8]   Athens, 1987:lll.

[9]   Cameron, 1964

[10]   Sutherland, 1949:9.

[11]   Geis, 1967.

[12]   Merton, 1964:225.

[13]   Bell, 1976:170.

[14]   Cullen, Maakestad, and Cavender, 1987.

[15]   See e.g., Nagel and Swenson, 1993.

[16]   Cressey, 1994.

[17]   See Wheeler, 1993 for a comprehensive bibliography of the group's publications.

[18]   Weisburd, Waring, and Chayet, 1995.

[19]   Daly, 1989.

[20]   Wilson, 1975:23.

[21]   Wilson and Herrnstein, 1985.

[22]   Gottfredson and Hirschi,1990.

[23]   Gottfredson and Hirschi, 1990:190-20l: see also Hirschi and Gottfredson, 1987.

[24]   Gottfredson and Hirschi,1990:90.

[25]   Benson and Moore, 1992; Reed and Yeager, 1996; Steffensmeir, 1989.

[26]   Jamieson, 1994:216-218.

[27]   Tillman and Pontell, 1995:1659

[28]   Shapiro, 1990:346.

[29]   Shapiro, 1990:357.

[30]   Shapiro, 1990:362.

[31]   Vaughan, 1996.

[32]   Lee and Ermann, 1999.

[33]   Benson and Walker, 1988; Hagan and Parker, 1985; Wheeler, Weisburd, and Bode, 1982.

[34]   Clinard and Yeager, 1980.

[35]   See, e.g., Simpson, 1986.

[36]   Stephen, 1883:149.

[37]   Szyajkowski, 1985:566.

[38]   Reiss and Biderman, 1980:11.

CHAPTER 3

State-Corporate Crime
in a Globalized World:
Myth or Major Challenge?

David O. Friedrichs

The Origins of the Concept of State-Corporate Crime

Individuals commit crimes. Organizations also commit crimes, at least in one interpretation. If one accepts the notion that organizations commit crimes, then some of these organizations are in the private sector, as in the case of corporations, and some are in the public sector, or part of the state. The concept of organizational crime – or crimes committed by or on behalf of organizations – has been quite widely accepted.[1] Since the 1970s the concept of corporate crime is also commonly invoked, and a substantial literature on corporate crime has developed.[2] Corporate crime is a major form of white-collar crime. Corporate crime may be defined as illegal and harmful activities carried out on behalf of a corporation by corporate personnel.[3] The concept of state crime – or state-organized crime – is somewhat less familiar but, especially in the final decade of the twentieth century, became more conspicuously a part of the criminological agenda.[4] State crime is a major form of governmental crime.[5] State crime may be defined as illegal and harmful actions carried out by state officials on behalf of the state, or some state agency.[6] State crime is best distinguished from political white-collar crime, which is defined as illegal activities carried out by officials and politicians for direct personal benefit.[7] The concept of state-corporate crime is among the more recent additions to the literature on white-collar crime.[8] What is the relation of state-corporate crime to existing types of crime? Some crimes fit quite neatly into the traditional categories of white-collar crime, or governmental crime. For example, a corporation engaging in illegal dumping of toxic waste in a waterway, in contravention to existing state law and without the knowledge of state officials, could be considered a pure example of corporate crime. A state agency engaged in genocidal actions, violations of international law in the context of war, or illegal surveillance of and harassment of dissident groups, could be regarded as pure examples of state crime. But many offenses do not fit so easily into these categories, and are best seen as hybrid or marginal forms of white-collar crime. Examples of such hybrid or marginal forms include finance crime (or illegal and harmful activity in the world of high finance), technocrime (or certain forms of computer and technologically centered crime), enterprise crime (or cooperative ventures involving syndicated criminals and businessmen), contrepreneurial crime (or frauds and scams appearing to be legitimate businesses), and avocational crime (or financially oriented, nonviolent crimes such as tax evasion and insurance fraud committed by members of the white-collar class, outside an occupational context). State-corporate crime, then, is one of these hybrid types. In a seminal paper, Ronald Kramer and Raymond Michalowski characterized this type of crime as occurring "at the interstices of corporations or governments;" more specifically, they defined it as follows: "State-corporate crimes are illegal or socially injurious actions that occur when one or more institutions of political governance pursue a goal in direct cooperation with one or more institutions of economic production and distribution."[9] State-corporate crime may involve agencies of the Federal, the state, or local government; it may involve major, Fortune 500 corporations as well as relatively small corporations. As a rule, of course, the potential for harm tends to be greatest when a cooperative criminal venture involving a Federal state entity and a large corporation occurs.

One possible objection to the state-corporate crime concept is that most, if not all, crimes carried out by either the state or corporations involve some level of implicit or explicit cooperation between states and corporations. To the extent that this is true we might think of these crimes as ranged along a continuum, with direct, explicit cooperation on one end of the spectrum and indirect, implicit complicity at the other end. And we can also recognize that some crimes are initiated by government entities, with corporations recruited or brought in at some point, while other crimes are initiated by corporations, with states or state agencies brought in at some point. In this sense we might distinguish between state-corporate crime and corporate-state crime. We might also acknowledge the existence of political-corporate crime, to capture crimes committed for the benefit of individual political officials, candidates, or parties, in conjunction with corporations (for example, by soliciting and accepting illegal corporate political donations in return for explicit or implicit political favors for the corporation.)

Another reservation about the concept of state-corporate crime would focus on the phrase "socially injurious actions." An assessment of a state-corporate venture as socially injurious could be viewed as a somewhat subjective judgment. Indeed, those with leftist or progressive ideological commitments tend to regard the whole industrial capitalist political economy as inherently injurious to people and to the notion of authentic communities. But in support of this dimension of state-corporate crime we must recognize that it is the state that primarily determines which forms of injury are officially designated illegal, and corporations tend to have disproportionate influence over this process, at least in relation to their own activities. Accordingly, rather than allowing states and corporations to avoid the uniquely stigmatizing label of "criminal" because their injurious actions have not been formally designated as criminal it seems better to apply this label somewhat more broadly even while acknowledging some element of subjective judgment in this process.

State crime and corporate crime, considered independently, have parallel dimensions as well as differences between them.[10] State crimes tend to be driven more by the objective of extending or retaining power, while corporate crimes are most often driven primarily by the objective of realizing financial gains or minimizing financial losses. Second, the nature of trust accorded state officials may have a different character than the trust extended to corporations, although both states and corporations have experienced erosion of public trust. Third, while both state crime and corporate crime can have violent consequences, the violence of state crime is often direct and intentional (as in the case of genocidal campaigns), while the violent consequences of corporate crime are not specifically intended but result from privileging profit over all other considerations. And fourth, the overall scope of harm from state crime is generally broader and more pervasive than the harm from corporate crime (for example, the deliberate extermination of millions of people during the Holocaust, and the total expropriation of their property).[11]

The concept of crime itself is, of course, central to all of the concepts discussed here. The term crime is invoked to mean quite different things, and may be used in a manner that is legalistic, political, humanistic, moralistic, or popular.[12] The approach taken here incorporates social constructionist assumptions (that what is defined legally as crime is relative), conflict theory assumptions (that power plays a central role in determining what is defined as crime), and critical theory assumptions (that the criteria of social harm should be central to any conception of crime).[13] Stuart Henry and Mark M. Lanier have formulated a "prism of crime" model that recognizes that crimes that cause great harm (e.g., corporate crimes) may have relatively little visibility as crimes, while crimes with great public visibility (e.g., theft) may cause relatively little harm. [14] The concept of state-corporate crime, then, refers to activities that do not always fall within the framework of legally defined crimes, and often have relatively low public visibility as crimes, but are nevertheless very harmful in terms of social consequences.

Constructing Crime, Myths About Crime, and State-Corporate Crime

When ordinary citizens think about crime it is surely not likely to be about state-corporate crime. Although we have some evidence of an increasing public perception of the serious harm of state crime and corporate crime, this perception has not necessarily translated into greater preoccupation with such crime.[15] It has been well-established by now that most citizens obtain their basic understanding of crime and crime control not from direct experience, but from the media.[16] And it has been established, as well, that the media presents a skewed portrayal of crime and criminal justice, with a strong emphasis on interpersonal violence and dramatic trials.[17] White-collar crime generally – and perhaps corporate or state-corporate crime in particular – receives relatively little attention either in the news or entertainment dimension of the media, especially on television, although coverage is somewhat greater today than in the past.[18] Various reasons have been identified for the relative neglect of corporate crime, including: the often indirect nature of the harm to victims; public resistance to viewing corporations as criminals; fear of lost advertising revenue from corporate sponsors, or of libel lawsuits by corporations; the absence of striking visual images in such crime; the intrinsic complexity of the cases, and adjudication of them; and the common lack of the necessary specialized expertise to understand corporate crime cases on the part of journalists.[19] And media executives may fear that investigating the state itself, or entities of the state, will jeopardize their broadcasting license, or important political interests of theirs.

If images of crime are often skewed, it follows that the public in varying degrees adopts various myths about crime and criminal justice.[20] We have many myths about conventional crime, and the criminal justice system response to such crime. A general myth, or widespread notion, holds that the greatest threat to our person and property comes from conventional offenders and from such criminal types as serial killers and junkies. States naturally tend to direct public attention toward conventional or anti-state crime, not toward the crimes of the state itself. Corporations have actively promoted another myth, that crimes of corporations are mainly technical violations of regulatory laws, and do not cause significant harm.[21] This is a myth, in any case, actively promoted by wealthy and powerful corporations. Corporations are especially well-positioned (for example, through their formidable sponsorship of media entertainment and reporting, various ties with media corporations, and in some cases direct control of the media) to promote a positive image of their activities. Street people, and conventional offenders, are certainly in a very different situation. Corporations project the claim that the activities of corporations are overwhelmingly beneficial to society. Corporations adopt the explicit or implicit claim that allegations of corporate (and state-corporate) wrongdoing are largely a myth, the product of leftist (or communist) propagandists and others with an axe to grind against the corporate world.[22] Those who allege state-corporate crimes may be dismissed as conspiracy theorists whose claims have no substance.

Corporations, business leaders, and conservative politicians also tend to promote the myth that corporations and businesses are victimized by greedy lawyers and plaintiffs, who sue them on frivolous grounds, in the hopes of taking advantage of their "deep pockets," that "runaway juries" award absurd sums of money to plaintiffs in cases directed against corporations, that businesses become unprofitable and go into bankruptcy in this environment, with harmful consequences for communities and consumers, and that a liberal/leftist conspiracy promotes laws intended to ruin businesses, and indeed destroy capitalism.[23]

It may be true that some allegations of state-corporate crime are false, that some accusers are promoting a political agenda, and that some initiatives against corporations (or the state) have harmful consequences. We can also acknowledge that both states and corporations engage in many beneficial activities. But it is a premise of this chapter that the notion of state-corporate crime itself does not refer to a myth; rather, it refers to significant, immensely harmful activities that represent a growing threat as we move through the twenty-first century.

Landmark Cases of State-Corporate Crime

Although the concept of state-corporate crime is of quite recent vintage, we can recognize seminal origins of state-corporate crime in very early cooperative criminal enterprises involving the state and private entrepreneurs. William Chambliss has characterized piracy as an early form of state-organized crime, although it also had some elements of state-corporate crime.[24] There is evidence that corrupt governors cooperated with pirates in Ancient Greece and Rome, and during the Middle Ages the Vikings operated as pirates on behalf of Scandinavian governments.[25] During the sixteenth and seventeenth centuries the British, French, and Dutch governments arranged for pirates such as Sir Francis Drake to attack Spanish and Portuguese ships returning from the New World laden with vast mineral riches; the state got a share of the loot in return for protection and sponsorship.[26] During the colonial period in America, corrupt governments in New York City and in Charleston, South Carolina, cultivated and protected pirates (including the notorious Edward Teach, or "Blackbeard") and profited accordingly.[27] Of course, state policy was not uniformly supportive of piracy, and during certain periods governments were actively hostile toward it.[28] But there can be no question that states and pirate organizations cooperated in carrying out various criminal operations.

The imperialistic and colonialist enterprises from the sixteenth century on could also be characterized as an early form of state-corporate crime. Indeed, starting with Columbus himself, the "conquest of paradise" (i.e., settlement of the Americas) enterprise was a joint state/private enterprise all too often directed toward wholly dominating the native population and systematically stripping them of their birthright.[29] Then the nineteenth-century "robber barons" – the Vanderbilts, Astors, Rockefellers, Goulds, and others – built up their immense corporate-based fortunes often with either direct assistance of political figures and state entities, or at least with negligent oversight by the state.[30] The Credit Mobilier Affair, which surfaced in 1872, is one specific instance of a state-corporate crime – or at least political white-collar/corporate crime – during this period.[31] Credit Mobilier was a holding company organized in 1864 to coordinate the westward expansion of the Union Pacific railroad. Shares in the company were made available to many congressmen at nominal cost (or were given as a gift) by the company's founders (including Congressman Oakes Ames), and Congress enacted a bond capitalization of the scheme that greatly enriched the shareholders.

In the twentieth century, the role of German corporations in the Nazi enterprise is surely one of the most dramatic cases of state-corporate crime. First, corporate leaders played a crucial role in Hitler's coming to power, by providing essential economic support for the Nazis and Hitler.[32] These corporate leaders apparently believed that Hitler represented their best hope for insuring that the communists did not come to power and destroy corporate capitalism. They also apparently believed – very mistakenly – that they would be able to control or manipulate Hitler to their advantage once he came to power. Second, corporations were directly involved in – and generally benefitted from – the "Aryanization" process initiated in the 1930s by the Nazis to effectively take businesses (including corporations) out of the control of Jews.[33] Although the Nazi state itself was the biggest profiteer from this Aryanization process, it is clear that many large German corporations also benefitted economically, as well as through providing various services to the Nazi state in connection with its systematic plundering of Jewish property.[34] Thirdly, some German corporations knowingly provided the instruments necessary for the implementation of the Holocaust – most infamously, the Zyklon B gas used in death camps such as Auschwitz and Majdanek was provided by subsidiaries of German chemical corporations, Degussa and IG Farben.[35] Of course the German corporations – Krupp as a well-known example – provided the armaments for the aggressive war initiated by Nazi Germany.[36] Then, fourthly, many major German corporations – not only IG Farben, but Siemens, Daimler-Benz, BMW, AEG-Telefunken, and others – used Jewish slave labor in their production process, with some 25,000 of these slave laborers dying at the IG Farben factory near Auschwitz alone.[37] Daimler-Benz, a prominent auto manufacturer, in addition to using slave labor, provided tanks, trucks, and airplane engines for the Nazi war effort, exploited opportunities in the occupied territories, and participated in the transit of people to the death camps.[38] In 1999, Volkswagen was being sued by former Polish and Russian slave workers for deaths of their children in nurseries run by the auto manufacturer.[39] And many other German corporations cooperated in various ways with the Nazi enterprise. Finally, after World War II, only a handful of the executives of these corporations were tried for war crimes – and received token sentences – and many of the corporations rebuilt with great success after the war and little if any acknowledgment of their complicity with the Holocaust.

The Holocaust was first and foremost a crime of the Nazi state, but it was also a case of state-corporate crime, and neither the Nazi war machine nor the Nazi death machine could have functioned without the willing participation of many German corporations. Furthermore, the build-up of the Nazi war machine did not solely involve German corporations. A Swiss legislator and sociologist has argued that the Swiss banks played an important role in Nazi Germany's "success" over a period of years by serving as a fence and money launderer on a large scale for Nazi Germany.[40] At the very end of the twentieth century, the Swiss banks acknowledged that they had held accounts of Holocaust victims for decades, without making the money available to their survivors.[41] American-based corporations also had some complicity. ITT was one of the first international conglomerates. ITT factories in Nazi Germany produced bomb sights for Nazi warplanes, among other products, and ITT communications operations also served the Nazis (Sampson, 1973). Remarkably enough, after World War II, ITT was able to obtain millions of dollars of compensation from the United States government (and taxpayers) for damage to its factories in Nazi Germany, on the grounds that it was not a party to the conflict between the United States and Germany and should not sustain losses! And by century's end, new questions were being raised about the knowledge of such companies as Ford and General Motors of their Germany subsidiaries during the Nazi period and their complicity with the Nazi war machine.[42] Altogether, the network of corporations that cooperated with the Nazi state seems to have been quite broad, cutting across various borders.

Many other examples, since World War II, could be cited where corporations cooperated in various ways with states engaged in actions leading to unwarranted deaths – sometimes on a very large scale – or massive financial losses. In the international context transnational (or multinational) corporations have long engaged in the systematic exploitation of less developed countries, typically with the corrupt cooperation of the political leadership of these countries.[43] If transnationals are not new they had become especially powerful and ubiquitous by the final decades of the twentieth century, and well-positioned to exploit profit-making opportunities in a "borderless" world.[44] Their immensely harmful activities have included the dumping of demonstrably unsafe products in less developed countries, exposure of workers to grossly unsafe working conditions, economic exploitation of workers, and destructive environmental practices.[45] Furthermore, the criminal activities of transnationals are carried out with the aid of not only the governments of these less developed nations, but agencies of the United States government as well. Over a period of decades the CIA intervened improperly in the affairs of many countries, funneling support to corrupt, totalitarian political leaders viewed as supportive of major corporate interests (as well as U.S. political interests), while aiding in the downfall of other political leaders regarded as threatening to U.S. corporate interests.[46] Transnational corporations lobbied successfully for CIA involvement in overthrowing the democratically elected, leftist government of Salvadore Allende in Chile in 1973, as they feared he would nationalize their businesses.

In at least some less-developed countries the political leadership has used its political power to corruptly acquire vast real estate and business holdings – including major corporations – for itself, family members, and friends or associates. For example, in the Philippines, during the long tenure of Ferdinand Marcos as president (until 1986), private corporations were taken over by the state and put into the hands of Marcos associates, or such associates were granted exclusive franchises on many industries ranging from sugar trading to casino operations.[47] This type of situation has been characterized as "crony capitalism." In Indonesia the family of President Suharto – forced out of office in 1998 – owned and controlled television and radio networks, airlines, banks, chemical factories, pharmaceutical companies, shopping malls, hotels, paper and pulp mills, shipping lines and taxi companies, or billions of dollars worth of assets.[48] This form of state-corporate crime victimizes competing corporations and businesses, as well as citizens and consumers generally insofar as public policy decisions are skewed to favor these well-connected corporations, and they are not likely to be constrained from exploitative practices by state agencies.

Indeed, in many countries around the world corruption is pervasive and institutionalized. Corruption is taken to be especially ingrained in less-developed countries.[49] Although corruption is most often thought of in terms of political office holders or government officials accepting bribes in return for favorable treatment of businesses, corruption has many different meanings.[50] It can be quite difficult to separate corporate or business interests, the personal interests of the political leadership and the well-connected, and the claimed interests of the state.[51]

Russia, since the dissolution of the Soviet Union, has been pervasively corrupt, with many interlinks between high government officials and bureaucrats and new, major corporate enterprises.[52] Although the People's Republic of China remains formally committed to communism, it is also ridden with corrupt relations between government officials and new corporate or business enterprises.[33] Of course much of this corruption does not fit under the heading of state-corporate crime – it is more often a form of political white-collar/corporate crime – but at least some such corruption is state-corporate crime insofar as illegal and harmful actions are undertaken in a cooperative venture between state agencies and corporate entities.

The Case of BCCI: Banking institutions are inevitably at the center of important financial transactions in modern society, and banking institutions are increasing transnational. The BCCI (Bank of Commerce and Credit International) case that emerged in the early 1990s has been characterized as "the largest financial fraud in history," and the bank itself as "the world's most corrupt financial empire," with losses estimated in the $15 billion range.[54] BCCI was founded in Luxembourg in 1972 by a charismatic Pakistani, Agha Hasan Abedi. It was the first multinational "Third World" bank. Operating secretively and with little regulatory oversight, it quickly established branches in over 70 countries around the world, acquired assets of some $20-30 billion, became a major force in world financial centers, and was backed up by the immensely wealthy ruler of Abu Dhai, Sheik al-Nahyan. In 1991 the bank was shut down after investigations in a number of different countries resulted in charges against the bank of corruption, bribery, money laundering, gun running, drug smuggling, terrorism, and massive outright theft. BCCI apparently catered to notorious dictators (including Saddam Hussein) and to international drug dealers (including the Medellin drug cartel). A complex web of strategies, including phony loans, unrecorded deposits, secret files, illicit share-buying schemes, and shell companies, were used to loot the bank of billions.[55] Bribery was one key to BCCI's success in infiltrating or taking over banks in many countries and in escaping accountability for so long. Clearly in many countries, political figures and officials in government entities, acting from various motives, facilitated the BCCI crimes. The BCCI is alleged to have served as a conduit for illegal funds in the Iran/Contra arms case, and in the transferral of vast funds out of the Phillipines by its former president, Ferdinand Marcos.[56] The BCCI case may not be a classic case of state-corporate crime, but it certainly incorporated elements of such crime. The case demonstrates that the distinctions between legitimate and illegitimate enterprises are often slight at best, and that the lines of demarcation between state (or governmental) crime, finance (or corporate) crime, and organized (or enterprise) crime are often blurred.[57] With the rapid expansion of the global financial network there is good reason to believe that other such major crimes involving state institutions and financial corporations will occur in the future.

In the American Context: Various elements of the American political and economic system are linked to state-corporate crime. The whole structure of political campaign financing gives corporations tremendous clout with the political leadership, insofar as they are a major source of campaign funds, especially through political action committee (PAC) donations.[58] Although many of the interests of corporations may be viewed as legitimate, legal, and in line with the interests of the state, corporations, in some cases, use their political connections to facilitate illegal and harmful activities, or to head off investigation and prosecution of such activity. Corporate lobbying, too, may in some cases draw political figures into cooperative roles

in connection with some form of corporate illegality and harmful conduct.[59] At what point does tax law favoring corporations and saving them
millions, enacted or implemented by political leaders indebted to corporations for economic benefits, become a form of state-corporate crime, imposing an unfair burden on ordinary taxpayers?[60] Corporations are also in a position to employ the best possible legal talent available, and these corporate
lawyers – typically well-connected politically – also use various tactics to foster state-corporate ventures that have harmful consequences for ordinary citizens.[61] The concept of "agency capture" has been applied to circumstances
where governmental agencies that are supposed to regulate an industry, and
the corporations active in the industry, are really overlooking corporate violations due to ties agency administrators have to these corporations.[62] Certain industries – for example, the defense industry – are characterized by
especially close and complex ties between government agencies and corporations.[63] At least a certain proportion of the billions of tax dollars wast-
ed or defrauded through defense contracts is best described as state-corporate crime. Altogether the many interlocks and interrelations between
political leaders, government bureaucrats, and corporations inevitably give
rise to harmful (and sometimes illegal) cooperative activities that could be
considered forms of state-corporate crime.

The Case of NASA/Morton Thiokol and the Challenger Explosion:
On January 28, 1986, the space shuttle *Challenger* exploded – killing six
astronauts and an American schoolteacher – as millions of Americans
watched on television. This famous incident has been described as a case of
state-corporate crime, insofar as a state agency, NASA, and a private corporation, Morton Thiokol, Inc., are alleged to have had motivations to press for
a launch despite unfavorable, cold-weather conditions and recommendations
against launching by aeronautical engineers.[64] The specific cause of the
explosion was traced to O-ring seals linking the rocket engine to the space
shuttle; these O-rings were apparently affected by the cold weather, and
failed. In one interpretation, managerial personnel at NASA and at Morton
Thiokol knowingly allowed the launch to go forward due to a desire to fulfill their political and economic agendas. On the one hand, NASA, a governmental agency, was under continual pressure during a period of diminished
political and economic support for the space program generally, to produce
a successful launch of the reusable space shuttle as soon as possible. On the
other hand, the Morton Thiokol corporation, the primary contractor on the
project, was eager to meet NASA's tight deadlines, and retain its profitable
contracts. Alternatively, in Diane Vaughan's monumental study of the launch
decision, it was not "evil managers," but organizational standards for acceptable risks that led to the launch in less than optimal conditions.[65] But whether
one focuses the primary blame on managers or on organizational culture and
standards, the *Challenger* catastrophe reflected a joint state-corporate enterprise that imposed excessive risks or harm on innocent parties, and in at least
this sense was a form of state-corporate crime.

A Fire in Hamlet: In September of 1991 an explosion and fire occurred at the Imperial Food Products chicken processing plant in Hamlet, North Carolina; 25 plant workers were killed and 56 were injured. Judy Root Aulette and Raymond Michalowski describe this as a case of state-corporate crime, due to the complicity of both a range of state agencies and the Imperial Food Processing corporation.[66] Although the rupture of a hydraulic line was the immediate cause of the explosion (and fire), Aulette and Michalowski identify a series of organizational decisions (both public and private sector) that contributed to the tragic losses of life, and the serious injuries. In a broader sociohistorical context, the state of North Carolina had long embraced a policy of overlooking exploitative or dangerous corporate practices in the interest of attracting corporations to the state. In the present case, negligent oversight by Federal agencies – OSHA (Occupational Safety and Health Administration) and USDA (United States Department of Agriculture) – state, and local agencies contributed to generally unsafe conditions at this plant and the specific circumstances where the plant management could get away with locking workers in at the workplace, ultimately trapping many of them when fire broke out. Aulette and Michalowski's modified conception of state-corporate crime defines it in terms of illegal or socially injurious actions resulting from the interaction of public and private institutions pursuing their goals. A study of the media coverage of this case found that newspaper accounts attributed the deaths to the lax enforcement of safety regulations but these accounts did not address these deaths as a case of crime, and they did not report criminal convictions in this case.[67] The notion of state-corporate crime continues to be resisted by the media.

The ValuJet Case: In a somewhat parallel case study Rick Matthews and David Kauzlarich address the crash of ValuJet Flight 592 in the Florida Everglades in 1996, killing 105 passengers and five crew members, as a case of state-corporate, or "state-facilitated," crime.[68] ValuJet was an airline company that had achieved rapid growth by providing very low-priced airfares, but this competitive pricing was achieved through some dramatic cost-cutting measures, including contracted-out maintenance. Guidelines for removal and disposal of oxygen generators from within aircraft were not followed by the maintenance company, Sabretech, and apparently an improperly inspected oxygen canister (without safety caps), placed on Flight 592 for transportation, caught fire and exploded, causing the crash. Matthews and Kauzlarich consider the FAA liable as well for failing to adequately enforce federal regulations that could have prevented this accident, motivated by an interest in seeing companies like ValuJet achieve success in the newly deregulated airline industry environment. In July of 1999, Federal and state charges of homicide were filed against Sabretech, and in the Federal case against three of its mechanics; apparently this was the first time criminal charges were filed in an airline accident case.[69] In the view of some commentators, these charges were politically motivated, failed to address the role of the airline and the

FAA itself, and would have the harmful consequence of discouraging cooperation in post-airplane crash investigations. Prosecutors are clearly more
comfortable charging a particular company, and individual employees, than
addressing such incidents as complex cases of state-corporate crime.

Crimes of the Nuclear State: As we move through the twenty-first century the possibility of nuclear war, and nuclear catastrophe generally, is surely among the most frightening and potentially most destructive of all threats
to humanity. In a pioneering work, David Kauzlarich and Ronald Kramer
have explored "crimes of the American nuclear state."[70] These crimes – a controversial designation in this context – include the use or threatened use and
the development of nuclear weapons by the United States government, in
defiance of international law. But at least some of the activities involving
nuclear energy are defined as a form of state-corporate crime. The hazardous
disposal of nuclear wastes involves cooperative activities between the
Department of Energy and private corporations. The long-term harmful
consequences of such disposal of radioactive material may well emerge in
the future.

Marginal and Contentious Cases: As indicated at the outset of this
article, we lack a complete consensus on where we should draw the line
between state-corporate crime and activities of states and corporations that
are disturbing to some but not criminal in any meaningful sense. For example, plant closings and corporate downsizing can cause much economic (and
psychological) devastation to communities, families, and individuals; these
activities are not illegal, but in one interpretation can be facilitated by governmental policies.[71] Of course many parties benefit from such corporate
activities, and some would say that the economy as a whole benefits. Does
such activity have anything to do with state-corporate crime, in any meaningful sense? And Robert Bohm has suggested that such conditions as the
grossly inequitable distribution of wealth; poverty; hunger; institutionalized
racism and sexism, and the like, should be criminal, even if they are not.[72]
If one accepts this provocative argument it follows that in many cases these
conditions can be linked to the policies and actions of both states and corporations, and in that sense state-corporate crime is involved.

The emphasis here has been on state-corporate crime as a global, or
national, phenomenon. William J. Chambliss has shown, however, that networks of politicians, businessmen, and organized crime figures engage in
cooperative, criminal ventures on a local level.[73] At least some of these
ventures could be described as a local version of state-corporate crime.

Explaining State-Corporate Crime

State-corporate crime is complex, and does not have a simple, one-dimensional explanation. The formidable concentration of power in the hands of the state, and corporations, is one important point of departure for the explanatory project. In totalitarian countries, or dictatorships generally, the power of the state is almost limitless. In many such countries corporations quite openly bribe, or collaborate, with the political leadership to engage in plunderous or harmful activities for the mutual enrichment of the corporation and the political leadership. In some countries the political leadership has quite directly owned or controlled many major corporate entities, and there is little meaningful separation between politics and big business. But even in democratic countries power is very disproportionately distributed. C. Wright Mills, a celebrated American sociologist of the mid-twentieth-century period, famously claimed that a "power elite" made up of the top people in the political, military, and corporate world, make the important decisions for American society based largely on their own, interrelated interests.[74] The extent to which power is concentrated in the hands of elites, or is divided between competing interest groups, continues to be debated.[75] That immense power is concentrated in the hands of the government and corporations has been quite thoroughly documented.[76] Corporate power in the present era – and the growing power of transnational corporations – is complex but pervasive.[77] State-corporate crime is most likely to occur in circumstances where power is most heavily concentrated in the hands of state officials and corporations, and where few if any meaningful constraints on this power exist.

State-corporate crime is not typically driven by the specific objective of doing harm (although in a case such as the Nazi state/corporate perpetration of the Holocaust, the intent to do harm – at least on the part of the Nazis – was quite central) Rather, in most cases, states and corporations are prepared to impose significant risks of harm to citizens, consumers or workers in the interest of advancing some state or corporate interest. The accumulation and maintenance of both wealth and power itself are the primary motivating forces for this form of crime. The desire to extend power and to accumulate material wealth would sometimes appear to be unquenchable.

The notion of trust is also at the core of state-corporate crime. In general the state – and to a lesser degree, corporations – enjoy a significant measure of trust from citizens. Indeed, a modern society could hardly function if this were not so. The degree of trust enjoyed by states and corporations facilitates the commission of state-corporate crime, which takes advantage of such trust. The state leadership, and corporate leaders, also benefits from occupying a highly respectable status that largely shields them from the constraints and indignities imposed upon street people, as an example.

State-corporate crime must be understood in terms of a complex interaction of micro-level to macro-level factors. That is, on the micro-level we have the social psychological forces that influence government officials and corporate managers to conform to pressures and expectations in their immediate environment. On the macro-level we have pressures for achieving goals that come from the organization of which they are a part, or the larger political economy. Government and corporate leaders are also responding to values emanating from the culture to which they belong. Any theory of state-corporate crime must integrate explanations on several different levels.

In traditional societies, the local community was a dominant force, with this community sometimes ruled by a tribal chieftain or baron. In modern society, the state impacts on the lives of citizens and becomes an increasingly dominant force in the lives of citizens. In an emerging postmodern society of the future, the world itself is likely to become an increasingly important element of our environment. The concept of globalization is quite widely invoked to describe the world in which we now live, with the claim that globalization will intensify as we move through the twenty-first century.[78] The term globalization does not have a single fixed meaning, but it refers broadly to a context in which global capitalism becomes quite dominant and a global, transnational system and social structure have emerged.[79] Paul Hirst and Grahame Thompson have usefully distinguished between an internationalized world economy and a globalized world economy.[80] An internationalized world economy is one where the principal economic forces are national economies, with much international trade and transnational ownership; in a globalized world economy a new global economy is the principal entity, and dominates economic activity. If the latter model is more accurate, it is one in which national states cannot exercise effective control over transnational corporations, which become increasingly powerful.[81] In such a circumstance, relatively weak national governments – or agencies, political leaders, and bureaucrats affiliated with such governments – are especially likely to engage in illegal and harmful actions with immensely wealthy and powerful transnational corporations. In this circumstance, state-corporate crime is especially likely to thrive.

Responding to and Controlling State-Corporate Crime

The fundamental paradox in the endeavor of controlling state crime is this: We rely primarily on the state itself to control crime. Given the substantial wealth and influence of corporations, it has also proven difficult to effectively control the crimes of these entities within society. It stands to reason, then, that when the state joins forces with corporations in some form of state-corporate crime, the challenges of effective control are likely to be especially great. In response to conventional crime we send out people in blue uniforms, wearing shields, carrying guns; we empower criminal court judges to impose tough sentences; we have prisons, with bars; and so on.

None of the strategies formulated to control street crime are especially applicable to the problem of controlling state-corporate crime, however.

State-corporate crime requires a response on many different levels. First, we must raise quite dramatically public consciousness of the problem. The public ideally imposes pressure on the state, and on corporations, to address harmful activities. In the extreme case the public engages in revolutionary action against state/corporate entities. Then, we can always promote ethics education and ethics codes in the hope that, in the long term, they will foster ethical behavior by government and corporate officials. However, historical evidence suggests we should not rely heavily on this approach making a measurable difference. Of course the state is not a monolithic enterprise. With a separation of powers, we can always hope that one branch of the state will act as an effective check on the activities of another branch, or we can establish independent bodies and commissions to pursue state-corporate crime.

Can law control state-corporate crime? Such crime increasingly crosses national boundaries and accordingly falls in "the space between the laws," in Michalowski and Kramer's memorable expression.[82] Indeed, transnational corporations typically seek to move operations to countries where laws that might act as a constraint on some of their profitable if harmful practices (e.g., environmental pollution) are weak, easily neutralized by bribery, or non-existent. On a national level, the limitations of law have been recognized in response to corporate wrong-doing – for example, in Christopher Stone's influential book on "where the law ends" – and these limitations are compounded when a powerful branch of the state is itself implicated in the wrong-doing.[83] On the global level, international law and international courts will increasingly have to become major means of responding to state-corporate crime, although such an internationalized response continues to confront formidable biases favoring state sovereignty and the challenges of enforcing laws against powerful states and corporations. Within particular nations only a meaningful separation of powers allows for the development and effective enforcement of laws addressing various forms of state-corporate crime.

Conclusion

White-collar crime is endlessly complex, and has many complex dimensions. We have to recognize that what we call white-collar crime can be configured in many different ways. In this article, a case has been advanced for recognizing state-corporate crime as one significant manifestation of white-collar crime. State-corporate crime focuses our attention on the complex of interlocks between states and corporations, that all too often results in illegal or socially injurious actions. A case has been made here for the proposition that state-corporate crime is hardly a myth but in fact is a major threat to our future well-being. The challenge of developing effective responses to state-corporate crime is great. Much depends upon meeting this challenge with some success.

Notes

[1]   Gross, 1980; Tonry and Reiss, 1993.

[2]   For example, see, Clinard and Quinney, 1973:206-223; Clinard and Yeager, 1980; Blankenship, 1993.

[3]   Corporate crime is now typically distinguished from occupational crime, or illegal and harmful activities carried out within the context of a legitimate occupation. Such crime, which includes the crimes of professionals, small businesses, and employees, is taken to primarily benefit the individual (or group of individuals), rather than the organization. However, the line of demarcation between individual and organizational benefit from illegal activity can be quite blurred.

[4]   For example, see, Chambliss, 1989; Ross, 1995; Friedrichs, 1998.

[5]   Governmental crime, in my view, is a broad category of crime encompassing involvement by the state, government officials, or politicians in illegal and harmful behavior (see Friedrichs, 1995). I regard governmental crime as having a cognate relation to white-collar crime.

[6]   It is important to acknowledge that the state is not best thought of as an entirely unified enterprise. Indeed, often one entity that is part of the state investigates and prosecutes another entity of the state.

[7]   Friedrichs, 1996a:143.

[8]   For a discussion of white-collar crime generally, see Friedrichs, 1996a.

[9]   Kramer and Michalowski, 1990.

[10]   Friedrichs, 1996b.

[11]   Many concepts relating to crime have been introduced in the preceding paragraphs. Students are sometimes impatient with discussions of concepts but it must be recognized that any attempt to make sense of, and achieve a clear understanding of, criminological phenomena must begin with the clear and concise definition of the relevant concepts. As John Gerring observes: "[C]oncept formation lies at the heart of all social science endeavor. It is impossible to conduct work without using concepts. It is impossible even to conceptualize a topic, as the term suggests, without putting a label on it." (Gerring, 1999:3).

For Gerring, the criteria of conceptual goodness include the following: familiarity, resonance, parsimony, coherence, differentiation, depth, theoretical utility, and field utility. The concepts introduced in this article – including the concept of state-corporate crime – hopefully meet these criteria, and help advance our understanding of crime.

[12]   I.e., legalistic crime – that is, activities prohibited by criminal law (statutory) or by the finding of a criminal court (adjudicated); humanistic and moralistic crime – that is, those activities that involve demonstrable harm to human beings or are at odds with a "higher" eternal law; and political or popular crimes – that is, acts offensive to those in power or at the focal point of public interest. (Friedrichs, 1996a:5-6).

[13]   Henry and Lanier, 1998; For a good discussion of the case for a more inclusive definition of crime see Kauzlarich and Kramer, 1998:10-15.

[14]   Henry and Lanier, 1998:609-627.

[15]   Evans et al., 1993; Cavender and Mulcahy, 1998.

[16]   Potter and Kappeler, 1998:3.

[17]   Potter and Kappeler, 1998:3; Bailey and Hale, 1998; Lofquist, 1997.

[18]   Cavender and Mulcahy, 1998.

[19]   See Friedrichs, 1996a:19-22.

[20]   Kappeler et al. 1993.

[21]   Clinard and Yeager, 1980.

[22]   Poclad, 1998:2.

[23]   Howard, 1994.

[24]   Chambliss, 1989.

[25]   Mueller and Adler, 1985:286; Peterson, 1989:51.

[26]   Chambliss, 1989; Peterson, 1989.

[27]   Browning and Gerassi, 1980; Adler and Mueller, 1985.

[28]   Jachcel, 1981:193.

[29]   Sale, 1990.

[30]   Josephson, 1934, 1962.

[31]   Noonan, 1984.

[32]   Turner, 1969.

[33]   Hilberg, 1961, Stallibaumer, 1999:1-27.

[34]   Hayes, 1998.

[35]   Hayes, 1987.

[36]   Manchester, 1968.

[37]   Hayes, 1987:209.

[38]   Gregor, 1998.

[39]   Cowell, 1999:A3.

[40]   Ziegler, 1998

[41]   Sanger, 1997:A1.

[42]   Rich, 1998.

[43]   Michalowski and Kramer, 1987. Michalowski and Kramer argue quite persuasively for the term "transnational" because it "implies an entity with an existence above and beyond the states in which it operates, while 'multinational' suggests only a business with operations in more than one country." (1987:34).

[44]   Hedley, 1999.

[45]   Mokhiber, 1988; Bonsignore, 1994.

[46]   Jeffrey-Jones, 1989; Prados, 1986.

[47]   Carbonell-Catilo, 1986.

[48]   Shenon, 1998; Colmey and Liebhold, 1999.

[49]   Theobald, 1990; Ward, 1989; Williams, 1987. While corruption is ordinarily taken to have harmful effects the argument is sometimes made that, in less-developed countries, it fulfills some positive functions as well.

[50]   Johnston, M. 1996.

[51]   As Yves Meny observes:

> Corrupt relations at the international level are particularly complex in that they combine private interests that are legitimate (those of the company) or less honorable (those of brokers) with the interests of political and administrative partners acting either on behalf of public interests considered to be legitimate (support for export, defence of national positions) or as parties standing to gain directly from the illegal transaction (Meny, 1996:321-336).

[52]   Erlanger, 1995; Lloyd, 1999.

[53]   Faison, 1998; Lee, 1990; Lo, 1993; Tang, 1996.

[54]   Truell and Gurwin, 1992.

[55]   Lohr, 1991.

[56]   Kappeler, Blumberg, and Potter, 1993:237-238. The Iran-Contra Arms case involved an illegal sale of weapons to Iran in return for funds used to arm counter-revolutionary forces in Nicaragua, undertaken by high-level officials in the Reagan Administration.

[57]   Kappeler, Blumberg, and Potter, 1993:237-238; Passas, 1993; 1996.

[58]   Eismeier and Pollock, 1988.

[59]   Birnbaum, 1992.

[60]   Barlett and Steele, 1998a; Barlett and Steele, 1998b.

[61]   Nader and Smith, 1996.

[62]   Friedrichs, 1996a:286-287.

[63]   Friedrichs, 1996a:84-85.

[64]   Kramer, 1992:214-243.

[65]   Vaughan, 1996.

[66]   Aulette and Michalowski, 1993.

[67]   Wright, Cullen, and Blankenship, 1995.

[68]   Matthews and Kauzlarich, 1997.

[69]   Wald, 1999; Bragg, 1999.

[70]   Kauzlarich and Kramer, 1998.

[71]   Friedrichs, 1997.

[72]   Bohm, 1993.

[73]   Chambliss, 1988.

[74]   Mills, 1959.

[75]   For a well-known argument on the elite side of this debate see Domhoff, 1967, 1970, and 1990.

[76]   For just one especially accessible account of this concentration of power see Mintz, and Cohen, 1976.

[77]   Bowman, 1996.

[78]   Kofman and Youngs, 1996; Robertson, 1992; Waters, 1995. The seminal roots of globalization go back to the voyages of discovery in the fifteenth century, Valaskakis, 1999.

[79]   Robinson, 1996.

[80]   Hirst and Thompson, 1999.

[81]   Valaskakis, 1999:155. As one commentator has put it, with reference to a globalized world economy:

>   Its most striking feature is the runaway quality of global finance that appears remarkably independent of traditional constraints of information transfer, national regulation, industrial productivity or "real" wealth in any particular society, country or region (Appadurai, 1999:230).

[82]   Michalowski and Kramer, 1987.

[83]   Stone, 1975.

CHAPTER 4

Toward an Understanding
of Academic Deviance*

Bankole Thompson

Introduction

Academic deviance has not been a subject of much scholarly focus and conceptualization in social science. This chapter is an exploratory theoretical study of academic deviance from that perspective. The justification for scholarly concern about this phenomenon is predicated upon its direct contraposition to the notion of the pursuit of excellence enshrined in the charter or mission statement of every institution of higher learning as its *raison d'être*. It is trite knowledge that the pursuit of excellence is academe's *Grundnorm*, deviations from which must logically be perceived as threats to the very survival of its ideals. Conceptualizing academic deviance in these terms is not an exaggeration of the nature and scope of the challenges it poses to the fundamental values and norms of academia. On the contrary, it is a recognition of a subtle and almost imperceptible threat to the core values of one of society's most valued and respected institutions which, if not addressed, may seriously undermine the credibility and legitimacy of the academic culture. The truth of this assertion will become evident as the chapter explores the diverse forms and dimensions of this emerging phenomenon, ranging from the seemingly innocuous to the manifestly illegal. What, then, is academic deviance?

* I wish to express my gratitude to Dr. Pete Kraska, Dr. Ken Tunnell, Dr. Thomas Reed, and Professor Vic Bumphus for their very valuable comments and suggestions. I also owe a debt of gratitude to Laurel Conners, one of my graduate assistants, for her own contributions.

Conceptual, Definitional, and Methodological Problems

As a concept, academic deviance is difficult to articulate with precision due both to its novelty, and definitional and methodological problems. Instructively, in the spheres of sociology and criminology, definitional and methodological issues have traditionally proved to be complex and intractable. One manifestation of this feature is that of scholarly efforts to conceptualize hitherto novel concepts like 'state crime' and 'political crime.' For example, to this end, Barak has observed that any systematic treatment of 'state crime' must grapple with conceptual, definitional, and methodological issues.[1] Likewise, Cohen takes the view that "early attempts to define the concept of state crime and links to human rights' violations failed because they were too wooly and polemical."[2] Similar controversies have surrounded the definition of 'political crime,' one being the possibility of a significant overlapping between 'state crimes' and 'political crimes.'[3] It is, however, not a contention here that academic deviance must be equated with the notion of criminality even though there exists the possibility of some overlapping between them especially where an act punishable under the general criminal law may also attract disciplinary sanction within the sphere of academia where the act is criminal in nature.

It is conceded that for the most part, academic deviance does not require the violation of laws. Even though this is the case, there is no logical reason why conduct which is in violation of academic values should not be characterized as deviant. But deviance is not necessarily coextensive with contravention of positive law. Likewise, an act within an academic setting which turns out to be morally reprehensible may still be properly described as deviant, even if it falls outside the proscriptive ambit of the criminal law, immoral acts not necessarily being the target of contemporary criminal prohibitions. Nor is there a perfect or necessary correlation between socially harmful conduct, in its widest sense, and conduct that is criminal. Analogously, no logical correlation is being posited here between academically deviant behavior and a criminal act, because "the criminal quality of an act cannot be discerned by intuition, nor can it be discovered by reference to any standard but one: is the act prohibited with penal sanction."[4] This reasoning is inapplicable to academic deviance because it is meaningless to inquire whether the act complained of is prohibited with academic sanctions, express prohibition in some academic code of conduct not logically being a condition precedent for an act to be designated as academically deviant. Nor can it be discerned intuitively.

Despite conceptual, definitional, and methodological problems about new deviant tendencies or activities, they have become, in contemporary times, appropriate themes for social scientific investigation and study. In effect, social science scholars have wrestled with such issues in their quest for an understanding of the nature, scope, and forms of hitherto unexplored brands of deviant behavior. Difficulties of this nature are commonly confronted in the context of scholarly efforts at conceptualizing and defining harmful activities that have never been conventionally characterized as deviant. It is suggested that an example of such harmful activities are those occurring within public institutions like the university which have, hitherto, been immune from legal scrutiny but which may objectively and reasonably be categorized as deviant even if not overtly illegal. An underlying premise of this chapter is that orthodoxy aside, there is nothing, in principle, precluding some scholarly focus from a social science perspective on harmful and prejudicial activities undertaken within universities with a view to exploding the myth that the culture of academia continues to be paradigmatic of excellence and immune from the imperfections associated with the outside world. In a sense, the subject of academic deviance is ripe for academic inquiry.

As a preliminary issue, it should be emphasized that, as a concept, academic deviance is problematical and open to intellectual challenge for several reasons. First, the concept itself may seem anomalous, given the entrenched perception that the university is predicated upon the doctrine of excellence. However, there is no logical inconsistency in maintaining that deviations from academic norms and values can and should be perceived notionally as academic deviance. Second, there is, as of now, no evidence or substantial body of evidence justifying scholarly attention to the concept as a social problem. This is attributable to the fact that the theme has never been regarded as a favorite subject of academic study largely due to the exclusive preoccupation, on the part of scholars, with the malfunctioning of other institutions in society except their own. Third, the probability that many academics would find any focal interest on the notion of academic deviance intellectually unpalatable, if not heretical, or even anomalous.

Based on the above assumptions, it is to be noted that there is bound to be controversy on the issue of a proper definition of academic deviance or even its existence at all primarily because it has never been seriously inquired whether admittedly harmful or prejudicial activities done within and on behalf of the university can, where appropriate, be suitably characterized as deviant. Conceptualization in this sphere has been mainly in the context of white-collar criminality in the ivory tower. Controversy of this nature is inevitable and constructive since the idea of academics policing themselves has been the rule rather than the exception. Therefore, conceptualizing and defining academic deviance is inescapably a formidable task rendered complicated by what may conceivably be its amorphous nature and complexity. What, then, is its doctrinal scope and nature?

Nature and Scope of Academic Deviance

Realizing the absolute lack of a definition of the term, the paradigmatic approach being adopted here is a juridical one, of linking the concept with a fivefold broad rationalization of activities that significantly (1) detract from the pursuit of excellence, as the supreme function of the academic community; (2) undermine professional autonomy, academic freedom, and the merit principle as three key foundational values of academia; (3) erode the principle of tenure as one long accepted core ingredient of the academic culture; (4) compromise integrity, objectivity, honesty, fairness, trust, and propriety as some shared norms and values that bind members of the academic community; and (5) violate the principle of legality in so far as it is recognized as applicable to decision-making process in institutions of higher learning.

Predicated upon the apparent inexhaustiveness of its categories as articulated, academic deviance, for the purposes of this study, may be defined as conduct within the academic sphere encompassing a broad range of prejudicial activities including: inefficiency; incompetence; negligence; lack of respect for properly constituted institutional authority; abuse of office; arbitrariness; patronage; nepotism; favoritism; corruption; partisanship; factionalism; discrimination; conflict of interests; circumvention or violation of properly established institutional principles, policies, procedures, and practices; disregard for the truth and the free spirit of inquiry; stifling academic freedom; abusing academic freedom; fraudulent research; engaging in any other conduct not consistent with the formal and informal missions and goals of the university; systematic replacing or supplanting of formally declared goals and objectives by fundamentally inconsistent informal ones; basing key personnel or related decisions on factors extraneous to the principle of merit; or performing other unsanctioned or prohibited institutional activity. Residually, it is also conceivable that there may be some overlapping between specific acts correctly characterized as deviant in an academic sense and specific acts of an illegal nature especially where the former amount to contraventions of positive law. But a complete understanding of the concept of academic deviance as articulated in this chapter can only be derived from an appreciation of the normative framework of academia.

The Normative Framework of Academia: Excellence, Integrity, Academic Freedom

Any discussion of the normative framework of academia must be predicated upon the recognition that the structure of the university as social group exhibits a high degree of regularity of behaviors creating a system of institutionalized norms. According to Chambliss and Seidman, two key implications of such an arrangement are: (1) that "action manifests consciousness and consciousness manifests actions," and (2) that the norms reflect the subjective internal conceptions that people hold about how those occupying certain positions ought to act. This reasoning imports the distinction between *role-expectation* and *role-performance*. The latter characterizes how those who serve the university in fact act either in pursuit of the norms defining their respective positions or in contravention of them.[5] In the institutional sense, therefore, the university is a complex interlocking network of norms. What, then, are these norms?

As already noted, any analysis of what the university stands for must begin with a recognition of its avowed commitment to the pursuit of excellence, its *Grundnorm*. This is the paramount standard within which the university operates. The commitment to this goal is frequently described as noble and worthy. However, this is not to contend that all who find themselves within the precincts of the ivory tower are motivated by this ideal. Logically, it is fair to presume the existence of this motivation. However, it can be shown empirically (a task beyond the scope of this study), using language reminiscent of Justice Oliver Wendell Holmes with reference to the law, that the life of academia today is not a quest for excellence, truth, and objectivity in the sphere of knowledge; rather it is one dominated by the competitive dynamics of the academic marketplace reinforced by socioeconomic nuances and subtleties. Despite the foregoing, it must be acknowledged that excellence is the normative hallmark of academia. Akin to this value is the pursuit of truth through free inquiry and the transmission of complex bodies of knowledge to those who come to the university, as the metaphor goes, seeking to drink deep of the fountain of knowledge. Knowledge that is not directed to achieving the truth or which is not acquired through the spirit of free and unfettered inquiry detracts notionally from the ideal of excellence.

The recognition of integrity as another key value vital to the academic function is implicit in the observation that "integrity is the soul of intellectual life"[6] and that "knowledge without integrity is weak and useless, and knowledge without integrity is dangerous and dreadful."[7] Not only does integrity, normatively, guide and inspire the teaching and learning process, it also permeates the array of institutional principles, policies, and procedures upon which university administration is pivoted. In addition, it is a core element of the principle of legality to which university actions, decisions, traditions, and practices must at all times conform.

A related value which is an integral part of the normative bedrock of the culture of academia is objectivity. Objectivity "calls for putting one's idiosyncratic predilections and parochial preferences aside in forming one's beliefs, evaluations, and choices. It is a matter of proceeding in line not with one's inclinations but with the dictates of impartial reason,"[8] and scientific data when available. To the community of scholars objectivity is a categorical imperative. In that regard, objectivity is seen as coextensive with rational cogency, applying the anthropomorphic conception of justice – the standard of the paradigmatic reasonable person.[9] Deviations from the objective standard in academia could be perceived as normative compromises even where expediency or pragmatism might have dictated those choices. For instance, it can be generalized that where decisions taken within the sphere of academia are based largely on the idiosyncratic predilections or parochial preferences of the decisionmaker, they clearly fall within the definitional scope of academic deviance. In essence, academic deviance occurs when wholly extraneous factors have influenced the decision-making process pertaining to some academic or academically related matter.

Another critical dimension of the normative context of academia is academic freedom. It is, as it were, the nerve center of the academic culture. Academic freedom has been variously defined. First, it denotes the right enjoyed by professors to pursue issues and problems in their fields of specialization and to communicate their teaching, research, and extramural utterances.[10] Second, it has been defined as the right to dispassionately search out the truth as a prerequisite for the satisfactory performance of the dual function of creating and transmitting knowledge.[11] Third, it is used to designate the right of all members of the community to express their ideas free from any political or ideological pressures that might censor their scholarship. A more comprehensive definition is the United Nations' perspective of academic freedom. It is threefold: (1) the right to teach freely according to accepted principles of professional responsibility and intellectual rigor and the right to disseminate research results; (2) the freedom to criticize one's institution and the educational system without fear of reprisal; (3) the right of faculty to undertake professional activities outside of their employment, particularly those that enhance their professional skills or allow for the application of knowledge to the problems of the community.[12]

However broadly or narrowly defined, the notion of academic freedom enjoys an inherent normative sacrosanctity underscored by the classic observation that "the university should have a place for extremes of thought on almost any question."[13] Academic freedom is, therefore, the pivot of the normative structure of academia. Admittedly, academic freedom does not give its possessors the right to impose any risk of harm they like in the name of freedom of inquiry.[14] And so, any such abuse can itself be perceived as violative of the norm. Equally important is the obligation that academic freedom imposes on faculty vis-à-vis students to develop an intellectual climate conducive to free expression and exploration of ideas. More specifically, it includes the following: freedom to read anything relevant to the intellectual task at hand; freedom to hear expressed a wide range of viewpoints; and freedom to express beliefs, to discuss, and to disagree with other students and with instructors on matters of opinion.[15] Failure to create such an intellectual atmosphere may constitute academic deviance.

Another indispensable and core feature of the normative hierarchy of academia is the doctrine of professional autonomy. Professional autonomy is the belief that individual faculty, and, by extension, academic departments, are by nature of their expertise in the best position to determine and organize their own work, accountable only to their professional peers.[16] "Professional" is a multifaceted concept, and it can be defined with any degree of precision when applied to any specific facet of the academic community. Nevertheless, it is certain that regardless of what is conveyed in one or another context, any usage would encompass the basic elements of professional behavior – disinterestedness, service, commitment to task, excellence, responsibility, and rationality.[17] Ideally, a key implication of professionalism is that members of the academic community are evaluated "almost entirely on the basis of one set of standards almost all members accept: professional performance."[18] The complexity of this norm requires, exceptionally, some further elaboration in an empirical context. Despite its centrality to the community of scholars, there is some evidence that faculty themselves attach little importance to it and as to the extent to which the norm actually operates within the academic system.[19] Baldridge et al. examined six dimensions of faculty professional autonomy: (1) the extent to which faculty employment contracts explicitly specify work to be performed or are relatively open ended; (2) the extent to which professional travel is tightly regulated; (3) locus of control over faculty teaching assignments; (4) the extent to which faculty are evaluated by their professional colleagues rather than by administrators; (5) locus of control over faculty hiring – departmental versus administrative; (6) locus of control over tenure decision – departmental versus administrative.

They found, in the first place, that the extent of professional autonomy varied considerably across the six dimensions. The majority of faculty experienced considerable individual freedom in their teaching assignments and their contractual obligations, and considerable departmental autonomy in hiring colleagues. However, a majority also reported a lack of individual autonomy in professional travel and of departmental autonomy in faculty evaluation and promotion. Moreover, faculty at different types of institutions showed very different levels of professional autonomy. Autonomy tended to be highest at research universities, followed in descending order by private liberal arts colleges and public comprehensive colleges and universities. In a subsequent analysis, institutional size and complexity – defined in terms of the higher degree offered, together with level of faculty expertise, defined by the proportion of faculty with the doctorate – emerged as the most decisive determinants of level of professional autonomy. Those larger, more differentiated institutions boasting a higher percentage of doctorally trained faculty in a large number and variety of departments tended to most fully recognize faculty prerogatives for independence.[20]

The principle of merit is another core ingredient of academia. As a juridical concept, merit means "to each according to his abilities," or in another and closely related sense, "to each according to his works.[21] In these two combined senses, merit advances and rewards according to ability and accomplishment, rather than according to status, preferment or chance."[22] It has been observed that where factors peripheral to the central functions of teaching and research intrude upon the application of the merit principle, institutionally this could lead to its total eclipse.[23] This is a significant observation especially when considered alongside the two key dynamics of the reality of the academic community: (1) the insignificant role played by faculty in determining who remains or does not remain within the community and (2) the fact that such a decision is the ultimate responsibility of the academic-administrators who may appear to be interested in questions or factors other than merit.[24] As a matter of logic, departures from the principle of merit can only be perceived as corrosive of a bedrock value of academia, almost analogous to an assault on the wall of Jericho. As an academic doctrine, merit is fraught with immense difficulties of application. Whatever problems are encountered with the concept arise more from subtleties and nuances of application rather than of analysis or conceptualization. It is at that boundary line, a delicate one at that, that it can be meaningfully asserted that issues of deviation can theoretically be characterized as academic deviance. In this context, the line between conformity and deviance can indeed be a fine one to draw. Then only the particular facts and circumstances can shed light on whether the principle has been followed or violated. Presumptions can also be useful in determining the issue. One such presumption is that whenever the academic system reflects fundamental disparities and inequities, the principle of merit goes into recession. In a community of scholars, scholarly performance is the only legitimate claim to recognition.[25] And so, when colleagues with lesser academic achievements are promoted over those whose academic accomplishments are greater, "the resulting demoralization is not limited to the persons concerned but tends to affect the entire milieu."[26]

Collegiality, too, is believed to enjoy some preeminence in academia being a logical corollary of the notion of a community of shared norms and values. As a defining characteristic, it is a precept inculcated in every new member of the community. Like many other kindred values and ideals, it is extremely difficult to measure. One valid perception is that, generally, it exists more in the realm of rhetoric than in reality. Despite its inherent elusiveness, it does not take any stretch of the imagination to figure out that where there is lack of trust, lack of respect for the opinions of others, and divisiveness among scholars, collegiality is more honored in its breach than its observance. The gravity of the breach may be directly proportionate to the acuteness and complexity of any scholarly ideological and political divergences existing among faculty.

Another important value of the academic culture is respect for properly constituted institutional authority and the principles, policies, and procedures by which they are constituted and regulated. It is expected that members of the community of scholars will uphold the hierarchy of the organic structure which establishes their community and its *modus operan-*

di. It is, likewise, expected that they will respect and abide by the body of principles, policies, and procedures that regulate the functioning of the various organs and institutions constituting the community. Highlighting the malfunctioning of organs within the hierarchical framework or criticizing the misapplication of policies and deviations from laid down decision-making processes or abuse of procedures cannot be equated with lack of respect for properly constituted institutional authority. To do so is tantamount to stifling academic freedom, a norm whose nature and scope has always been a matter of acute controversy, but which, nonetheless, lies at the heart of the culture of academia.

Analysis and Conclusion

Predicated upon the functionalist hypothesis in sociology that "every society has a set of agreed-upon customs (rules, norms, and values) which most members internalize," it is deducible that the university, as a social group or institution, is governed by a network of shared norms, values, and traditions which most members internalize. Within such a culture, the expectation would be that of academic conformity. Academic deviance, therefore, emanates from the fact that some members of the university do get socialized into behavior that objectively deviates from the prescribed norms, but which serves their individual or collective interests and may not be in conformity with those of the institution. Such socialization, depending on its regularity and frequency, may crystallize into a culture of patronage with a high potential for supplanting the agreed-upon and established culture of meritocracy. Admittedly, where it is contended that a culture of patronage plausibly rests on the notion of 'being a team player,' the line between academic conformity and academic deviance may sometimes, depending on the particular facts and circumstances of each case, become extremely difficult to draw. How, then, does academic deviance relate to academic conformity? The interaction or relationship between the two concepts, it is submitted, is antithetical and dichotomous. Notionally, it is one of mutual exclusivity.

One of the underlying assumptions here is that academic deviance may manifest itself in diverse, complex, and subtle forms. Within the parameters of the broad categorizations of academic deviance articulated earlier, it is postulated that several specific acts done within and against academic institutions which can be accurately characterized as deviant include violations of due process, infringement of academic freedom, circumvention or disregard of written policies and procedures governing decision-making processes, application of extraneous criteria in the decision-making process, unethical conduct, neglect of institutional obligations and responsibilities to students, deliberate indifference to students' needs and interests, lowering of standards in pedagogy and scholarship, grave breaches of collegiality, erosion of objectivity and reasonableness in decisionmaking, discrimination and unfair practices, undermining the integrity of the reappointment, promotion and tenure process, acts of a fraudulent or criminal nature, proclivity to violate rules and regulations, erosion of standards of excellence, and contraventions of standard academic practices.

Breaches of collegiality, antagonistic rivalry, and demonstration of pettiness among colleagues, and lack of respect for the opinions of others can result in a culture of divisiveness. Where this is carried into the pedagogical or research arena and conveyed to the students, a new and equally pernicious culture emerges: one of academic superiority, arrogance, resentment, and contempt for the judgments of other colleagues. Admittedly, a feeling of academic self-appreciation is not wrong or damaging. Another effect of this trend is the undervaluing of meritorious academic productivity of colleagues who genuinely strive to exceed normal expectations in their teaching, scholarship, and service. Such activities clearly fall within the definitional scope of academic deviance proposed here because of their potential cumulatively to threaten the survival of the core values of the ivory tower depending on their level of intensity. When these cultures become chronic they can militate against the pursuit of genuine and legitimate institutional goals and objectives. Needless to mention that, in their acrimonious and malignant form, they can completely destroy true collegiality.

Another context in which academic deviance may become perceptible relates to the notion of autonomy and some of its implications for the academic community. Predicated upon the notions of faculty governance, collegiality, and appropriate academic leadership, institutional autonomy must be balanced by institutional accountability. When this is not the case, not only is there a likelihood of a gradual diminution of accountability on vital issues of commitments to quality and excellence, fairness to students and minorities, and to support of academic freedom, but also a systematic wiltering away of faculty governance, a core doctrine of the university as a community of shared norms and responsibilities and the tenet that universities "are built on faculty and their intellectual capital is derived from faculty."[27] Arguably, within a much narrower compass, conduct transgressing the bounds of academic propriety in relation to pedagogical, research, and service-oriented matters may ordinarily be labeled as academic misconduct. It is submitted that where, extraordinarily, such conduct reaches the level of a gross deviation from widely accepted academic standards and practices, it may, analogous to the notion of medical malpractice, properly be construed as academic malpractice. This reasoning rests on the presupposition that academia is governed by a tradition of ethics. It seems, too, that proclaiming excellence but systematically neglecting to sustain it or promoting mediocrity may well be symptomatic of academic dysfunctionalism, itself a species of academic deviance. When deviance within academia assumes scandalous proportions, it becomes impossible to claim for the ivory-tower immunity from the imperfections of the outside world. The logical recourse, then, is to attempt to pierce the academic veil and explore the extent to which specific goals such as power and prestige have created situations whereby conflicts of values and deviant activity have become acceptable means of achieving such goals.[28]

In the ultimate analysis, without detracting from the utility of the rationalizations of academic deviance articulated here and the proposed theoretical framework for understanding it, it should be emphasized that whether a specific act constitutes academic deviance or not is not merely a philosophical issue. It is, inevitably, a determination predicated upon the facts and circumstances of each particular case in the light of the governing institutional norms and values or any other applicable regime of rules and principles. Perhaps, future research into this phenomenon may well focus on providing an alternative theoretical framework for understanding the problem. It may also be in the direction of investigating empirically the nature and extent of the problem in a manner similar to the study of white-collar criminality in academia. Further, it may be worthwhile investigating in the future the extent, if any, to which, as the present author asserts, academic deviance has become a subtle and almost imperceptible threat to the core values of academia which, if not addressed, may erode its credibility and legitimacy.

Notes

[1] Barak, G., 1991.

[2] Cohen, S., 1996:1-21.

[3] Friederichs, D., 1998.

[4] *Proprietary Articles Trade Association v. A-G for Canada AC 310* (1931) per Lord Atkin quoted in Thompson, 1999.

[5] Chambliss, W. and R. Seidman, 1982.

[6] Anderson, M., 1992.

[7] Anderson, M., 1992.

[8] Reschler, N., 1997.

[9] Reschler, N., 1997.

[10] Metzger, W., 1955; Finklestein, M., 1989.

[11] Lewis, L., 1975.

[12] *Academe*, Bulletin of the American Association of University Professors Vol. 85 No. 4 (1999).

[13] Lazarsfeld, P. and W. Thielens Jr., 1958.

[14] *Academe*, Bulletin of the American Association of University Professors Vol. 85 No. 4 (1999).

15   Eastern Kentucky University Faculty/Staff Handbook 1998-2000 (Richmond, KY: Eastern Kentucky University 1998).

16   Lazarsfeld P. and W. Thielens Jr., 1958.

17   Lazarsfeld P. and W. Thielens Jr., 1958.

18   Lazarsfeld P. and W. Thielens Jr., 1958.

19   Finklestein, M., 1989.

20   Finklestein, M., 1989.

21   Seabury, P., 1972:41; Lewis, L., 1975.

22   Seabury, P., 1972:41; Lewis, L., 1975.

23   Lewis, L., 1975.

24   Lewis, L., 1975.

25   Caplow, T. and R. McGee, 1977.

26   Caplow, T. and R. McGee, 1977.

27   Bracey, D. et al., *Study Team Report of the Criminal Justice Graduate Program Review* (Kentucky: Eastern Kentucky University, March 2000).

28   Simon D. and D.S. Eitzen, 1990.

CHAPTER 5

A Critical Model for the Study of Resource Colonialism and Native Resistance

Linda Robyn

During certain points in time, the pattern of history repeats itself in current events. Such moments take on a new meaning when a people and a region are shaped and changed through economic advancement of the state and powerful multinational corporations. Indigenous peoples (also called First Peoples, First Nations, American Indians, Native Americans) are on the frontline of contemporary colonial struggles. They are sitting on resources the rest of the world wants, and wants at the lowest possible cost. Their territories are considered frontier lands, unowned, underutilized, and therefore, open to exploitation. Usually, indigenous populations are small, politically weak, and physically isolated. Until recently, resistance to corporate greed by indigenous people who historically have had most of their power stripped away has been relatively ineffective.

Resource acquisition and profit-maximizing activities by some of the most powerful institutions in the industrial global economy have been defined in the past by genocide, social hierarchy, and out-of-control technology. Nonrenewable resource addiction, life-threatening pollution, massive habitat destruction, and endless material growth – the results of these types of activities – are considered crimes from a critical perspective because the dominance of indigenous peoples by powerful institutions, and the suppression of indigenous knowledge, ultimately hurts us all.

The Chippewa of Wisconsin, along with several grassroots organizations, are no longer willing to submit to the multinational corporations' ongoing war of aggression against native peoples and the natural world. The Chippewa's unwillingness to acquiesce to the most powerful institutions in the world has been met with various institutional sanctions, including criminalizing those who dare to resist.

Today, in order to maintain control over others' (in this case, the Chippewa of Wisconsin) land and resources, corporate/state actors must effectively neutralize efforts of those who would oppose this control. Michalowski's work on the dynamic relations between the capitalist economic mode and the hierarchical working of state control help analyze resistance as deviance. Michalowski writes that "it is the political economy of a society in connection with its cultural history that determines the definition of what acts are adaptive, rebellious, or maladaptive."[1] Michalowski points out that "to understand the 'criminality' of any particular individual or group (in this case resistance by the Chippewa) requires critical examination of the objective yet dynamic connections between individual experience and the historically specific character of material and social relations."[2]

In applying Michalowski's analysis to the scenario occurring between the Chippewa and the corporate/state actors in Wisconsin, being an American Indian of any tribe is not merely a condition or state. It is also a manifestation of specific social and material relations between Indian people and white Americans that extends back to the time when Europeans arrived and set out the treaties that formed the resource colonies that exist today. Resistance as deviance and social control is located in recurrent historical struggles to control material existence. A critical view of these hierarchical social structures argues that these historical creations do not exist naturally. The age-old structures between powerful institutions and the Chippewa exist as they are produced over and over again as part of the everyday struggles of people. A critical approach to the events occurring between the Chippewa and corporate/state institutions provides a framework for challenging these recurrent historical struggles, the hierarchical structure of government, and its application of the law.

Culture Conflict

The continuing loss of Indian land today through mining and other capitalistic enterprises is rooted in the first contacts between the Native American and Europeans. When two different races of people come together, lives are changed; sometimes for the better, but often for the worse. The Europeans' search for gold, precious metals, and fossil fuels demonstrates such a meeting with an outcome that adversely transformed a region and a people through social conflict which is still occurring today.

The Chippewa/Ojibwa suffered more than the loss of their native lands at the hands of the first European explorers. Chippewa culture, spirituality, and language were also at the mercy of the Europeans. Some tribes were totally eliminated through genocidal practices. Even though settlement in permanent villages occurred with treaties ending their nomadic lifestyle, the Chippewa have survived and have managed to keep their culture alive, despite the persistence of the paternalism of the French, British, and Americans.

Without a doubt, the wearing away of traditional Chippewa culture by white Americans has left its mark in many areas, but although times and traditions change, the roots of the Chippewa have remained strong. Through failed attempts of the federal government to make the Chippewa reservations self-supporting and assimilate its residents into mainstream America, the importance of their culture became clear. The resistance to total assimilation and their strong tribal cohesiveness have been a nurturing source of strength allowing the Chippewa to survive the interference of destructive government policies for the past 300 years.

That their traditional culture and beliefs were able to survive at all through centuries of European domination demonstrates the high degree of strength found in their strong sense of ethnic identity. The traditional beliefs of the Chippewa endure in the old and new ways of life representing a strong legacy and a firm foundation of great importance to the Indian people.[3]

The history between Europeans and Chippewa lead to the perception of the Chippewa as an exploitable group, or disposable resource. In retrospect, the historical relationship that evolved between these two peoples lends insight to the reason why exploitation is occurring today. The Chippewa, and many other American Indian tribes, believe in a strong sense of balance. Before the first Europeans came, the Great Lakes region of the Chippewa was a vast land mass. The trees, earth, and the sense and sight of the environment itself influenced the intellect and thinking process of the Indians in creating the notion of balance. This precarious balance still exists, and the relationship between plants, animals, the elements, the air, water, wind, and the earth, are all equally and evenly placed within the whole. For many Chippewa even today, the way of life revolved around the environment. One does not, and indeed cannot, own the other if a healthy balance is to be maintained. Rather, only what is necessary to survive is taken from one another.[4]

As it is with balance, the spiritual connection with the natural world is sacred. There is a balance of power between humans, animals, all of the environment, heaven, and earth. All these pieces tied together make up the whole. Spiritually, or "The Way" guides the balance.

The French who came to the Great Lakes region during the sixteenth century, followed by the British, and then the American settlers, did not respect, let along try to understand, the ways of native peoples. The exploitation that occurred as the settlers in the 1800s demanded more and more land resulted in massive land losses to the Chippewa. The ceding of lands in exchange for services (economic extortion) caused the loss of almost all of the Chippewa lands. At the center of all treaties was the American businessmen's desire to acquire land to further their capitalistic economic gains. In time, the lands ceded often suffered dire environmental consequences at the hands of the big money moguls; a practice that has continued to this day. To understand this, some facts need to be considered.

Many American Indians are very rich spiritually, but suffer severe economic hardships as a result of being forced to live within a nation whose mainstream culture is so different from their own. Hunting, gathering, and fishing were enough for the Indians of the Great Lakes region to survive many years ago, but the development and destruction of the land and resources by the descendants of the first explorers and settlers means that these methods, as a sole means of survival, are no longer available. Therefore, most American Indians have had to find other ways to survive. Sometimes they have been successful, but all too often, they suffer from the consequences of economic extortion and dependence on the white culture.

American Indians have been victimized into giving up their lands, or allowing the use or development of their lands, in return for economic relief. More times than not, this economic relief has led to the failure of capitalism to work to the advantage of the Chippewa as well as to other problems such as alcohol and drug abuse.

The incongruence in the values and in the understanding of progress of two different cultures was a major factor in the loss and destruction of Chippewa lands. The American Indian values expressed the strong relationship between family members, kinship ties, the environment, and the unity of all things. European values allowed land and environment to be viewed as commodities to be exploited, and they imposed their will upon the land with little thought of the consequences. The values of the Indians emerged from their woodland cultures and spirituality. There was a timeless value placed on all things. Native values are circular with all things being related as revealed from the outer world and their religion.

The Anishinabe (Chippewa/Ojibwa) people developed a code of ethics and a value system that guides the behavior of many in accordance with Natural Law – or mino bimaatisiiwin – translated as "the good life" or "continuous rebirth." Mino bimaatisiiwin "guides behavior toward others, toward animals, toward plants and the ecosystem, and it is based on tenets of reciprocity and cyclical thinking."[5]

In contrasting the value system of the Chippewa with capitalistic values, it is reciprocity or reciprocal relations that define responsibilities and ways of relating between humans and the world around them. LaDuke writes:

> Simply stated, 'the resources' of the ecosystem, whether corn, rocks, or deer, are viewed as 'animate' and, as such, gifts from the Creator. Thus, one could not take life without reciprocal offering, usually tobacco or saymah, as it is called in our language. Within this act of reciprocity is also an understanding that 'you take only what you need and leave the rest.' Implicit in the understanding of Natural Law is also the understanding that most of what is natural is cyclical: whether our bodies, the moon, the tides, seasons, or life itself. Within this natural cycling is also a clear sense of birth and rebirth, a knowledge that what one does today will affect us in the future, on the return.

> These tenets, and the overall practice of mino bimaatisiiwin, imply a continuous inhabiting of place, an intimate understanding of the relationship between humans and the ecosystem, and the need to maintain balance. For the most part, social and economic systems based on these values are decentralized, communal, self-reliant, and very closely based on the land of that ecosystem. This way of living has enabled indigenous communities to live for thousands of years upon their land as, quite frankly, the only examples of continuous sustainability which exist on Turtle Island (North America). We hope there will be more.[6]

The European-American values of power, materialism, economic efficiency, and immediacy have led to confusion and misunderstanding about other people and their ways. European-American views toward family and religion are different than the views of many American Indians. Christianity is not connected to the earth or environment as is the religion of "The Way" of American Indians. The most disturbing aspect of this culture conflict is that both sides see their values and their way of looking at life as the only correct way. In this context, the unequal balance and hierarchical social structure produced by the expansionary needs of capitalism is, to many American Indian people, highly destructive to their perception of the need for balance between physical and spiritual worlds. Leonard Peltier expressed the American Indian point of view well when he stated,

> Today, what was once called worthless land suddenly becomes valuable as the technology of white society advances. White society would like to push us off our reservations because beneath the barren land lie valuable mineral and oil resources. It is not a new development for white society to steal from nonwhite peoples. When white society succeeds it's called colonialism. When white society's efforts to colonize people are met with resistance it's called war. But when the colonized Indians of North America meet to stand and resist we are called criminals.[7]

The sharp contrast between these two sets of cultural views is a major point of contention between state-corporate actors and the Chippewa today. These differences also begin to describe the state-corporate relationships with the Chippewa in Wisconsin today.

State-Corporate Relationships to the Chippewa in Wisconsin

The strained relationships between state and corporate actors, and the Chippewa are rooted in the historical background of treaties and their negative impact on corporate goals of profit. Despite heightened tribal nationalism regarding Indian resources, multinational mining corporations continue to pressure tribes into colonial-style mineral agreements, like the Exxon discovery site.[8]

With treaties blocking the corporate goals of power and profit, the state and corporations have unethically "quietly leased" portions of reservations in an effort to bypass agreements written into treaties. This indicates the strength of the treaties and the weakness of the state of Wisconsin and corporations in their efforts to abrogate the treaties in other ways. Even though treaties have been violated time and time again, they are strong enough to keep the state from overriding the resistance of the Chippewa, or methods of "quiet leasing" would not be necessary.

The resistance by the Chippewa to corporate attempts to dissolve treaties and grab the resources has risen from the past history of Indian/white relations involving exploitation, racism, broken promises, discrimination, and victimization. The relationship has been unequal in the past with the Indians having very little impact on the "white" side of the equation. That situation is changing today with the assertion of treaty rights.

Today, one corporation after another is meeting with stiff resistance from the tribes. These large corporations have developed sophisticated strategies to override and "neutralize" their opposition, but the Chippewa are the ones with the treaties – and treaties will protect their lands – a major stumbling block for the state and corporations today.

The economic stakes involved in mining are staggering. At the same time that the public has become more aware of the serious environmental costs of mining, the anti-Indian movement has become more politically sophisticated and has extended its influence into mainstream politics at both the state and national level. The bottom line, however, is the inseparable connection between the political assault against Indian treaties and the corporate assault on the environment which continues into the new millennium.

Resistance of the Chippewa to Exxon

Because of their environmentally destructive nature, mining operations tend to be highly visible, more so than those of an oil company. One consultant to a multinational corporation states, "The development of a mine assaults the physical, the cultural, and the economic environments, all by its very nature. Therefore, mining companies have a very different socio-political vulnerability pattern than oil companies, even though both are extracting nonrenewable resources.[9] As the higher-grade resources are exhausted, new mining ventures exploit lower-grade deposits in less accessible and more fragile environments.[10] This was the situation confronted by Exxon Minerals in Crandon, Wisconsin. The unequally matched battle between the Sokaogon Chippewa and Exxon Minerals began in 1975 and ended in December 1986 with Exxon's withdrawal from its proposed project.[11]

Exxon first stated its intention to mine a zinc-copper deposit near the town of Crandon, just one mile from the Sokaogon Chippewa's wild rice lake, in 1976. If this mine were to be built, acid runoff and seepage could destroy the lake. Exxon's own environmental report stated that the "means of subsistence on the reservation may be rendered less than effective.[12] The Chippewa became even more concerned when Exxon's own biologist mistook their wild rice for a "bunch of weeds."[13]

Because of its proposed geographic location at the headwaters of the Wolf River, 58 million tons of toxic acidic waste over the 20-year life of the mine would have been generated, contaminating both surface and groundwaters. The Sokaogon Chippewa would not be the only tribe affected. The Menominee, 30 miles downstream, were in the direct path of the pollutants that would be generated from this mine. A report prepared for the Menominee states that "The development of the [Exxon] orebody poses a potential threat to the Wolf River basin . . . Ground-water contamination will be especially hard to detect and contain. The residual effects may not, in some cases, express themselves until years after the development has occurred. If Exxon's plan to contain the tailings fails, pollutants could ruin life in the Wolf River."[14]

Even though this report told of the environmental devastation that would occur with the building of this mine, and that the Menominee were in the direct path of the pollutants that would be generated from this mining operation, Exxon deliberately did not mention the tribe on their maps showing American Indian lands and the local study area.[15] Any contamination of the ground or surface water in the area posed a threat to survival. Exxon's own geologist stated that "contamination is bound to occur no matter how wisely a mine is designed or how diligent are the operators."[16]

These concerns raised the issue of Chippewa treaty rights. Sokaogon Chippewa tribal leaders claimed that the orebody Exxon wanted runs underneath their reservation, which lies in the middle of a 92,000-acre tract of land promised to them by the United States government following an 1854 treaty.[17] Exxon gave a check for $20,000 to the Sokaogon tribal chairperson in September 1975 for the right to explore on their 1900-acre reservation. At the same time, Exxon made offers, including one of $200,000, for 40 acres of corporate-owned timberland just one mile away. When the tribal council found out about this offer, they took Exxon's check, tore it to pieces, and reasserted the Sokaogon Chippewa's treaty claim to lands surrounding the discovery site.[18] This marked the beginning of a decade-long conflict between Exxon and the Sokaogon.

This decade-long environmental conflict would not have occurred if Exxon could have limited the contest between itself and the Sokaogon. From the perspective of the history that has taken place between the Chippewa and the state of Wisconsin since its inception, we can see how multinationals have overwhelmed native peoples in the past in an attempt to control resources found on their lands. Not only is this practice found between multinationals and the Chippewa, but between multinationals and native peoples worldwide. To reduce corporate political and financial risks as much as possible, multinationals limit the scope of the conflict so that the victims are completely exposed to the corporation while the corporation has only a small part exposed to the opposition.[19]

Because of the loose regulations on industrial tailings ponds, environmental threats were of major concern to many non-Indian residents as well. Also of concern was the precedent that would be set for other corporations to follow if Exxon's proposed mine became a reality. Other multinational corporations who are looking at northern Wisconsin as a colony where rich deposits of base metals and radioactive minerals could be mined at minimal costs without cleaning up afterwards include Kerr-McGee, Universal Oil Products, Amoco Minerals, Noranda (Canada), Kennecott, Phelps Dodge, BHP-Utah, and from Germany, Urangesellschaft.[20]

An article in *American Metal Market* noted, "Exxon Corporation expects to begin serious prospecting of a rich 70-million-ton zinc and copper orebody at Crandon, Wisconsin, next year while it works to neutralize objections from the environmentalists, residents, and Indian tribes.[21] When concerned citizens realized Exxon would likely be given the go-ahead for the proposed mine, they began to use existing organizational networks in place and to seek out allies who were also worried about the mine. The Sokaogon Chippewa were the closest allies and worked together with the citizens alliance to challenge Exxon's proposal. "The multiple environmental concerns if this Indian-citizens alliance became a central focus of town politics thereafter."[22]

Environmental concerns from several groups raised the issue of treaty rights that would become a "monkey on the back" of Exxon in the form of stockholder resolutions and a federal lawsuit. Church groups who own stock have asked corporations to state their position publicly on issues such as divesting in South Africa, ending nuclear weapons production, and corporate responsibility regarding environmental concerns. These kinds of resolutions put forth by stockholders to the corporations rarely succeed in gathering large numbers of votes, but they do succeed in dramatizing issues and forcing corporations to state their position on them. This tactic has been used successfully by the Sokaogon Chippewa and the Forest County Potawatomi tribes with the help of the Wisconsin Resources Protection Council (WRPC) and church stockholders. Exxon filed its mining application in December of 1982 with the Wisconsin Department of Natural Resources. The Sinsinawa Dominican Sisters of Wisconsin, who own stock in the corporation and in conjunction with six other religious groups, entered a stockholder resolution with Exxon requesting a postponement of further investment in the project until claims made by the Chippewa were settled.[23]

"Sister Toni Harris of the Sinsinawas reports a successful 'encounter' with Exxon—6% of the vote or 49 million shares were registered in favor of the resolution. Exxon's Board of Directors had advised shareholders to vote against the resolution. The resolution urges that potentially affected tribes be treated as sovereign nations and equal authorities in decisions which impact their communities."[24]

In 1984 the Sokaogon tribe threatened Exxon with another resolution in an effort to force the corporation to invest in pyrite-removal technology for the tailings ponds – an effort that would curb environmental pollution. Exxon's vice-president of shareholder relations and other members of its staff met with the Chippewa and the Dominican Sisters to persuade them to withdraw their resolution. Exxon Minerals refused to invest in the technology, and in return, the Chippewa refused to withdraw their resolution. Through a petition to the Securities and Exchange Commission, Exxon asked to disqualify the resolution. The Securities and Exchange Commission suppressed the resolution, but the Chippewa "once again demonstrated that they could effectively translate widespread local discontent with the project into political action that reached into the center of the parent company's decision making process. Many of the tactics used in the Exxon conflict – private legal action, petitions and referenda, and shareholder campaigns – have been widely used by environmentalists in their efforts to delay, modify, or block new industrial projects."[25]

After a decade of opposition, Exxon finally abandoned its plans to construct their proposed mine. Exxon cited low metal prices as the reason for backing out and denied that pressure from Indians and environmentalists had anything to do with their decision.

Chippewa treaty rights were not the only, or even the decisive, factor in Exxon's decision to withdraw from the project, but the treaties were a formidable blockage in the path of the mining project's major supporters. For Anthony Earl, governor of Wisconsin from 1982-1986 and active supporter of the Exxon-Crandon project, the Chippewa treaties were a powerful defensive blockage against environmental destruction that would come from the proposed mine. "The implications of that mine on the Wolf River and the people who live downstream were among the most serious questions raised about that mine. And that was on account of the treaties."[26]

Resistance of the Chippewa to Kennecott

Kennecott announced its plans to mine a six-million-ton copper deposit, known as the Flambeau deposit, near Ladysmith, Wisconsin, in 1970. If Kennecott and its partner, Rio Tinto Zinc, were allowed to go ahead with this project, other mining corporations would follow suit. Though small in size, the Flambeau deposit became important because it would allow northern Wisconsin to become a domestic mining district.[27]

At the time of the proposed mine, not enough was known about mining to raise any significant objections. "At first, most of us thought a copper mine would bring prosperity to this area," said Roscoe Churchill, retired school principal, part-time farmer, and Ruck County supervisor.[28] Doubts about the mine began to surface when William Bateson, a University of Wisconsin economist at the Institute for Environmental Studies, calculated that the Ladysmith mine stood to gain $20 million worth of copper and $5 million worth of gold and silver each year. Rusk County would gain only $4,688 each year while Kennecott's after-tax profits were conservatively estimated to be around $5 million annually.[29]

Churchill and others also discovered that long-term jobs with the mine would last only eight years and employ about 40 people. Concerns about environmental consequences of the mine also began to raise doubts. The mine would be only 300 feet from the pristine Flambeau River, one of Wisconsin's prime walleye fishing areas. The Lake Superior Chippewa also held hunting, fishing, and gathering rights in the northern third of Wisconsin, precisely where this mine would be located. Massive sulfide-type rock surrounded the orebody to be mined. "When massive sulfides are exposed to air and water during mining, they form sulfuric acid, which can contaminate both groundwater and surface waters. Contamination of this sort could devastate the dairy farming economy of Rusk County as well as the tourist trade."[30]

A hearing concerning an environmental impact statement for the proposed mine revealed that Kennecott planned to run the project through with the help of the state. An environmental impact statement (EIS) must be prepared by the Department of Natural Resources (DNR) before major development projects can proceed. The town of Grant, Wisconsin, hired Kevin Lyons to represent their township on mining issues. Lyons describes how this public hearing was conducted: "Before testimony began, the Wisconsin Department of Natural Resources hearing examiner ruled that the only lawyer allowed to ask questions would be the Kennecott lawyer, who would be questioning his own witnesses. The examiner also ruled that there would be no cross-examination of the Kennecott witnesses by anyone. The Kennecott lawyer then called and examined his witnesses, all of whom supported the EIS . . . At the end of the hearing, the examiner rule[d] that the EIS was adequate.[31]

In the meantime, Churchill organized a meeting of concerned citizens. They learned as much as they could about the environmental devastation that would occur if plans for this copper mine were allowed to proceed. Visits were made to other copper mines and findings reported throughout the county through public meetings and the "Letters to the Editor" column of the *Ladysmith News*. Churchill's visits confirmed that no high-sulfide metallic mine has ever been successfully reclaimed anywhere in the world. Current mining proposals are all based on experimental technology that has never been operational. Even the most modern mining companies frequently violate pollution standards and have a very poor record of environmental safety.[32]

Armed with information about poisoned rivers and streams in other areas of the country and Canada, the newly formed Rusk County Citizens Action Group (RCCAG) prepared a legal appeal of the DNR's approval of the environmental impact statement for the proposed mine. They sought legal counsel and, as the final permit hearing on Kennecott's mine application drew near, the Rusk County Citizens Action Group had put together a defense team with Kevin Lyons representing the town of Grant; and Frank Turkheimer, attorney for the Natural Resources Defence Council (NRDC). NRDC is a well-respected national environmental organization that utilizes scientific research and citizen education to protect natural resources, combined with legal action. Citizens of the state in the proceedings were represented by Intervenor Peter Peshek.[33]

Investigations revealed that the DNR had accepted Kennecott's environmental impact statement without ever verifying critical interpretations of groundwater quality, soil permeability, seepage of toxic metals, and so forth.[34] In their report, Kennecott reported that no potential danger of pollution to the river existed because the heavy metals and toxic materials would go into a small artificial lake (some 300 feet from the river) and remain there permanently. Peshek later gained access to a letter from Kennecott which stated exactly the opposite.[35]

The Department of Natural Resources' deliberately misleading environmental impact statement helped put an end to the permit proceedings. But the biggest blockage to the state and Kennecott was, by far, the public education efforts of the Rusk County Citizens Action Group. But, this is not the end of the story. In the face of Kennecott's defeat and Chippewa resistance to Exxon's proposed mine at Crandon, corporate strategy to gain future access to resources in Wisconsin needed to be re-evaluated. One option involved coopting and splitting the opposition and building an alliance between the state of Wisconsin and the mining corporations to neutralize opposition to mining. Two powerful organizations are involved in this strategy with the goal of profit for each organization.

Through lobbying efforts of Kennecott, lawyers from Wisconsin regulatory agencies, key legislators, and environmental lobbyists formed a new consensus decision-making process to try once again to begin mining in northern Wisconsin. This new corporate-state alliance to promote mining focuses public attention on corporate compliance with environmental laws. The goal of this strategy is to gain approval of projects without major legal delay, political attention or public scrutiny. The idea is to delay environmental opposition by meeting the letter of the law, more or less. When used in other states, this tactic has swayed, intimidated, awed, outraged, and finally, split state environmentalists.[36]

This process would involve Indian tribes, local citizens, and environmentalists in negotiations with mining companies and the state about rules that would allow mining companies to begin their projects. "The assumption underlying the consensus process is that mining is inevitable no matter what the social and environmental costs may be. And if it is inevitable . . . it is better to have the state effectively regulate the social, economic, and environmental effects of such projects."[37] Lawyers for Exxon, Kennecott, and Inland Steel; the DNR; Wisconsin's Environmental Decade; the public intervenor; and lawyers for three of the affected townships comprised this elite planning group with Exxon assuming a leadership position and providing funding from the very beginning. Roscoe Churchill pointed out, however, that the citizens who were supposedly represented in the "consensus" were given no active part in the drafting of mining rules, especially AB 800, the groundwater rules for mining.[38]

The consensus process legitimates the political inequality of access to information and organizational resources between the mining companies and the public during the formulation of public policy. Mining companies have the best of both worlds with their dominant role in shaping mining rules and regulations while diverting potential opposition from outside political organizing, public education, and legal battles. Disagreements among consensus participants are not brought to the attention of the public through the media – a key feature of the consensus process. "This strategy of consensus decision making is in reality a subversion of democratic decision making whereby potential conflicts which may otherwise arise between corporate and community interests are either suppressed or neutralized in the legislative and regulatory processes."[39]

Naming this decision-making process "consensus" leads one to believe that everyone participating has an equal voice in these decisions. But it may, as one political scientist observed, "only serve to hide the fact that powerful interests and their legislative partners are using the process to force their will upon weaker interests."[40] In other words, unequal methods used by those privileged by power of forcing weaker interests to comply with powerful corporate groups are being facilitated with help from the state. Corporate and government collusion is occurring in a variety of different ways. For example, a pamphlet prepared by UW Green Northwoods Taskforce reports that:

- Wisconsin's "tough mining laws" have eroded since the early 1980s during Tony Earl's administration, and continue to do so under Governor Tommy Thompson.

- In 1988 Kennecott drafted an amendment to Wisconsin statutes allowing corporations to circumvent local mining moratoriums by entering into a "local agreement" with a subdivision of local government, signed into law by Governor Thompson in 1989. Thompson also signed a bill giving permission to mine Wisconsin's state parks.

- The DNR (whose top staff are Thompson appointees) granted six variances enabling Kennecott to bypass what little remains of Wisconsin's mining statutes – one enabling Kennecott to mine 140 feet from a river instead of 300 feet. (According to Wisconsin ordinances, you can't even put a swimming pool 140 feet from a river).

• Nearly all the studies used by the DNR in the final Environmental Impact Statement were conducted by Kennecott or with reference to Kennecott compiled data.

With lessons well-learned in the wake of their previous defeat, Kennecott planned to revive its mine permit for the Flambeau deposit in 1987. This time, Kennecott came back with a corporate counteroffensive against local environmental activism that they believed would help get the permit through. Kennecott's plan included three components:

(1) a divide-and-conquer approach to local politics using sophisticated mass media promotions, behind the scenes political influence and gifts and donations to community groups;

(2) legal threats; and

(3) pressuring the DNR into putting the mine permit application on a fast track for approval.[41]

In an attempt to revive the previously defeated mining attempts, Kennecott convinced some Ladysmith business people that a scaled-down version of the project would be a definite boost to downtown businesses. Ladysmith town officials invited the town of Grant and Rusk County to join them in a united effort to see what Kennecott had to offer, and perhaps negotiate a mining agreement. Two elected officials from each of the three governments were selected in a very informal process, and meetings began in December of 1987. The negotiations were held in closed session. Kennecott lawyers were in attendance, but the general public was not permitted to take part.

As part of the negotiations, Kennecott said that "the local communities must agree to provide Kennecott with relief from the local approvals such as the Rusk County ordinance."[42] The local impact committee had no authority to negotiate with Kennecott, but that was not seen as an obstacle. There was no environmental impact statement prepared by the DNR, committee members did not have the benefit of legal council, and therefore, had very little information about the social, economic, and environmental impacts of the project.

Roscoe Churchill was vice-chair of the board for Rusk County, and the town of Grant passed a moratorium on mining in 1982. Kennecott anticipated the possibility of resistance. "If an agreement cannot be worked out which would provide for local approvals, there appear to be only two potentially viable alternatives to satisfy the local approval requirements" according to the company's strategy paper.[43] "These are either to have the entire parcel annexed by the city or to initiate litigation challenging the existing local law."[44]

If Ladysmith annexed the mine site, Grant would be deprived of any proceeds from the mine. Committee members were reminded that Kennecott's lawyers had a petition ready to annex the entire property to Ladysmith. If the threat of annexation was not sufficient to force the committee to reach an agreement Kennecott could live with, the lawyer for the committee said Kennecott probably would have legal grounds to sue if they did not alter tough local mining laws. The threat of a huge lawsuit against a small city within an economically poor country is quite frightening.[45]

Now that Kennecott had intimidated the local negotiating committee with a lawsuit, all they needed was passage of legislation allowing them to proceed. With legislation drafted by a Kennecott lawyer, and with help from a pro-mining state senator, the bill became an amendment to the state budget bill. No public hearings were held, and very few legislators were even aware that it was part of the budget bill. Then in May of 1988, pro-mining Governor Tommy Thompson signed this bill into law with hardly any public notice.[46]

Kennecott used their overwhelming economic and political power to make the mine seem inevitable, and managed any environmental opposition through their vice president, Larry Mercando. Mercando visited churches and civic clubs where he declared the mine to be environmentally safe. Even so, large numbers of citizens still protested the mine. In an effort to keep protestors in their place in the social hierarchy they were referred to by Mercando as "outsiders" and as "un-American." Projecting such an image to the public would make it seem as though to be patriotic and a good citizen of the Ladysmith community, one must be in favor of the state.

Kennecott did not limit its efforts to neutralize environmental opposition with Mercando. They also hired a public relations firm to publish a weekly supplement to the local town paper. The company also spread money around the community by contributing thousands of dollars to local charities, schools, and governments.[47]

By bribing the local community and intimidating the environmental opposition, Kennecott tried to establish an offensive position. Kennecott also let it be known that Rusk County and the town of Grant could be sued for zoning codes that restrict mining. The threats of a lawsuit and lost tax revenues worked to Kennecott's advantage. Grant's town chairperson, Bob Plants, feels that the mine has been forced on his community. "They know all the loopholes, and they have the best lawyers. Sometimes you have to see the light of day and realize that some things are going to happen whether you want them to or not."[48]

One major obstacle to this corporate power play came back to haunt Kennecott. During negotiations and in gathering information for the environmental impact statement, neither Kennecott nor the DNR consulted with the Lake Superior Chippewa. Mercando viewed the treaty rights as unimportant. He told a reporter that Kennecott owned the land and the mineral rights.[49] However, with treaty rights, the Chippewa could legally stand to intervene in the efforts of corporations trying to gain mine permits that could endanger treaty-protected resources.

Promises from the mining company and the state of Wisconsin that the health of people and other species would not be damaged (at least not more than what is considered "acceptable") was not enough for the Chippewa. Chippewa treaties can protect the land for both Indians and non-Indians. While the treaties do not cover mineral rights, they can be used as legal tools to protect the natural resources reserved for the Chippewa.[50]

This is possible because treaties are legally binding agreements made between two nations; the United States and the Chippewa tribe. Treaty rights were never sold by the Chippewa, nor were they granted or given by the federal government. The Chippewa kept the right to obtain food and other necessities on ceded lands in order to be sure future generations would always have a source of food and survival.[51]

Armed with knowledge of Kennecott and Rio Tinto Zinc's (RTZ is a subsidiary of Kennecott) infamous environmental track record and with knowledge of the protection treaties can produce, Gaiashkibos, tribal chair of the Lac Courte Oreilles Chippewa, traveled to London in May of 1990 to attend RTZ's annual general meeting to address the environmental concerns of the Chippewa.[52] Gedicks quotes Gaiashkibos as stating he intended to tell RTZ's Board of Directors "that the tribes and environmentally concerned people of Wisconsin will not accept degradation of ground or surface water, not the stockpiling of hazardous and toxic materials simply so a foreign company can exploit the natural resources of our region. The track record of Kennecott and RTZ in the United States, Canada, and around the world is one of pollution, dead rivers, dead fish, boom-and-bust economies, and displaced native peoples. That is unacceptable in northern Wisconsin.[53] When he asked if RTZ would respect Chippewa rights in Wisconsin, board chair Sir Alistair Frame answered, "We will deal directly with the federal and state government. Next question."[54] Gaiashkibos tried to ask a follow-up question, but Frame turned off his microphone. London's very famous "Financial Times" publication noted that such rude treatment of the head of a sovereign nation overshadowed the announcement that Standard and Poor's and Moody's had awarded RTZ the top ratings for its bonds. Gaiashkibos replied that "What we've observed today confirms our worst suspicions about the intentions of RTZ. We have been told firsthand that RTZ couldn't care less about our rights or concerns.[55] Further challenging the mining project, Gaiashkibos stated "The company is saying it will be here for six years. Their liability goes for another 30 years. We're going to be here forever."[56]

The outcome of the Kennecott/Ladysmith mining controversy is still uncertain. Whatever the outcome, Kennecott faces opposition from Wisconsin's six Chippewa bands – Mole Lake, Lac du Flambeau, Red Cliff, Lac Courte Oreilles, St. Croix, Bad River, several treaty rights support groups, national environmental organizations, and local grassroots environmental organizations.

Resistance to the Kennecott/RTZ mine has been fierce. In 1992, Anishin-abe treaty rights activist Walt Bresette climbed over a 10-foot high security fence carrying a war club once used by Black Hawk and "counted coup" on some earth movers.[57] Bresette, a member of the Red Cliff band of Lake Superior Chippewa and a founder of the Wisconsin Greens, hit the machines with his war club but did no physical damage.

With the help of three other activists, Bresette then removed an American flag flying about a 50-foot pile of topsoil at the site being cleared for mining alongside the Flambeau River. The protestors neatly folded the flag and planned to hold it hostage until RTZ agreed to postpone further mine con-struction. The protestors were charged with trespassing and theft. These are the first activists to be charged in connection with opposition to the mine.

Bresette said, "It's obviously a faulty permit, so I don't recognize the authority of this mine to move forward. There's no proper environmental impact statement completed on this. The DNR is a rogue government. They are bypassing democracy in this process . . . The State of Wisconsin has abdicated its fiduciary responsibility to protect the Lake Superior Chippewa. Endangered species are threatened."[58]

After the arrests, the Sierra Club filed a lawsuit asking the court to order the DNR to follow the Wisconsin Environmental Policy Act and con-duct public hearings on the supplemental environmental impact statement before allowing mining to proceed. Damaging testimony came from a DNR diver who is now a staff biologist for the Great Lakes Indian Fish and Wildlife Commission. The diver testified that he was prohibited by his DNR superiors from surveying the Flambeau River to determine possible damage to the endangered species from sediments that washed into the river after failure of the mining company's erosion control system in September, 1991.

Siding with the state and mining corporation and despite evidence of the DNR's failure to comply with the requirements of the Wisconsin Environ-mental Policy Act along with its disregard for the public's right to participate in the mine permitting process, Dane County Circuit Judge Angela Bartell dismissed the lawsuit on June 13, 1992. One of the reasons for the dismissal was that citizens waited longer than 30 days to appeal the January, 1991, decision to grant the permits. Lac Courte Oreilles lawyer, Larry Leventhal, stated Bartell's ruling "essentially says if an agency hides information from the public, it won't be held accountable for it."[59]

Lawsuits such as the one above slow down ecologically devastating mining projects, but more often than not, mining corporations can outspend and outmaneuver their opponents. When this happens, mining corporations are discovering that their opponents have other weapons in their arsenals. Aggressive litigation, mass demonstrations, shareholder resolutions, nonvi-olent direct actions against polluters are all forms of "counting coup" on earth destroyers and placing massive blockages in the path of the state and corporations. This combination of blockages has been successful in defeat-ing RTZ mine projects in the past and may work in northern Wisconsin.

Even though the outcome of this particular controversy is still uncertain, with treaty rights as a powerful tool to protect the lands, at the very least mining corporations can no longer barge into a community and dictate when and how valuable resources will be removed. Mining corporations can no longer disguise their disregard for community concerns under the guise of a "consensus" decision-making process. If the multifaceted concerns of local communities are not respected by mining corporations, there will be no mining in northern Wisconsin.[60]

A Critical Perspective of the Mining Controversy

In a society built upon hierarchical power such as the United States, a critical perspective would assert that the control of resources is governed by the interests of those most privileged by power, i.e., the state of Wisconsin and the multinational corporations. This perspective demonstrates that American Indian people have been historically ritually stripped of their power, except for treaty rights. Resistance of the Indian people through assertion of treaty rights to keep their land base and protect their resources threatens the privilege and control of powerful multi-national corporations and the state. The Chippewa have fiercely resisted destruction of the environment and the destruction of treaty rights.

A critical perspective also argues that resistance by those less powerful to established social order is often labeled as deviant. Those who have resisted the projects described in this chapter have been portrayed as deviant and "un-American" as a device to mobilize public opinion in favor of mining corporations. According to Spitzer, potentially deviant "problem populations," such as those resisting corporate intrusion upon their lands described here, came from within the capitalist political economy through critical awareness not only of environmental concerns, but also awareness of unequal power structures and unequal economic gains.[61]

In examining this story through a critical perspective, a scenario unfolded of how a small minority of relatively powerless people have empowered themselves with knowledge of the environment and economy to resist injury and harm they believe will be brought about by those in positions of economic and political power. Classifying this behavior as deviant is to suppress the resistance of those who threaten such privilege.

The effects of social control through colonization are demonstrated through the formulation of treaty-making between the colonizers and the colonized, giving those situated in the higher classes the upper-hand in decisions as to which direction the mode of production takes. Through the treaties, it is abundantly clear that one class of people were ensured the ability to ritually authorize and perpetuate its control over others.

The conquest was complete and, as Marx and Engels theorized, these unequal structures created social divisions between those who controlled and those who were controlled on an economic level. As Pfohl writes, the primary targets of social control are those who resist, disrupt, or otherwise threaten the existence of structured economic inequality.[62] The powerful corporate-state efforts to economically and politically order society in a way that will benefit some to the exclusion of others would have us ask "who makes the rules and why?"[63]

Indigenous Knowledge and New Policy Implications

Policy is built on a variety of philosophical and epistemological arguments, ultimately grounded in subjective choice, and developed using political skills of strategy and persuasion. The central question that arises from this scenario is, "what philosophical and epistemological frame of reference is best suited for policy leading to environmental justice and power relations based on reciprocity rather than hierarchical domination?" Using a critical perspective to answer that question stresses the significance of values in rethinking how environmental policy should be dealt with, and is tested by placing views about the environment into an American Indian "way of life." In other words, there is a need to reconceptualize those values deemed to be "authoritative." Allocative decisions for society should be grounded in doctrines and principles stressing reciprocal power, and a holistic way of viewing the environment that includes indigenous knowledge as its base.

For much of this century, positivist philosophies dominated social science with the belief that questions and problems posed in the social world could be understood and solved using the same techniques as those applied to questions about the physical world. Some have come to question the ability of positivist approaches to deal with complex social issues like those considered in United States public policy.[64] The basic problem with the positivist approach is its inability to provide a way to transcend political interest in order to obtain policy knowledge.

What is suggested here is how policy analysis might benefit from a methodology which acknowledges that scientific knowledge is dependent upon the normative assumptions and social meanings of the world it explores. Dryzek suggests that policy analysis should address ethics and normative theory and the apparent normative basis of the status quo in the decision-making process – that is, the values and interests represented in the existing regime and policy process.[65]

Along the same lines, Mary Hawkesworth (1992:295-329) argues that in order to effectively examine policy, the underlying values that drive decisionmaking must be acknowledged.[66] Most importantly, for Hawkesworth, sources of power must be critically examined. Indeed, the critical study of any subject should take into account the hierarchies of power that are inherent in the society.

A critical perspective challenges policy analysts to place themselves within an environmental justice framework which would attempt to uncover the underlying assumptions that may contribute to and produce unequal protection. A framework such as this addresses the ethical and political question of "who gets what, why, and how much."[67] Addressing ethical and political questions such as these is important because one frame of reference by itself does not inform the whole of the problems associated with negative environmental impacts on people of color and low-income groups.

The critical perspective used in the scenario of the Chippewa in Wisconsin challenges the policy analyst to choose among social values, and because values underlie decisions, the policy analyst should recognize that the choice of a frame of reference is culturally bound and dependent; a point made by discussing the American Indian "way of life."

A Way of Life

A power-reflexive critical perspective offers a new frame of reference for policymaking grounded in the doctrines and principles of American Indian views on the environment. The American Indian perspective demands critical thinking about the policies of the private and public sectors developed by those privileged by power in response to environmental issues. The critical perspective used in the case of the Chippewa questions the assumptions upon which current policies are based and examines traditional solutions as well as advocating new ways of thinking about the environment. It allows for different realities and reciprocal relations of power based upon mutual respect, and that these different realities should be reflected in decisions and policies made to include indigenous peoples.

Formulating environmental policies from a critical perspective includes taking into consideration questions about the responsibilities toward the environment and how these responsibilities ought to be reflected in the policies adopted by the government and private companies as well as in the habits of the population as a whole.

For many Chippewa/Ojibwa people, the environment is not an issue. It is a way of life. As with other tribes, the Chippewa consider themselves inseparable from the natural elements of their land.

Environmental sustainability is the "ability of a community to utilize its natural, human and technological resources to ensure that all members of present and future generations can attain a high degree of health and well-being, economic security and a say in shaping their future while maintaining the integrity of the ecological systems upon which all life and production depends. The four pillars of sustainability are: economic security, ecological integrity, democracy, and community."[68]

This definition of environmental sustainability is relatively new, but many American Indians have been practicing the "new" concept of sustainability for a very long time. American Indian concepts of the environment include holistic views, which have come into conflict with the dominant capitalistic nature of early European settlers and continue to do so today. Since the beginning of the United States, control of the land and natural resources have been a constant source of conflict between Euro-American settlers and indigenous nations. Disputes over land usage and ownership have defined the totality of government-Indian relationships from the first contact to the present day. The European perspective of exploitation of land and its resources will continue into the foreseeable future. Mining projects, development proposals, and get-rich-quick schemes have been inflicted upon tribes for years. Millions of dollars are at stake with large multinational corporations and the federal government clamoring to do business on reservations.

The 291 Indian reservations within the United States from Florida to Wisconsin to Alaska are among the most exploited and environmentally degraded lands anywhere in rural America. With sanctioning of certain power arrangements by the federal Bureau of Indian Affairs, corporations and federal agencies have pressured, bribed, cajoled, and enticed their way in to mine for strategic minerals that would environmentally devastate the sacred rice beds of the Sokaogon Chippewa; to strip-mine coal, as on the Crow and Navajo reservations; to drill for oil, as on the Blackfeet Reservation; to site garbage dumps and medical waste incinerators, as on the Salt River and Gila River reservations. This process of exploitation and expropriation goes on and on.[69]

The belief that Natural Law is supreme law and should provide the guiding principles upon which societies and peoples function is what distinguishes the American Indian perspective on the environment from the dominant paradigm of Eurocentric environmental exploration. The holistic view of sustainability for the Chippewa/Ojibwa people is that laws made by nations, states, and municipalities are inferior to Natural Law and should be treated in this manner.

The basic practice of mino bimaatisiiwin, continuous rebirth, mentioned earlier in the chapter, helps us understand the relationship between humans and the ecosystem, and our need to maintain balance. Social and economic systems based on these values tend to be decentralized, communal, and democratic, allowing the people to rely on the land of that ecosystem.

Holistic environmental paradigms based on indigenous knowledge stand in sharp contrast to life in an industrial society. Natural Law is preempted in industrial society as "man's domination over nature" becomes the central way of life. In contrast to the American Indian cyclical process of thinking, this linear concept of progress dominates industrial societies. Progress is defined in terms of economic growth and technological advancement and is key to the development of "civilized" societies. From this perspective, the natural world is seen as something that is wild and in need of taming and cultivation. Those not part of this mentality were and are seen as primitive and in need of being civilized. Civilizing those not part of the dominant paradigm is the philosophical basis of colonialism and conquest.

Social interpretations of this way of linear, scientific thinking have resulted in particular actions taken, like Darwinism and Manifest Destiny, in which some humans have the god-ordained right and duty to dominate the earth and other peoples. As Winona LaDuke argues, the difference in these two paradigms demonstrates the scope of the problem and the reality that a society based on conquest cannot survive.[70]

LaDuke reports that during the last 100 years, industrial society has caused the extinction of more species than have disappeared in the Ice Age and the nineteenth century, and in the past 400 years, an estimated 2,000 indigenous peoples have been made extinct. LaDuke feels that, worldwide and in North America, native peoples are at the center of the present environmental and economic crisis, and not coincidentally. Even though native peoples represent a demographic minority of the total population in North America, native peoples still maintain land occupancy over substantial areas of the continent. LaDuke points out that in many regions in the United States, native peoples are the majority population in parts of New Mexico, Arizona, northern Minnesota, the Dakotas, and Montana. The native population is the majority in two-thirds of Canada, roughly one-third of the North American continent. Much of the northern population is native in areas such as Quebec, Newfoundland, Labrador, Ontario, and the west coast in British Columbia. The native population of the Arctic and subArctic is substantial as well. In this context, American Indian perspectives regarding native thinking, survival of native communities, issues of sovereignty and control over natural resources are becoming central to North American resource politics.

Even though American Indian perspectives are beginning to inform environmental politics and policy to a greater extent, at this point in time, American Indian philosophies and values are not included in those policy decisions that benefit large corporations and serve the interests of the state. There is a vast social distance between all involved that causes a breakdown in communication as well as misinterpretation of each other's actions. Walter Bresette, activist and member of the Red Cliff band of Chippewa, argues that Indians and non-Indians alike are being victimized by large corporations that reduce economic options.[71]

Activist and author Al Gedicks writes, "the sooner we stop labeling 'native issues' as something separate and distinct from our own survival, the sooner we will appreciate the critical interconnections of the world's ecosystems and social systems."[72] Environmental concerns can be absolutely crucial within the context of reservation politics; even before the most hostile of tribal councils, the kind of "Mother Earth" talk that would make Anglo mining executives or legislators roll their eyes can make all the difference.[73] In dealing with American Indian people when making important decisions, such as formulating environmental policy, corporate America and the federal government would be wise to realize that there is a growing respect for tribal elders and the "old ways." Utilitarian business practices and government actions that benefit all involved cannot be accomplished by ignoring this fact.

Environmental protection or harms follow the path of least resistance. Environmental harms are connected to many things such as the air we breath, our food, water, lifestyles, and legal decisions. Developing economically sustainable alternatives will depend on many variables such as research, effective organizing and lobbying, legal representation, effective use of the media, interactive skills involving native rights and environmental movements, and an earnest inclusion of native beliefs, knowledge, and values concerning the environment.

Including these values singularly or in combination, depending on the context, into the political deliberative and allocative process can help bring about environmentally sound, long-term sustainable economic alternatives. With the inclusion of these values, socially harmful interaction between economic and political institutions can be decreased while at the same time helping restore the balance which is so important to native peoples. Clearly, incorporating these kinds of values and beliefs into policy decisions challenges the harmful and wasteful projects of profit-maximizing corporations and growth-at-all-costs government policies.

Through use of a power-reflexive critical analysis, we can see that powerful rituals that give us our "common sense" notions of business as usual, are socially constructed. These rituals control our perceptions, our evaluations, and our interactions with others. From a power-reflexive perspective, the world experienced by the Chippewa has been artificially given to them by the material and symbolic power of ritual. Conversely, state-corporate actors and their interactions with the Chippewa are historically situated in colonial-style treaties. This has allowed Chippewa resistance to the environmentally destructive forces of mining to be seen as an action that challenges state-corporate senses of what things are and what they should be.

With a power-reciprocal, multicultural view, we can begin to deconstruct the notion of technology, short-term wasteful project of profit-maximizing corporation and government policies, as being "natural," and we can then liberate ourselves from the problems these have created. As Mander writes, the only group of people so far, who are clear-minded on this point are native peoples, simply because they have kept their roots alive in an older, alternative, nature-based philosophy that has remained effective for tens of thousands of years, and that has nurtured dimensions of knowledge and perceptions that seem outdated to many.[74] It is crucial that Eurocentrism be reassessed for its impacts on the environment, tradition, and native peoples because native societies are the ones that hold the key to future survival.

Notes

[1]   Michalowski, 1990:196.

[2]   Michalowski, 1990:196.

[3]   Danziger, 1990:215-217.

[4]   Ramirez, 1992:78.

[5]   LaDuke, 1993:x.

6   LaDuke, 1993:x-xi.

7   Peltier, 1992:3.

8   Dorgan, 1977.

9   Davies, 1982.

10   Gedicks, 1993:61.

11   Gedicks, 1993:58.

12   Gedicks, 1993:61.

13   Gedicks, 1993:61.

14   Beal, 1978.

15   Gedicks, 1993:62.

16   May and Shilling, 1977:44.

17   Gedicks, 1993:63.

18   Dorgan, 1977.

19   Nader, 1982:9.

20   Gedicks, 1993:64.

21   Crown, 1980:1; cited by Gedicks, 1993:67.

22   Crown, 1980:1; cited by Gedicks, 1993:67.

23   Honor Digest, July/August 1994, 5(5):10.

24   Honor Digest, July/August 1994, 5(5):10.

25   Gedicks, 1993:75.

26   Mayers and Seely, 1990.

27   May and Schilling, 1977:39.

28   Gedicks, 1993:85.

29   Gedicks, 1993:85.

30   Gedicks, 1993:87.

31   Lyons, 1979, pp. 1-2, cited by Gedicks, 1993:88.

32   Pamphlet published by Anishinabe Niiji, no year given.

33   Gedicks, 1993:89.

34   Peshek and Dawson, 1981:12.

35   Peshek and Dawson, 1981:25.

36   Gedicks, 1982:50.

37   Gedicks, 1993:92.

38   Gedicks, 1993:92.

39   Gedicks, 1993:93.

40   Amy, 1985:15.

[41]   Gedicks, 1993:96.

[42]   Gedicks, 1993:97.

[43]   Gedicks,1993:98.

[44]   Gedicks, 1993:98

[45]   Seely, 1991, cited by Gedicks, 1993:98.

[46]   Gedicks, 1993:99.

[47]   Churchill, Remarks from Mining Conference, 1992.

[48]   Gedicks, 1990:10.

[49]   Kewley, 1990.

[50]   Madison Treaty Rights Support Group, pamphlet, no year of publication given.

[51]   Great Lakes Indian Fish and Wildlife Commission, June 1993:1-2.

[52]   Gedicks, 1993:106.

[53]   LCO News Release, 1990; cited by Gedicks, 1993:106.

[54]   Gedicks, 1993:11.

[55]   Gedicks, 1993:11.

[56]   Bauerlin, 1991:3.

[57]   Green Net, Detroit Summer Coalition, 1992:1-3.

[58]   Green Net, Detroit Summer Coalition, 1992:1.

[59]   Green Net, Detroit Summer Coalition, 1992:3.

[60]   Gedicks, 1982:51.

[61]   Spitzer, 1975.

[62]   Pfohl, 1994:436.

[63]   Taylor, Walton, and Young, 1973:220.

[64]   Fisher and Forester, eds., 1993.

[65]   Dryzek, 1993:214-215.

[66]   Hawkesworth, 1992:295-329.

[67]   Bullard, 1994:119.

[68]   Cortese, Kline, and Smith in Second Nature Partnership Training Manual, Feb. 1994.

[69]   Knox, 1993:50.

[70]   LaDuke, forward in Gedicks, 1993, p. xi-xiv.

[71]   Bresette, W. Remarks from the Mining and Treaty Rights Conference, October 1992, Tomahawk, WI.

[72]   Gedicks, 1993:202.

[73]   Knox, M., 1993:50.

[74]   Mander, 1991.

CHAPTER 6

Toxic Crimes and Environmental Justice:
Examining the Hidden Dangers of Hazardous Waste

Michael J. Lynch
Paul B. Stretesky
Danielle McGurrin

Introduction

The chapters in this book focus on crimes that criminologists tend to neglect: corporate crime and white-collar crime. Among the most neglected of these crimes are toxic crimes, which we provisionally define as illegal or immoral activities that harm the environment and human health through the production and disposal of hazardous waste. Toxic crimes stand out from other crime for four reasons.

First, as noted, little attention has been directed toward this form of harm. Indeed, it is no exaggeration to say that if criminologists have neglected corporate crime in general, then criminological literature on toxic crimes is practically nonexistent.

Second, criminologists not only neglect the harms caused by corporate crime, but have also neglected the laws which criminalize these behaviors. This is an important omission because many criminologists argue that legal rules and practices are a defining characteristic of behaviors we call crime (and hence, behavior worthy of study). Criminologists who study corporate crimes are often criticized for examining behaviors that fall outside of the criminal law. This criticism does not, however, apply to many toxic crimes because numerous legal rules and regulations exist which define these activities as illegal.

Third, toxic crimes possess the potential to cause massive catastrophes, have long-term human health implications, and devastating environmental consequences that cause more human (and environmental) injury and death than street crimes. In fact, the level of harm associated with toxic crimes is so extensive that this fact alone provides sufficient justification for focusing attention on them.

Fourth, toxic crimes, while broadly felt within American society, have their most detrimental impacts on minorities and the lower classes. Toxic crimes contain patterns of class, race and ethnic bias, and the study of toxic crime is an important avenue for researching and exposing racial and class bias in law-making and law enforcement. Lax enforcement patterns, the locations of hazardous waste production and management facilities, and corporate manipulation of environmental laws, all contain race, class, and ethnic injustices that criminologists who study toxic crimes can expose and explore.

The study of toxic crimes is a fertile area of research outside of criminology, and, since the early 1980s, researchers in several disciplines have examined the issue of environmental justice (EJ). EJ studies pay particular attention to how the risks associated with producing and managing hazardous waste affects minorities and the lower classes. EJ studies, now two decades old, are only now becoming a matter of criminological interest. Criminological neglect of environmental justice studies is surprising because, theoretically, both areas share a commitment to interdisciplinary research strategies. Further, the absence of environmental justice studies in the criminological literature speaks to the (un)willingness of criminologists to take issues of (1) racial (and class) discrimination, and (2) corporate harm, seriously.

In this chapter, we examine the issues reviewed above by defining toxic crimes, providing examples of this form of crime, reviewing the general rules that apply to these offenses, the punishments provided to those found guilty of toxic crimes, and by reviewing evidence of the biases contained in the pattern of toxic crimes evident in the United States. We employ case studies to illustrate these points.

Defining Toxic Crime

It is difficult to provide an exact definition of the term "toxic crimes" because of the variability of the actions to which this idea applies. Numerous laws define toxic crimes, and it would be easy, though misleading and limiting, to define toxic crimes as acts that violate *laws regulating the production and management* (i.e., storage and disposal) of hazardous waste. It would be even more misleading to restrict the definition of toxic crimes to behaviors that violate *criminal laws*, even though numerous criminal laws defining toxic crimes exist.[1] In short, a legal definition of toxic crime provides an appropriate starting point for *a limited range* of criminological studies examining acts recognized as harms by law, and enforced by agencies such as the Environmental Protection Agency (EPA). A strict legal definition, for example, excludes harmful behaviors not yet recognized as crimes; harms where there are conflicts concerning the nature of toxic harms and their definition; and, harms that citizens' attempt to have recognized as detrimental through protest and other noncriminal remedies. Examples of these latter actions include civil lawsuits filed by people alleging that hazardous waste production and management practices have particularly adverse impacts on minority and lower-class communities (i.e., lawsuits alleging the existence of environmental injustice).

To overcome the limits of the legal definition of toxic crimes, we define toxic crimes *as corporate behaviors that unnecessarily harm or place humans and the environment at risk of harm through the production and management of hazardous waste in the course of a legitimate business enterprise*. We include the word "corporate" in our definition to exclude behaviors individuals perform that threaten human and environmental health. Individuals, for example, may illegally dump oil or radiator fluids they flush from automobiles, or paints or household solvents by disposing of these chemicals in their trash, or by pouring them down the drain. While these acts are serious and illegal (as defined in federal and state regulations*), the harms they create pale in comparison to the organized production and disposal of hazardous wastes by legitimate businesses*. In addition, we focus on corporate behavior to illustrate the organized nature of corporate efforts to deceive the public about the extent of harm caused by corporate production and disposal of toxic chemicals.[2] We briefly address this issue below.

The Organization of Toxic Corporate Crime

Numerous studies exist that illustrate the processes corporations employ to mask the harms associated with the production and management of toxic chemicals. Stauber and Rampton, for example, expose how corporations use mass media, advertising, and public relations firms to craft public campaigns that deny the harms associated with toxic chemical production and disposal.[3] Fagin and Lavelle examine how corporations use "scientific studies" prepared by toxic chemical manufacturers to counter the claims made by public health officials and activists concerning the negative impact of toxic chemicals on human and environmental health and well being.[4] Toxicologists, chemists, and biologists have examined similar claims, and brought to light the strong scientific evidence that contradict corporate safety claims.[5] Also of significance are works on these issues by women, including: (1) Lois Gibbs, a mother whose family was victimized by the toxic dumpsite at Love Canal. Gibbs organized the group Citizens Clearinghouse for Hazardous Waste, which remains active today in the fight against toxic crime.[6] (2) Rachel Carson, a former government biologist for the U.S. Fish and Wildlife Service turned activists. In 1962, Carson released her book, *Silent Springs*, which warned of the impending environmental consequences of corporate dumping of toxic waste. Carson's book is also important because it is credited with founding the environmental movement in the United States. (3) Dr. Ellen Steingraber, a biologist and cancer survivor, whose recent book, *Living Downstream*, uses personal narrative and an extensive knowledge of science and toxins to provide one of the most significant, modern examinations of the effects of toxic waste in the United States. These works, and many others, tell the story of the forms of intentional harm and corporate deception with respect to toxic chemical crimes.[7]

Equally important to our discussion of the organization of toxic crime is the fact that corporations could avoid exposing us to toxic hazards if *corporate decisionmakers would choose different methods of production and waste management*. Corporations possess the ability to minimize the impact of toxic crimes by relying on alternative, nonpolluting technologies. We provide a few examples below.

Consider non-organic pesticides, which we often believe are necessary to our survival. Natural, safe alternatives to highly toxic synthetic chemical pesticides and herbicides exist. *Neem* is one example of a natural pesticide that does not harm people or the environment in its natural state.[8] *Neem* is a tree extract used in India for centuries to repel more than 200 different types of insects.[9] Research has confirmed that *Neem* is *as effective* at removing insects from crops as highly toxic pesticides such as DDT and Malathion.[10] W.R. Grace, a multinational corporation, recently patented *Neem* extract, effectively curtailing the ability of people across the globe, especially Third World Farmers who have traditionally relied upon *Neem* to protect their crops, from using *Neem* without paying W.R. Grace a fee.[11]

In other countries like Cuba, organic farming is promoted by national policies. According to Rosset and Benjamin "[t]he Cuban experiment is the largest attempt at conversion from conventional agriculture to organic or semi-organic farming in human history."[12] Cuba turned to organic chemicals in response to an agrochemical embargo, heavily endorsed by the United States, which began in 1990. Cut off from agrochemicals, many feared the Cuban population would suffer from famine. This, however, did not happen. Beginning in 1990, Cuba instituted a system of organic farming that uses insects to control insects, and microbial antagonists to combat soil diseases.[13] These organic methods of farming have proved effective. For instance, Rosset and Benjamin report that by the end of 1991 an "estimated 56 percent of Cuban crop land was treated with biological controls, representing a savings, after costs, of 15.6 million dollars per year."[14] Cuba now uses less potent and smaller amounts of synthetic agrochemicals than it did 10 years earlier, and has demonstrated to the world that organic farming does not compromise productive output.

In short, alternatives to dangerous pesticides exist. These alternatives can be easily employed to reduce the harms posed by the use of synthetic agrochemicals. The corporations that produce synthetic agrochemicals, however, have established policies that limit the use of organic chemicals, and which facilitate our reliance on harmful agrochemicals.

Environmental Justice

The distribution of environmental risk among diverse populations is at the heart of EJ research. As noted earlier, Environmental Justice (EJ) researchers examine the distribution of environmental hazards such as treatment, storage, and disposal facilities and environmental benefits such as parks and playgrounds across diverse populations; that is, in relation to the racial, ethnic, and class composition of communities.

Criminologists interested in patterns of environmental victimization address EJ concerns by asking the following question: Are toxic/hazardous waste facilities and dangerous production processes evenly/randomly distributed across diverse populations?

The study of EJ bears an important connection to the study of toxic crimes. We defined toxic crimes as involving the purposeful or patterned activities of corporations engaged in the production and management of toxic/hazardous waste. The question EJ research addresses speaks directly to whether or not corporate toxic waste production and management has a specific pattern (is purposeful), or is random and unplanned. If, for instance, research finds that toxic waste facility locations have a statistical relationship to the class, and/or racial and/or ethnic characteristics of areas in which these facilities are located, we can conclude that: (1) there is a pattern to these corporate activities; (2) that such extensive patterns are not random; and (3) that this pattern is the result of institutionalized discrimination. Before we review the extant environmental justice literature, it is necessary to provide an overview of the typical data employed in these studies.

Environmental Hazard Data: General Overview

In this section we provide an overview of EPA data on corporate chemical pollution and manufacturing. Case study data from Hillsborough County, Florida – the county in which the city of Tampa and the University of South Florida are located – is included to illustrate the nature of the information found in the EPA data.

EPA data used to study corporate violations of environmental regulations include the following information: the location of environmental hazards, the quantity of toxins chemical manufacturers produce and dump into our environment, and a list of chemicals involved. When joined with other data sources, such as those kept by the Census Bureau, EPA data can be used to investigate the issue of environmental justice – that is, how chemical production and disposal is distributed across geographic areas inhabited by different racial, ethnic, and class groups in the United States. A further discussion of this procedure with illustrative data is presented later in this chapter.

Numerous qualitative and quantitative data sources on environmental harms exist. Local information on environmental hazards may, for instance, be obtained from city or regional planning commissions and newspapers, as well as state agencies charged with protecting the environment. Theoretically, these agencies collect information on worse-case scenarios; the worst possible outcomes associated with a chemical accidents/disasters within their jurisdiction. However, the EPA maintains the most comprehensive database on environmental hazards.

EPA data is similar to Uniform Crime Report data to the extent that it provides a means of tracking violations of law over time and by jurisdiction. While EPA data has its limitations, and access to some EPA information has been restricted by corporate lobbying efforts, it remains a rich source of data on environmental hazards and pollution.[15] Criminologists have largely neglected EPA data in their study of corporate crime.

By federal mandate, the EPA keeps records on environmental toxins in several separate databases. Four primary EPA databases related to corporate environmental pollution are discussed below. Much of this information is available on-line from the EPA (www.epa.gov), or through the "Right to Know Network" (www.rtk.net).

Biennial Reporting System

Beginning in 1989, the EPA has published hazardous waste information in the Biennial Reporting System (BRS) under the authority of the Resource Conservation and Recovery Act (RCRA). BRS data covers waste generating facilities and RCRA permitted Treatment, Storage and Disposal Facilities (known as TSDFs). TSDFs are required to report the *amount* and *type* of waste they generate, ship off-site, or receive for treatment, storage, and disposal from other facilities to the EPA. The BRS, designed to track the production and disposal of hazardous waste, allows users to determine how much waste is generated, shipped, and either stored or disposed of in each reporting year at each facility. Each permitted TSDF facility reports the amount of waste it generates and ships, whether there is on-site treatment, storage, and disposal of hazardous waste, and whether they have plans to develop such facilities to the EPA for inclusion in the BRS. A major limitation of federal BRS data is that only a fraction of facilities recorded in state or regional information systems are found in the federal listing. This shortcoming has led some researchers to suggest that *Toxic Release Inventory* (see below) be included as an additional source of information on the location of hazardous waste facilities.[16] Other commercial sources of information on hazardous waste facilities also exist. For example, the *Environmental Services Directory* (Environmental Institute, published annually) contains a list of all known commercial hazardous waste facilities and can be consulted to obtain location and profile information on hazardous waste facilities. Several examples of the kinds of information available in the BRS follow.

In 1995, one Hillsborough manufacturer, Chromally Casting, reported generating 904,920 pounds of waste, self-managing (treating, storing, or disposing) 816,000 pounds of waste, and shipping the remainder to other facilities. Because of the amount of waste it generates, Chromally Casting is classified as a large quantity waste generator (LQG). While Chromally Casting produces a good deal of hazardous waste, other companies in Hillsborough produce and process even more waste. Alumax Entrusions Inc., for example, produced more than 58 million pounds of waste, or 40 percent of all reported toxic waste produced in Hillsborough, and managed more than 99 percent of this waste itself.

In 1995, there were 35 BRS facilities in Hillsborough. These facilities produced a total of 72,581.76 tons (approximately 145 million pounds) of waste, and shipped 12.5 percent (9089.87 tons) of this waste to other facilities. It is important to know how much waste corporations ship, because high levels of waste shipment are likely to increase the possibility of a hazardous waste spills or accidental chemical releases. The BRS includes only a limited range of information about the toxic chemicals corporations produce, store, and dispose. A more complete picture of the production of toxic waste can be constructed by referring to other EPA data.

Toxic Release Inventory

Under the authority of the Pollution Prevention Act, the EPA began collecting *Toxic Release Inventory* (*TRI*) data in 1987. *TRI* data are collected annually through EPA mandated forms filled out by manufacturers. The *TRI* records releases and transfers of toxic chemicals from manufacturers with (a) 10 or more workers, (b) that process in excess of 25,000 pounds, or use more than 10,000 pounds of one of (c) the 350 chemicals identified in the Pollution Prevention Act. The *TRI* lists pollution releases according to the form of release, which include: (1) air, (2) land, (3) water, and (4) underground releases. When combined with BRS information, the *TRI* helps track how corporations manage the toxic waste they produce or receive for disposal.

In 1997 in Hillsborough, 42 facilities reported information to the EPA for inclusion in the *TRI*. Of these facilities, 31 reported releasing or disposing of nearly five million pounds of chemical pollution into the environment. While this figure represents a great deal of toxic waste, it does not represent all toxic waste emissions into Hillsborough's environment, since the *TRI* only covers specific kinds of chemical releases. The *TRI* data also indicate that the level of releases reported by these 31 facilities varied from nearly three million pounds to two pounds. The average number of pounds released per facility was 150,473. Five companies reported releases in excess of this mean, while one-half of reported releases in excess of 12,000 pounds.

The *TRI* contains other important information that can be used to assess the release of hazardous waste into the environment. We illustrate the nature of this information by focusing on the releases reported by one company, CF Industries, Inc., a phosphorus production facility. Of the total *TRI* emissions reported for Hillsborough, 64.4 percent (3,001,963 pounds) were produced by CF Industries. Given its level of *TRI* emissions, CF Industries ranks among the top 10 percent of the dirtiest production facilities in the United States in 1997. CF Industries reported its releases in aggregate form, and provided no specific information concerning the amount of top-ranked cancer-risk toxins it released into the environment. CF Industries reported releasing 298,763 pounds of chemical-pollution into the air; 2.7 million pounds of chemical into the ground; and, 3,200 pounds of chemicals into the water. Clearly, CF released a large quantity of toxins into the environment, and we have already noted that CF is among the "dirtiest" polluters in the United States. Below, we place these releases in a more extended context.

U.S. industries generally claim to have made significant inroads in the area of protecting public health by reducing toxic emissions into the environment. How do CF Industries' reported *TRI* releases stack up against this claim? Employing the EPA's *TRI* data from 1988 to 1997 for CF Industries, the answer is: not well. Total environmental releases at this facility *rose* from 1,699,306 pounds in 1988 to 3,001,963 pounds by 1997, *an increase of nearly 77 percent*. Toxic airborne releases at the facility declined by 40 percent, while toxic land releases increased by 125 percent. This pattern of releases indicates *a shift in releases* at *CF* that *redistributed* (and increased), *rather than eliminated, toxic releases*. Thus, rather than getting "cleaner," *CF Industries* got dirtier over the past decade. Adding to this "dirty" image, 18 percent (more than 54,000 pounds) of CF's toxic air releases were suspected (though unspecified) carcinogens, while 100 percent were suspected respiratory toxicants.

Comprehensive Environmental Response, Compensation and Liability Information System Data

Comprehensive Environmental Response, Compensation and Liability Information System (CERCLIS) data is collected by the EPA under the provisions of Comprehensive Environmental Response, Compensation and Liability Information Act. CERCLIS data covers hazardous waste sites, hazardous waste site inspections, preliminary hazard assessments, and remedial action status for waste facilities, and contains information about toxins stored or present at a specific hazardous waste site. The most hazardous CERCLIS sites are those that the EPA has determined pose a substantial health threat to the people living nearby. These sites are placed on the National Priority List (or Superfund list) and are eligible for federal aid in cleanup. CERCLIS data have been collected for more than 20 years, dating back to 1980. Specifically, CERCLIS data details the "site identifiers" (owners, site address, description of on-site activities, etc.), type of hazard(s) found at a site, investigative actions taken (discovery, pre-remedial, preliminary assessment, screening site inspection, remedial action, removal actions, NPL status) and dates of actions, agency responsible for actions, whether further actions are planned, actions outcomes (fines, etc.), and whether a specific incident precipitated an action.

In 1997, there were 102 identified CERCLIS sites in Hillsborough. Each site had undergone both a discovery action and a preliminary screening assessment. Based upon preliminary screening results, 70 percent (N = 72) of these sites were also subjected to a screening site inspection. Taken together, the discovery, preliminary screening, and screening site inspection constitute what the EPA defines as "pre-remedial" actions. Following completion of pre-remedial inspections, 50 sites were listed as requiring no further (remedial) actions. Below, we examine the more serious remedial actions taken by the EPA.

The EPA took 60 remedial actions at 15 sites. Fourteen sites were referred for a "hazardous ranking determination." Based upon the results of this determination, 12 sites were proposed as Superfund sites. Between 1980 to 1997, 12 sites were added to the Superfund list, while one was removed. There are currently 11 Superfund sites in Hillsborough, and one proposed Superfund site (Normandy Park Apartments).

Overall, 16 CERCLIS sites were found to be in violation of EPA standards, and had EPA enforcement actions. In addition, those 16 sites (15.7 %) had 73 violations, or an average of 4.5 violations per site. Five sites had only one enforcement action, and two sites had two actions. The remaining nine sites faced the majority (64) of enforcement actions (7.1 per site). One site had 13 enforcement actions held against it by the EPA. The 16 sites where remedial action was required were subjected to either consent or unilateral consent decrees. There was an average of two consent decrees per site. The EPA entered into only one litigation against CERLCIS sites in Hillsborough for this time period.

Under remedial actions, 18 sites (17.7%) were subject to 100 financial obligations by the EPA, amounting to $9,078,684. The average financial obligation per incident was $90,787, with a range of $1,686,000 to $14 per incident. On average, there were 10 financial obligations per year for this period, and 5.5 financial obligations per site, averaging $543,720 per site (ranging from $4,453,620 to $321 per site). The number of obligations per site ranged from one to 21. Five sites had only one financial obligation, while two sites had 40 of the 100 financial obligations levied against them. Taken together, these data indicate that a small percentage of sites were responsible for the majority of "serious" EPA actions against corporations that pollute the environment.

Accidental Release Information Program Data

Accidental Release Information Program data contains information on "unplanned" accidental chemical releases (ACRs) into the environment that occur at fixed facilities and which have off-site consequences. Off-site consequences included death and injury to humans, public evacuations, and environmental damage to soil, water, air, or wildlife. Though chemical accidents are unplanned, they should not be considered random events since facility conditions (e.g., following a maintenance and inspection schedule), adherence to legally required procedures (e.g., organized routines and safety inspections and criteria), production levels, and even location and community characteristics can be used to predict the location of these accidents.[17]

Unlike other sources of EPA data, the information contained in the ARIP includes the exact date and time an incident occurred and ended. This information is important because it can be used to establish a sequence of events necessary to examine hypotheses that specify a causal order (time sequence) for events.[18] Like other EPA data, ARIP reports include information on a facility's location, which can be used to examine the geographic distribution of ACRs and their relationship to community characteristics. ARIP reports also contain information on the company (company name, owners, number of employees, Dun and Bradstreet number), spill quantity, the chemical(s) released, the chemical's concentration or purity, whether deaths, injuries, or public evacuations resulted from the accident, and the costs associated with the accident.

Using EPA Data to Study Environmental Justice

In this section we illustrate how criminologists can study the distribution of environmental hazards across diverse populations using data on Superfund sites in Hillsborough. We choose Superfund sites for this example for three reasons. First, the EPA estimates that as much as 90 percent of all toxic waste in the United States is disposed of illegally.[19] Second, our review of Superfund sites in Hillsborough turned up numerous EPA violations at all of the sites. Third, the EPA has estimated the potential adverse health effects of contaminated hazardous waste sites are considerable.[20]

It is important to note that each of the four EPA data sources discussed contain street addresses and latitude and longitude coordinates that can be used to locate the particular environmental hazards investigated using a Geographic Information System (GIS) such as ArcView or LandView. The location information in the EPA data is particularly important in the study of environmental justice as it allows for the testing of the distributive justice hypothesis that minorities and the lower classes are more likely to reside near environmental hazards than affluent whites and thus be will more likely to be adversely impacted by illegal corporate activities.

In our particular example, we are interested in determining if Superfund site locations can be predicted by the racial, ethnic, and class characteristics of census tracts in Hillsborough. Based on previous environmental justice research, we hypothesize that Superfund sites in Hillsborough will more likely be situated in low-income and minority communities than in white and upper-income communities. To test this hypothesis, we used GIS software to located each Superfund site in a geographic unit (e.g., census tract, zip code, county) for which population characteristics can be drawn from census data. Next, the racial, ethnic, and class characteristics of the geographic units containing Superfund sites are compared to the racial, ethnic, and class characteristics of the geographic units that do not contain those sites. For smaller geographic units (such as census tracts or blocks), each unit may also be referenced according to the distance it is situated from the nearest Superfund site (or other environmental hazard) using GIS software.

For purposes of defining a neighborhood's racial and ethnic composition, we divided Hillsborough into African-American, Hispanic, non-Hispanic and white census tracts. These divisions were based on population averages for Hillsborough County; census tracts exceeding the average African-American composition of the population (13.2%) were defined as African-American census tract; those with fewer than 13.2 percent were defined as white census tracts. Similarly, census tracts with more than 12.6 percent Hispanics (the average for Hillsborough) were defined as Hispanic census tracts, while those below this figure were defined as Non-Hispanic census tracts. The same procedure was used to define census tracts as poor (those where more than 15.4% of the population – the average for Hillsborough County – were below the poverty level) and nonpoor (those were less than 15.4 % of the population were below the poverty level. We then mapped the location of Superfund sites to assess if there was a relation between site location and the racial, ethnic, and class composition of census tracts in Hillsborough census tracts (using 1990 Summary Tape File 3a census data; see Figure 6.1).

Visual analysis of Figure 6.1 suggests that Superfund sites are clustered near census tracts that are disproportionately African-American and Hispanic, supporting the hypothesis that in Hillsborough these groups are more at risk of being impacted by this type of toxic crime. Formal statistics provide a better means of measuring these relationships, and for simplicity's sake, we used difference in means and Wilcoxon Rank-Sum tests to compare the mean and median distance in miles census tracts are situated from the nearest Superfund site for African-American/non-African-American, Hispanic/non-Hispanic, and poor/non-poor census tract pairs (see Table 6.1).

As indicated in Table 6.1, census tracts defined as African-American are situated, on average, 2.30 miles from the nearest Superfund site while tracts defined as white are situated, on average, 6.24 miles away from those hazards. Since risk decreases with distance, these results indicate that in Hillsborough, African-Americans are generally at greater risk of being adversely impacted by chemical substances found in Superfund sites than whites. This same pattern also holds true for the poor residents of Hillsborough (poor census tracts are, on average, 3.29 miles from a Superfund site, while non-poor tracts are 6.29 miles away). Clearly, in Hillsborough County, corporate violations of EPA regulations have placed African-Americans and the poor in greater peril than whites and the non-poor. How do our findings stack up against the findings from previous research? We address this issue in the next section.

Figure 6.1

Geographic Distribution of Superfund Sites and the Percentage of Minority Residents (African-American and Hispanic) in Census Tracts in Hillsborough County, Florida (1990).

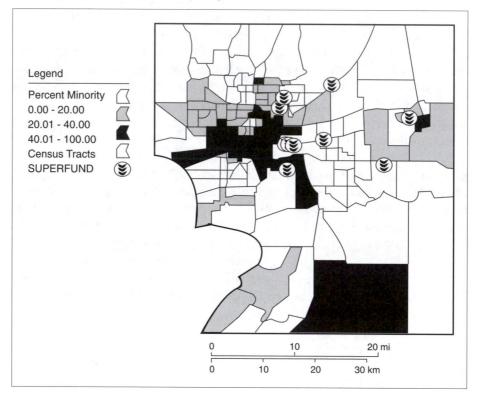

Race, Class, and Environmental Justice: History and Evidence

In the environmental justice literature, two studies stand out for their impact on national and state policy. The U.S. Government Accounting Office conducted the first empirical study of EJ in response to protests over the proposed placement of a hazardous waste facility in North Carolina.[21] The second study, conducted by the United Church of Christ (1987), the first national level study of EJ, is perhaps the most widely disseminated environmental justice study. We review each of these important studies briefly.[22]

Table 6.1
Independent-Sample t-tests[1] for a Difference of Means, and Two-Sample Wilcoxon Rank-Sum Tests for a Difference of Medians, Comparing Distances (in miles) Between Census Tracts That Have a Greater Proportion of African-American, Hispanic, and Poor Residents Than Hillsborough as a Whole to Census Tracts That Have a Smaller Proportion of African-American, Hispanic and Poor Residents Than Hillsborough as a Whole (1990).

Tract Demographic Characteristics	Mean Distance to Closest Superfund Site	Number of Tracts	t-Test	Wilcoxon Z-Statistic
African-American Tract	2.30 miles	50	8.10*	6.93*
White Tract	6.24 miles	114		
Hispanic Tract	5.70 miles	49	1.29	0.62
Non-Hispanic Tract	4.75 miles	115		
Poor Tract	3.29 miles	60	4.27*	5.62*
Non-Poor Tract	6.29 miles	104		

* $p < 0.001$
[1] Assuming unequal variances.

The GAO Study. Protests over a proposed chlorobiphenyl (PCB) landfill in Warren County (North Carolina) prompted the U.S. General Accounting Office to investigate the issue of environmental justice. Warren County residents argued that North Carolina officials selected their county for the hazardous waste facility because it was predominately African-American and poor. GAO researchers found that three of the four off-site hazardous waste landfills in eight states that make up EPA's Region 4 were located in predominately African-American census tracts even though the region as a whole is only 20 percent African-American.[23] For example, the GAO determined that *Chemical Waste Management*'s site (Alabama) was located in a tract that was 90 percent African-American; Warren County's landfill was located in a tract that was 66 percent African-American; *Industrial Chemical Company*'s landfill (South Carolina) was located in a tract that was 52 percent African-American; and, *SCA Services'* landfill (South Carolina) was located in a tract that was 38 percent African-American. The GAO also found that the census tracts containing the landfills had an average median family income of only $14,233, and that nearly 33 percent of the residents in those tracts lived in poverty (see Bullard, 1983, for a similar findings of racial inequality in Houston, Texas). The GAO study prompted further investigation into environmental justice issues. In 1987, the United Church of Christ (UCC) conducted the most notable of these investigations.

The UCC's Commission for Racial Justice conducted a national level study that examined the distribution of 415 commercial hazardous waste facilities and 18,164 uncontrolled toxic waste sites (e.g., CERCLIS sites) across U.S. ZIP codes. UCC's researchers found that "race proved to be the most significant among the variables tested in association with the location of commercial hazardous waste facilities."[24] UCC also determined that median family income and housing values were inversely related to the location of hazardous waste facilities – though the income/hazardous waste relationship was weaker than the African-American/hazardous waste relationship. In 1994, the Center for Policy Alternatives released an update of the UCC analysis which revealed that between 1980 and 1993, the percentage of minorities living in ZIP codes containing commercial hazardous waste facilities *increased* from 25 percent to 31 percent.[25]

The widespread attention given to the GAO and UCC studies generated futher EJ studies. These studies were sponsored by various private industries such as Waste Management Incorporated and The Institute for the Chemical Waste Management, government agencies such as the EPA, nongovernmental organizations such as the Center for Policy Alternatives, and independent academics. The findings from these studies are diverse and cover a wide variety of data sources, geographic areas and units, and diverse variables. These studies are best categorized according to the type of environmental hazard examined.

The Location of Commercial Waste Facilities

The majority of studies focus on the location of commercial hazardous waste facilities (under the Resource Conservation and Recovery Act of 1976). Mohai and Bryant examined the economic and racial characteristics of residents living near 16 residential commercial hazardous waste facilities in the Detroit (Michigan) metropolitan area.[26] Rather than use ZIP codes or census tracts, Mohai and Bryant examined the demographic characteristics of a sample of households. Their dependent variable was distance (measured in miles) from the household to the nearest waste facility. The researchers found that the households situated nearest to hazardous waste facilities were more likely to be low-income and African-American. With respect to race, the researchers determined that 3 percent of whites in the Detroit metropolitan area lived within one mile of a facility, as opposed to 11 percent of minority residents. The researchers also found that race was a stronger predictor of distance to the nearest hazardous waste site than income. Their findings are supported by multivariate ordinary least squares regression analysis, and Adeola's study of household distances to waste sites in Baton Rouge, Louisiana.[27]

In 1994, Anderton, Anderson, Oaks, and Fraser published the first national-level study to contradict previous environmental injustice claims.[28] Anderton et al. examined the distribution of 454 commercial hazardous waste facilities located in metropolitan census tracts across the United States using difference of means (and medians) tests and logistic regression to determine if there were statistically significant differences between the racial, ethnic, or economic composition of tracts that contain commercial hazardous waste sites and those that did not. Anderton et al. refuted the findings of earlier environmental justice research, and concluded that: "Census tract-level results in SMSAs do not appear to substantially support earlier research suggesting appreciable [racial, ethnic, or economic] inequity in [commercial hazardous waste facility] locations; in fact, they contradict that research."[29] One exception to the general findings occurred in EPA Region 10 (containing the state of California), where the percentage of Hispanics residing in census tracts was positively related to the location of commercial hazardous waste facilities. This result, however, was the only evidence of environmental injustice in their study. The researchers suggest that the UCC's findings are likely the result of aggregation bias, which is typical when large geographical units such as ZIP codes are studied.

More recent studies, however, support the earlier GAO and UCC findings. For instance, Boer et al. examined the relationship between hazardous waste facilities and the racial, ethnic, and economic characteristics of census tracts in Los Angeles County (California).[30] The researchers found that the percentage of African-Americans and Hispanics were positively associated with hazardous waste facilities across census tracts. Their results also indicated a non-linear income effect meaning that "wealthier communities have the economic and political power to resist negative environmental externalities."[31] The researchers concluded that the communities most likely to be impacted by hazardous waste facilities are those that are "working-class communities of color."

Been (1994), concerned that results presented by GAO (1983) and Bullard (1983) were due to their failure to account for issues of causal order, expanded upon those studies to examine the demographic characteristics of the communities containing hazardous waste facilities over a 30-year period using 1970, 1980, and 1990 census data.[32] Been discovered that the demographic characteristics of census tracts near the four sites studied in the GAO study changed little over this time period. That is, the census areas containing the sites were predominately African-American at the time the facilities were sited. In contrast, Been determined that in Houston, Texas, waste sites were not as likely to be sited in minority census tracts, but rather that nearby tracts became predominately African-American over time. Been proposed that the results of the GAO study suggest that the rate of residential mobility in rural areas, such as those in the GAO sites, is generally slower and that market dynamics may have less of an impact on rural communities that contain hazardous waste facilities.

Yandle and Burton also examined changing demographic patterns for 142 hazardous waste facilities in census tracts in metropolitan areas within Texas.[33] This research addresses issues of causal order by examining demographic patterns around hazardous waste sites at the time they were sited. The researchers found that areas in which facilities were sited were predominately poor and largely white. While poverty remained significant over time, percentage minority did not.

The first national-level study to specifically examine the issue of causal order in the siting of hazardous waste facilities in detail was conducted by Oakes, Anderton, and Anderson).[34] The researchers were interested in determining the degree to which "disadvantaged communities bear inequitable environmental burdens from the disproportionate and intentional siting of locally undesirable land uses in minority and poor communities."[35] Using a "case control approach," Oakes et al., examined census data from 1970, 1980, and 1990 to determine if the percentage of African-American, Hispanic, or poor residents in census tract areas: (1) predicted the siting of a new facilities (discriminatory siting hypothesis); or (2) changed significantly after the siting of new facilities (market forces hypothesis). The researchers found that neither hypothesis was plausible.

Hamilton (1995) studied ZIP codes to determine if a relationship between the percentage of nonwhite persons and plans for hazardous waste facility expansion existed. Hamilton found that facilities with plans to expand their capacity were more likely to be located in nonwhite ZIP codes than facilities without such plans (25% versus 18%).

TRI Facilities

Researchers have also examined the environmental justice hypothesis using data derived from the Toxic Release Inventory. For instance, Ringquist studied environmental justice by examining whether the nation's TRI facility (approximately 30,000) locations and release patterns were related to the racial and income characteristics of residents living in all U.S. ZIP codes.[36] Controlling for alternative explanations, Ringquist found that the distribution and density of TRI facilities and the concentrations of TRI pollutants was positively related to the percentage of minorities residing in U.S. ZIP codes. For class indicators (income and poverty) the results were mixed, providing weak support for economic effects. Specifically, with respect to income, Ringquest (1997:822) found that "While wealthy neighborhoods are not more likely to have a TRI facility, they are more likely to have multiple facilities. . . If exposure to risk increases with the number of facilities, then all other things equal, wealthier neighborhoods are exposed to higher levels of environmental risk from TRI facilities."

Other researchers have examined TRI data at the state or local level. For instance, Bowen et al. analyzed toxic releases into the environment in Ohio and found a strong, positive relationship between percentage of nonwhite residents in the county and the amount of toxins released.[37] However, the researchers failed to find a similar association at the census tract-level of analysis and argued that their county-level results are likely the result of aggregation bias. When Bowen et al. examined different types of toxins being released, they found a weak, but statistically significant, relationship between median household income toxic releases. As median income increase, toxic releases decreased. Bowen et al. conclude that toxic chemicals are likely to be released in areas that are predominately poor rather than areas that are predominately nonwhite.[38]

Pollock and Vittas focused their work on the state of Florida – addressing the relationship between race, ethnicity, and distance (in miles) from census blocks to TRI sites.[39] After controlling for urbanization, population density and property values, the researchers determined that poor African-Americans are more likely to reside in census blocks that are closer to industrial waste than are poor whites. They also found that poor Hispanics were likely to live the farthest away from toxic release sites. Pollock and Vittas conclude: "occupational and housing patterns account for much of the variation in proximity to pollution [but] there is persistent inequity in potential exposure across racial groups."[40]

Abandoned Waste Sites

Researchers studying the issue of environmental justice have also examined the geographical association between race, ethnicity, economic indicators, and abandoned hazardous waste sites. The most notable study was national in scope and conducted by Anderton, Oakes, and Egan.[41] In that study, the researchers examined the spatial distribution of all CERCLIS sites (including a separate comparison for Superfund sites) for all U.S. census tracts in 1990. The researchers found that CERCLIS and NPL sites are unlikely to be located in nonwhite census tracts, and that non-NPL CERCLIS and Superfund sites were also less likely to be located in African-American and Hispanic tracts. They also found that the poor were less likely to live in NPL tracts and more likely to live in non-NPL CERCLIS tracts. These same patterns persisted for NPL tracts in a multivariate analysis. However, when the researcher examined non-NPL CERCLIS sites while controlling for potential confounders, they found a relationship between the percentage of African-Americans, percentage of Hispanics, the percentage living below the poverty line, and the incidence of those sites. Anderton, Oakes, and Egan note, however, that none of the race, ethnic, or economic effects is so large to be considered *strong evidence* of environmental inequality.[42]

Hird examined the relationship between residential, political, and economic characteristics of census tracts surrounding 788 of the nation's Superfund sites.[43] Hird suggests that Superfund sites are more likely to be found in counties that are more affluent rather than economically disadvantaged. Hird also found, however, that Superfund sites are more likely to be located in counties with a higher percentage of nonwhites. Kreig's results concerning race and income shed some light on Hird's findings.[44] Kreig studied the distribution of NPL sites in the greater Boston Area. He found that the relationship between race, income, and the number of Superfund sites varied by the area of the city in which the sites were located. For instance, race was positively and significantly related to the location of Superfund sites in older industrial areas, while income was positively and significantly related to the location of Superfund sites in newer industrialized areas. These results suggest that the location of Superfund sites and the distribution of risk associated with those sites can be linked to structural shifts in the economy. Race and class inequalities often associated with the type of manufacturing employment, then, are also related to distribution of risks across diverse populations.[45]

Stretesky and Hogan investigated the spatial distribution of 53 Superfund sites in the state of Florida using census tract data.[46] While their 1990 cross-sectional analysis revealed that Blacks and Hispanics were more likely to reside in or near a tract that contained an NPL site, their 1980 analysis was somewhat less definitive, though still indicative of race and ethnicity effects. When the researchers examined 30-year changes in the ethnic and racial composition of census tracts, their results indicated that environmental inequities were intensifying over time. For instance, in Superfund census tracts the percentage of African-American residents increased from 15 percent to 20 percent between 1980 and 1990, while the percentage of Hispanic residents in those tracts increased from 13.4 percent to 16.3 percent. At the same time, state averages for minority populations remained constant. Stretesky and Hogan conclude that "environmental injustice is more than just direct discrimination, clearly, social processes beyond the siting decisions themselves are furthering such inequality."[47] The researchers point to institutional factors such as housing, employment, and educational discrimination to explain their results.

Lavelle and Coyle evaluated the location of the nations Superfund sites and the association of the community characteristics with enforcement efforts at those sites.[48] The researchers found that the NPL prioritization and length of remediation were positively related to the percentage of the minority population and persons living below poverty in ZIP codes that contained Superfund sites.

Accidental Chemical Releases

Stretesky and Lynch (1999) performed the only EJ study to examine the distribution of accidental chemical releases, employing data from *the Accidental Release Information Program* to examine the distribution of serious chemical accidents across Hillsborough (Florida) census tracts.[49] The researchers found that, on average, chemical accidents are more likely to occur near census tracts that are African-American and low-income than tracts that are white and more affluent. However, the multivariate analysis indicated that income alone was significantly and inversely related to the distance (in miles) any particular tract was located from the nearest accident. Stretesky and Lynch conclude: "accidental chemical spills do not appear to be random events; rather, they seem to be distributed according to the economic characteristics of census tract areas in Hillsborough County."[50]

Taken together these studies provide mixed support for environmental justice claims concerning hazardous waste facilities and landfills, toxic releases into the environment, and chemical spills. Unsettled debates (e.g., the use of control variables, the issue of causal order, the meaning of discrimination, the geographic units studies, and the type of hazard examined) have added some confusion to these findings. Further, it should be noted that several of the studies that fail to support race and class effects have been funded by waste production and management industries, adding to the controversies in this field of research. There is clearly much work that criminologists can do in the area of environmental justice.

Above, we reviewed the issues of EJ by presenting a unique analysis of the relationship between race, class, ethnicity, and Superfund site locations in Hillsborough County, Florida, and by summarizing the findings of other empirical studies. While empirical studies of EJ are important, they can omit facts that can only be relayed through case study approaches. Below, we review the information from several select case studies on EJ.

Case Studies

Case Study 1: Escambia Treating Company Site, Pensacola, Florida

From 1942 through 1982 the Escambia Treating Company (ETC) operated a pentachlrophenol (PCP) and creosote-based wood treatment facility in Pensacola, Florida. When the company closed, it left behind 40 years of waste including unlined landfills and containment ponds, unlabeled leaking barrels, electrical transformers, asbestos insulation, and widespread air, soil, and groundwater contamination.[51] The Escambia site occupies 26 acres in a mixed residential-industrial area comprised largely of low-income African-Americans, single-family homes and large, federally subsidized apartment buildings. The ETC site is separated from residential communities by a fence. For years, ETC waste ponds overflowed into nearby streets and yards following heavy rain.

In 1991, nine years after ETC closed, the EPA added the site to the Superfund program due to high levels of dioxins present in the immediate and surrounding areas. Under a site inspection, (stage 3 of the Superfund Process), the EPA excavated the contaminated area and stockpiled the wastes onsite. According to EPA technical advisor Joel Hirschhorn, this was an attempt to remove the threat to shallow groundwater.[52] Ironically, Hirschhorn reports, not only was the removal action ineffective in reducing dioxins in shallow groundwater, the excavation left behind highly contaminated surface oils that leaked into the local environment. In effect, the EPA's removal action and its subsequent stockpiling of these wastes on site actually caused, rather than staved off, preventable health threats.[53]

By 1992, the EPA had sufficient evidence to propose the Escambia site for the National Priority List (NPL). By this time, the 255,00 cubic yards of contaminated stockpiled soil had become known as "Mt. Dioxin." Oddly, the EPA waited until 1994 before it proposed the Escambia site for the NPL. According to Hirschhorn (1997), the EPA intentionally delayed Superfund listing of this site because of its apprehension about securing funds for what would become (at more than $4 million), one of the most costly removal actions in the Superfund program.[54]

After the 1994 NPL, the EPA delayed action at the site in violation of the National Contingency Plan. Four years later, the EPA still had not taken any action. Responding to both the EPA's reckless sample collections and their sustained indifference to expediency, CATE was able to secure permanent relocation for all 358 Escambia site families. However, CATE continues to fight for a fair price for the homes of Escambia residents, as many families await relocation and hope that the government makes good on its promise to make their communities safe.

Case Study 2: Marzone Inc./Chevron Chemical Company Site, Tifton, Georgia

From 1950 to 1983, Chevron operated a pesticide formulation plant (Marzone) in Tifton, Georgia, less than one-quarter of a mile away from a largely African-American residential area. Nearby residences consisted of very low trailer homes, more affluent middle-class homes, and some newly constructed homes very close to the site. Because of their role, Chevron was identified as a "cooperative" responsible party for Superfund cleanup activities. Chevron used its economic power to insure that it would be actively involved in the decision-making process.[55]

Chevron formed the Marzone Project Team (MPT; which would later include the EPA and the Georgia environmental agency as its members), as a coordinated effort that enabled them and their contractors to dominate the Superfund process. By taking the lead role in the cleanup, Chevron systematically excluded community representatives that attempted join in negotiation over the cleanup process.

According to Hirschhorn, the EPA Technical Assistance Grant (TAG) Advisor and community groups expressed growing concern to the EPA that the Marzone Project Team was moving the Superfund process at an accelerated rate without input from the residents.[56] Further, they were concerned that the large public relations effort sponsored by Chevron was misinforming the public regarding reported dioxin contamination. Finally, and of greatest concern, was the EPA's failure to conduct comprehensive soil testing prior to any remedial actions.

For 10 years, the EPA refused to test for dioxin contamination as Chevron and other parties conducted several removal actions. The refusal was particularly troubling because the EPA's own Superfund Preliminary Analysis in 1984 identified three herbicides at the Marzone site (Dilvex, 2, 4-D, and 2,4,5-T) that were linked with dioxin impurities. The EPA was finally convinced to conduct several rounds of supplemental RI soil testing in 1996, two years after its 1994 Record of Decision (ROD) for the remedial cleanup.

After first dismissing the findings of dioxin contaminated soil in 1995, the EPA eventually acknowledged widespread dioxin contamination at the Marzone site one year later. The EPA refused however to acknowledge that the dioxin contamination resulted from pesticide materials and wastes. According to Hirschhorn, at one point the EPA sent a letter to residents maintaining that no pesticides had been used at the Marzone operation. The main dioxin culprit, the EPA asserted was wood-burning waste, and that the pesticide materials were merely "background contamination."[57]

Armed with evidence supporting Chevron's use of pesticides (both from official site documents and extensive interviews with former pesticide workers at the Chevron operation), a community group, *People Working for People* (PWP), petitioned the U.S. Justice Department for a criminal investigation and for assistance from EPA's National Ombudsman. Meanwhile, the EPA has to deny dioxin-related claims, and, in violation of the 1994 *Executive Order on Environmental Justice*, has refused to base its risk assessment upon the full range of multiple and cumulative exposures of dioxin found in its and PWP's repeated empirical research studies.

From an environmental justice perspective, Hirschhorn notes the importance of linking the unyielding positions of the EPA with the presence of an encroaching responsible party (i.e., Chevron), whom the environmental agency relied upon for funding the Marzone cleanup. Hirschhorn concludes that the EPA had learned from the Pensacola relocation initiative, that by limiting community organization involvement, staving off soil testing, and relying upon less stringent risk measures and improper testing methods, it could avoid the protracted and costly cleanup associated with other Superfund site cleanups, such as the one in Pensacola, Florida.[58]

According to Hirschhorn, future Superfund initiatives must obtain comprehensive soil testing as early as possible to quantify exposure to toxic chemicals and to connect exposure to potential health threats.[59] Also, the EPA must address its institutional culture by educating Superfund staffers and managers of its environmental justice mandates. And finally, the autonomy and integrity of EPA decisionmakers should be safeguarded by not permitting polluters to control the cleanup process. In order for the process to have any meaning, community organizers must be able to participate fully in securing the safety of their residents, and when necessary, to be compensated fairly and expediently by permanent relocation.

Case Study 3: Environmental Racism in Chester, Pennsylvania

Chester, Pennsylvania, a 65 percent African-American, low-income community 15 miles Southwest of Philadelphia is home to 43,000 residents and four municipal and hazardous waste facilities. Ninety-five percent of Chester's African-American residents live in neighborhoods closest to these facilities. With a poverty rate of 25 percent, Chester ranks three times higher than the national average.[60]

The United States' largest medical waste autoclave, fourth largest garbage incinerator, a sewage treatment plant, and a sludge incinerator all reside only yards from Chester homes. The incinerator, operated by Westinghouse until 1997 (presently by Ref-Fuel), burns more than one-half of its waste from out-of-state producers (including New York, New Jersey, Maryland, and Delaware). The plant has had numerous air emission and odor violations, but has received very few fines. One such example occurred in 1993, when a highly radioactive pellet of Cesium-137 was lost. According to the plant, the pellet was either vaporized in the incinerator or melted down in the steel plant of one of Westinghouse's contractors (Luckens Steel Co.). Thus presently, the radioactive remnants are either contained in the air and ash from the incinerator, or are a part of the metal consumer products made by Luckens Steel Co.; no fines were assessed for this violation.[61]

Next door to the trash incinerator stands the largest infectious and chemotherapeutic medical waste autoclave in the United States, Thermal Pure Systems. Thermal Pure, near bankruptcy, ceased operations a few years ago and has recently sold the plant. Before closing, Thermal Pure brought in roughly three times the amount of medical waste than is produced in the state of Pennsylvania. According to the Campus Coalition Concerning Chester, it wasn't unusual to see medical waste lying in the grass outside the perimeter of the plant where children played.[62] Many workers at the plant were stabbed by needles while handling the waste, and many suffered recurring rashes, infections, and other health ailments related to the handling of or exposure to toxic waste. One particularly egregious example occurred in July 1995 when Thermal Pure allowed 33 trucks of medical waste to sit, unrefrigerated, in the baking sun for four days (the legal limit is 24 hours).

The Delaware County Regional Water Quality Control Authority (DEL-CORA) Sewage Treatment Plant facility is located near the Thermal Pure Plant. DELCORA treats sewage from Delaware County and from local industries in Chester such as Sunoco and British Petroleum (now Tosco) refineries. This highly toxic industrial sludge is then burned in DELCORA's sludge incinerator, which releases many harmful pollutants including high levels of arsenic and dioxin, in excess of EPA standards. Additionally, three other county sewage plants also burn their waste in DELCORA's incinerator.

Reacting to these numerous health threats, the citizens group Chester Residents Concerned for Quality Living (CRCQL) began to investigate potential linkages between facilities bringing waste to Chester. In 1994, after two years of research, CRCQL found that the land under the American Ref-Fuel and Thermal Pure Plants, as well as three other Chester plants, were owned by a Pittsburgh investment firm, Russell, Rea, and Zappala (RR&Z). Further, they found that corporate officers Andrew Russell and Donald Rea serve as executive officers at some of these waste facilities. They also discovered that Charles Zappala's older brother, Stephen, serves a Supreme Court Justice in Pennsylvania. This connection would prove significant when a lower court victory by the Chester residents against Thermal Pure (for accepting 10 times the state's legal limit on medical waste), was overturned by the Pennsylvania Supreme Court. Using a rare archaic law called "King's Bench," the High Court used their power to overturn the lower court's ruling thereby permitting the facility to continue its operations.[63]

In 1996, CRCQL filed the first environmental racism lawsuit in the United States against the state of Pennsylvania, under the Civil Rights Act of 1964. The lawsuit maintained that the state discriminated against the African-American community when it did not consider the racial composition of Chester or the number of existing facilities in permitting a fifth waste treatment plant. While the appellate process was underway, the proposed plant, Soil Reclamation Services (SRS) was eventually denied an operations permit, and the lawsuit was declared moot by the U.S. Supreme Court.[64]

Although there are many issues that remain to be addressed (i.e., Chester has the highest infant mortality rate and the highest percentage of low-weight births in the state; Chester's overall mortality rate and lung cancer mortality rate are 60 percent higher than those in the mostly white Delaware County; and 60 percent of the children in Chester have unacceptably high levels of lead in their blood), some small victories have been achieved. Notably, 1997 marked the first time a permit for a hazardous waste facility (Cherokee BioTechnology) in Chester was denied. Later that year, permits were denied to SRS (discussed above), and Ogborne Waste Removal.[65] While these three examples cannot compensate for the state's history of complicity with industry and the lack of enforcement in Chester, it does suggest that the State EPA is finally responding to community concerns and is aware that its citizens will be watching to see that state agencies conducts decisionmaking in a lawful and responsive manner.

Case Study 4: Environmental Justice in Louisiana

Beside the Mississippi River in southern Louisiana lies a predominately African-American community, called Convent in St. James Parish. Convent is the center of the 85-mile stretch of more than 140 petrochemical and industrial plants widely known as "Cancer Alley." The small town of Convent is home to 2,052 residents, 80 percent of whom are African-American, and over 40 percent of whom live at or below the poverty line. In 1996, the St. James Parish community gained national attention when the giant Japanese chemical corporation Shintech announced plans to spend $700 million to build three chemical factories and an incinerator next to the homes and schools in Convent. The proposed industrial complex would manufacture 1.1 billion pounds of polyvinyl chloride (PVC) and according to Shintech's own admission, would release 611,700 pounds of toxic contaminants into the air each year, many of which are Class-A carcinogens. As stated by Greenpeace Toxics Campaign Officer, Charlie Cray and environmental justice attorney, Monique Harden (1998), this level of industrial toxins – nearly 1.5 tons – equals 300 pounds of poisons for each person in Convent, per year.

Unfortunately, the St. Parish community is no stranger to pollution. In 1995, 10 facilities within 4.5 miles of the two elementary schools in Convent emitted more than 16 million pounds of toxic air pollutants, and an average of 250,00 pounds of industrial poisons per square mile; the national average is 382 pounds per square mile. In an effort to reverse this trend, Convent residents filed a Title VI complaint under the Civil Rights Act of 1964, with the U.S. EPA. The complaint charged Civil Rights violations related to the Louisiana Department of Environmental Quality's 1997 decision to issue air permits to Shintech. Convent residents had the backing of the Louisiana State Advisory Committee (LSAC) who, in 1993 reported to the U.S. Commission on Civil Rights systemic bias by state and local regulatory agencies against many black communities along the industrial corridor. Despite this, remedial governmental and corporate compliance was hardly forthcoming.

In fact, as Cray and Harden reveal, a corporate backlash led by the National Association of Manufacturers (who secured support from the Environmental Council of States – an association of state environmental agencies; the U.S. Conference of Mayors, and several corporate-sponsored think tanks) have attempted to derail the Title VI claims, and have been quite vocal in calling for its elimination.[66] One notable example includes Louisiana's Governor Mike Foster who has publicly stated that the Louisiana's Department of Environmental Quality's job is to make it as easy as possible "within the law" for Shintech to get their permits. According to the Tulane University Environmental Law Clinic (Mensman, 1999) Foster received a $5,000 campaign contribution from Shintech Inc. in 1996, the maximum legally permissible campaign contribution. After Shintech applied for its permit to build its plastic plant in Convent, Foster offered Shintech a 10-year exemption from local property taxes. Additionally, he helped Shintech receive more than $130 million in other tax rebates, which would ultimately be subsidized by Louisiana taxpayers (Cray & Harden, 1998).[67]

The Tulane Environmental Law Clinic helped Convent residents challenge many of these questionable practices, and were instrumental in assisting community members in petitioning the EPA. Residents charged that Shintech's PVC plant would violate the Clean Air Act of 1990 and the Civil

Rights Act of 1964. In response, Louisiana's powerful business lobby persuaded the state Supreme Court (who received more than $420,000 in support on recent judicial races from Shintech backers), to place extremely tight restrictions on what the student legal clinics could and could not do. Rules now state that clinics may only help individuals with a yearly income of $10,056 or less, or $20,563 for a family of four. By limiting whom the legal clinics are allowed to serve, citizens are rendered even more vulnerable in securing environmental justice claims.[68]

In September 1998, Shintech announced that it would not build a PVC plant in Convent. Instead, Shintech plans to build a smaller, $250 million PVC plant in the nearby town of Plaquemine. Meanwhile, the battle continues as the power of civil rights laws to stop polluting industries from targeting communities of color are employed. The need to phase-out PVC and other toxic substances is also at stake. If the past is any predictor of future outcome, environmental justice suits will only increase as more and more communities become aware of this toxic discrimination.

Case Study 5: Normandy Park Apartments, Temple Terrace, Florida

The eight-acre tract of land occupied by the Normandy Park Apartments (Hillsborough County) has been owned by Gulf Coast Recycling (GCR) since 1953. From 1953 through 1963, GCR operated a battery recycling and secondary smelting facility on this site. Here, batteries were split, and the lead plates smelted for recycling.[69] In 1970, GCR built the Normandy Park Apartments.

In 1991, the Hillsborough County Environmental Protection Commission investigated the Site in response to citizen complaints. Sampling revealed the presence of lead in soil (35,000 mg/kg) and groundwater (16.7 mg/L). One year later, the Florida Department of Environmental Protection (FDEP) referred the site to the EPA for further study. The EPA found widespread lead contamination, cadmium, arsenic, and antimony throughout the site in levels harmful to human health, wildlife, and the environment. Lead contamination was the most widespread. Lead and antimony levels exceeding federal drinking water standards were also found.[70]

After conducting the required CERCLA baseline risk assessment, and analyzing the site clean-up goals and five possible alternatives, the EPA proposed the following plan under stage 8 of the Superfund process: soil excavation, onsite screening, ex-situ solidification/stabilization, off-site disposal, monitored natural attenuation, and institutional controls. The case remains open. Further, there is little evidence of EJ claims being made in this case. We bring this situation to the reader's attention to demonstrate how corporate misbehavior (knowingly building an apartment complex on a former heavy metal recycling operation without attempting cleanup) can endanger human health.

Conclusion

Traditionally, criminologists have focused their research efforts on street crimes of the poor, excluding corporate crimes of the powerful from their scrutiny. This neglect has been justified by numerous claims. Among the most important of these claims are the ideas that corporate crimes are not as harmful as street crimes, and that there is a lack of data that can be used to study corporate crime.

In this chapter, we have demonstrated the weaknesses of these excuses by reviewing the kinds of data that can be employed to study two kinds of corporate crime: toxic crimes and crimes of environmental justice. These areas of research are only beginning to enter the criminological domain, and we hope that criminologists and their studies will increasingly turn their attention to these important issues.

Notes

[1]   See, Clifford, 1998.

[2]   Lynch and Stretesky, 1999a.

[3]   Stauber and Rampton, 1995. See also, Greer and Bruno, 1996; Karliner, 1997.

[4]   Fagin and Lavelle, 1996.

[5]   E.g., Carson, 1994; Colborn, Dumanoski, and Myers, 1997; Ehrlich and Ehrlich, 1996; Stiengraber, 1998.

[6]   Lois Gibbs, 1982; 1995.

[7]   E.g., Colborn, Dumanoski, and Myers, 1997.

[8]   Rifkin, 1998.

[9]   Rifkin, 1998; Shiva, 1997.

[10]   National Research Council, 1995; Stone, 1992.

[11]   Rifkin 1998; Shiva 1997.

[12]   Rosset and Benjamin, 1994:82.

[13]   Rosset and Benjamin, 1994.

[14]   Rosset and Benjamin, 1994:37.

[15]   Lynch and Stretesky, 1999b.

[16]   Anderton, 1996.

[17]   See, Stretesky and Lynch, 1999.

[18]   Stretesky and Lynch, 1999.

[19]   Nader and Brownstein, 1980.

[20]   General Accounting Office, 1995.

[21]   General Accounting Office,1983.

[22]   United Church of Christ, 1987.

[23]   General Accounting Office,1983.

[24]   United Church of Christ, 1987:xiii.

[25]   See also Gould, 1986.

[26]   Mohai and Bryant, 1992.

[27]   Adeola, 1994.

[28]   Anderton, et al., 1994. See also, GAO, 1995; Greenberg, 1987.

[29]   Anderton et al., 1994:244.

[30]   Boer et al., 1997.

[31]   Boer et al., 1997:793.

[32]   Been, 1994; GAO, 1983; and Bullard, 1983.

[33]   Yandle and Burton, 1996.

[34]   Oakes et al., 1996.

[35]   Oakes et al., 1996:125.

[36]   Ringquist, 1997.

[37]   Bowen et al., 1995.

[38]   Bowen et al., 1995.

[39]   Pollock and Vittas, 1995.

[40]   Pollock and Vittas, 1995:294; see also Stretesky, 1997.

[41]   Anderton, Oakes, and Egan, 1997.

[42]   Anderton, Oakes, and Egan, 1997:17; see also Zimmerman, 1993.

[43]   Hird, 1993.

[44]   Kreig, 1995.

[45]   Stretesky, 1998.

[46]   Stretesky and Hogan, 1998.

[47]   Stretesky and Hogan, 1998:284.

[48]   Lavelle and Coyle, 1992.

[49]   Stretesky and Lynch, 1999.

[50]   Stretesky and Lynch, 1999:843.

[51]   Citizens Against Toxic Exposure (CATE), 1997.

[52]   Hirschhorn, 1997.

[53]   CATE, 1997; Hirschhorn, 1997.

[54]   Hirschhorn, 1997.

[55] Hirschhorn, 1997.

[56] Hirschorn, 1997.

[57] Hirschorn, 1997.

[58] Hirschorn, 1997.

[59] Hirschorn, 1997.

[60] Ewall, 1998.

[61] Ewall, 1998.

[62] Ewall, 1998:C-4.

[63] Ewall, 1998:C-4.

[64] Kearns, 1998.

[65] Kearns, 1998.

[66] Cray and Harden, 1998.

[67] Cray and Harden, 1998.

[68] Wardynski, 1999.

[69] Denman, 2000.

[70] Denman, 2000.

CHAPTER 7

The Scandalization of America:
Political Corruption in the Postmodern Era

David R. Simon

Modern American Scandal

Between 1860 and 1920, the United States suffered only two major crises of corruption involving corruption on the federal level. This amounts to about one scandal every 50 years. However, beginning in 1963 with the investigation into the assassination of President John F. Kennedy, the American federal government has experienced repeated scandals. As shall be demonstrated, the press has failed to uncover either (1) the root cause(s) of these scandals, or (2) some of the most basic facts concerning them.

The scandals themselves are serious social problems, causing all manner of social harm. The press's coverage, or rather the lack of it, has added to the harms by increasing public cynicism toward the truthfulness of government.

Item: When President Kennedy was assassinated in Dallas, Texas, on November 22, 1963, a cover-up of the investigation into the crime was personally ordered by President Johnson, Assistant Attorney General Katzenbach, and FBI Director Hoover. They allegedly felt those communist elements from either Cuba or the Soviet Union (or both) might be involved, and feared a war would result. These officials agreed that the public must be convinced that Lee Harvey Oswald acted alone in killing the president.[1] This was President Johnson's motive in setting up the Warren Commission in December, 1963. Moreover, the Warren Commission did indeed find that Oswald had acted alone in killing the president, and that Dallas nightclub owner Jack Ruby had acted alone in killing Oswald (who at the time was surrounded by nearly 200 armed law enforcement officers) in the Dallas police station.

Subsequent investigations into the crime by the House Special Committee on Assassinations, (HSCA) 1975-1978, found numerous inconsistencies in the case. The HSCA found that President Kennedy "was probably

137

assassinated as a result of a conspiracy."[2] Probable suspects included members of organized crime.[3] The HSCA concluded that Mafia bosses Marcello of New Orleans and Trafficante of Florida had the "means, motive, and opportunity" to assassinate the President, and/or that anti-Castro activists may have been involved.

The precise nature of the conspiracy concerning actual assassination, and those persons or organizations that employed them were never determined, and, consequently, numerous theories have been advanced. Between 1966 and 1993, more than 600 books and 2,000 articles were written about the Kennedy assassination. The dominant view in these writings is that government agencies killed their own president. They did this because the president was gong to make peace with the Soviet Union and end the Cold War. There is also speculation that Kennedy was going to disengage the United States from its involvement in Vietnam. The JFK assassination is important in that it marks not only the first major postwar scandal, but from the beginning of the investigation, and despite all evidence to the contrary over the past 30 plus years, the dominant media has always supported the Warren Commission's major conclusions.

Following President Kennedy's death, the United States escalated its presence in Vietnam (1964-1975). The Pentagon Papers, investigative reporting, and leaks from within the government had the effect of turning public opinion against the war and the government. A number of governmental transgressions were revealed, including:

- the manipulation of Congress by President Johnson with the Gulf of Tonkin incident;

- the indictment of high-ranking officers for war crimes similar to those committed by the Germans and Japanese during World War II;

- the deliberate destruction of civilian targets by U.S. forces;

- intelligence agency suppression of information regarding enemy troop strength and sympathizers in South Vietnam;

- falsified reports by U.S. field commanders regarding the destruction of enemy targets;

- the spraying of more than five million acres of South Vietnam with defoliating chemicals, much of it with Agent Orange (a chemical that caused great physical harm to many American troops).

- the execution of more than 40,000 so-called enemy agents by the Central Intelligence Agency (CIA) under the Phoenix Program (most without trial); and unauthorized bombing raids against North Vietnam.

From early 1969 until May 1970, President Nixon assured the U.S. citizens that the neutrality of Cambodia was being respected. Yet Nixon had secretly ordered the bombing of so-called enemy sanctuaries in that country during that period. He was able to keep the bombings secret through the use of a double-entry bookkeeping system arranged between the White House and the Department of Defense.

The press's coverage of the Vietnam Era was at times inadvertent. The truth of the Gulf of Tonkin incident was never really explored by the media, nor were the war's secret origins. The war pictures on the nightly news were received by a skeptical public in ways not intended by the media, and the nature of U.S. and South Vietnamese atrocities during the war were given very little attention until after Mei Lai. Moreover, coverage of the war was nearly nonexistent between 1972 and 1975, in part due to White House pressure on the media.

In 1975, governmental investigations revealed that the CIA had violated its charter by engaging in domestic intelligence, opening the mail of U.S. citizens and spying on congresspersons and newspaper reporters. Moreover, this organization plotted the assassinations of a number of foreign political officials.

The Senate Intelligence Committee revealed that every U.S. president from Eisenhower to Nixon had lied to the American people about the activities of the CIA. Following Watergate in 1975, investigations into the postwar activities of the CIA and the FBI revealed that both agencies had engaged in systematic violations of the civil liberties of thousands of American citizens. Such violations have continued to this day.

Since 1947, the FBI has committed more than 1,500 illegal break-ins of headquarters of American organizations and foreign embassies. During the Reagan administration (1981-1988) alone, the FBI spied on various citizens' groups and citizens opposed to administration policy in Central America. Such groups included the United Auto Workers, Maryknoll Sisters, and the Southern Christian Leadership Conference.[4]

After Rev. Martin Luther King, Jr.'s 1963 "I have a dream" speech, the FBI illegally spied on Rev. King, bugging his house and hotel rooms. The FBI even tried to induce Rev. King to commit suicide by threatening to reveal evidence that he had carried on adulterous affairs.

The CIA has been involved in a variety of illegal activities both inside and outside the United States. From 1947 to 1975, the CIA illegally experimented on a variety of American citizens, scientists from the Army Chemical Corps, and some of its own agents (without their knowledge or consent) with knockout drops, incapacitating chemicals, and LSD (an hallucinogenic drug). The CIA even hired San Francisco prostitutes to give their customers drugs.

Abroad, the CIA has been involved in various assassination plots against foreign heads of state, including Cuba's Castro, Lamumba (Zaire), Trujillo (Dominican Republic), Diem (South Vietnam), and Allende (Chile) between 1950 and 1974. This practice continued into the 1980s when, in 1985, CIA director William J. Casey secretly arranged for the murder of Shiite Muslim leader Sheik Mohammed Hussein Fadlallah in a deal with Saudi Arabian intelligence.[5]

Public confidence in government was also lowered when it became known that every president since Franklin Roosevelt had used the Federal Bureau of Investigation (FBI) for political and sometimes illegal purposes. After J. Edgar Hoover's death, we learned how the FBI had been used by its longtime chief to silence critics of Hoover and the FBI. Hoover had also involved the FBI in a number of illegal acts to defeat or neutralize those domestic groups that he thought were subversive. Again, the dominant media accepted the Rockefeller Commission's argument that these abuses of power were aberrations rather than long-established patterns of behavior within what has been termed "the secret government."[6]

The Watergate scandal, and its aftermath, 1972-1974, brought down the Nixon administration. Watergate was also a most significant contributor to low public confidence in government in the past quarter century. The litany of illegal acts by governmental officials and/or their agents in Watergate included securing illegal campaign contributions, dirty tricks to discredit political opponents, burglary, bribery, perjury, wiretapping, harassment of administration opponents with tax audits, and the like. Again, the press did a superficial job of uncovering and investigating the incident, and to this day many important unanswered questions about it remain.[7]

What was the initial reason why the Nixon White House authorized a break-in to and bugging of the Democratic National Committee office? To this day, we still do not know what the people who bugged the Democratic National Headquarters were trying to find out.[8]

In 1987, news broke concerning what was to be the most damaging scandal of the Reagan administration, the so-called Iran-Contra affair. The root of the scandal involved the diversion of funds from profits on missiles sold to the Iranian government. The profits were diverted to the Nicaraguan Contras, a counterrevolutionary force virtually created by the CIA.

At first the entire episode was blamed on marine Lt. Colonel Oliver North. Virtually all high-ranking officials of the Reagan Administration claimed they were "out of the loop" concerning any knowledge of the events. Subsequent investigations and trial testimony, however, pointed to a massive cover-up by White House aides and others:

Item: North's 1989 trial revealed that a 1984 national security group meeting composed of Vice President Bush, the Joint Chiefs of Staff, several cabinet officers, and President Reagan, a Contra aid discussion based on solicitation of "third" parties (foreign governments) took place. This was adopted as a strategy of getting around the Boland Amendment that forbid further military aid to the Contras.

Item: President Reagan personally solicited the largest contributions for Contra aid from foreign nations, and a number of Latin American governments were requested to cooperate by falsifying arms sales transactions so knowledge that the weapons were for the Contras could be hidden. Those nations agreeing to falsify such documents were promised increased U.S. foreign aid.

Item: Both the illegal arms sales and illegal solicitation of funds were orchestrated by a secret group, the Enterprise, set up apart from the CIA and other governmental agencies to assure secrecy. The Enterprise was composed of retired military and intelligence personnel, arms dealers, and drug smugglers.

A report issued in 1994 by Special Council Lawrence Walsh indicated that Reagan administration officials covered up many aspects of the scandal to insure "plausible deniability" of knowledge of the scandal by President Reagan. Walsh's report also concluded that former President George Bush had lied to the press and the American people concerning his knowledge of various aspects of Iran Contra.

The press left uncovered and unanswered a number of important issues. Some of the most important of these questions involved possible CIA and Enterprise involvement in smuggling illegal narcotics into the United States and using the proceeds from such sales to arm the Contras.[9] The entire issue of drug trafficking by both the CIA and the Contras has been almost ignored by major media outlets.

Likewise, the Bush administration left office with a host of unanswered questions concerning its deviant activity. According to Hagan and Simon:[10]

Item: Brett Kimberlin, while serving time as a federal prisoner for drug offenses, was on two separate occasions placed in detention and incommunicado from the media in order to silence him. Kimberlin claimed that in the early 1970s he frequently sold marijuana to Quayle who was then a law student. During the 1988 Presidential campaign, Kimberlin was invited twice by reporters to discuss these charges. In both instances, before he could speak, he was put into detention by order of J. Michael Quinlan, then director of the Federal Bureau of Prisons. This was unprecedented – never before had a bureau director isolated an individual inmate. A report issued by Senator Carl Levin (Democrat, Michigan) and Chairperson of the Subcommittee on Oversight of Government Management concluded that Kimberlin was silenced for political reasons. According to one source, the DEA had informed the Bush campaign that it had a file on Quayle alleging cocaine use.

Item: The Inslaw case charges that the U.S. Department of Justice, beginning during the Reagan Administration, stole proprietary software from the Hamiltons and tried to force their small company out of business in order to pirate its software and sell it for the benefit of Reagan cronies. Two court cases have ruled in favor of the Hamiltons and against DOJ. The software that they had developed that was the subject of dispute was PROMIS (Prosecutor's Management Information System), which enabled the computerization of law enforcement and criminal justice system files. The Hamilton's defense attorney, Elliot Richardson, discovered that Inslaw's lucrative contracts and software had been planned to be passed on to then-Attorney General Meese's friends. Further intrigue was added to the Inslaw case when, in 1990, freelance writer Danny Casolaro mysteriously "committed suicide" while hot on the trail of what he described as an outlaw intelligence operation behind Inslaw.

The Iran-Contra Conspiracy and "Operation Polecat"

At the State Department, the Iran operation was described as "Operation Polecat" because they thought it stunk so much. George Bush at first lied and claimed that he had been "out of the loop" and unaware of Iran-Contra activities. Even though as Vice President, Bush headed a Vice President's Task Force on Terrorism, which urged that it was futile to make deals with hostage-takers, he later admitted that he was aware of the hostage deal, but did not admit to knowledge of diversion of funds to the Contras. Ironically, by violating their own rules and dealing for hostages, the Reagan-Bush team proved their own point. Such secret operations released three hostages, but encouraged the taking of more.

The entire cover-up, lying to Congress, and hiding of evidence, had been intended to protect Ronald Reagan from possible impeachment. In June, 1992, Special Prosecutor Walsh indicted former Secretary of Defense Caspar Weinberger, in order to attempt to prove a conspiracy to cover up Reagan's involvement. The charges were that Weinberger had lied to Congress and obstructed justice based upon entries in his diary.

Finally came the "Christmas Eve Massacre" (December, 1992) in which lame-duck President George Bush issued pardons to most of those convicted or under investigation claiming that they "did not profit or seek to profit from the conduct," that they were acting in what they believed to have been the national interest and that the Iran-Contra investigation represented an unnecessary "criminalization of policy differences." Bush did not pardon Secord, Hakim, and Cline, who were convicted in Iran-Contra, and whose motivations appeared to be more of a mercenary nature. The pardons left Lawrence Walsh little choice, but to close down the probe.

The message sent by George Bush in issuing the pardons was that government officials are free to violate the law whenever they believe their behavior is for the good of the country and even if it is in violation of the Constitution.

Iraqgate and the Banca Lavoro Affair

In the Iraqgate, or the BNL Affair (Banca Nazionale del Lavoro) it is alleged that the Bush Administration helped provide financing and arms to Sadaam Hussein in an effort to win him over, and then covered up the policy after he invaded Kuwait. Banca Nazionale del Lavoro is an Italian bank whose Atlanta branch was used by Iraq to finance its arms buildup. Billions in loans to Hussein to finance his military were guaranteed by the U.S. Department of Agriculture in a labyrinth of deceit. All told, the Reagan and Bush administrations provided Iraq's Hussein with more than $5 billion in loan guarantees, brokering him into a major military power and, of course, invader of Kuwait. The news story of this event was broke, not by an American source, but the *Financial Times of London*.

Moreover, there is the evidence that Bush secretly played an important role in a covert mission designed by William Casey to maximize Iraq's military power in the first place, and to escalate the Iran-Iraq War as part of an elaborate strategy to facilitate the arms-for-hostages deal.

Item: In March, 1993, the United Nations Truth Commission on crimes committed against civilians in El Salvador's 12-year civil war released its official report. Among the conclusions was that the majority of the political murders in that nation's civil war occurred at the very least with the reluctant agreement and financial support of the Reagan and Bush Administration. More than 80,000 people, one in 70 Salvadorans and mostly unarmed civilians, were murdered in the war. Since the release of the report in March, 1993, the Clinton Administration and more specifically, Secretary of State Warren Christopher has appointed a panel to investigate charges that members of the State Department misled Congress about the El Salvador atrocities throughout the 1980s. The CIA, in its own report, described one leader, Roberto d'Aubuisson, as a drug trafficker, arms smuggler, and plotter in the assassination of Archbishop Oscar Romero.

Item: During the presidential re-election campaign of 1992 (more specifically September 30 and October 1), rival Democratic candidate Bill Clinton's passport files were searched in an attempt by Republicans to attack his anti-Vietnam War activities while he was a student at Oxford University in England. Also searched were his mother's records as well as those of Independent candidate Ross Perot. Before leaving office, Bush dismissed Assistant Secretary Elizabeth Tamposi, who was the most apparent official responsible for the search. A special prosecutor was appointed by the Attorney General Barr, in part, to investigate whether the Bush Administration instigated the illegal search.

In February, 1993, the General Accounting Office panned the Bush Administration for its inaction in investigating bank fraud particularly as it related to the Savings and Loan debacle. The Bush Administration created only two of the 26 special task forces it had promised and managed to collect just 4.5 percent of the $846 million in fines and judgments imposed in the fraud cases. This was a miserable effort indeed considering that the S&L scandal with estimated losses of $500 billion represents the largest series of white-collar crime in American history. Considerable circumstantial evidence shows important links between some S&L executives and other investors and organized crime. What is more disturbing, however, is that many of these same S&L executives are also linked with the Central Intelligence Agency (CIA). A number of writers claim that the CIA laundered drug money through Mafia-linked S&Ls in order to buy arms for the Contras. Much of the information regarding CIA-Mafia activity in the S&L crisis was uncorked by Houston Post reporter Pete Brewton. Brewton almost single-handedly discovered that the failure of at least 22 S&Ls was linked to Mafia-CIA activity. The pattern in these failures concerns a small group of operatives, men like former casino owner Herman Bebe, who has ties to New Orleans boss Vincent Marcello, and Mario Renda, a financier with ties to Bebe.[11]

Bush's sons also may have been involved in the Iran-Contra and S&L scandals. John Ellis Bush ("Jeb") of Miami, Florida, received considerable financial support from Miami's right-wing Cuban community. Along with business partners, he defaulted on a shared $4.6 million loan from Broward S&L, which later collapsed. Later, federal regulators reduced the estimated amount owed by this group to $500,000, stiffing taxpayers for the remaining $4 million. One of his business partners, Camilo Padreda, had previously been accused of and indicted for looting Jefferson S&L (McAllen, Texas). Another partner of Padreda's, Hernandez Cartaya, has been associated with CIA operatives and contractors who had systematically misused ("looted") at least 26 S&Ls as part of Iran-Contra operations. In 1989, Padreda pleaded guilty to defrauding HUD of millions of dollars during the 1980s.

While working for Miguel Recarey, Jeb Bush's employer facilitated the largest Health Maintenance Organization Medicare fraud in U.S. history involving overcharges, false invoicing, and outright embezzlement. Recarey was convicted and has since fled the country. This same medical business is also believed to have been tied into Iran-Contra operations. A Health and Human Services (HHS) agent who was continually blocked in his investigation by Washington claims Recarey and his hospital were treating wounded Contras from Nicaragua; part of the $30 million a month given by the government to treat Medicare patients was used to set up field hospitals for the Contras.

George W. Bush Jr. ("Junior") operated out of Dallas, Texas. In 1983, his failing Spectrum 7 Oil Company was taken over by Harken Energy, which gave him a job with generous stock options and benefits. It was underwritten by Stephens, Inc. (Little Rock, Arkansas), which was heavily involved in both the Nugan Hand Bank scandal (Australia) and international money laundering with BCCI. Harken took advantage of having been tipped-off regarding Persian Gulf troubles. Again, the mainstream press has virtually ignored the CIA-Mafia link in the S&L scandal.

Clintongate

On its face, the Clinton-Lewinsky scandal of 1998-99 may not appear to fit the pattern we are describing here. From all appearances, it was a scandal about an individual (i.e., President Clinton) and his illicit sex life, and not an outward manifestation of organizational behavior or of how an investigation functions to cover up a scandal. Yet in many ways, a cover-up did take place.

During Watergate, the Senate Judiciary Committee carefully reviewed Nixon's case before being passed onto the Rodino Committee in the House. There, all manners of evidence were introduced against Nixon. The Clinton hearings, in contrast, will go down in history as the most nonsensical in our history. This is because:

- Not a single material witness was called; no direct evidence of any kind was introduced.

- The prosecutor in the case was turned into a witness.

- Convicted perjurers were converted into experts on perjury.

- Biased members of the military testified as to Clinton's fitness as commander-in-chief and then stated that a pay raise for the military would help morale.

- The House Majority Whip has asked senators to take seriously secret, sealed hearsay evidence of a rape in their trial of the president. This despite the fact that the charge was already denied by the alleged victim and no such evidence was introduced during the Judiciary Committee hearings on the matter.

After the trial began, an entire additional set of contradictory messages was promulgated by both sides.

- The Republicans insisted that Clinton's attorneys were the best paid and most skilled in the nation, while the House Managers were merely inexperienced citizen lawyers.

- Representative Sensenbrenner gave an entire diatribe concerning how Clinton had violated Paula Jones' civil rights by obstructing justice and committing perjury. Yet, as it turns out, Sensenbrenner was the only House Manager who voted against a 1991 civil rights bill involving the sexual harassment of women.

- The GOP Managers claimed over and over that the scandal was not about Clinton's private life, but in fact all the lies of which he was accused were indeed about his private behavior.

Clinton probably had committed impeachable offenses, but Congress did not dare investigate them. I speak here of the matters related to illegal campaign contributions from Lippo Group and other foreign corporations, and the possible give-away of classified material to the Chinese Army (again, for campaign contributions). Congress will not go near this issue because it would open a Pandora's Box of scandal, the likes of which is beyond Watergate. Politicians of all stripes would be involved. This is because the American political system has institutionalized this form of corruption in numerous ways.

Finally, the greatest contradiction in this scandal may be that it has served as a gigantic distraction from actually doing some thing to help the 80 percent of the population who do not own the nation's wealth, who do not give great amounts of money to political campaigns, and whose welfare is greatly threatened by congressional inaction. As Charles Lewis, of the Center for Public Integrity, notes, the United States remains the only modern democracy with no healthcare system that covers everyone.[12] Tobacco kills 400,000 Americans a year and makes millions ill or birth defective, yet Congress has protected big tobacco. Despite all its conspiracies and lies to keep the truth about smoking from the public, tobacco is only now beginning to pay some of the public costs from the billions in profits it has reaped. Adverse drug reactions kill 160,000 Americans per year and cause one million hospitalizations, yet go unaddressed. Congress protects the food industry, while thousands die each year from poisoned food. This is exactly why congressional failure to deal with the question of campaign financing has such scandalous consequences, and is yet another example of how modern corruption is much more organizational in nature than corruption in previous eras.

Conclusion: The Scandalization of America

All of the scandals listed above share common characteristics:

(1) They were all the result of secret actions of government agencies (especially the FBI, CIA, executive office of the president) that were either illegal or unethical, and caused severe physical, financial, and or moral harm to the nation. All have taken place since the passage of the National Security Act of 1947, which institutionalized the most secretive aspects of what President Eisenhower termed the military-industrial complex, and C. Wright Mills characterized as the power elite and higher immorality.[13] The key here is that organizations with immense resources, not merely corrupt individuals, were involved in criminal acts and their cover-up.

(2) All the episodes discussed were the subject of official government hearings or investigations. The Watergate and Iran-Contra hearings were nationally televised. Despite official investigations, the original causes of most of these episodes remain unknown. Thus, motives for President Kennedy's assassination, the reason(s) for the Watergate break-in, and the possible involvement of Vice President Bush, President Reagan, and CIA director Casey, in planning the Iranian arms sales and diversion of funds to the Contras, remain matters of heated debate. Indeed, one of the hallmarks of the official investigation of modern scandal is that they tend to become part of the scandals themselves, leaving unanswered questions concerning the causes of and mysterious events surrounding scandals to linger.

(3) Moreover, numerous unanswered questions concerning events within each scandal remain shrouded in mystery. What was Lee Harvey Oswald's true identity? Why did Jack Ruby shoot Oswald in front of more than 70 armed officers? Did the Nixon Administration hire Arthur Bremmer to assassinate George Wallace in 1972? Why was the FBI the first agency to meet

Dorothy Hunt's airplane following its bombing? Did the 1980 Reagan campaign arrange an "October Surprise" of its own that eventually became the Iran-Contra scandal? These and many other questions still await answers.

(4) Finally, recent political scandals, especially Iran-Contra and the Savings and Loan episode, interrelate, not only to each other, but to other types of crime and deviance as well. There is an emerging body of evidence that much of what is mistakenly called the American "street-crime" problem is actually part of a complicated network of relationships among criminals and organizations at all strata of society.[14]

Notes

[1]   Simon, 1993.

[2]   Summers, 1980:14.

[3]   Select Committee on Assassinations of the U.S. House of Representatives, Volume IX, 1979:53.

[4]   Simon, 1999:257ff.

[5]   Simon, 1999:270-272ff.

[6]   Moyers, 1988.

[7]   Simon, 1992.

[8]   Colodny and Gettlin, 1991.

[9]   Simon, 1996: 303-04.

[10]   Hagan and Simon, 1993: 3-18.

[11]   Pizzo et al., 1991:466-71; Weinberg, 1990:33; Brewton, 1992.

[12]   Lewis, 1998.

[13]   Mills, 1956.

[14]   Simon, 1995; 1999.

CHAPTER 8

Downsized by Law, Ideology, and Pragmatics – Policing White-Collar Crime

Anne Alvesalo

Useful information to the police when a crime has been committed:

- description of what has happened and where;

- exact time and place of the crime;

- whether the offender is still present or whether he/she has escaped;

- name of the offender;

- personal description of the offender (age, height, physique, distinctive features on the face, colour of the eyes, teeth, speech, hands, movement, clothes);

- how and to which direction the offender escaped;

- if the offender has a vehicle, the registration number and other identifying marks of the vehicle (make, color, model); and

- how dangerous the offender is (arms, state of mind, threats, use of alcohol or drugs).

– Instructions for the victim in the Internet pages of the Finnish Police.[1]

Introduction

Why is it that non-enforcement of law designed to control illegal business activity is the norm, and enforcement activity tends to focus upon the smallest and weakest individuals and organizations?[2] There are many studies – both theoretical and empirical – describing and analyzing the obstacles of white-collar crime control, and the failure of the criminal justice system's ability to control the crimes of the powerful is well documented. This chapter attempts to introduce a way of analyzing the problems of white-collar crime control by suggesting that in trying to understand the difficulties of capturing white-collar crime in the network of the criminal justice system, one should study how law, ideology, and pragmatics are intertwined and how the processes in which all these elements are present reproduce and reinforce the problems of control. As Nicola Lacey has pointed out, to understand the frontiers of criminality is not to assume that someone or something has been "doing" the criminalizing or "constructing" the frontiers. In any society one should take into account a multiplicity of actors and processes and of interpretive and enforcement as well as overtly law-creating processes.[3]

White-collar crime has not been a principal concern of traditional law enforcement agencies, and one of the ways it differs from conventional crime is that the detection and investigation of these crimes has been, and still is, the concern of a wide range of regulators, and police involvement has remained limited.[4] There are overlapping systems of control; in addition to the police, there are varieties of civil, administrative, and other regulatory mechanisms, which deal with both criminal and other illegal activities of the powerful. The problems of regulation both in general and of particular agencies, and also the other levels of control; legislators, prosecutors, and courts have been explored by many scholars.[5] However, of all areas in white-collar crime, we probably know least about traditional law enforcement conducted by the police which, from this point forward, will be referred to as "policing."[6]

To explore the policing of white-collar crime is fruitful for many reasons. Albeit the existence of the numerous regulators involved in preventing this area of deviance, the fact remains that the police force is the organization that is at least *supposed* to bear responsibility for crime prevention.[7] Furthermore, despite the fact that there are many harmful activities of the business world that are not criminalized, *there are also those that are*, and thus should be dealt with by the police. Bearing this in mind, the analysis of the processes and obstacles in policing offers possibilities to understand the problems of white-collar crime control on a more general level as well. After all, the police activities present the primary level – the possibility to react – of the official criminal justice system, where reality is transformed into legal crime categories.

The Context of this Exercise

The incentive in this chapter for the examination of the obstacles in police enforcement in this article is influenced by the fact that ongoing empirical research is concentrated on the policing of white-collar crime in Finland. Data has been gathered through participant observation of police investigation in cases of white-collar crime. The emphasis of law and legal ideology in this article is influenced by my primary observation on the problems in policing; the features in the way contemporary criminal law and doctrine deals with reality make it difficult to police white-collar crimes. This happens on both on the level of *criminal policy*, e.g., in the making decisions on scope of using the police forces to combat white-collar crime and also on the level of *investigation*; in practice, it is problematic for the police to build cases of incidents that constitute white-collar crimes as crimes, *even if those acts, or combinations of acts are criminalized.*

The setting of this empirical study is interesting, if not peculiar. It is widely accepted amongst those researching the area of white-collar crime that control efforts tend to be relatively weak and sanctions following regulatory activity are light.[8] Nils Christie has questioned the possibility of law-and-order campaigns against white-collar criminals: *"Who has heard of a society using police force against its rulers?"*[9] It is an exceptional phenomenon that both in 1996 and 1998, the Finnish Government produced action plans to combat 'economic crime,' a rubric covering a broad range of illegal business activities.[10] During the 1990s, the role of the police in the detection and investigation of white-collar crime has expanded considerably; the amount of investigators has tripled. What is also uncommon is that white-collar crime investigation has, to some extent, become a part of local, "normal" police work. Along with the intensification of enforcement, new laws have been passed; not only reformed or new criminalizations, but laws that have as their aim to make the control of economic crime more effective.

In 1996, the Finnish supreme police command produced a definition that is used by the Finnish police when they make the report of an offence and register it as a white-collar crime: *"a criminalized act or omission which is committed in the framework of, or using an enterprise or other corporation. The act is done with the objective of attaining unlawful direct or indirect financial benefit. A criminalized systematic act that is analogous to entrepreneurship and has the objective of considerable benefit is also defined as white collar crime."* One of the aims to produce a definition was to separate traditional individual acts from the "real" white-collar crimes both on the level of the work of white-collar crime squads and in statistics. Whether or not the action plans are a success in the end,[11] this framework has offered an interesting possibility to study both the policing of white-collar crime and the role of law in it. The aim here, however, is not to report on the empirical findings of this author's study, but more to offer one viewpoint into understanding the difficulties of the police in "managing" white-collar crime.

Law, Criminalization, and Policing

The examination of policing is interesting also from the point of view of analyzing what constitutes the (criminal) law. The legal realists pointed out that, in order to "find" the law, one should not look at legal texts "law in books," but at the factual, referring to what happens in courts. As Oliver

Wendell Holmes, one of the "mental fathers" of American realism, said in 1897: ". . . *The prophecies of what the courts are likely to do in fact and nothing more pretentious are what I mean by law.*"[12] This notion can be drawn further: to get an understanding of what constitutes the criminal law and crimes *in fact*, one should also look at what the police are doing; that, too, is "law in action." It is important to make this distinction because, as Nicola Lacey has pointed out, when we talk about behavior that breaches criminal laws, it is not clear whether we mean all that behavior that could be – according to existing legal categories – proceeded against, or whether we are referring to behavior which in fact comes to the notice of criminal justice agencies; it is not possible to separate creation, interpretation, and enforcement in the social practice of criminalization.[13]

Criminologists are aware of the selectivity of the criminal justice system; not only that some harmful incidents are criminalized, others are not, nor that certain people are reported to the police, charged, tried, and sentenced, and others are not, but also that some criminalized incidents are selected for control and others are not. Studies on policing have demonstrated how the activities of the police determine largely both the people and the criminalized acts that are caught in network of the criminal justice system. From this point of view, one could say that the prophecies of what the police are likely to do in fact and nothing more pretentious are what I mean by crimes defined by the criminal justice system. Recognizing the fact that criminal processes are much more diverse than those represented by the police, especially in areas of white-collar crime, one needs to refrain from making such a definition. However, an examination of the problems that the *police* have in dealing with even criminalized acts of the powerful demonstrates how the criminal justice system fails to deal with contemporary social problems called white-collar crimes; it exhibits the tension between the equal treatment that law promises and the unequal treatment that it delivers.

Law and the ways it fails to deal with white-collar crime should not be analyzed merely from the point of view of law as an external mechanism of regulation. In addition to the recognition of the relevance of "law in action" in defining law (and crime), also the pervasive ideological role of law is central in understanding it. As Hunt has pointed out, law should be perceived as a constituent of the way in which social relations are lived and experienced.[14] Sargent notes that law has a special role within the liberal state as an idealized expression of social relations. One should recognize that legal ideology has its role in creating social reality, and shapes the experience of social actors.[15] Scholars of the critical legal studies movement (cls) have also analyzed ideology and legal consciousness; law can be fruitfully analyzed as an *ideological form*, and that legal ideology plays some contributory role in the reproduction of human subordination.[16] Analyzing the criminal justice system and its ideological messages, Reiman has noted that the justice system supports certain conceptions of crime. The image that the misshapen mirror, the criminal justice system, shows is a distorted image of the dangers, and the police react to the those dangers and reinforce the misshapen image of crime.[17] As Melossi has pointed out, the police are inevitably an integral part of a structure of power and ideology; their job is one of sustaining an unstable compromise between the social production of activities that are usually identified as crimes.[18]

According to Reiman the criminal justice system communicates "subtle yet powerful messages in support of established institutions." The powerful magic of the criminal justice system is that it focuses on *individual* criminals, and it portrays criminal law as politically *neutral*.[19] Sargent has stressed how law represents an influential discursive medium in which ideologies are expressed and disseminated. He emphasizes the social character of law as both the product of a historical process, and as a set of ideological discourses affecting the way in which social relations are defined and experienced. The ideological discourses, which underlie the form of trial and the criminal law conceptions of responsibility, together with the judicial sentencing practices, play a crucial role in individualizing and de-politicizing the experience of social actors confronted by the criminal justice system. By emphasizing the values of individual responsibility and freedom of choice, these ideological discourses serve to reinforce popular notions of the objectivity and neutrality of the law, despite the evidence of its particularized and unequal application in practice.[20] However, the conservative power of legal doctrine is not to be found in legal outcomes per se, but in the reification of the very categories through which social conflict is defined.[21]

On the Relevance of the Definition

One of the reasons referred to in almost all of the writings on the obstacles in controlling white-collar crime is the inconsistency of the concept "white-collar crime." As the diversities have been scrutinized by numerous scholars,[22] I will restrain from burying myself in the concept discourse. Instead I will address some major disagreements in the definition matter and the implications of the ambiguity of the concept for the policing of white-collar crime. The classic definitional disagreement is the question, should only criminalized acts be included in the concept, or also administrative and civil wrongdoings.[23] The fact is that many forms of business illegalities have avoided criminalization, which is an ideological message *per se*, not to mention the pragmatic implications. The police can only carry out a criminal investigation where, on the basis of a report made to it or otherwise, there is reason to suspect that an *offence* – a criminalized act – has been committed. As Lieutenant Howard E. Williams declares in his guide for white-collar crime investigation, *"For the criminal investigator to view violations of civil law or administrative regulations as crimes is unacceptable."*[24] Furthermore, even if there are some criminalized white-collar crimes, but the non- or de-criminalizations remain the rule in this area of deviance, this reinforces – not only in the general public but also within the police – the idea that white-collar crime is a marginal problem, and that it should be dealt with by other regulatory agencies.[25] Benson and Cullen point out how investigators assess the facts both in relation to a moral framework of harm and blameworthiness and in relation to law; legal culture does shape how investigators react to corporate wrongdoing.[26] Because this chapter concentrates on the analysis of policing, it is functional to limit the definition of white-collar crime here into activities that are criminalized by law.[27] The legal criminalizations, after all, are the basic points of reference for the criminal justice system – and the police – to react.

The other questions[28] that have arisen in the discussions on the definitional issue are the following: Should organized or professional crime be included, or only criminal activities that are conducted within legal business?; What are the objects of protection?; Who or what (corporations) can be perceived as offenders of white-collar crime?; and Should the misuse of governmental power be included in the concept of white-collar crimes? Behind this debate are several factors, and the importance of it is not definitional clarity *per se*. In general, definitional questions raise issues regarding the legitimate nature of academic work.[29] The role of the academic, and the choice of definition, is significant. Snider has stated that, *"In the most basic sense, corporate crime has disappeared because those who originally defined it as an object of sociological and criminological knowledge conceived it as an illegal act proscribed by government."*[30] However, the content of the concept is crucial in determining the scope of acts and omissions that are pinpointed to policing, even if one examines the *legally criminalized* acts.

On the level of police work, the academic definitional problems are present. But those who deal straightforwardly with actual cases don't have realistic possibilities to make theoretical distinctions of the crimes and select only those cases that would fulfill the exact definition, e.g.: *"individual or collective illegalities that are perceived as helping to achieve, or are congruent with, the organizational goals set by the dominant coalition within an organization".*[31] For example, if a report of tax fraud or a health and safety violation is made of a small subcontractor – whose company consists of a pickup truck and a couple of men, who is using illegal labor and who never planned to pay any taxes – the investigator will take the case, even if the suspected crime would not satisfy the distinguished corporate crime scholar. The importance of the definition that the academic corporate crime scholar pursues becomes real, however, in how the police proceed in the investigation of such cases: will they remain in investigating the crimes of the subcontractor and illegal employees only, or will they perceive those crimes as the first step in solving the "real" white-collar crime and proceed by efforts to establish liability for also the main contractor, who benefits from the situation?[32] In this sense, the understanding of the essence of "real" white-collar crime within the police has its importance and influences the level of enforcement.

Thus, regarding the relevance of the definition in policing, it has its importance when observing the processes and outcomes of criminalization on the level of legislation. The relevance of definitional unclarity – or definitional choices supporting certain ideologies – can be elaborated with the following example. One of the main areas of restructuring in the first phase of the total reform of the penal code in Finland were reforms regarding white-collar crime. However, regardless of the extensive debate about the definition, white-collar crime was not seen useful as a basis of systematization of the penal code. The definition was said to be unclear and ambiguous; inaccurate, because it is not based on the classification built on the concept of "legal good" as property offences are, but expresses more a "examination of fields of life." The result was not only that white-collar criminalizations remained dispersed in the penal code, but also that some crimes committed by employees against corporations were included under chapter 30 of the penal code titled "business crime."[33] The systematization of the Finnish penal code has been criticized as a watering-down of the definition of white-collar crime.[34] To emphasize the special character of economic crimes committed by organs or persons acting on *behalf* of the company would have meant that these crimes are clearly distinguished from crimes *against* the enterprise. This possibility was rejected unanimously by the law-drafters, because it was seen equally important to disapprove crimes committed by employees against the enterprise.[35] This argumentation exemplifies how certain ideologies are laid down by law, in this case through the systematization of the penal code.

These kind of examples of unclear definitions and their consequences on determining the scope and quality of acts that are seen as white-collar crimes do not influence only the ideological and discursive level; they have many direct and indirect implications on policing as well. An unclear definition has its influence on getting knowledge of the phenomenon. If one looks at crime statistics, which are usually based on the systematization of the penal code it is very difficult to draw any conclusions of the scope of white-collar crime because they are not differentiated from traditional crimes, individual actions. For example frauds include many different kinds of traditional crimes, but they also include serious economic crimes. Using FBI crime data on fraud, Hirschi and Gottfredson seek to show that there are no differences between white-collar and conventional offenders – and on this basis propose the abandonment of any concern for "white-collar crime" within criminological study.[36] In his critique of Hirschi's and Gottfredson's analyses, Steffensmeier points out how the Uniform Crime Reports (UCR) of the FBI have little or nothing to do with white-collar crime.[37] This is the case in other countries as well: there are no statistics available on white-collar crime, which makes the study of the phenomenon problematic,[38] and creates a self-fulfilling effect: the image and extent of the "crime problem" is largely created through crime statistics, and also the distribution of resources to different areas of policing is influential to public perceptions of "the crime problem."[39] Struggles for resources between organizational sub-units is inevitable, and it makes sense to assume that resources are allocated on the perceived importance – often defined by the amount of detected crime – of the sub-units work.[40]

The criminalized acts that are selected to "white-collar crime control" can vary from individual credit frauds or embezzlements and commercial espionage to bankruptcy or securities frauds and occupational health and safety crimes. If there is unclarity in the definition, it is possible to water down the control of the intended form of deviance.[41] Even if the decision-makers intention was to combat the more serious forms of white-collar crime, a broad definition gives flexibility for limiting the scope of investigation to minor events, or for replacing a definition by another one. An elaborating example of the latter is the following: despite the action plans against economic crime (i.e., white-collar crime) 1996-1998 and 1998-2001, already in the beginning of 2000, it was suggested that the number of drug investigators should be doubled, and that the personnel could be taken from white-collar crime investigation. The Finnish minister of interiors – to which the Finnish police is subordinate – argument on the matter was that *"…drug offences are the most serious problem in our society […] which are drug offences and which are economic crimes is totally mixed up nowadays. Because drug offences are organized, they are systematic, and they are often connected to economic crime."*[42] This kind of logic [sic!] and argumentation can lead to a new interpretation of white-collar crime, i.e., that it should be perceived as one category of drug-related crime, and accordingly, the investigative resources of white-collar crime can and should be used in the investigation of money laundering of drug traffickers. The tendency to use investigators who are specialized in financial matters in drug-related crime rather than white-collar crimes is not exceptional: in 1993 the value of drug confiscation orders made on the level of policing in England and Wales was £11,952,000, and the value of non-drug offences (including confiscation orders made by the serious Fraud Office) was £1,941.[43] On the level of prosecution in the United States, Benson and Cullen found that corporate crime cases receive lower priority than do drug or gang cases.[44]

The Role of Criminal Law in Enforcement

The information available, that of research, statistics, legal knowledge, knowledge of criminal tactics and techniques, of white-collar crime can be said to be in its infancy. Those who go into policing are strongly influenced by the emphasis on dramatic forms of conventional criminality; the training of police also reinforces this idea.[45] The police lack resources to investigate white-collar crime and are mostly recruited, trained, and motivated to investigate traditional offences.[46] Recent studies have acknowledged that the limited capacity of the criminal justice system in white-collar crime can also be explained because of system overload.[47] My aim here is to look at how law and ideology and their entanglement in the pragmatics of enforcement play a role in both producing and reinforcing the problems inherent in investigating white-collar crime.[48] Despite the fact that legislative changes happen, the traditional ideas such as criminal liability as a system of personal accountability, and crimes as incidents that happen at a certain time in a certain place, are built-in to criminal law and doctrine as a whole, and have their implications on the pragmatics of enforcement.

The units or squads and the areas of responsibilities within the police are often divided on the basis of the criminal law, either using the concept of the legal goods or crimes, such as property offences, violent crime, robbery, drugs, or homicide. Especially in the local police districts, it is not always clear whose responsibility it is to investigate different forms of white-collar crime. Even if there are specialized units for white-collar crime, the types of crimes investigated vary enormously, and division of labor between other units of different crimes are not obvious. In Finland, for example, environmental crimes are investigated in white-collar crime and violent crime units; in both they are rare and considered oddities.[49] It is likely that the unclear duties and "enemies" of white-collar crime investigators make it difficult for them to create an identity, subculture or working culture within the police, and to illustrate their importance in "fighting crime." It is difficult enough, because the daily work of white-collar crime investigation itself is commonly not considered as "real police work" within the police;[50] investigators have nicknames such as "cardigan soldiers" or "sandal men," and their cases are called "paperclip cases" or "piles of appendices."[51]

Studies on policing demonstrate how much of detective work is to transform an incident into a case and an individual into a defendant by the collection, categorization, and presentation of evidence.[52] Looking at the instructions for victims of "useful information to the police when a crime has been committed" in the beginning of this article, one should note that the problems in attaining useful information begin before one gets as far as to the first tip: in most cases it is not clear whether a crime – or which crime – is in question in the first place. In traditional crime it is usually easy to construct the course of events and the criminalized conduct, and many standard practices, processes, and legal rules defining the use of police powers are evolved from this standpoint. In their analysis of the Ford Pinto case, Cullen et al. have demonstrated how, at each stage of the criminal justice system, even if existing legal statutes would allow, circumstances exist that limit the practicality of using the criminal law in cases of corporate crime.[53]

In policing white-collar crime, the essential point is to separate illegal business activities from legal ones; business per se is not criminal. The police need various forms of professional expertise and knowledge that are not required in traditional policing. In fact, the investigation of white-collar crime is hardly possible without using expertise and powers of other officials.[54] One significant feature of investigation is that law is an important daily tool for white-collar crime investigators.[55] This is naturally the case in all policing, but the use of law has different dimensions than in traditional crime. During investigation, white-collar crime investigators are constantly reading the criminal code in order to recall the exact rubrics of criminalizations. Also, knowledge of laws concerning business operations is necessary.[56] The problem is figuring what the crime is, even if one knows – or has an idea – who the offender is. As an investigator said, "In traditional crime investigation, the police are searching for the *criminal*, but in cases of white collar crime they are searching for the *crime*."[57] As an "incident" or "act," white-collar crime differs totally from traditional crime; the basic activity that is happening is legal and even considered desirable; white-collar crime could be defined as exaggerated business. Though some criminologists have defined *all* crime as "merely the exaggerated form of common practices,"[58] there is a difference between traditional and white-collar crime, when one looks at how the *criminalizations in law texts* are formed. In traditional crime, the starting point is that the activity is forbidden as such, whereas in white-collar crime they are connected to activity that is encouraged as such. The ways of conducting business are regulated outside the criminal law, and only certain ways of doing business activities are criminalized. This leads to the fact that the *criminal act itself finds its definition often with the support other legislation* or even business practices, through concepts such as "good book-keeping practice" or "permissible risk," "insolvency," "careful management" or "economically reasonable behavior."[59] The result is that those whose conduct is criminalized are able to define the borders of the criminalizations.

Even if the things that have happened are known, and even if they can be proven true, there still lies the problem of making these elements formulate the legal definition of a crime. In addition to the construction of the crime, the police face the problem of constructing criminal liability with individually based preconditions of culpability, such as intent. So, the police usually know the "name of the offender,"[60] but not if he or she is legally responsible for it. The difficulty to construct corporate liability is the ultimate example: it is extremely laborious to formulate the legal argumentation in accordance with individualistic criminal law and doctrine. Despite legislative changes establishing corporate liability, the fact remains that the idea *universitas delinquere non potest* is built-in to criminal law and doctrine as a whole. For example, in the Netherlands there was a legal breakthrough already in 1976 through paragraph 51 DPC in the penal code, according to which *all* offences can be committed by natural persons and corporations. However the characteristics of the point of view of criminal liability as a system of personal accountability and corporations of legal fictions of private law is still present in the Dutch penal code. The definitions of offences and the grounds of impunity, for the most begin with the words: "The person who". . . . or "He, who . . . ."[61] The Finnish solution to corporate liability is that corporations cannot be formulated as offenders, largely because in the legislative process it was seen as impossible to construct corporate fault. *"The use of punishment always demands necessarily that the crime, as well as the individual behind it, can be identified."*[62] It seems, however, that the imagination for legal constructions is also flexible: according to the reasoning of the legislator, even if corporations are not culpable, they can possess liability, and criminal sanctions can be imposed on corporations even where no individual offender is found. However, *"the ghost of mens rea is always present when we talk about corporate criminal liability."*[63] The problem of liability is also at hand in crimes that are based on individual responsibility. Finding the liable person in organizations,[64] such as the limited liability company, is difficult in itself because the responsibilities of different actors are complex and often defined by civil legislation, internal arrangements, or contracts of the company or companies in question.

Police seldom detect white-collar crimes themselves, but get the report from other officials, usually months or years after the crime has been committed.[65] This is due to many reasons, but one important reason is that there is no "exact time and place of the crime." Thus, it is very difficult to make a "description of what has happened and where." The difficulty of defining the exact time of the offence leads to many pragmatic problems. For example, the periods of limitation to prosecute are mostly calculated from the day the crime was committed, and the uncertainty of whether the crime has fallen under the statutes of limitations may lead to a decision not to proceed in the investigation. The *forum delicti* rule – the principle that crimes should be investigated and prosecuted by the authorities in the locality where the crime has been committed – causes problems in deciding where the case should be investigated and prosecuted. In order for a crime to be formulated, all the essential elements of the crime have to be constructed. In cases of white-collar crime, the crime described in the law text does not mean that the elements have happened at the same time, but some act can be committed long before another and the separable acts are not usually crimes. This has its implications in constructing the incidents as crimes. Kelman's analysis on *narrow and broad time frames*[66] in legal argumentation demonstrates well the problems that follow from the fact that white collar crimes are not incidents that "happen" at a certain time in a certain place. Particular acts are construed as crimes and prosecuted. However, these incidents have a history: things occur before and after incidents that are *considered relevant*, things such as events preceding or post-dating the criminal incident. Narrow time frames – to focus solely on the isolated criminal incident – buttress the traditionally asserted intentionalism of the criminal justice system. In white-collar crime the use of narrow time frames hamper the construction of crime because the relevant acts that constitute the crime are spread, i.e., happen at different times. Kelman points out, for example, how commentators who attack the use of strict liability invariably use narrow time frames.[67]

Conclusions

The purpose of this chapter was to demonstrate how the complex and diverse social practice of criminalization has its role in the control of white-collar crime. Poor systematization and legislation and their inherent ideologies have their role in determining the scope and quality of acts that are seen as white-collar crimes. Ambiguous concepts and their implications and the ideologies which underlie criminalizations both on the level of criminal policy and pragmatics of enforcement, and *vice versa*, have their role in downsizing control. Criminal law and doctrine are originally designed for conventional criminality committed by an individual at a certain time in a certain place. The legal criminalizations of white-collar crime include concepts that find their content from ideologies inherent in the activities (i.e., "doing business"), which find the limits of acceptable behavior from laws and practices, including different goals and ideals than the particular criminalization. Competing values, which are also found in law, manifest themselves in the practices of criminalizing white-collar crime, where – as often interpreted – the "side effects" of the core business, legitimate activities are the objects of control.[68]

What is also essential in analyzing the problems of policing of white-collar crime is the fact that the formal functioning of economic organizations, and crimes committed by them, or in their organizational framework, do not occur in one exact tangible place and time by a certain person, but are often constituted by chains of events. In understanding the particularity of white-collar crime and its control, it is crucial to note that the "ontology" of the organization, what they are doing and crimes committed in or by them – their legal existence – is established through documentation such as contracts, bookkeeping, entries in the trade register, or in the records of the board of directors. The possibility of creating "paper reality" offers many possibilities to commit many types of offences behind the veil of seemingly legitimate business; crimes which would not even be possible without using an economic organization. Incidents that constitute the crime are usually legal constructions which have "happened" through documentation, and the police's task is to show that this "paper reality" is untrue.[69] This creates a particularly heavy burden of proof for the police; the white-collar crime defendants have an exceptional possibility create "reality," which is true until proven otherwise. The tools needed in the collection of evidence – e.g., home searches – can be used if there is reasonable suspicion of both a crime and a suspect. The problems that lie in the "search of the crime" derail the possibilities to conduct an effective investigation on the whole. The vicious circle in the investigation of white-collar crime is that, without a crime, the police cannot collect evidence, but without evidence they are unable to construct the crime.

In terms of understanding the problems of controlling white-collar crime, this chapter illustrates that it is worth studying how the entanglement of law, ideology, and pragmatics reproduce and reinforce the problems of control. Ideological, political, and socioeconomical tensions can be found in the processes of criminalization, as I have demonstrated with some empirical examples. This happens not only in the level of policy, in making decisions of the scope and quality of crimes that are policed, but also at the point where the police try to construct a case of an act definable as a white-collar crime. As has been mentioned, the conservative power of legal doctrine is not to be found in legal outcomes per se, but in the reification of the very categories through which social conflict is defined. It is particularly interesting to focus on the recurring rhetorical structures in legal texts and legal arguments in the criminal justice system's "primary level of criminalizing," policing with the goal to connect the theoretical explanations of law found in legal texts with the daily experiences in order to show how law fails to deal with contemporary social problems called white-collar crimes. Law is not apart from society; it is one of the elements that constitutes reality. It has a great influence on how we see the world. One should not overestimate the role of law, but nor should one underestimate its power in the study of crime and crime control.

Notes

[1] *http://www.polisi.fi/english/index.htm.*

[2] Snider, 1993:120-124.

[3] Lacey, 1995:4, 9.

[4] Friedrichs, 1996:271; Schlegel and Weisburg, 1992:15; Rudovsky, 1982:243.

[5] A selection of the key theoretical approaches, concepts, and empirical findings and debates, see Slapper and Tombs, 1999:163-194. On the lack of studies on policing white-collar crime, Schlegel and Weisburd, 1992:14.

[6] On the concept of policing, see e.g., Reiner, 1989:3-4.

[7] In Finland, the police are responsible for crime prevention and investigation (Police Act §1). If there is reason to believe that a crime has happened the police have to conduct an investigation.

[8] Snider, 1993:120-124.

[9] Christie, 1986:52.

[10] Government decisions 1.2.1996 and 22.10.1998 on the action plans to combat economic crime and the black economy. The operationalization of these programs has entailed considerable resource allocation. Funds have been granted to different institutions, including the police, customs, execution and tax authorities, and prosecution. In addition, new control agencies and methods of working have been established and training and education programs for police have been developed.

[11] See Alvesalo and Tombs, 2001.

[12] See e.g., Friedman, 1967:293. See also Alvesalo, 1998b:5-14.

[13]   Lacey, 1995:16, 25.

[14]   Hunt, 1985:11.

[15]   Sargent, 1990:100.

[16]   See Hunt, 1986:12.

[17]   Reiman, 1998:53.

[18]   Melossi, 1994:200.

[19]   Reiman, 1998:156.

[20]   Sargent, 1989:43, 60.

[21]   See e.g., Minda, 1995:113.

[22]   See e.g., Friedrichs, 1996:1-183.

[23]   On "the Sutherland – Tappan" debate see Slapper and Tombs, 1999:3.

[24]   Williams, 1997:7.

[25]   In Finland in the beginning of the 1990s, the local police's perception of the problem of the investigation was the "lack of time and resources" often referring to the fact that investigators cannot be taken from "normal" or "real" police work to the investigation of white-collar crime. Also it was suggested that e.g., tax authorities should have their own investigators, so that the police need not to be used for the investigation of white-collar crime. Laitinen and Alvesalo, 1994:21-22.

[26]   Benson and Cullen, 1998:193.

[27]   Snider, 2000:9. I acknowledge the deficits in using the legal definition and this choice is not a claim on how white-collar crime should be defined in general, but more based on what my present object of study is. Furthermore, I agree with Tombs and Slapper, who have drawn their definitional boundary to acts and omissions which existent bodies of law proscribe and/or require; their declared political point is to emphasize how *"despite the fact that we are discussing bourgeois legal categories, capitalistic corporations by and large do not and cannot adhere to them."* Slapper and Tombs, 1999:19.

[28]   Alvesalo, 1994:70, Friedrichs, 1996:9.

[29]   Slapper and Tombs, 1999:1.

[30]   Snider, 2000, 8.

[31]   Slapper and Tombs, 1999:14-15, the authors note, however that *"... the distinction between occupational and organizational crimes can be overdrawn..."*

[32]   The Finnish white-collar crime investigators have a saying: "A thief is a person who has not had time to establish a limited liability company." The revised version of this is "A thief is a person who has not had time to change his employees into a limited liability company." This refers to the tendency to replace workers with sub-contractors in order to avoid the legal obligations of the employer. It is both legally and in practice difficult, but not impossible, to establish liability to the main contractor.

[33]   Lahti, 1991:882.

[34]   Also e.g., in Germany the prosecution of white-collar crime is quite arbitrary; white-collar crimes are defined in more than 200 separate statutes, and their definition is often vague. Salvesberg, 1994:35.

[35]   Träskman, 1987:125.

[36]   Hirschi and Gottfredson, 1987:971.

[37]   Steffensmeier, 1989:347-356.

[38]   Corporate Crime Reporter Vol. 12, No. 46, 1998:15. Exceptionally, in Finland such statistics have been produced since 1996. The police have been instructed to register offences described in ref. 7 as white-collar crimes. The system is not watertight because the registration is dependant on each individual policeman or woman. The prosecutors and courts do not, however, have the same system. In addition, when the official crime statistics are published in the statistical yearbook, the classification of crimes is based on the Penal Code.

[39]   See Lacey, 1995:12; Melossi, 1994:206, Chambliss, 1982:238.

[40]   Benson and Cullen, 1998:191.

[41]   Träskman, 1987:125.

[42]   Minister Kari Häkämies 2.2.2000 in the National (YLE) radio news.

[43]   Levi, 1995:4.

[44]   Benson and Cullen, 1998:165.

[45]   Friedrichs, 1996:272; Honkonen, 1999:178-180.

[46]   Cullen, Maakestad, and Cavender, 1987:319-334 have separated three major obstacles – ideological, structural, and legal – that limit the use of criminal law against corporate illegality in the Ford Pinto case.

[47]   Pontell, Calavita and Tillman, 1994:393.

[48]   See Alvesalo, 1999b.

[49]   Laitinen and Alvesalo, 1994:21; Alvesalo (unpublished manuscript).

[50]   See e.g., Levi, 1995:38; Korander (unpublished manuscript) and Honkonen,1999:180 have noted how within especially the uniformed police the way of thinking is that [police]man is not supposed to degrade himself in the "feminine" role of the ridiculous 'clerk' who has to do foul paperwork, keep indoors and study legal technicalities. Even 'normal' detective work is perceived to some extent as not being real "policeman work."

[51]   Alvesalo (unpublished manuscript).

[52]   Dixon, 1997:270.

[53]   Cullen, Maakestad, and Cavender, 1987:319-334.

[54]   Alvesalo (unpublished manuscript). The police conduct investigation with e.g., tax-authorities, customs, bailiffs, and officials of the bankruptcy ombudsman's office.

[55]   Alvesalo, 1999:6.

[56]   Salminen, 1998:15; Alvesalo (unpublished manuscript).

[57]   Alvesalo (unpublished manuscript); Pontell, Calavita and Tillman, 1994:402; Slapper and Tombs, 1999:98.

[58]   E.g., Box, 1983, drawing from Durkheim.

59 See e.g., Nuutila, 1996:147, 160-172 and his analysis on how the "operational environment," e.g., arranging safety at the workplace, is used as a model to connect norms and facts in the process of "finding the crime." Häyrynen, 1998:35 has pointed out how the borders of criminalizations in security market crimes are influenced by the rules of the Stock Exchange.

60 Benson and Cullen, 1998:174; Pontell, Calavita, and Tillman, 1994:402.

61 de Dodler and Hartmann, 1999:76-79.

62 Oikeushenkilön rangaistusvastuu, 1998:14. The following institutions considered that the reform was not needed: the Court of Appeal of Turku, The Central Association for Employers, The Central Association of Industry, The Central Chamber of Commerce, The Central Association of Small Industry, The Central Association for Wholesalers and the Advisory Board of the Banks.

63 Jaatinen, 1999:108.

64 Salvelsberg, 1994:34.

65 Pontell, Calavita, and Tillman, 1994:403.

66 Kelman, 1981:600.

67 Kelman, 1981:605.

68 Slapper and Tombs, 1999:90.

69 Alvesalo (unpublished manuscript). See also Benson and Cullen, 1998:174; Talvela, 1998:136-140.

CHAPTER 9

Globalization, State-Corporate Crime, and Women:
The Strategic Role of Women's NGOs in the New World Order

Nancy A. Wonders
Mona Danner

Scholarly work on corporate crime has become more common over the last two decades, yet little of this work addresses the unique and often disproportionate impact corporate harms have on the lives of women. This sparse attention to the relationship between corporate actions and women's lives is more than a minor oversight, as we will detail in this chapter. In fact, we argue that the hyper-exploitation of women is a key engine driving globalization; the costs associated with corporate crime under globalization are born disproportionately on the bodies of women, particularly in developing countries. Under globalization, corporate crime has been given new momentum. Harms that are widely defined as illegal within the West are instead regarded as necessary costs for developing countries to bear if they wish to participate in the New World Order. Simultaneously, protections extended to citizens in the West are rapidly eroding as developed countries struggle to maintain economic superiority. In this shifting balance of power, nation-states are increasingly collaborating with transnational corporations in ways that cause harm to workers and citizens; harms that we believe disproportionately affect women. Like others, we use the term "state-corporate crime" to capture this collaborative relationship.[1] Because there is little incentive for either states or corporations in a globalized world economy to be concerned with the rights of women, we believe that international organizations, particularly nongovernmental organizations (NGOs) within the United Nations, must play an increasingly important role in protecting the lives of women.

In order to explore the impact of globalization and state-corporate crime on women, we begin by analyzing the changing power relations that have accompanied globalization. We then offer a brief exposition of the nature and differential impact of certain state-corporate harms on women, focusing particularly on economic dislocation, unfair labor practices, environmental degradation, and militarism. We follow this discussion with an investigation into the role that women's NGOs have played in creating a broader human rights agenda that provides better protection for women from the harms associated with globalization. Ultimately our goal is to reveal the increasingly gendered nature of much state-corporate crime under globalization, as well as to emphasize the need for intervention strategies to be globalized if they are to be successful in protecting all women's lives.

Globalization, Changing Power Relations, and State-Corporate Crime

Globalization is a term that is used to refer to the historic convergence of diverse national economies into a single, capitalist world economy dominated largely by transnational corporations.[2] Although many argue that this trend toward a single economic system has a long history,[3] most authors argue that globalization also represents significant changes in the character of capitalism.[4] For our purposes, we would like to highlight two of these changes: first, the vastly increased economic and political power of transnational corporations under globalization, and; second, the concomitant decline in the political power of nation-states under globalization.

With few exceptions,[5] the vast majority of literature on corporate crime has remained focused within the boundaries of individual nation-states. Today, however, such a limited focus is misleading and potentially dangerous. One of the hallmarks of globalization is the expansion of corporate control beyond the boundaries of nation-states. As others have already evidenced, the most significant and powerful corporations in the world today are transnational in character, with operations in many different countries. Korten summarizes contemporary corporate power this way:

> The world's 200 largest industrial corporations, which employ only one-third of the world's population, control 28 percent of the world's economic output. The top 300 transnationals, excluding financial institutions, own some 25 percent of the world's productive assets. Of the world's 100 largest economies, 51 are now corporations – not including banking and financial institutions.[6]

It is worth noting that corporate control is also highly gendered; "white males still hold 95 percent of the top management jobs in the country's largest corporations. The situation is remarkably similar around the world: women hold only 2 percent of the senior executive posts in most West European countries, and a discouraging 0.9 percent in Japan."[7] Seager[8] urges us to ask "what are the linkages between the power of men as leaders of capitalist enterprises and the power that derives from the broader exercise of male privilege?" In response to this query, we posit later in this chapter that men's dominance over the global capitalist economy has tended to weaken women's economic and political position both within countries and internationally. This point is especially important in developing countries, where women's economic position has been historically strong, as we will discuss shortly.

Another mechanism creating heightened power for corporations is the rapid technological change accompanying the last two decades. With the rise of new computer technologies, the Internet, and virtual business transactions, corporate power might better be described as "hyper-national," operating outside the physical boundaries of geographic space or national boundaries. The implications of this shift are clearly profound, leading some to argue that this is the dawn of a new age, what Rifkin[9] calls "the age of access," at least as revolutionary as the Industrial Revolution. In this new age, important economic, political, and cultural decisions are being made primarily by large corporations that control not just the economic sphere, but also the means of human communication in an increasingly virtual world. "In a world in which access to human culture is increasingly commodified and mediated by global corporations, questions of institutional power and freedom become more salient than ever before."[10] It is not our purpose here to elaborate all of the changes globalization and technological change have wrought, but we do wish to emphasize what numerous authors have already established: the economic and political power held by transnational corporations has increased dramatically over the last decade.

This increased power has also led to greater corporate control over economic development, commercial activity, and, more significantly, its regulation. In the West, over the past 50 years, a body of regulatory law has been developed to try to curtail the most damaging aspects of corporate capitalism. In the United States, for example, national regulations attempt to protect worker's health and safety, food and product safety, the environment, and many other areas of social and economic life. While these regulations have never achieved the rigor some might like, they represent a radical contrast to the global situation. The language of "industry capture" is probably too weak to describe many of the global organizations that discipline international economic practices today. Global commerce is dominated by a relatively small number of global players who also serve as self-designated coaches and referees. The most powerful corporations exert significant influence over important international trade and development organizations such as the World Bank, the International Monetary Fund, and, of increasing importance, the World Trade Organization (WTO).[11]

The WTO was created to represent and foster transnational commercial interests. The WTO has positioned itself as an economic *and* political organization, with the ability to finance and support countries that agree with its directives, and to oppose and withhold funds from countries that do not. Health and safety regulations are largely viewed by the WTO as trade barriers, and the presence of internal safety standards within a particular country can lead to significant sanctions. As Wallach and Sforza point out:

> With the establishment of the WTO, judgments over such key areas as food safety have been pulled from the hands of domestic legislatures and effectively ceded to the international corporate interests that helped write the WTO rules. Following an adverse WTO ruling, Europe must now absorb $115 million annually in WTO-authorized trade sanctions to maintain a ban on beef containing residues of artificial growth hormones.[12]

Through the WTO and other disciplinary organizations for the global economy, countries concerned about protecting their citizens from the potential harms caused by global capitalism are punished and regulated. The ability of an individual country to control its own economy becomes directly linked to its willingness to collaborate with transnational corporations. In their effort to entice corporate investment in their countries, Wallach and Sforza[13] argue that "*nations* are serving as corporations' servants, agreeing to challenge laws that the corporations oppose." Thus, national destinies are directly linked to transnational interests in the New World Order.

An obvious corollary of the increased power of corporations under globalization is the declining power of nation-states. Many scholars argue that nation-states are increasingly unable to control their own economies, let alone the global economy.[14] For the developed world, participation in the global economy has tended to require dilution of existing regulations in order to discourage de-industrialization and corporate flight to more hospitable (less regulated) countries. For developing countries, where regulation never existed, the competition for corporate investment has all but invited and sanctioned harmful corporate practices. Cohen describes the dilemma this way:

> As nations compete for the favours of capital, the ability to assert any type of discipline over corporate behaviour comes into direct conflict with the increased mobility of capital. Unless all nations, party to an agreement, behave in the same way with regard to corporate discipline, the corporations will not be disciplined at all. Any one nation, by acting on its own, will be disadvantaged by behaving in a stricter way. Since there is no mechanism for nations to act collectively, individual state action is critically weakened.[15]

In all nation-states, then, there is tremendous ideological and economic pressure for corporate harms to be ignored, tolerated, and even, at times, embraced "for the good of the country."

Given this changing balance of power, particularly the dependence of national economies on close economic relationships with transnational corporations, it should be clear that few corporate harms in the globalized world are strictly "corporate" crimes. In many cases, a better conceptualization of harms caused by global corporations is offered by the term "state-corporate crime." A number of scholars have employed the term state-corporate crime to effectively illustrate the interdependence between nation-states and corporations in generating particular harms.[16] In our work, we draw on the conceptualization offered by Aulette and Michalowski:

> State-corporate crimes are illegal or socially injurious actions that result from a mutually reinforcing interaction between (1) policies and/or practices in pursuit of the goals of one or more institutions of political governance and (2) policies and/or practices in pursuit of the goals of one or more institutions of economic production and distribution.[17]

As Friedrichs[18] notes, "the premise for the concept of state-corporate crime is that modern states and corporations are profoundly interdependent." He goes on to say that "above all, the concept of state-corporate crime compels us to recognize that some major forms of organizational crime cannot be easily classified as either corporate or governmental, and that the interorganizational forms of crime that bring together corporations and government entities may be especially potent and pernicious."[19]

In employing the concept of state-corporate crime, we are not arguing that corporations and governments necessarily bear equal responsibility for the harms generated by certain capitalist practices. In the modern world, the power of transnationals frequently exceeds state power, particularly in developing countries where international, commercial, financial, and regulatory organizations exert strong influence over national policy decisions. At the same time, it has been argued elsewhere[20] that many harms against women could be viewed as political crimes, predominately characterized as crimes of omission since the state tacitly supports these harms by failing to protect women's basic human rights. In this chapter, we extend this argument by illustrating the way that many corporate harms fostered by globalization can only occur because nation-states collaborate with or ignore the perils associated with corporate practices in their country. In making this argument we recognize that nation-states are frequently bullied, threatened, and/or punished into compliance with corporate desire.

As will be clear in the examples that follow, the International Monetary Fund (IMF) and World Bank have played a critical role in solidifying the relationship between internal national interests in developing countries and global economic interests. Over the last two decades, many developing countries have had difficulty paying their debts to Western countries. The IMF and World Bank developed Structural Adjustment Programs (SAPs) as a mechanism to ensure timely payment of debts by pressuring countries to move more rapidly into a privatized, commodified, global capitalist economy. "Essentially, such programs require countries to increase productivity and exports while decreasing government spending on social welfare."[21] The goal of SAPs is to catapult developing countries into the world capitalist economy. Although some countries are essentially coerced into accepting SAPs, the consequences of their complicity with transnational imperatives, at the expense of their citizens' health and welfare, must be problemmatized. According to Aulette and Michalowki,[22] state-corporate crime is frequently characterized by a situation "where government omissions permit private business to pursue illegal and potentially injurious courses of action which, *in a general way,* facilitate the fulfillment of certain state policies." Though state power may be waning, nation-states still represent one of the only strategic sites for curtailing the harmful impacts associated with globalization. Governments must be held accountable for both actions that clearly collaborate in creating corporate harms and their failure to protect the basic human rights of their citizens.

Our goal in the section that follows is to reveal the way that many of the corporate harms affecting women are generated by processes of globalization consistent with the concept of state-corporate crime. In this section we discuss four types of harm that emerge from the interrelationship between corporations and nation-states under globalization. We have elected to focus in particular on the disproportionate effect these harms have on women. This is not to diminish the impact of these or other harms on men or, importantly, on children who frequently pay the heaviest price for state-corporate crimes; instead, our goal is to highlight the way that women's traditional location in the social, political, and economic space of both developed and developing countries has been exploited to great advantage and wealth by global corporations. Indeed, the exploitation of women has been a critical engine of economic development and expansion for both transnational corporations and nation-states. While corporations reap great profits and countries shore up their economies, many women suffer, if they are lucky enough to survive.

The Impact on Women

A number of scholars have written extensively about the unique impact that globalization has on women's lives.[23] In this section we draw on this literature to illustrate the way that corporate harms against women often reflect collaboration between governmental entities and corporations: state-corporate crime. To illustrate this point, we target four categories of harm that emerge directly from the economic and political collaboration of transnational corporations and nation-states and which have disproportionate impact on women. These include: (1) economic displacement as a result of the privatization and corporate control of land in developing countries; (2) unfair labor practices and unsafe working conditions for women who must now work at waged labor in order to survive; (3) environmental harm; and (4) militarism. This list is not exhaustive of state-corporate harms that affect women, but it is illustrative of the gendered character of much state-corporate crime under globalization.

Economic Displacement

One of the central features of globalization is the mass movement of people within countries and across borders.[24] As transnational corporations seek to dominate the economic landscape of every country, people engaged in traditional survival practices, particularly agricultural production, are displaced. By now it is well established that this displacement has disproportionately affected women.[25] Women have historically served as the primary workforce in agricultural production in developing countries.[26] As global corporations leverage land in developing countries, whether for purposes of agribusiness, cash crops, or natural resource exploitation, traditional agricultural workers, overwhelmingly women, are driven from the land. Privatization of the land occurs through several strategies, but most commonly requires collaboration between developing nations and large corporate or private interests. Governments "sell" land that, though not necessarily "owned" by indigenous people, was under their control for generations. Although this land is frequently (but not always) purchased by corporations, the economic displacement caused by corporate control of indigenous lands is clearly not figured into the price paid to developing countries.

Corporate control of land in developing countries has a decidedly gendered character. As Lorentzen and Turpin note, this control:

> . . . often means the transfer of resources into men's hands, even where women do the bulk of the labor. In much of Africa, colonial laws and development policies generally allocate land only to men. Women have lost their traditional rights to the land, even though they do up to three quarters of the agricultural labor.[27]

In other words, economic displacement has also had political ramifications, reducing the real power of women to control their lives or to make decisions over the geographic space within which they reside. In countries where women are structurally or practically restricted from political influence, this loss of economic power further weakens their ability to exert control over their own life chances.

This economic displacement has led numerous scholars to note that women's migration far exceeds men's in the current period.[28] Women migrate to cities and, increasingly, to other countries, to sell their labor for a paycheck; a radical change from the relative self-sufficiency offered by agricultural production. This displacement serves corporate power and national interests in another way by creating a large pool of available, even desperate, workers for industrial production. In this way, women have become the new industrial workforce for the global economy. As numerous authors have noted, women constitute a significant industrial army for the New World Order.[29] But unlike the parallel labor position that was once occupied by men working in industrial production in the West, women rarely have any legal protections from the harsh realities of corporate capitalism: no unions, no family wage, no workplace regulations.

Unfair Labor Practices and Unsafe Working Conditions

A critical feature of Structural Adjustment Programs has been the pressure put on developing countries to foster labor market flexibility. As Millen and Holtz explain:

> . . . international financial institutions (IFIs) considered some forms of governmental intervention in labor, such as minimum wage laws and job security protections, to be impediments both to labor mobility and to a competitive investment climate: by "flexibilizing" their labor markets, governments could create more friendly business environments in their countries.[30]

In pursuit of labor market flexibility, many countries have resisted pressures to create or enforce laws protecting the basic rights of workers and have instead either supported or ignored a number of exploitive labor practices that are inconsistent with international human rights standards.

In many developing countries, it is not uncommon for women to be recruited for factory work before the age of 14.[31] Labor practices approach indentured servitude as families send young daughters off to work in the nearest factory, sometimes paying the factory back a portion of wages earned to cover lunches or housing.[32] In developing countries, there are few restrictions on the hours that can be worked and wages are uniformly low. The poverty wages paid to women workers have consequences not only for their health and welfare, but for their children as well, since women are frequently the primary providers for their families.[33] As Peterson and Runyan[34] note, "by the early 1990s, one-third of the households in the world were headed by women, and the highest numbers of these were in the Third World (reaching more than 40% in parts of Africa and the Caribbean)." Despite the fact that many women bear primary responsibility for the economic well-being of their families, it is typical for women to earn less than men. In the free trades zones established by some countries to attract transnational corporations, women's wages are 20 to 50 percent lower than men's.[35] In most developing countries, nation-states collude with corporations by forbidding unions or labor organizing, and in some cases have used internal military force to violently crush unionizing efforts.[36]

In addition, working conditions in many factories are hazardous, and in too many cases, deadly. The lack of governmental regulation over workplace safety creates an important incentive for global corporations to locate in a particular country. In the electronics industry, women frequently work with hazardous chemicals without the benefit of protective gear or adequate ventilation. Steady[37] reviews a range of research that supports this point, including one study that found that one-third of all women in Taiwan were harmed by exposure to environmental toxins in the workplace. She also notes additional studies that report similar damage to women workers in the *maquiladora* industry in Mexico and in factories in the Caribbean.

Some corporate practices violate women's basic right to control their own bodies. Some factories in Honduras require that women and girls take birth control injections or pills so that they do not become pregnant; similarly, mandatory pregnancy tests are given to women working in the *maquiladoras* in Mexican free-trade zones.[38] In the U.S. commonwealth of Northern Mariana Islands, there are even reports that some pregnant women workers have been forced by transnational apparel companies to have abortions.[39]

As we noted earlier, the lack of governmental regulation or minimum standards of protection is best characterized as a crime of omission rather than commission, but the effects are no less dangerous for women. The impact of many of these harmful labor practices in developing countries has been exacerbated by Structural Adjustment Programs (SAPs). Although global corporate culture creates the pressure for counties to accept SAPs, it is the collusion between corporations and nation-states that leads directly to economic displacement and the consequent hyper-dependence of women on wage labor to survive. At the same time, SAPs have all but eliminated basic social welfare programs, guaranteeing that women must accept the conditions associated with paid employment, however dangerous or harmful they might be. Importantly, developing countries have also responded to the demands of the global marketplace by reducing the percentage of governmental expenditures for social welfare. In all countries affected, research has evidenced that reductions in social welfare disproportionately harm women and children.[40]

Environmental Harm

Research has overwhelmingly established that the consequences of environmental harm caused by corporations fall disproportionately on those already the most disadvantaged; women are, of course, among this group.[41] Environmental harm takes many forms and many of these cause increased risk, danger, and sometimes death to women.

The most obvious form of environmental harm is pollution caused by the toxins associated with industrialization. In developed countries, women and children, particularly those of color or those who belong to immigrant groups, are disproportionately poor and are, therefore, less able to escape the hazards associated with housing located near industrial centers, landfills, or hazardous waste sites.[42] Pollutants of all kind pose particularly serious for women in their childbearing years, who are more likely to suffer miscarriages, problem pregnancies, and to have children with birth defects. For women in developing countries, the impact of corporate pillage of the environment is even more damaging. In many of these countries, environmental degradation has a more visible face than buried toxins or groundwater pollution; more often the corporate practices in these countries, including clear cutting, strip mining, the use of toxic pesticides that would be illegal in the West, strip the land permanently of the natural resources necessary to sustain life.[43] Typically these practices are sanctioned or ignored by the government as a way to encourage corporate investment.

Corporate agribusiness has had particularly devastating effects in some developing countries. Governmental collaboration with agribusiness has been a common feature of the "Green Revolution." Viewed as another strategy designed to make developing countries global players, the Green Revolution has been characterized by the shift from farming practices designed to feed local populations to the production of luxury crops for sale on the global market. Despite promises of greater wealth and economic stability for indigenous populations, this practice can better be characterized as a form of state-corporate crime given the harm it has caused to indigenous populations, particularly women.

The harmful consequences of this strategy are well documented and include reductions in biodiversity, permanent damage to the land because of the mechanization of farming practices, pesticide poisoning, and malnutrition and hunger among indigenous peoples who cannot eat coffee beans, flowers, tobacco, or other luxury crops and survive.[44] One example of this shift from the production of indigenous crops to luxury crops is provided by many Latin American countries now growing flowers for export. "Persistent exposure to highly toxic chemicals is now causing serious health problems in a number of Latin American countries, especially for women engaged in flower production, who suffer high miscarriage rates, and recurrent headaches and dizzy spells."[45]

Land degradation is another consequence of the over-farming practices commonly employed by agribusiness, because paying for new land is sometimes cheaper than employing environmentally sensitive farming practices. As Turpin and Lorentzen explain:

> Ecological degradation affects women disproportionately. The increased burden placed on women is not from environmental deterioration per se, but rather from a sexual division of labor that considers family sustenance to be women's work. Thus, fuel gathering, food preparing, water collecting, and subsistence farming are generally considered women's tasks. In much of Africa women produce 80 percent of the food. Women comprise 60 percent of the farmers in India, 64 percent in Zaire, and 98 percent in Nepal.[46]

Deforestation by agribusiness has created near deserts in some parts of the world where water and firewood were already scarce. This has caused local populations, but particularly women, to travel further and work longer hours in search of water and firewood.[47] The seriousness and extensiveness of this problem is hard to appreciate for those who live in the West. Yet, research has established that the struggle to obtain water and firewood has been exacerbated as a result of corporate agribusiness in countries as distant from each other as Bangladesh and El Salvador; in some cases this means that women must devote more than seven hours a day to this activity alone.[48]

Militarism

Another consequence of globalization is the heightened role militarism plays as an ordinary strategy to ensure stability for corporations, to "free" markets, and to quell nationalist or ethnic resistance to globalized change. Weapons are also a profitable commodity, and weapons makers are also global corporations with close links to particular nation-states, especially the United States. As Millen and Holtz point out:

> In a number of volatile areas of the world, the United States has been the major supplier to governments that are involved in ongoing ethnic conflicts. From 1993-1994, in 45 of the largest 50 ethnic or territorial conflicts, U.S.-supplied weapons were used on either one or both sides. American-made weapons have killed millions throughout the world, particularly in middle income and very poor countries – Haiti, Guatemala, Somalia, Liberia, Sierra Leone, Indonesia, Mexico, Colombia, and the Philippines, to name a few. Between 1993 and 1997, the U.S. government sold, gave away, or let industry sell $190 billion in weapons to almost every country in the world.[49]

Several large defense contractors within the United States, such as Lockheed, have been especially fortunate beneficiaries of militarism and conflict throughout the world.[50] The relatively recent decision to market weapons as a consumer product links corporate arms dealers to nation-states in the facilitation of armed conflict around the world. This decision was made without the involvement of ordinary citizens around the world, those most likely to suffer when the bombs fall and the land mines explode.

A hidden feature of the apparently male face of militarism is the disproportionate cost of militarism to women's bodies. Indeed, as Lorentzen and Turpin[51] point out, women are "more likely than men to become war's casualties or refugees"; in the 1990s, 90 percent of all casualties during war were civilians and the majority of these were women and children. They go on to say that other harmful consequences of war also fall disproportionately on women; for example, "more than four-fifths of war refugees are women and young girls, who often experience additional violence during their flight."[52]

Militarism also has other adverse consequences, including the diversion of resources away from basic health and welfare to armaments and environmental damage and pollution. Thus, militarism creates other casualties among the citizenry beyond the immediate dangers associated with guns and bombs. The diversion of national resources to militarism is a highly political decision with little direct benefit to women whose participation rates in state militaries is uniformly low worldwide. As Peterson and Runyan[53] point out, "women are not direct recipients of military spending." But to the extent that militarism has costs, it is clear that these costs are disproportionately born by women.[54] These costs include the direct harm caused to women by geographical displacement, physical violence and injury as war casualties, and the sexual assault of women during wartime; they also include the indirect costs associated with state-corporate policies to foster weapons production and militarism at the expense of other social and economic goals more beneficial to women's lives.

Women's Rights, the United Nations, and NGOs Under Globalization

Several avenues have been identified as strategies to exert greater control over the harmful behavior of transnational corporations, including company self-enforcement, national and local government intervention, and nongovernmental organizations (NGOs).[55] Because of the historic discrimination and oppression of women around the world, there is little incentive for corporations or nation states to be concerned about the unique impact that state-corporate crimes may have on women. For this reason, women's international nongovernmental organizations have been the driving force behind the protection and advancement of women in the face of globalization. Women's NGOs both challenge and collaborate with the United Nations as the UN represents the most important single arena for forming and enforcing international agreements that may mediate the effects of globalization.

In this section we offer a brief history of the critical role women's NGOs have played in raising awareness and creating policies designed to address harms against women in the international arena. The policies, conventions, and treaties that emerge from the United Nations provide one of the only standards by which state-corporate crimes can be identified and to which they can respond.[56] For this reason, we also argue that women's NGOs will continue to have a strategic role to play in the future if women are to have collective power and representation in a globalized world.

The Historic Role of Women's NGOs

Founded in 1945 as an international governmental club, the membership of the United Nations is composed entirely of delegations of government officials. The Preamble to the United Nations Charter details its *raison d'être* as the promotion of peace and the end of war, "faith in fundamental human rights . . . in the equal rights of men and women," and economic and social development, in addition to a system of justice to enforce international laws. The Charter contains provisions for the involvement of nongovernmental organizations; NGOs are formal organizations composed of private individuals or associations, neither governmental organizations nor social movements. Women's NGOs may rightly claim nearly all of the credit for establishment in 1946 of the UN Commission on the Status of Women, and for the numerous declarations, conventions, and treaties that speak to the need to protect and empower women in the international arena in fulfillment of UN goals. It is important to note that conventions, treaties, and covenants are all international agreements among nations; thus, they represent "the strongest legal tool(s) the UN has to offer."[57]

International conventions and treaties emerge from United Nations Conferences. UN Conferences are generally a series of working sessions and meetings organized totally around the production of a final document. Frequently, NGOs lobby for such conferences. Because of the work of women's international NGOs, the UN authorized the International Women's Year and Conference in 1975 in Mexico City. At the close of the Conference, the UN Decade for Women, *Equality, Development and Peace* was declared to run from 1976-1985. Three more World Conferences followed in Copenhagen (1980), Nairobi (1985), and Beijing (1995).

Nongovernmental organizations hold forums in conjunction with world conferences. NGO Forums provide opportunities to learn, educate, connect, and organize; they also send the message to the UN Conference that the constituencies are watching.[58] Women's NGOs are responsible for the International Women's Year and Decade, the four UN Conferences on Women, the international women's movement, and the more formal NGO infrastructure. Without women's NGOs, few of the conventions, policies, or programs on women in and around the UN ever would have occurred.[59]

Indeed, in combination with the UN Commission on the Status of Women, women's NGOs were responsible for insuring that the final version of the *Universal Declaration on Human Rights* refers to all "human beings" rather than all "men," as written in the early drafts. The *Declaration*, adopted in 1948 in part due to atrocities committed during World War II, serves as the foundation for UN women's rights documents.[60] Article 2 states that "everyone is entitled to all the rights and freedoms set forth in this Declaration without distinction of any kind such as race, colour, sex . . ." While the *Declaration* is quite broad in its recitation of rights – from political rights, to the right to travel, immigrate, marry, work, and rest, among many others – it has traditionally been used to emphasize civil rights in the political arena. This focus on the right to participate in the political process and to be protected from abuses by the state, though seemingly gender-blind, ignores the realities of women's lives and their disadvantaged position in the various dimensions of social life.[61] As we have noted above, women's structural location makes them more vulnerable to exploitation and less able to resist state or corporate abuses.

Because it was not a treaty or convention, the *Declaration* was not legally binding. It took another 30 years before the international covenants on civil and political rights and on economic, social, and cultural rights were adopted. However, while both covenants prohibited discrimination, they failed to mention gender-specific human rights issues and referred to women only in reference to motherhood.[62] During this time, conventions specific to women were adopted, including those related to trafficking in persons and prostitution (1949), equal pay (1951), women's political rights (1952), employment discrimination (1958), and marriage (consent, minimum age, registration; 1962), among others.[63]

The failure to recognize discrimination and violence against women as human rights issues continued through the First World Conference on Human Rights, held in 1968, and up to the UN resolution announcing a Second World Conference to be held in 1993.[64] In response, women's international NGOs launched the Global Campaign for Women's Human Rights. The first major initiative of the Campaign was a petition drive, eventually yielding more than a million signatures from around the world, calling upon the World Conference "to comprehensively address women's human rights at every level of its proceedings" and to recognize "gender violence . . . as a violation of human rights."[65]

Over the next two years, the Campaign held public hearings documenting the prevalence and types of gender violence. These hearings culminated in the Global Tribunal on Violations of Women's Human Rights in 1993 in Vienna immediately prior to the World Conference. The Tribunal was organized around five primary areas of women's human rights abuses, which encompass the impacts of globalization discussed above: human rights abuses in the family, war crimes against women, violations of women's bodily integrity, socioeconomic violations of women's human rights, and political persecution and discrimination. As a result of these actions on the part of women's NGOs, the 1993 Vienna Declaration on Human Rights recognized violence against women as a violation of human rights. Later that same year, the UN General Assembly adopted the Declaration on the Elimination of Violence against Women and in 1994, the UN Commission on Human Rights appointed a Special Rapporteur on Violence Against Women. Finally, the *Platform for Action for Equality, Development and Peace*, adopted at the Fourth World Conference on Women (Beijing, 1995) continually references equality as an integral part of women's human rights.

Women's NGOs continue to push the United Nations to acknowledge the central role of women to UN goals. For instance, Chapter 24 of *Agenda 21*, the UN treaty on sustainable development which came out of the 1992 World Conference on the Environment (in Rio de Janeiro and known as the Earth Summit), recognizes the manner in which environmental degradation affects the lives of women; as we have noted, deforestation and polluted runoff, for example, mean that women in rural areas must walk farther in search of fuel and water, thus impeding their ability to care for themselves and their families. Thus, *Agenda 21* calls for the end of gender-based discrimination throughout the society, as well as the involvement of women in environmental and economic program planning, funding, management, and review. In addition, governments are urged to ratify and implement all UN conventions. Many of these documents provide a basis in international law to protest the state-corporate crime described earlier in this paper.

The Limits of International Law and NGOs

The success of women's NGOs in securing women's inclusion in United Nations activities and treaties is impressive, yet human rights abuses of women remain rampant with respect to economic displacement, unfair labor practices, environmental harms, and militarism. Several reasons exist for this contradictory state of affairs. Chief among them is that the UN has no authority to compel its government members to sign or ratify UN conventions and little success in enforcing them in those nations where they have been ratified. For example, the *Convention for the Elimination of All Forms of Discrimination Against Women* (CEDAW), adopted by the UN General Assembly in 1979, formed a core component of the Second World Conference on Women as it was signed there by member states (Copenhagen, 1980). As a treaty, CEDAW must be ratified within countries. Thus far, 165 nations are parties to CEDAW; the United States is not. Although the United States signed CEDAW in 1980, Senator Jesse Helms, chair of the Senate Foreign Relations Committee, has refused to release it for a ratification vote.

In the past, it was quite common for governmental officials, corporate officers, and even human rights organizations to candidly identify women's human rights as trivial, not as important, or for later consideration; a cultural, private, or individual but never political issue; inevitable or too pervasive to counter.[66] Indeed, only in the past 30 years have data been disaggregated by gender in order to assess women's participation in education, employment, healthcare, politics, etc.; in this most fundamental way, women simply did not *count* and, even today, the data remain political and problematic.[67] While blatant rhetoric about women's lesser worth is more rare today, many activists believe that women's rights are viewed as "special" within the UN and are marginalized in human rights activities.[68] Men's dominance over national and international political bodies, as well as traditional patriarchal attitudes, have slowed the pace of change.[69] Women's policies and programs exist in "bureaucratic mire."[70] UN agency funding dedicated to women is limited; "no more than 15 percent of funds are allocated – a magical ceiling that stunts the gender redistribution of resources."[71] Further, women's NGOs are frequently poorly resourced, especially in light of the many needs.

It is also evident that globalization exacerbates the conditions under which ideologies about women justifying outright discrimination and violence against them may be used to serve global capitalist interests. This takes several forms. Claims about respect for cultural differences represent one particularly complex justification for the denial of women's rights. Culture has been used to defend various practices that clearly violate women's human rights;[72] the Taliban in Afghanistan illustrates this phenomenon. In the mid-1990s, the Taliban referenced Islamic law to impose strict rules on women that required that the windows of women's homes be darkened so they could not be seen, banished girls and women from education and employment, prohibited women from being in public unless accompanied by a male relative and shrouded by a burqa (or chadari), and prohibited women and girls from being examined by male physicians which, because women could not work, effectively meant that healthcare for women ceased to exist. Penalties for violating Taliban decrees are severe and include beatings and even death.[73] Although arguments about cultural difference are often critically important, too frequently corporations and states use such arguments strategically as a way to ignore women's rights, when the real issue is the well-cultivated link between patriarchal values and profits. The truth is that sometimes there is simply too much money to be made to pay attention to women. The profits in laying a pipeline across Afghanistan have enticed international oil companies to go into business with the Taliban. Despite human rights advances, corporations do not sign conventions and governments that do remain acutely aware that technological and transportation advances mean that corporations can quickly move to more profitable areas should they object to governmental regulatory efforts.

Another problem with the effectiveness of NGOs and international law in addressing the harms caused by globalization is the reliance of NGOs on traditional human's rights discourse, particularly the focus on individual political and civil rights. In these arenas, women's NGOs have been successful in securing greater rights for women, but these rights do not necessarily fundamentally alter the threats to economic, social, and cultural rights posed by the New World Order.[74] For this reason, an expansion of the human rights agenda will be required if women's NGOs hope to continue to improve women's lives in a globalized world.

The Future of Women's Human Rights in the Face of Globalization

In this chapter, we have argued that globalization has had many unfortunate consequences for women. As transnational corporations become stronger and nation-states relatively weaker, the incentives for state-corporate crime become greater. We recognize that it is controversial to argue that the development policies and ordinary business practices of globalized corporate capitalism constitute state-corporate crime; indeed, it is just such controversy that we wish to ignite. Because of the weakened power of nation-states under globalization, we all must play a role in problemmatizing what seem to be inevitable trends within the global economy, particularly given the harmful consequences of globalization for women and children. The international arena offered by the United Nations serves as a strategic site for contesting this inevitability and raising the human rights standards by which corporations and countries must do business. In a globalized world, United Nations treaties and conventions take on ever greater importance, which is also why they are now more hotly contested. The increasing power of corporations relative to nation-states may also flow over into the UN as governmental delegations seek to protect corporate interests in order to encourage economic investment in their nations. Thus, the role of NGOs within and across nations is likely to be even more important in the future.

NGOs, especially women's and human rights organizations, use UN agencies and international conventions and treaties to insist that women not be completely forgotten or overly exploited in the face of globalization. NGOs "expand the public policy agenda, both confronting and nudging at governments, international development organizations, and the people that staff bureaucracies in those institutions."[75] In numerous ways, treaties and data about women define issues and strategies for action, make women visible, and can be used to hold governments accountable. And while the forces allied against women's interests are formidable, NGOs have been effective.

Bunch[76] reminds us that "the women of the Plaza de Mayo in Argentina did not wait for an official declaration but stood up to demand state accountability" for the disappearances of their loved ones. In so doing, they expanded the concept of human rights. Because of the Global Campaign for Women's Human Rights, practices once deemed unimportant or private, such as discrimination or rape during war, are now on the international public agenda. Activism by U.S. university students against garment industry sweatshops has been successful in pressuring sports apparel makers to adhere to higher standards to protect workers, most of whom are women.[77]

The Feminist Majority Foundation's[78] Campaign to Stop Gender Apartheid helped stop the United States and the United Nations from officially recognizing the Taliban until women's human rights have been restored. They have also been effective in curtailing corporate investment in oil and telecommunications in Afghanistan. The United States would have normalized relations with the reigning Taliban to aid U.S. corporations if not for the outcry of women's NGOs. In these myriad ways, women's NGOs remain critical in mediating the effects of globalization.

Given the crucial role women's NGO have played and must continue to play if women's basic human rights are to be protected, it is clear that additional resources ought be directed to these organizations.

In the area of economic and social rights – where NGOs and women's groups are working out ways to be more effective – the mobilisation of enormous resources will be required to overcome human wrongs, such as the illiteracy of several hundred million girls and women worldwide. The political will to allocate these resources for transformation will be the real deciding factor in this global struggle for human rights.[79]

In emphasizing the role of women's NGOs, we are not implying that international law is the only arena for reducing the harms caused by state-corporate crime. Still, we would argue that it is an important one. "Although law is one of the disciplinary techniques of global governmentality, it is a site where the limits of the readability of narratives of difference, community, and democracy are constantly contested."[80] We believe that women's NGOs have served and must continue to serve women by contesting the boundaries of state-corporate action; in doing so they play an essential role in advocating all human rights.

Notes

[1]   Kramer and Michalowski, 1990; Aulette and Michalowski, 1993.

[2]   Amin, 1990, 1997; Greider, 1997; Hoogvelt, 1997; Mander and Goldsmith, 1996.

[3]   Friedman, 1999; Hirst, 1996.

[4]   Korten, 1995, 1998; Karliner, 1997.

[5]   See, for example, Michalowski and Kramer, 1987.

[6]   Korten, 1998:15.

[7]   Seager, 1993:82.

[8]   Seager, 1993:82.

[9]   Rifkin, 2000.

[10]   Rifkin, 2000:11.

[11]   Millen and Holtz, 2000.

[12]   Sforza, 1999:18.

[13]   Wallach and Sforza, 1999:18.

[14]   Cohen, 1996.

[15]   Cohen, 1996:401.

[16]   Kramer and Michalowski, 1990; Kauzlarich and Kramer, 1998; Aulette and Michalowski, 1993; Friedrichs, 1996.

[17]   Aulette and Michalowski, 1993:175.

[18]   Friedrichs, 1996:154.

[19]   Friedrichs, 1996:156.

[20]   See Caulfield and Wonders, 1993.

[21]   Peterson and Runyan, 1999:136.

[22]   Aulette and Michalowki, 1993:175.

[23]   See for example, Sassen, 1997 or Peterson and Runyan, 1999.

[24]   Wonders and Michalowski, 2000.

[25]   Shoepf, Schoepf, and Millen, 2000; Lorentzen and Turpin, 1996.

[26]   Steady, 1998.

[27]   Lorentzen and Turpin, 1996:4.

[28]   International Labor Organization, 1996; Kempadoo and Doezema, 1998.

[29]   Sassen, 1997.

[30]   Millen and Holtz, 2000:186.

[31]   Millen and Holtz, 2000; UNDP, 1996.

[32]   UNDP, 1996.

[33]   Steady, 1998.

[34]   Peterson and Runyan, 1999:135.

[35]   Millen and Holtz, 2000.

[36]   Millen and Holtz, 2000.

[37]   Steady, 1998.

[38]   Millen and Holtz, 2000; Human Rights Watch, 2000a.

[39]   Millen and Holtz, 2000.

[40]   Peterson and Runyan, 1999.

[41]   Bullard, 1993; Steady, 1998; Peterson and Runyan, 1999.

[42]   Bullard, 1993; Steady, 1998; Seager, 1993.

[43]   Madeley, 1999; Millen and Holtz, 2000.

[44]   Madeley, 1999.

[45]   Madeley, 1999:46.

[46]   Turpin and Lorentzen, 1996:3.

[47]   Turpin and Lorentzen; Madeley, 1999.

[48]   Turpin and Lorentzen, 1999; Rodda, 1991.

[49]   Millen and Holtz, 2000:212.

[50]   Millen and Holtz, 2000.

[51]   Lorentzen and Turpin, 1996:6.

[52]   Lorentzen and Turpin, 1996:6.

[53]   Peterson and Runyan 1999:121.

[54]   Nikolic-Ristanovic, 1996.

[55]   Millen and Holtz, 2000.

[56]   Michalowski and Kramer, 1987.

57   International Women's Tribune Centre, 1998:7.

58   Prügl and Meyer, 1999.

59   Winslow, 1995.

60   Tomasevski, 1993:98.

61   Young, Fort, and Danner, 1994.

62   Tomasevski, 1993:100.

63   Pietilä and Vickers, 1990:117.

64   Bunch and Reilly, 1994.

65   Bunch and Reilly, 1994:131.

66   Bunch, 1990:488.

67   Danner, Fort, and Young, 1999.

68   Gallagher, 1997:285.

69   Connors, 1999.

70   Staudt and Timothy, 1997:333.

71   Staudt and Timothy, 1997:333.

72   Mayer, 1995; Rao, 1995.

73   Feminist Majority Foundation, 1999.

74   Connors, 1999.

75   Staudt, 1997:vii.

76   Bunch, 1990:497

77   Human Rights Watch, 2000b.

78   Feminist Majority Foundation, 1999.

79   Ashworth, 1999:272.

80   Otto, 1999:174.

CHAPTER 10

States, Corporations, and the 'New' World Order

Frank Pearce
Steve Tombs

In a 1973 essay titled "Crime, Corporations and the American Social Order," and then in 1976 in *Crimes of the Powerful: Marxism, Crime and Deviance,* it was argued that representations of the "crime problem" in the United States were distorted in two major ways.[1] First, the illegal activities of corporations and the wealthy minority that, to a large extent owned and controlled them, received little publicity although it was possible to show that, for example, violations of anti-trust laws produced staggering sums in illegal profits, and that the same was true of the illegal tax evasion engaged in by their wealthy owners. This meant higher prices and higher taxes for the rest of the population. It was also argued that corporations had, on occasion, used gangsters to undermine trade unions and to intimidate working people and that they had collaborated with the American government in illegally undermining independent governments in other societies. Indeed there was a nexus involving American corporations, the U.S. government and organized crime that had played a significant role in structuring the environment within which corporations operated. This, in turn, suggested that it was worth exploring in more depth the political economy of the United States in the context of its national and international activities. Such an exploration showed that neither American corporations nor the U.S. state act much in accord with standard representations of their activities. Corporations may pay lip service to competitive markets but in practice they act systematically to control, at whatever cost, the markets within which they operate. The American state may be formally democratic but it is so constrained and beholden to corporate capital that it is very narrow in the interests it pursues and often cruelly indifferent to the well-being of most citizens at home and abroad. Sometimes this involves illegal activities, often it means creating a legal framework which allows and, indeed, encourages the destructive activities of corporate capital.

Thus, one of the key tasks of this earlier work was to explore the nature of the U.S. capitalist economy at least in terms of what was presented as the co-existence of, on the one hand, an "imaginary" and, on the other, a "real" social order. The phenomenon of corporate crime – its nature, scale, opportunity structure, "regulation," and relative invisibility – was placed within this disjuncture between "the way things are supposed to happen and what actually occurs."[2] In this chapter, we turn our attention again to the contours of capitalist economies, attempting to discern their essential features alongside some specificities of particular capitalist social orders (notably the U.S. and the U.K.), focusing upon the disjuncture between representation and reality. We shall say little about corporate crime *per se* in this chapter. Other contributions to this volume more than adequately address a whole series of relevant empirical, conceptual and theoretical issues, while together and separately we have also dealt with many of these issues elsewhere.[3] Finally, the specific nature of links between neoliberal political economy on the one hand and corporate crime on the other have recently been addressed cogently and at some length by Snider.[4] Rather, our aim is to return to some of the concerns of *Crimes of the Powerful*, focusing upon the nature of contemporary capitalism – and the nature of states and corporations within this – thereby examining the extent to which there has emerged a "new" social order in the 25 years since the publication of that text.

It is no coincidence that this previous work on the political economy of corporate crime was written and appeared when it did. Post-Watergate America, in which the state was plunged into something of a crisis of legitimacy and in which powerful organizations were also affected by more than a whiff of both corruption and criminality, was a ripe context for the emergence of a "social movement" against corporate crime.[5] And so in the early to mid-1970s, more than three decades after Sutherland had famously attempted to turn the attention of American criminology to corporate crime, there appeared to be something of an academic and indeed popular interest in the criminal and socially irresponsible activities of corporations. A quarter of a century later, however, a leading academic commentator has written the obituary of corporate crime research in the academy.[6]

The period since the publication of *Crimes of the Powerful* has witnessed a key series of economic, political, social and cultural shifts, central to which has been the emergence of neoliberalism, a particular version of capitalist ideology and organization. Thus summing up the period from the mid 1970s to the mid 1990s, Gottschalk highlights the following features, which are now widely associated with the prescriptions of neoliberal economists:

> Deregulation and the unleashing of market forces became the norm. Restrictions were lifted on the movement of capital. National financial bubbles emerged, grew and burst. The iron curtain fell, while market economies appeared to gain a strong foothold. Policies shifted to the right, and proponents of the "Welfare State" found themselves increasingly on the defense.[7]

Reflecting upon the 1990s, Anderson has defined the "principal aspect" of this decade as "the virtually uncontested consolidation, and universal diffusion, of neo-liberalism," [8] with this "neo-liberal consensus" finding "a new point of stabilization in the 'Third Way' of the Clinton-Blair regimes."[9] For some commentators, the end of the twentieth century signaled the once-and-for all triumph of the political shell of liberal democracy and a free market economic order,[10] and the death of all forms of socialism and social democracy.[11] If such apocryphal claims are taken at all seriously, one should expect to find severe implications for the willingness or ability of nation-states to regulate capitalist corporations effectively.

In this chapter, we review some of these shifts, as the means of most adequately raising, let alone answering, a key political question – to what extent is the effective control of corporations, and thus the more effective prevention of, or responses to, corporate crime, more or less possible at the start of the twenty-first century? In other words, understanding corporate crime and its control 25 years after the last documented large-scale "social movement" around these phenomena requires addressing a logically prior theoretical question – have there occurred qualitative changes in the nature of capitalism, or key actors and institutions within it, particularly here states and corporations, which render such control less (as is popularly held to be the case) possible?

The structure of the chapter is as follows. We begin by highlighting some of the economic and social characteristics that have accompanied the emergence of neo-liberalism, a school of economic thought which has risen to pre-eminence in the period under consideration, focusing particularly upon the economies of the USA and Britain, where neo-liberal ideas have been most thoroughly put into practice. Having examined several aspects of disjuncture between "representational" and "real" social orders, we devote much of our paper to an extended analysis of key aspects of processes of economic globalization, both ideological and material. Intimately linked with the emergence of neoliberalism, it is economic globalization that has increasingly become the leitmotif of our times: we examine the central substance of globalization claims, their key effects, and consider their implications for capitalist diversity and state activity, including not least the regulation of corporations. We conclude with a series of observations regarding the appropriate mode of analysis for considering the prospects for the more effective control of corporate crime.

Neoliberalism and Its Consequences

Compared to most citizens in most other countries, and compared to their own previous standard of living, average citizens now living in the 29 OECD (Organization for Economic Co-operation and Development) countries have a dramatically better standard of living. On average: they work fewer hours, live longer, are healthier and better housed, have access to a greater volume and range of goods and services; they are more mobile and, through their easy access to a range of mass media, are exposed to a greater wealth of information; they have a better education and better medical care, and, through unemployment benefit, welfare, worker compensation and pensions, they have greater security. Changes in the Gross Domestic Product (GDP) per capita within OECD countries over time and the differences between their current GDP per capita and that of other countries provide telling evidence of their relative prosperity.

The past quarter of a century has seen the emergence to dominance of a particular version of capitalist economics, in which free markets and minimal states are central.[12] Such ideas commonly referred to as neo-liberalism and associated with the work of the Chicago School in particular – have been enormously influential in the re-organization of the British and American economies (and, of course, internationally), in terms of the organization of interactions between national economies, and as tools of powerful international organizations in their dealings with developing economies. Because increasingly the only way of producing and distributing goods and services is by capitalist enterprises in a global market economy, with increasingly limited state interference, the world now looks like a more "rational" place.

If, from the perspective of neoliberalism, much of the world now seems more rational, we should at the time – note that it is now a much more unequal and, for the vast majorities of peoples, harsher place than was the case in the mid-1970s. To note, as we did above, that the average standard of living of people in the OECD countries, as measured by their GDP per capita, has improved over time and is much better than that of non-OECD countries, is a statement at such a level of generalization that it obscures a great deal. Most obviously, if there is any emerging global political economy, then this emergence has, with the exception of the four Asian tigers (Hong Kong, Korea, Singapore, and Taiwan) and China,[13] been accompanied by increasing disparities in wealth between developed and "Third World" countries,[14] with the latter group seeing their relative role in world trade declining, their debt burden increasing and balance of payments deficit continuing.[15] The share of global income of the world's poorest 20 percent dropped from 2.3 percent in 1989 to 1.4 percent in 1999; by contrast, the share of the richest 10 percent grew from 70 percent to 85 percent.[16] The gap in per capita income between the industrial and developing world "tripled between 1960 and 1993."[17] World consumption in 1997 was twice the level it was in 1975; yet the average African household consumes less today than in 1972.[18] Twenty percent of the world's people account for 86 percent of the world's private consumption expenditures, the poorest accounting for just 1.3 percent.[19]

Indeed, 1997 and 1998 saw a generalized crisis across Asian economies, somewhat altering the security of capitalist optimism even here.[20] The neo-liberal "way out" of this economic decline is likely to impact even more detrimentally upon the quality of life within developing economies. Thus the logic of the economics of the IMF-World Bank-WTO-US Treasury nexus is that less developed countries should exploit any competitive advantage open to them, whether this be access to natural resources or low wages and lax regulation. To provide one illustration of this, Laurence Summers, while chief economist at the World Bank (and as we write, Treasury Secretary in the US Government), wrote in a 1991 internal memo that waste and dirty industries should be transferred south:

> Just between you and me, shouldn't the World Bank be encouraging more migration of the dirty industries to the LDCs . . . I think the economic logic behind dumping a load of toxic waste in the lowest wage country is impeccable and we should face up to that . . . I've always thought that under-populated countries in Africa are vastly under-polluted; their air quality is vastly inefficiently low compared to Los Angeles . . .[21]

In fact, and rather contradicting Summers' claims regarding the under-polluted nature of developing countries, the UN has consistently documented that the vast majority of environmental damage falls upon the poorest peoples of the world, while consumption is overwhelmingly concentrated amongst a handful of the richest countries.[22]

Further, globalized economic activity, and the increasing mobility of capital, has heightened the insecurities that individuals and communities, even nations, experience about their economic future.[23] The commodification of most productive activity and an orientation towards international markets makes all countries dangerously vulnerable to global economic fluctuations.[24]

If we turn to conditions *within* OECD countries, it is clear that figures relating to increasing living standards are *averages*, and must therefore be supplemented with some analysis of the distribution of income and wealth within these countries. What we find is that increasing inequalities across nation-states as well as within them are also a key hallmark of the past two decades.[25] Thus, within all OECD nations there are significant inequalities. But these are hardly uniform. In the U.K. and the U.S., where the neoliberal experiment emerged and has been most thoroughgoing,[26] as well as in some parts of Europe, economic and social inequalities have been increasing since the beginning of the 1980s, even if these are often officially masked.[27] Esping-Anderson's review of poverty and income inequality across OECD states concludes that trends towards greater poverty and income inequality in the 1980s were the most marked in those welfare regimes that he had characterized as pursuing the "liberal deregulatory" strategy: for example, during the 1980s, the lowest decile earners lost, relative to the median, 8 percentage points in Australia, 11 in Canada, 13 in New Zealand, 23 in the U.K. and 29 in the United States.[28] Gottschalk claims that where the United States stands out in trends in inequality from the mid 1970s to the mid 1990s is "in the magnitude of the increase in earnings of those at the top of the distribution"; amongst industrialized countries, the U.K. had the next largest increases in this index of income inequality.[29] Froud et al., by contrast, claim a distinctiveness for the U.S. and U.K., but base this not on the larger share of income to more affluent households, but on the peculiarly low shares to the poorest households: "their poorest households in the bottom quintile manage on not much more than 4.5 percent of total household income, just one tenth of what the top quintile receives."[30] What is not at issue is the peculiarity of the U.S. and U.K. in terms of inequality. Let us take some brief indicators of trends in inequality in these two countries.

If we turn first to the U.S., we find, for example, that: when adjusted for inflation, most U.S. households had less net worth in 1999 than they did in 1983; since the mid 1970s to the end of the 1990s, the top 1 percent of U.S. households doubled their share of national wealth, owning 40 percent of national wealth, more than owned by the "bottom" 95 percent; when adjusted for inflation, average weekly wages for workers in 1998 were 12 percent lower than in 1973, a period in which productivity grew by almost 33 percent; during this same period, household debt had grown from 58 percent to 85 percent of income.[31] While the CEO of a U.S. company could expect to earn 35 times that of the average worker in 1973, by 1998 that had risen to 200 times.[32] By 1997, the value of the minimum wage was 30 percent lower than it had been in 1968.[33] In 1999, Forbes Magazine calculated that Bill Gates was the wealthiest individual in the world;[34] this personal fortune of $60 billion was, in 1998, a sum greater than the GNPs of all Central American states plus Jamaica and Bolivia combined.[35]

As for the U.K., a review of studies of the pattern of (income) inequality since the 1970s has led one researcher to conclude that:

> the picture that emerges is one of a U-shape: falling inequality during the first half of the 1970s, followed by an upturn sometime after 1976. At first the increase is slow but seems to increase rapidly in the second half of the 1980s. Between 1979 and 1988/9, 39 percent of the rise in average equivalised disposable household income went to the richest 10 percent of the population . . . If capital gains [and fringe benefits] were included in the income definition, this would be even higher.[36]

While the U.S., the U.K., and Canada all experienced marked increases in wage inequality during the two decades from the mid 1970s to the mid 1990s, these increases were *somewhat* mitigated in the U.K. and Canada due to social transfers to households.[37]

If we take poverty rather than inequality, we also find that the experience of the U.S. and U.K. in recent years is a peculiar one.[38] Thus an OECD study of people's experience of poverty found the U.K. to have the worst record of poverty amongst OECD nations, followed by the United States. Between 1991 and 1996, 38 percent of the U.K. population spent at least one year below the poverty line (26% in the U.S.), with 20 percent of the population in any one year living in poverty (14% in the U.S.). The U.K. also had the poorest record on long-term poverty – more than 6 percent of the population were below the poverty line for all six years of the OECD study (4.6% in the U.S.).[39] Such levels of poverty have been attributed particularly to the legacy of the harsh economic policies of the 1980s.[40] On Britain, Bradshaw has recently calculated that "in the twenty years since 1979 absolute poverty has remained stable and relative poverty has increased nearly threefold."[41]

In their comparative-based effort to provide a summary of reasons for the most marked trends in income inequality being found in the U.S. and the U.K., Gottschalk and others have cited the weakening of social protection mechanisms, regressive tax reforms, the abandonment of Keynesian macroeconomics and any commitment to full employment, the withdrawal of the public sector from economic activity, deregulation of labor markets, and thus increasing and enduring levels of unemployment. Such policies were, they rightly note, championed earliest and more fervently by the governments of Reagan and Thatcher in the U.S. and U.K.[42] In many respects, then, the U.K. and the U.S. are distinctive amongst OECD economies.[43] There are very good empirical reasons for suggesting a direct relationship between trends in inequality and neoliberal economic policies.

This much is also claimed by Brenner in his review of the world economy in the post-war period, though it is an observation made with a further sting in the tail:

> Since the victories of Reaganism-Thatcherism at the end of the 1970s, capitalism has greatly deepened its domination, especially in the U.S. Wage growth has been effectively repressed. Fiscal austerity, combined with tight credit, has brought universal deflation. The rich have benefited from several rounds of tax reduction. Industry after industry has been deregulated to weaken unions which had benefited from their formerly administered prices. The global flow of capital has been progressively unfettered so that multinational corporations and banks can better scour the world to find the most profitable location for their activities. Finance has been unshackled, to create ever more baroque means to squeeze more money from money. The brutal stabilization programs of the World Bank and the IMF have been accepted as gospel. What is more, the statist regimes of the former Soviet Union and Eastern Europe have collapsed, and China has taken the capitalist road. Yet, despite all this, things are not going smoothly for capitalism.[44]

These claims are of particular interest, for while inequalities have widened across and within nations, Brenner indicates here that all is not rosy in the neoliberal garden. When he refers to things "not going smoothly" for capitalism, the key issue here is the rate of profit. While there are long-standing disagreements as to how to measure, let alone explain, the rate of profit, there seems to be agreement that the period since the recession of the early 1970s has been one of declining rates of profits across all advanced capitalist economies.[45] That the rate of profit should continue this long-term downwards spiral is perhaps even more remarkable given the political and economic changes that have worked almost unanimously to the benefit of capital, those changes summarized in the quotation from Brenner, above. Certainly during this period, as we have indicated, the rate of exploitation of labor has increased,[46] as wages have been screwed down, the social wage reduced, and productivity increases cranked out of workers across the world. Moreover, while there is *some* evidence that the 1990s saw small signs of recovery in the rate of profit in the U.S.,[47] even this minor trend reversal is disputed,[48] while there are few claims for generalized increases in profit rates in capitalist economies beyond the U.S. The booming stock markets – not least in the U.S. and the U.K. – of the past decade are hardly in themselves any indication of economic health. Indeed, as Pollin has recently argued as regards the U.S., the growth of Wall Street stocks, and in particular the unprecedented mismatch between the performance of stock prices and the real economy, has created a dangerously fragile financial structure that is unsustainable.[49]

In this context, it is important to note that while in both the U.S. and the U.K. the corporate sectors are not only highly concentrated, they seem firmly set on inexorable paths towards even greater concentration. Within each economy there were a series of merger movements in the last century,[50] none of which, it should be emphasized, could be accounted for adequately in terms of the greater efficiency of those companies who benefitted the most.[51] A perhaps more plausible interpretation of these trends is to be found in the desire to secure ever greater market share and greater absolute corporate incomes whilst cutting costs, as a means of staving off (or perhaps redistributing the effects of) long-term declines in rates of profitability. Following Marx, the level of competition/oligopoly serves as a means of redistributing surplus-value amongst firms – it cannot affect the level of surplus value, and thus the rate of profit, at the level of the economy as a whole.

Certainly in the U.S., the fourth of these merger improvements (between 1980-1988) was generated, on the one hand, by deregulation and the opportunities it offered the large corporations for consolidation of their control over the national economy and the possibility for corporate raiders and others to maximize the current value of assets. It was also stimulated, on the other hand, by a concern with international competition, with indigenous capital concerned with its own competitiveness and overseas capital concerned with securing access to U.S. markets. This last merger movement was the most significant in terms of the sheer number of mergers and the dollar amounts involved. The movement peaked at just under 4,500 mergers per year, with an eight-year total of 26,671 mergers and acquisitions involving assets worth $1,083.4 billion. It is worth noting here that corporate take-overs and reorganizations are expensive and involve an extremely high opportunity cost in terms of a poor use of money that could have been used for investment in new plant and technology.[52] The U.K., too, witnessed an unprecedented wave of mergers in the latter half of the 1980s. As Hughes writes, this movement "generated a level of take-over activity which in terms of both values and numbers of companies acquired outstripped the previous U.K. post-war peak of 1969-1973."[53] Thus while the average annual number of acquisitions and mergers during the earlier period was slightly more than 1,000, there were almost 2,000 in both 1988 and 1989.[54] The 1990s saw further mergers and the emergence of oligopoly on a global scale. In the U.S., it is a moot point whether one refers to the continuation of the merger wave of the 1980s, or identifies a new wave of mergers in the late 1990s. Certainly, however, recent years have witnessed spiraling merger activity. 1996 saw a record level of merger and take-over activity, a level then surpassed by almost 50 percent in 1997 ($1 trillion worth of activity), and a further increase of some 30 percent in 1998.[55] Many sectors and markets are highly concentrated. For example, oil, an industry of immense economic and geo-political significance,[56] and historically dominated by the so-called "Seven Sisters," has become even more concentrated following a flurry of merger activity. Snider notes how "monopolistic markets are now the norm in automotive, airline, computing, aerospace, electronics and steel."[57] In five industries crucial to the agricultural economies of developing countries – coffee, corn, wheat, pineapple, and tea – just five multinationals control 90 percent of world exports.[58] Such data rather cast into question the version of capitalism depicted by neoliberalism, which posits competition within markets that have relatively low barriers to entry, a classic if consistently unrealized aspect of capitalist ideology.[59] Indeed, while the annual value of mergers increased by 550 percent between 1992 and 1999, during the same period, "the total budgets of the two primary antitrust enforcement agencies – the Federal Trade Commission and the Justice Department's Antitrust Division – decreased by 7 percent in constant dollars while the GNP grew by 112 percent."[60] Between 1976-1997, only 150 of 3,700 planned mergers in the U.S. were investigated; in only 14 cases were court actions filed against them.[61]

The "contradiction between reverence for competition as a sacred principle and the actual practice of decreasing competition under the millennial rhetoric of globalization"[62] is stark indeed, though this is not confined to the U.S. Both Europe and Japan also found themselves in the midst of a further wave of merger mania at the end of the century.[63] Indeed, Europe has become the main arena for merger activity.[64] More generally, mergers in western economies totaled $468 billion in the first quarter of 1999, against a record value of activity of $859 billion in the whole of 1998. As mergers and acquisitions have reached record levels within the U.S., Europe, and Japan, so too did cross-national deals: in 1997, according to UNCTAD, "cross-border mergers and acquisitions amounted to $342 billion,"[66] a nine-fold increase in the buying up of firms based in developing countries by Western multinationals since 1991.[67] The key rationale provided for this latest wave of mergers has been neither diversification nor simply attempts at rationalization (cost-cutting), rationales provided in previous merger booms – this time, the mantra has been the need to organize globally to compete globally.[68] The same rationale has allowed states to portray their more recent excesses in corporate welfare as part of the need to develop "national champions" to compete in the so-called global marketplace. Yet this practice of state welfare to corporations has long been central to the development of corporate capital, and operates on an international not simply domestic scale. Ruigrock and van Tulder[69] have noted how most of the world's largest corporations have relied extensively on various forms of support from governments in order to achieve their strategic aims and/or secure market positions.[70] And referring to U.S. Government support for U.S. industry, Chomsky notes how one review of Reagan's Presidency stated that "the post-war chief executive with the most passionate love of laissez-faire presided over the greatest swing towards protectionism since the 1930s."[71] A similar argument is made regarding the level of state subsidy of corporations under Thatcher in the U.K.[72] Beyond national governments, the IMF has been identified as a key source of corporate welfare.[73]

One net effect of these general restructurings has been to augment the dominance of existing, and the creation of some new, extraordinarily large economic actors. An examination of the most recent available data on the Gross Domestic Product of all 29 OECD member states[74] alongside that for the annual revenues of the world's largest corporations provides some instructive relative insights here. On the basis of such data, *of the 50 largest economies, 23 are states, 27 are corporations*; General Motors, the world's largest corporation according to Fortune's 1999 list, has a revenue in excess of the GDP of 11 OECD states (the Czech Republic, Finland, Greece, Hungary, Iceland, Ireland, Luxembourg, New Zealand, Norway, Poland, and Portugal). In a rare moment of perspicacity, John Edmonds, General Secretary of the British GMB Union, has recently noted that "General Motors packs more punch than some European Member States."[75]

In sum, several features characterize the international economy in the past quarter of a century. First, the existence of marked and, for the most part, increasing inequalities between and within nations; amongst these general experiences, there are marked differences, so that certainly within nations inequalities appear to have become much more marked precisely where commitments to neo-liberalism have been most vehement. Second, this period has witnessed a decline of the general rate of profitability alongside corporate restructuring towards ever-increasing concentration. Third, we notice that within the global economy as a whole and within the advanced national economies in particular, very large corporations are now the major economic actors.[76] *If* social power is measured simply in terms of economic muscle, such data would raise questions about the ability of nation-states to regulate effectively the activities of transnational corporations in particular, and business in general. However, important as it is to recognize changes in the scale of and relationships within – corporate capital, we cannot simply read off from such insights conclusions regarding their increasing power vis-à-vis other actors, not least states. This is one of the questions at issue in debates around the phenomenon of economic globalization, and it is to a consideration of some of the more relevant dimensions of this contested "process" that the remainder of this chapter turns.

Globalization: States, Corporations, and Regulation

There is now an enormous social scientific literature that constitutes a series of debates as to the nature, dimensions, and consequences of the phenomenon of globalization.[77] Thus Hay has recently referred to "the voluminous literature on globalization which, though equally portentous in its conclusions, is decidedly less clear about the mechanisms, processes, and actors involved."[78] If part of the appeal of the term globalization is its very looseness, so that it can mean so many different things for different people,[79] it is also the case that its most common usages "emanate squarely from the universe of neo-liberal ideology and social practice."[80] Thus, in summarizing the state of the literature thus far, it is these common usages that constitute what Hay identifies as "a certain orthodoxy," which:

> posits an increasingly "borderless world" in which labour and ("footloose" multinational) capital flow freely – down gradients of unemployment and social protection, and taxation and labor cost, respectively. The result is a much more fully integrated global economy in which the Darwinian excesses of international competition drive out "punitive" taxation regimes, "over-regulated" labor markets, social protection, all but residual welfare regimes and Keynesian economics. This in turn serves to establish a pervasive logic of international economic and political convergence – a convergence on neo-liberal terms . . .[81]

Tellingly, Hay refers to this version of globalization arguments as the "business school globalization thesis."[82] It is clear that many of these arguments and their implications can be and have been subjected to various forms of empirical and theoretical critique – in which Hay himself engages, and as we have attempted elsewhere.[83] However, it is neither possible nor desirable for us to rehearse such debates here. Rather, we wish to make several observations on globalization-claims and their implications in terms of states, law and, more specifically, the possibilities of effective regulation of corporate crime.

On States and Markets

One of the problems of arguments around globalization, it seems to us, is that there is tendency to move immediately to empirical evidence in order to develop a case "for" or "against" greater economic globalization, and on the basis of detailed considerations of data thereby to draw conclusions regarding states, markets, and corporations. But prior to any consideration of particular points of detail within globalization arguments, it is important to enter into some theoretical consideration of the nature of states, markets, and corporate activity. We seek to utilize some of the insights of a Marxist analysis here, a mode of analysis which itself seems to have been organized off academic agendas in the past two decades.

The first point to make is that, both historically and indeed contemporaneously, it is clear that capitalist forms of production may be organized in a series of quite different ways within a variety of political and social "shells," producing quite different effects.[84] That is, capitalism as a system is neither unified nor homogenous – which is not to deny certain essential features which define it. Within the construction of different forms of capitalism, the state plays a key role.[85] For instance, state activities are preconditions for the risk-taking activities of entrepreneurs.[86] States help to constitute capital, commodity, commercial and residential property markets, produce different kinds of "human capital" and constitute labor markets, and regulate the employment contract. Further, the state plays a role in constituting economic enterprises through specifying rules of liability and possibly specifying rules of incorporation. These are put in place by regulatory instances that include, but are not exhausted by, regulatory agencies.

These schematic observations partly explain why regulation is a necessary function of a state even in the quintessential market economy, even while advocates of marketization consistently deny such a role for the state and regulation. Despite its common rhetorical framing, then, regulation is always productive and indeed implicitly moral,[87] even in the case of regulatory instances that rely strongly upon the power of markets and the coercive effect of civil courts through actions initiated by private legal subjects, and where regulatory agencies are reduced to an advisory role. Thus, the recent deregulation associated with the "discourses of enterprise" has not meant that problematic areas of economic and social life were "rectified" merely by removing extant forms of intervention, but that these have given rise "to all manners of programs for reforming economic activity in order to construct such a virtuous system, and to a plethora of new regulatory technologies that have sought to give effect to them."[88] In other words, as well as deregulation there has been re-regulation. Indeed, the property rights to be found within all such market systems depend upon custom and tradition, the action of state bureaucracies, and of the legal system.[89] The latter is not merely enabling but is also constitutive and depends on the "myths" of sovereignty and consistency,[90] and the reality of coercion.[91] Furthermore, some form of displacement of free markets as both an organizing and regulative principle, is, in fact, the historical norm. The 'free market' is modified through oligopolisation, (whether viewed negatively, [92] or as a condition of viability[93]), by state regulation,[94] nationalization[95] or through networks.[96] As Sayer has recently demonstrated, not only has there never existed, but there cannot exist, any economy which is adequately characterized by the term "free market." While "the ideological notion of latent or implicit markets which only need freeing figures strongly in neo-liberal rhetoric,"[97] this contrasts with the overwhelming empirical and theoretical evidence attesting to markets as social constructions. The creation, maintenance, and development of "markets" requires co-ordinated, extensive and ongoing involvement of the state and other institutions.[98]

The state, as we have argued elsewhere,[99] can in some ways be conceived of as a set of apparatuses through which a power bloc is in part constituted and through which it *seeks* to secure, maintain, and extend its dominance over an economy, polity, and society. It will try to do this in a way that most other groups tend to accept its leadership, i.e., the power bloc will try to become hegemonic. Yet the struggle for dominance is never finally achieved; conflict and struggle are constant, if at times more or less present threats.

Indeed, viewing capitalist societies as fundamentally and essentially class societies allows us – or forces us – to conceive not simply of corporate crime, but also its regulation, more adequately. Instructive here is the work of Rianne Mahon, who has sought to understand the activity of the state and of regulatory agencies within the context of a theory of the state which draws upon the work of Gramsci[100] and Poulantzas.[101] While there are important differences between the versions of Marxism developed and represented by these two theorists, for each the state itself is understood not simply as a thing, to be captured or used as an instrument, not an entity external to classes and class power, but as a relation. Indeed, it is through the state that the interests of various fractions and classes are combined and recombined: in the development of the unity of a historic bloc, in the constant struggle to secure hegemony, the formation of authority is a continuous process of incorporating the interests of various forces through the state. Thus the articulation of class struggle in the state produces the authority of the hegemonic class/fraction. Poulantzas argues that:

> The notion of the general interest of the people, an ideological notion, covering an institutional operation of the capitalist state, expresses a real fact: namely that this state, by its very structure, gives to the economic interests of certain dominated classes guarantees which may even be contrary to the short term interests of the dominant class but which are compatible with their political interest . . . their real hegemonic domination.[102]

The relative autonomy of the state allows this securing of hegemony; it also permits the state to function as "political organizer of the various dominant fractions and to arrange the 'corporate' compromises that provide the conditions for the expanded reproduction of capital and of the bourgeoisie as the dominant class."[103] Thus the state "expresses and organizes the political relations of class domination. It is not captured by the dominant class."[104] Rather, inscribed in the state is " 'an unequal structure of representation' historically produced by the class struggle . . . through which the 'unstable equilibrium of compromises' is arranged."[105]

One consequence of this theorization of state-capital is the understanding that any real economy, polity, and society has dynamics which are and must be independent of, or not subject to the rational ordering of, the dominant power bloc. In these respects, the broad brushes of the "end of history" theorists proclaiming the triumph of an increasingly global, homogenous version of capitalism – are necessarily always lacking. No social group, no class, has ever made society in its image, nor controlled it. Thus although members of the most powerful blocs of social actors can realize their will better than most of us can, and often at our expense, the best that even a "dominant bloc" can do is to modify a pre-existing social order in such a way that it can maintain or increase its comparative advantage over other groups. If currently predominant forms of economic, social, and political organizing – neo-liberalism, monetarism, privatization, and the development of the workfare state – have increased "the structural power of capital,"[106] these forms of organizing can never give dominant blocks complete control of our societies.

'Globalization' as Hegemonic Project

It is in the context of these more theoretical considerations that we can now return to arguments regarding a recent series of significant changes in the nature of capitalist societies, changes that are said by many to mark a new phase of capitalist development (even, for some, a stage of post-capitalism), changes that render the efforts of states, regulatory agencies and oppositional social forces increasingly redundant. This "new orthodoxy," or "common sense,"[107] now widespread in political, cultural, popular, and academic contexts,[108] proclaims, in its strongest variants, the emergence of a new, globalized economic order. And this is an economic order that bears a striking affinity with many of the prescriptions of neoliberalism regarding the primacy of markets, capitalist production, and the minimized role of nation-states. However, it should also be emphasized that, whether or not, and in what forms, globalization actually "exists," it is clear that the discourses of globalization now exert enormous power over governments of advanced capitalist economies, not least the current British and U.S. governments. Despite intense academic debate about the actual nature and reality of globalization tendencies themselves, there is no doubt that the *discourses* of globalization have assumed the status of a hegemonic truth, a new orthodoxy.[109] It is the "perceived diktats"[110] of this orthodoxy which governments invoke as they seek to attract or retain private capital through various forms of de- and re-regulation, impose massive cutbacks in the social wage, and more generally reproduce the "political construction of helplessness;"[111] and it is this orthodoxy to which transnational capital points as it seeks to increase its leverage over national-states, and both intra- and international sources of resistance.[112]

Thus, for our considerations, the key implication of the hegemony of discourses of globalization is that Governments can exert less political control over economies – economic management is relegated to the task of over-seeing the operation of "free" markets – and over the key actors in these economies, namely corporations and, most significantly, multi- or transnational corporations. Having accepted – more or less willingly – the diktats laid down through the discourses of globalization, governments *discipline themselves* to the extent that they either eschew, or at best exercise supreme caution in imposing, additional "burdens" – that is, regulation, or more specifically the costs arising from so-called "social" regulation and the effects of corporate competitiveness – upon business. Such discourses have found a perfect complement in the deregulatory initiatives of recent British and U.S. governments: this was clearly the case with successive Conservative Governments who, as key architects in an international neoliberal project,[113] played a crucial role in promoting the discourses of globalization, both materially and ideologically; but it must be recognized that the current Democratic (in the U.S.) and Labor (in Britain) administrations remain committed to this legacy. Blair, for example, has consistently portrayed his Government as subject to the whims of an international market within which Britain can be a key player only by ensuring the continued development of deregulated labor and capital markets.[114]

What we want to suggest here, is that the emergence of arguments and claims around globalization themselves represent part of a project of hegemonic reconstruction. One immediate observation is that if the idea of globalization has become a very powerful one, then this has emerged, not in any "free-floating" sense, but as it is propagated in forms that are linked to certain agents, institutions and practices. If we view globalization as "hyper-liberalism,"[115] it is possible to link this idea to the claim by some that there has occurred a conscious process of hegemony (re)construction, key agents of which have been large multinational companies, right-wing governments and politicians, particularly from the U.S. and Britain, and right-wing academics.[116] By the early 1980s, there had emerged a consensus:

> about the needs of the world economy and appropriate economic policies for developing countries. Reflecting the demise of Keynesianism and the ascendancy of supply-side economics in the U.S. and some parts of Europe, the consensus was based on the

twin ideas of the state as the provider of a regulatory framework for private sector exchanges (but not as a *director* of those exchanges), and of the world economy as open to movements of goods, services, and capital, if not labor.[117]

Thus globalization tendencies are symbiotically linked to deflationary macro-economic policies.[118] Of course, such policies, in the name of "adjustment," have been rigorously pursued within many national states under pressure from the IMF, the World Bank, the G-7, the OECD, the Bank for International Resettlement, the European Bank for Reconstruction and Development, UNCTAD, and, more recently if at least post-Seattle somewhat infamously,[119] by the World Trade Organization.[120] Moreover, the role of such institutions embraces normative as well as material elements.[121] Thus, more generally, Gill and Law argue that "during the 1970s and the 1980s, the emphasis, certainly with regard to economic policy, has shifted towards *a definition of questions and concepts* which is more congruent with the interests of large-scale, transnational capital."[122]

Consistent with our reading of the Gramscian notion of hegemony,[123] we would argue that the construction of this new hegemony relies not just on material power (the ability of capital and national states to distribute benefits and disadvantages), but also on a moral and intellectual leadership, so that the ideas associated with globalization become predominant to the extent that they seep into popular consciousness, ruling out alternatives, and integrating into the ranks of the (relatively) advantaged some "subordinate" groups whilst (often safely) consigning to economic and social marginalization and exclusion whole segments of populations.[124] In particular, this hegemony seeks to organize off political agendas notions of state regulation of, or intervention in, corporate activity; indeed, such notions are de-legitimized notwithstanding the fact that states maintain intense levels of activity in these respects, a point upon which we shall expand below. We should be clear that academic discourse plays a not insignificant role here, and more generally in constructions of the "feasible" or "acceptable."[125]

Thus the utilization and development of the idea of globalization has involved the creation of a new set of economic and political "realities;" realities which constrain the possible, the desirable, the feasible within and beyond national states. This has profound implications for those who would seek to improve protective regulation, and places constraints upon the operation of capital. In this sense of the creation of new discursive terrains, terrains which set these limits, then it makes sense to speak of an increase in the structural power of capital.

As Hay and Watson have noted, here with particular reference to Britain and the Blair Government:

New Labour clearly acts *as if* the globalization hypothesis were an accurate description of reality. This, in turn, has very real effects The intrinsic link between the material and the ideational is, in this instance perhaps particularly significant. It is not globalization *per se* which is driving change in contemporary Britain. Given that production relations have yet to be globalized . . . how could it be? Rather change is a function of the distinctive and dominant *political understanding* of globalization now internalized by New Labour. The meaning and significance attached to 'globalizing trends' tendencies and processes may be as significant in accounting for outcomes as those trends, tendencies and processes reflection (as, and when, they exist).[126]

Thus, to the extent that globalizing trends – and representations of these – become more significant, then this *does* have consequences for the nation-state, consequences which are generally constraining of any national-state autonomy. There is no doubt that even without accepting some of the more exaggerated claims around globalization, enormous class and social power accrues to transnational corporations in particular, and to capital in general, and to the extent that arguments for globalization reflect real trends, then this class and social power is likely to be augmented. Any augmented power of particular corporations – and corporate capital in general – makes democratic demands less articulable, less realizable and hence, if they are designed to constrain capital, much less effective. Employers in both public and private sectors are convinced that it is too expensive to regulate or pay "decent" wages or benefits, and that the requirement of competing in a global marketplace *demands* "roll backs" and benefit reductions. They also appear to be convinced that governmental regulatory structures are inefficient, produce essentially counter-productive effects, and indeed to some extent that the very idea of regulation is always-already illegitimate, morally problematic, or at best an option of last resort. Bargaining takes place in a world where reducing the deficit has become the number one economic priority (even if the deficit is due to borrowing for productive investment), an article of faith now with governments of every political stripe.[127] These ideological changes mean progressive ("pro-regulatory") forces have lost legitimacy and the indirect leverage this provides, and have lost bargaining power. This diminished power should also be understood in the context of structural changes in the nature of capital, allied reductions in the percentage of work forces in unions, and, of course, a series of very direct (and often savage) material assaults upon organized labor across advanced capitalist economies.

Yet we need to be clear that these trends, and their promotion through the arguments and agendas of advocates of neo-liberalism, are by no means unidirectional, and certainly not inevitable; they are "at best" a set of emerging institutional arrangements, more a hegemonic project than a hegemonic reality. In particular, we need to be clear about the disjuncture between the idea of globalization and the actual nature of economic and extent of globalization. In other words, there are marked disjuncture between representation and reality, a disjuncture which often masks the fact that emerging institutional arrangements reflect some degree of political choice, although of course such choices have always been subject to a variety of internal and external constraints. If the arguments of this section are accepted, then two points follow: First, that states make choices, so that economic, political, and social arrangements could be other than they currently are, that is, there *are* alternatives; second, that there are always pressures and forms of resistance from counter-hegemonic forces. It is to a consideration of these questions that the following sections turn.

States 'Versus' Footloose Capital: An Unequal or Illusory Contest?

A key issue therefore becomes the extent to which capital in general, or particular capitalist corporations, notably Transnational Corporations (TNCs), can now act "autonomously"of, and in successful "opposition" to the needs, desires and interests expressed through particular nation-states. Our basic argument in this and the subsequent section is that the national-state remains crucial within any development of a globalizing economic order.[128]

Capital is hardly operating in an autonomous, "footloose" fashion – if globalization is a nascent trend, then it is a trend that is dependent upon legal, regulatory, and institutional arrangements in which state forms play a key facilitating and organizing function. Thus as Hirst and Thompson have recently argued,[129] we should not become too carried away with the concept of a global economy because activities by nation states, regional organizations like the European community, and international bodies (not to mention military alliances) all play key and often opposing roles in the organization of economic activity. That is, to the extent that activities by national and international bodies other than nation states are becoming more significant,[130] this does not necessarily entail any reduction in the power or autonomy of any particular national state.[131] Beyond this empirical observation, it is clearly over-simplistic and erroneous to conceptualize national-international and/or state-capital relationships in a "zero-sum" fashion, conceptualizations that themselves are only possible on the erroneous views of national-international as independent spheres of corporate activity and of state and capital as separate, independent entities.[132]

Of particular relevance for us, and for more general considerations of the nature and possibility of more effective forms of regulating capital, are those claims that relate to the mobility of capital, particularly transnational capital. In their constructed ideal typical globalized economy, Hirst and Thompson provide a vivid statement of the supposed new realities engendered by the emergence of TNCs as "the major players in the world economy."[133] Thus, "The TNC would be genuine footloose capital, the main manifestation of a truly globalized economy."[134]

We should be clear on this point that the nation-state under capitalism has *always* been more or less constrained[135] – and there is particular irony when this fact is "forgotten" by commentators of the left. Thus it is certainly the case that national-states are, as they always have been, engaged in a constant, "competitive process of attraction-and-immobilization"[136] of capital, one element of which is to provide the most "favorable conditions for the reproduction of capital within [their] boundaries."[137] In the 1980s, many would agree that this process had taken the form of competitive deregulation or, perhaps more accurately, competitive re-regulation, with many national states attempting to "redefine market rules under new conditions."[138]

Within the political, and certainly neoliberal, rhetoric of globalization, the idea of globalization is often presented as an argument against the development of protective regulation, or in favor of complete "liberalization." The assumption upon which such arguments are based is that the development and enforcement of "social" regulation will prompt capital to seek out less regulated contexts in which to locate. Now by definition, if more corporations are organized cross-nationally, and if greater numbers of domestic economies are now open to capitalist investment, then there is a sense in which the issue of (re)location augments the power of capital vis-à-vis any particular nation-state; that is, any threats of relocation carry in generalized terms at least greater force. On the other hand, we should not ascribe to capital an excessive capability, nor exaggerate the extent to which investment and productive activity necessarily seeks out less over more regulated contexts: though it will do so where all other things are equal, corporate considerations of geography, sunk costs, "human capital," general infrastructure and so on, mean that it is rarely the case that all other conditions are in fact equal.[139] This is not to deny, of course, that various companies and capitals have used – successfully – the "reality" of globalization to threaten particular location/ relocation decisions, thereby influencing the conditions in which they operate. But, as we have indicated above, in a blurring of representation and reality, national states have used such threats in order to legitimate certain policies or practices.[140]

One very straightforward illustration of the "new" problems engendered for states through some of the changes associated with globalization will suffice here. Central to any state's ability to manage its economy is the raising of revenues through taxation, and corporate taxation should form an element of any fiscal strategy. But of course the international organization of corporations allows them to transfer funds internally so that levels of taxation payable to any particular nation-state become drastically reduced. Thus, citing figures from a report by the U.S. General Accounting Office, Mokhiber and Weissman note that in each of the years 1989-1995, almost a third of the largest corporations operating in the U.S. "paid no U.S. income tax. More than six out of 10 large companies [assets of $250 million or more, or sales of at least $50 million] paid less than a million dollars in federal income tax in 1995."[141] Such levels of payment are made possible through the strategies of transfer pricing available to companies operating multinationally, and would require new national legislation or international agreements to prevent them.[142] States have proven reluctant to introduce more effective national legislation, while such forms of international regulation are notoriously difficult to develop.[143] At the same time as their ability to evade taxes is increased, transnationals exert pressures on governments to reduce the tax "burden." It is surely no coincidence that the years since 1980 have seen across almost all OECD states reductions in levels of corporate taxation.[144] The classic recent instance of this pressure and its possible (but not necessary) outcome were the consistent commitments of Conservative and then Labor Governments to introducing and then maintaining reductions in levels of taxation of oil companies, more latterly in the context of explicit (if highly unrealistic) threats of relocation on the part of the latter,[145] leading Lloyds List to describe the U.K. as "the most oil investor friendly nation in the world."[146]

Yet such instances should not be taken as implying either a zero-sum contest between state and capital, nor that the transnational manifestations of the latter are inevitably in a position of such power so as to render the former impotent or irrelevant. It is worth noting here the extent to which even in the U.S. and U.K., where the past two decades have seen considerable areas of deregulation, there has also occurred complex forms of re-regulation. Some of this can clearly be seen to be contrary to the immediate economic interests of corporations of capitals in particular,[147] while other areas of state regulatory activity simply serve to illustrate the nonsense of the term "free markets" or of the claim that corporations can act autonomously of states. Also instructive here is Vogel's recent study of the extent to which, and the ways in which, *freer* markets tend to be constructed through "*more* rules."[148] Rejecting claims associated with economic globalization – namely that states are increasingly powerless vis-à-vis capital and the view that MNCs can increasingly play the game of "regulatory arbitrage' – Vogel documents a series of case studies which elaborate upon four ideal-typical forms of re-regulation: pro-competitive, juridical, strategic, and expansionary re-regulation. While the first two of these ideal types "undermine governmental control over industry," the latter two actually "enhance government control."[149] Focusing particularly upon the U.K. and Japan, but also examining France, Germany and the U.S., Vogel demonstrates the enormous amount of work that states must put in order to (re)construct markets,[150] and also attempts to document empirically and then theorize the bases of the "remarkably different ways"[151] in which states have reacted or indeed driven or exacerbated a seemingly universal logic of economic globalization.

Somewhat differently, whilst in the 1980s financial markets in London and New York were significantly internationalized and deregulated, scandals such as the Polly Peck in the U.K.[152] and the Savings and Loans crisis in the U.S.[153] have prompted the development of new national modes of regulation. The role of criminality on the part of bank owners and directors, and more generally within the business sector, in the bank crises at the heart of the

Finnish recession of the early 1990s – the largest in OECD history since the 1930s – is a key factor in explaining the emergence of what appear to be an unprecedented series of initiatives against economic crime launched by the Finnish Government in 1996. And this in a small, open economy which seems to most closely approximate the type of state vulnerable to the demands of national and international capital.[154] The changing fortunes of environmental regulation and deregulation,[155] the cleanup of toxic waste in the U.S., and the regulation of occupational safety and health all provide examples of situations too complex to sum up in a simplistic anti- or pro-regulatory formula, or a regulation/deregulation dichotomy.[156]

Finally, a focus on finance capital is instructive on the ability of capital to really act without a regulatory framework, in a footloose manner, in classic globalization-thesis form. Amongst "evidence" or signs of globalization, the case of financial capital is often taken as the paradigmatic instance of any economic globalization.[157] But if the sphere of finance appears to be the area which best fits the most excessive of all claims of globalization analysts, then this is not because finance is more developed along some inevitable route, but because it is quite a special case altogether. Thus, "finance is a different kind of beast," argues Weiss. "Trade, investment and multinational production are not on a par with financial flows. Although they are frequently discussed together as roughly equivalent indicators of an aggregate globalizing tendency, they differ substantially."[158] In particular, finance is "special" due to its exceptional mobility, and to the related fact that financial flows operate in a fleeting fashion across national borders, thereby contributing little or nothing to the economic interconnectedness of "real" economies.[159] The vast majority of the flow of finance is for speculative rather than productive reasons: by 1995, about 95 percent of international financial transactions were speculative, with about 80 percent of these transfers making "round trips of one week or less."[160] As Hay and Watson note, capital flight is much more likely where investment is of a speculative rather than a productive nature.[161]

In other words, the claim that the expansion of international financial activity is "at the forefront of the economic globalization trend in recent years"[162] does not necessarily mean that other areas of economic activity are likely to "catch up" with or emulate the nature of contemporary finance activity. Indeed, if finance is an exceptional case, it is perhaps the one area in which there has occurred a genuine undermining of whatever abilities nation-states have ever possessed to make autonomous economic and political choices; such flows can be, and certainly have been, constraining upon state "autonomy" and also in certain instances highly destructive, even if the "autonomy" and vulnerability of different nation-states clearly varies.

But there is an even greater irony in investing too much significance to finance as the harbinger or model of a generalized, global free-market economy. If the phenomenon of the increasing globalization of financial flows seems to provide the greatest support for such claims, it is at the same time the very phenomenon which has most called into question the desirability or even possibility of untrammeled global economic activity to the extent that there has emerged debate about the need for the introduction of new forms of national and international regulation of financial capital.[163] The Asian crisis, followed swiftly by the massive U.S. bailout but subsequent collapse of Long Term Capital Managements, no doubt go a long way to explaining such calls. Calls for international capital controls have in recent years reached such a crescendo that they have been enjoined by one of the world's archetypal individual capitalists and financial speculators, George Soros;[164] by the end of the 1990s, there had emerged a generalized political and academic discourse regarding the means of regulating international finance in general,[165] and of restricting short-term speculation in particular (notably via the so-called Tobin tax).[166]

Bringing Politics – and Resistance – Back In

If the period since the mid-1970s, then, has undoubtedly been one of significant economic changes across the globe, it is clear from our particular attention to the role of, and consequences in, the U.K. and the U.S. that *politics matters* a great deal in the creation, encouragement, or facilitating of these trends and the mediation of these effects of "economic" change.[167] And by "politics," we should be clear that we do not mean merely, or even, the nature of Governments, but more importantly the balance of class forces, the nature and history of institutions, the character of particular national-state formations and so on.[168]

The fact that states are not victims of, nor passive agents within, generalized economic processes,[169] is further indicated when we recall our argument above regarding the peculiarity of trends in inequality and poverty in the U.S. and U.K., and the wider contextual point that OECD countries have experienced quite different trends in both inequality and poverty during this period.[170] Indeed, in one OECD state, Finland, a relatively recent but paradigmatic example of a corporatist welfare state,[171] the 1980s were a decade of *equalizing* incomes[172] and *decreases* in poverty.[173] Thus, in a recent study of the changes in the welfare states – and both the sources and effects of these changes – in all OECD countries, Navarro documents a heterogeneous range of experiences. But, perhaps unsurprisingly, such experiences tended not to differ randomly across these states, but rather could be grouped in terms of a rough typology amongst these states which are cast as Social Democratic, Christian Democratic, and Anglo-Saxon political economies (along with a fourth category, Conservative Fascist Dictatorships). Similar differential but clustered – experiences are also developed in Esping-Anderson's recent work on the paths taken by differing welfare regimes in the so-called "post-industrial" age.[174]

Thus Navarro is led to conclude that:

> *The changes in the welfare state respond primarily to political rather than economic forces* The current emphasis on globalization as the cause of these changes has an apologetic function, defending the inevitability of such changes. Yet globalization is not a cause but a symptom of the state of class relations in the developed capitalist countries . . . the social democratic countries have actually been among the most integrated internationally, without "globalization" being a handicap for the extensive development of their welfare states. Actually the extensive welfare state development was a *condition* for their competitiveness and integration into world markets.[175]

As we have noted, the political forces in the ascendancy in both the U.S. and the U.K. for the past quarter of a century have been neoliberal. This was of course the case under Reagan then Bush, and Thatcher then Major, but we should be clear that Clinton and Blair have each headed governments explicitly committed to maintaining the fundamentals of the neoliberal consensus.[176] As Sim has noted, "New Labor, in government, has sought and acquired an accommodation and settlement within the existing balance of forces that dominate the global capitalist marketplace. Like their Conservative predecessors, New Labor looks to the USA for guidance."[177] Continuing, he notes:

> the government wholeheartedly accepts the so-called Washington consensus – that deregulation, privatization, hire-and-fire labor markets, balanced budgets and low taxes are not the only key to policy success but unstoppable . . . the Government remains starstruck by business.[178]

In respect of Britain, at least, it could be argued that New Labor has been *more* supine in the face of "business" than the Conservatives. The modernization process to which Blair and colleagues subjected the Labor party in recent years in their desperate quest for electoral success, and then a second Governmental term, has had as a central element the constant need to prove itself to be a business friendly party,[179] something which the Conservatives, as the "natural" party of business, have not had to do so explicitly.[180]

Both Clinton, then Blair, have been strongly influenced by the arguments of former U.S. Secretary of Labor Reich.[181] Whilst speaking from a claimed left-of-center position, Reich accepted most of the "truths" of cruder versions of globalization. The following is, for us, a faithful and useful summary of the assumptions inherent in Reich's now celebrated text, *The Work of Nations*:

> the disintegration of national economies must be accepted by governments as a fact of life, even though it may condemn the majority of citizens to chronic economic insecurity and gradual immiserization; that globalization provides a secure foundation for the success and prosperity currently enjoyed by a minority of cit-

izens due to their skills or, more often, their ownership or control of capital and knowledge; and that attempts to resist or reverse globalization are politically futile and economically undesirable.[182]

The mantle of key peddler of the truths of globalization has been assumed in Britain by Giddens,[183] who himself acknowledges his debt to Reich. Given Giddens' role as his advisor, it is little wonder, then, that Blair has pledged to "accept globalization and work with it."[184] Indeed, far from simply accepting and working with globalization, the so-called Third Way is *predicated* upon the existence of a "global economy, where financial irresponsibility by governments leads to immediate financial punishment by markets."[185] Thus Anderson has written that the Third Way has become "the best ideological shell of neo-liberalism today,"[186] combining (indeed, at times *exceeding)*[187] the harshness of the Right's economic and social policy with a more humanized rhetoric and – at the margins practice.[188] The most insidious consequence of the adoption of neo-liberalism in its Third Way guise is that the view that "there is no alternative" "acquires full force once an alternative regime demonstrates that there are truly no alternative policies."[189]

This acceptance of globalization rhetoric on *both* sides of the Atlantic has real material consequences, as we indicated above in terms of recent trends in inequality and poverty. And the point is that there is no inevitability in accepting the "logic" of globalization, even (or perhaps particularly) in an advanced capitalist state. Thus, in contrast to Blair, Clinton, Cardoso, and others who have embraced the Third Way response,[190] the French Prime Minister and leader of the French Socialist party, Lionel Jospin, has at one and the same time accepting the 'reality' of globalization while deriving no necessary political logic from this:

> We fully recognize globalization. But we do not see its form as inevitable. We seek to create a regulatory system for the world capitalist economy. We believe that through common European action – in a Europe fired by social democratic ideals – we can succeed in the regulation of key areas This need to take control in adapting to reality paces a special responsibility on the state. The state is in a position to provide the necessary direction, without taking the place of other actors in society. Often it is the only agent that can clear away or navigate around the archaic forces standing in the way of changes that society wants.[191]

One does not wish to exaggerate the differences between the different politics of pro-capitalist governments, but differences there certainly are, and these have real consequences for real peoples. Moreover, to emphasize, this is not simply a matter of "choice." The relative freedom of British and American Governments to pursue harsh neoliberal agendas was the result of a sustained attack on the organized labor movement and other forces of resistance. But the balance of class forces that has characterized recent experience in Britain and the U.S. is not reproduced across the globe – it is perhaps no coincidence in the light of Jospin's comments above that one of the most notable periods of activity on the part of organized labor in Western Europe in recent years was witnessed in France in the Winter of 1995.[192]

In other words, we must consider the differing and various forms of resistance to which the (supposed) effects of globalization have met with both in particular nation-states, and internationally. Indeed, such myopia to the ability to resist seemingly ineluctable economic processes provides a further clue as to the ideological nature of globalization discourses. Thus as Lazarus writes, and following our argument in earlier sections of this chapter, "globalization directly serves the interests of some people and . . . there is an intimate structural connection between the obscenely burgeoning prosperity of this minority and the steady immizeration of the vast majority of the world's population."[193] Citing Gills, he continues,

> No argument that depoliticizes the processes of globalization should be politically or intellectually acceptable. On the contrary, global-ization should actually serve to focus our attention precisely on the type of political responses it sets in motion, rather than feed the idea that politics is becoming the predictable epiphenomena of tech-nological processes. In reality, the politics of globalization is all around us, and like all politics, it is a fairly fluid and open situation, the outcomes of which will be determined by "struggle" or contest, and by the balance of forces on each question Above all, no account of globalisation should "write out" the response to these processes by popular forces and social movements, including traditional labor movements and oppositional political parties.[194]

For us, bringing back politics into critical discussions of globalization also entails recognizing the realities – and possibilities – of resistance. It is of course possible to set out a whole series of events and processes – both in different nation-states and indeed (and significantly) internationally – in which forces of resistance have either halted (such as at Seattle or over the issue of Multilateral Agreements on Investment) or indeed reversed (such as over GM foods) the progress of seemingly ineluctable trends towards the globalization of neo-liberal fantasies. Moreover, other processes such as the emergence of international activism around capitalism *per se*, or further signs of the inter-nationalization of trades unionism, provide cause for optimism. Interesting-ly, however, what has been relatively lacking on the Intellectual Left in recent years are any real efforts at theorizing adequately the nature (and lim-its) of such resistance in an internationalizing capitalist social order.

However, there has in recent years appeared some important academic work which rather undermines the easy (if no less forgivable) embracing of globalization rhetoric and which allows some reinsertion of the political into considerations of states and state activities. Certainly, if there have been sig-nificant political differences in the relationships between particular nation-states and globalizing economic forces, then we should not be too sur-prised to find that there are an increasing number of theoretical and empirical studies which document and theorize the variety of ways in which states continue to manage economies and key corporate actors within them – as well as work which examines the extent to which different forms of welfare states or regimes may be sustained under changed international economic and political circumstances. In other words, the logic of globalization towards nation-state convergence in an international neo-liberal economic order is being significantly disputed.

As we have noted, Navarro, Esping-Andersen, and Therborn have all sought to document, and explain, the differential responses of states in terms of the provision of welfare services and the direction of distinct welfare regimes. Somewhat differently, Hobson, Weiss, and Evans have all sought to both describe and theorize the variety of ways in which states can and do manage their national economies, and in so doing wholly undermine claims to the effect that there are no alternatives for national governments other than to bow to some neoliberal necessity.[195] Similarly, the edited collections by Blomstrom and Meller, Borrego et al. and Crouch and Streeck are paradigmatic of a body of work that has sought, respectively, to examine retrospectively divergent paths of capitalist development, and to map the contours of future capitalist diversity.[196] Further, albeit in different ways, these writers all argue convincingly that to the extent that there are globalizing tendencies in the international economy, then these are the *product* of the activity of nation-states, while at the same time offering different possibilities for domestic management.

Now, to the extent that such texts illustrate the range of possibilities open to national governments and nation-states, they are welcome correctives to the motivated or simply downright sloppy work around "globalization." But whether they draw upon the new institutionalism, policy network analysis or other theoretical and conceptual frameworks, many of these authors tend to be characterized by a neo- or radical Weberianism. For us, these theoretical frameworks entail certain forms of problematic myopia.

Thus, commenting on the work of Evans, Woodiwiss notes that for all its detailed attention to "embeddedness," this rather focuses upon "actors, institutions, and the strong or weak ties that bind them together," as opposed to seeking to understanding embeddedness as a phenomenon at a more macrostructural level, one central constituent element of which is class structure.[197] Whilst not commenting specifically on the texts mentioned above, Moran's concern that even "sophisticated" political economy restricts its focus to "the state as a set of elites" and globalization as "a process centering on states and certain corporate actors" is appropriate here. Thus,

> state-society relations are predominantly conceived as involving relations between the state and certain class elites . . . notably fractions of (internationalized) industrial and finance capital . . . the organized working class simply does not appear . . . [and] logically the role of democratic class conflict or alliance is missing as a dynamic of social change.[198]

Moreover, while much of this work deals with state-capital-economy relationships sensitively, there remains a tendency to treat these phenomena as analytically and empirically distinct entities, however inter-related, inter-dependent, and so on they are considered to be.[199] By contrast, what are required are analyses which recognize that states, markets, capitals are *social relations*, which is not to reduce these phenomena to, but to seek to theorize them in respect of, fundamental class relationships. As Burnham has noted,

> By viewing states and markets as differentiated forms of the same fundamental social relations we reinstate the class character of both and emphasize the weakness of counterpoising the "democratic state" and the unbridled avarice of the market.[200]

Thus Radice has recently criticized "globalization skeptics" including many of the authors highlighted above for the conspicuous absence of both "capitalism" and "labor" from their considerations. Capitalism is "a word more-or-less banished" from their lexicon, yet if "globalization can best be understood as an aspect of capitalism, then labour needs to be at the center of its analysis."[201] We concur with many of these observations, and would summarize them thus: what has been lacking are Marxist analyses of the nature and limits of divergent state trajectories in a so-called universalizing era; that is, work which attempts to theorize capitalist differences within a recognition of the essential features of capitalism as system of production.

Arguments which seek to expose the class-based nature of the discourses of globalization are for us crucial. They clarify that what is at issue is not simply re-inserting the political into considerations of globalization, but of re-inserting a class-based politics of resistance. A further point follows. For we have, as have other globalization skeptics, attempted to emphasize the continuing importance of states in a supposedly globalized era. But this is not to champion the state *per se*, for states are intrinsic to the maintenance and reproduction of capitalist social relations, themselves the driving force of globalization! So we need at one and the same time to recognize the continuing significance of the state, while not descending into any untheorized and apolitical commitment to national state politics in the contexts of the harsh winds of globalization. This constitutes a key dividing line between two groups of globalization skeptics, whom Radice has labeled progressive nationalists and socialist skeptics.[202] The tendency amongst the former is "to seek to promote a conventional progressive agenda within a fundamentally national political arena. They contest what they see as the predominant neoliberal ideology of globalism, which is used by economic and political elites to defend their wealth and power."[203] Policy-debate, then, centers on the ability of the state – "presumed to be acting in the national interest" to generate "order and progress" on a national level, in the context of the disorders generated by nascent "world markets."[204] By contrast, a socialist critique of globalization starts form the premise that globalization is an aspect of capitalism, to be understood via the categories that allow us to grasp capitalism as a mode of production.[205] Further, within this (Marxist) framework, states are neither neutral, protectors of any national interest, nor instruments to be wrested from capitalist control they, too, are objects of political struggle.

Some Concluding Observations: On Capitalism, Corporate Crime, and Criminology

In the superficial plausibility of globalization rhetoric, we must not lose sight of the fact that we are still concerned with capitalist economies. Fundamental aspects of these are antagonisms borne out of differential relationships to the means of production, and the necessity for capital to constantly seek to maximize the extraction of surplus value. One element of this is the constant pressure from capital and its representatives towards lower costs of production – in a moment of candor, one American union-busting lawyer, Alan Lips, told *People Management* magazine that "Unions and employers are natural enemies" and that corporations should "threaten to exercise the employer's economic power to coerce rejection of unions."[206] It is also to be expected that, all other things being equal, corporations will push for less rather than more regulation, and will operate with more rather than less destructive effects. These persistent realities obviously have implications for any understanding of the prevalence of corporate crime.

The emergence to dominance of neoliberalism in general, and the prevalence of the discourses of globalization in particular, have combined to increase both the structural power of capital and what Snider has referred to as "the social credibility of capital,"[207] and in this way tend towards the removal of (the control of) corporate crime from state agendas. As the legitimacy of business organizations has increased, so has the legitimacy of their control declined.[208] If one sets these processes in the context of the difficulties that have historically attached to labeling the illegal activities of corporations as crime – not least, if most regrettably, due to the support of a succession of academics[209] – it is no surprise that this task has become much more difficult in the past two decades. Neoliberalism has also raised the naked pursuit of profit to the status of almost moral exigency, which has the effect of legitimating virtually any activity because it is engage in by business, and de-legitimating opposition and resistance the bases of pro-regulatory forces for its very "anti-business" rhetoric and practice. And, of course, the discourses of globalization have the consequence of rendering regulation of such activity impractical even if it were desirable. Where external controls (both material and ideological) on profit maximization are weakened, then we can reasonably expect to see an increased incidence in illegal corporate activity.[210]

These points being made, there are some senses in which it is non-sensical to speak of the increasing incidence of corporate crime under conditions of rampant neoliberalism for one of the effects of the increasing struc-

tural power and social credibility of capital is that corporate crime as a phenomenon disappears:

> because its survival as an object of study is contingent on the pas-
> sage and enforcement of "command and control" legislation, cor-
> porate crime can "disappear" through decriminalization (the repeal
> of criminal law), through deregulation (the repeal of all state law,
> criminal, civil and administrative), and through downsizing (the
> destruction of the state's enforcement capacity. All three have
> been used.[211]

While Snider's claims cannot be disputed, we should also emphasize that
there exist and have existed countervailing trends, even while much of the
literature on globalization in particular, and the general dominance of neoliberalism in general, serves to cast the freeing of capital from state regulation
as inevitable and/or desirable. We have attempted to unpack the discourses
of globalization and their relationship to neoliberal fantasies one consequence of which is to re-open debates around, and the possibility of, regulation of corporate activities. We have argued that viewing capitalist societies
as class societies forces us to conceive not simply of corporate crime, but also
of regulatory agencies within the context of a theory which sees inscribed in
the state of the state "an unequal structure of representation" and an "unstable equilibrium of compromises."[212] Within such an analysis, a regulatory
agency is most likely to have its origins in an issue that cannot be "resolved"
within existing structures of law. The creation of such a body provides "a
framework for facilitating an exceptional compromise in the face of a political challenge that can only be met by altering the juridical rights of capital."[213]
Thus a regulatory agency must be "independent apparently insulated from
partisan politics and the regular administrative apparatus:"

> . . . because the kind of issue which gives rise to the establishment
> of a regulatory agency – giving it its status as "special case" – is a
> potentially explosive one, the threat may resurface, possibly neces-
> sitating renegotiation of the agency's terms, powers, and rela-
> tionships to other parts of the state apparatus. That the particular
> compromise is institutionally located at an apparently greater dis-
> tance than the rest of the apparatus from the overtly political
> institutions (the assembly and the executive) indicates the impor-
> tance of neutralizing / insulating the compromise. Yet it is pre-
> cisely the special political nature of the issue that may lead to a
> future rupture.[214]

A theoretical understanding of a regulatory agency as a hegemonic
apparatus forces us to ask a rather different series of questions to those
raised within and around criminology: what (issue) created the need for
compromise; what is the hegemonic fraction; what place does the regulat-

ed industry hold in the social formation; what is the nature of the compromise; and what are the conditions of existence of this compromise – crudely, how stable is this? Of course, these questions must be treated through reference to the empirical,[215] although it is also clear that developing our understanding of the nature and limits of regulation then requires a further shift back to a more abstract, theoretical level, now interrogated and refined through theoretically informed empirical analyses.[216] The point is, however, that neither our questions nor our answers are entirely foreclosed. Understanding regulatory agencies as hegemonic apparatuses means that their effects are not pre-determined, that there is always space for more (and, of course, less) effective regulatory strategies, forms, modes of enforcement. The strength or weakness of regulation therefore is interpreted dynamically, within the context of struggle between members of classes and a range of social forces.[217] Thus such an approach allows us to be more sensitive to the different forms in which different corporate activity is, and can be, regulated. It points us towards the need to understand regulation from the point of view of states, economies, societies. An approach grounded in a Marxist political economy can meet these tasks. Further, such an approach allows us, indeed forces us, to account for "globalization" processes without being seduced by the epoch-making claims of some of their cruder "analysts."

The basic argument of this chapter – following previous work[218] – is that corporate crime can only be understood in the context of wider political economy. One essential feature of corporate existence across all political-economic contexts is the need, at least in the long run, to maximize profitability, and it is impossible to disassociate this fact from the incidence of corporate crime. However, it is also clear that there are aspects of particular political economies which need to be taken into account in understanding the particular incidence of criminal activity on the part of corporations. Such tasks are, it seems to us, beyond the reach of criminology. From a Marxist perspective, Hirst, O'Malley, Pearce and Pearce and Tombs have all challenged the notion that such administrative categories as crime and criminals, could be the theoretical "object" of social scientific analysis.[219] Thus for us, a more adequate means of grasping corporate activity, including corporate crime, and of assessing the means for its more effective regulation is to be achieved through political economy, and indeed through Marxist political economy. Of course, just as the hegemonic project of neoliberalism/globalization seeks to deny a role for states and regulation, so at the same time has one of its effects been to marginalize Marxist modes of argument and analysis from academic and popular agendas. We have sought to demonstrate that such forms of analyses remain as, if not *more*, central now, at the start of the twenty-first century, than they were a quarter of a century ago, a time when they were much more in fashion but about to face an ideological assault from various forces of the Right.

Acknowledgments

Our thanks go to Joe Sim and Dave Whyte, each of whom commented at length on an earlier version of this paper. Despite our incorporating many of their suggestions, neither will be in full agreement with the argument contained herein, and neither of course bears any responsibility for errors and inconsistencies.

Notes

[1]   Pearce, 1973, 1976.

[2]   Pearce, 1976:79-80.

[3]   Pearce, 2000; Pearce and Tombs, 1998; Slapper and Tombs, 1999.

[4]   Snider, 2000.

[5]   Katz, 1980; Geis et al., 1995:6-7.

[6]   Snider, 2000.

[7]   Gottschalk et al., 1997:1.

[8]   Anderson, 2000:10.

[9]   Anderson, 2000:11.

[10]   Fukuyama, 1992.

[11]   Dahrendorf, 1990; Gray, 1998; Callaghan and Tunney, 2000.

[12]   Pearce and Tombs, 1998:3-33.

[13]   Indeed, 1997 and 1998 saw a generalized crisis across Asian economies, somewhat altering the security of capitalist optimism even here (see, for example, Brenner, 1998:213-226, Singh, 1999, Weiss, 1998).

[14]   Amin, 1997; Korzeniewicz and Moran, 1997; Marfleet, 1998; Robinson, 1998/99.

[15]   Magdoff, 1992:63-70; Sivanandan, 1998/99.

[16]   Giddens, 1999:4.

[17]   Roy, 1999:8.

[18]   United Nations Development Programme, 1998:2.

[19]   United Nations Development Programme, 1998:2.

[20]   See, for example, Brenner, 1998:213-226; Singh, 1999; Weiss, 1998.

[21]   Cited in Mokhiber and Weissman, 1999d:1.

[22]   United Nations Development Programme, 1998:4-6; Smith, 1997.

[23]   Madeley, 1999.

[24]   Waring, 1988.

[25]   MacGregor, 1998:94; Marfleet, 1998; Robinson, 1998/99; Sivanandan, 1998/99.

26   Cerny 1996/97.

27   Cashmore, 1989; Currie, 1990, 1997; Council of Churches for Britain and Ireland, 1997; Oppenheim and Harker, 1996; Phillips, 1991; Wilson, 1992; Zeitlin, 1989.

28   Esping-Andersen, 1999:154; see also Fritzell's five nation comparison; Fritzell, 1993.

29   Gottschalk, 1997:18.

30   Froud et al., 1999:161.

31   Mokhiber and Weissman, 1999e:1-2; Navarro, 1999:4; for further details, and dimensions, see also Brenner, 1998; Moseley, 1999a; Pollin, 2000.

32   Elliot, 1999:2.

33   Pollin, 2000:21.

34   Pollin, 2000:21.

35   Mokhiber and Weissman, 1999e:1.

36   Gardiner, 1997:37.

37   Gottschalk, 1997:25-29; see also Navarro, 1999:42-45, Tables 8 and 9.

38   Denny, 2000.

39   Denny, 2000.

40   Denny, 2000.

41   Bradshaw, 2000:55.

42   Gottschalk et al., 1997:5.

43   Froud et al., 1999:161, and passim.

44   Brenner, 1998:235.

45   Brenner, 1998; Callinicos, 1998, 1999; Fine et al., 1998; Moseley, 1997, 1999a, 1999b.

46   Moseley, 1998.

47   Brenner, 1998:235-262; Moseley, 1997, 1999b.

48   Callinicos, 1998:21-3, 1999.

49   Pollin, 2000.

50   See Jones, 1982.

51   Jones, 1982; Pearce and Tombs, 1998.

52   Adams and Brock, 1991:108-109; Treanor, 1999.

53   Hughes, 1992:309.

54   Hughes, 1992:309; see also Sawyer, 1992:252-255.

55   Mokhiber and Weissman, 1999a:120-2.

56   Whyte and Tombs, 1998.

57   Snider, 2000:189.

58   Coates, 1999.

[59]   Pearce, 1976.

[60]   Mokhiber and Weissman, 1999b:1.

[61]   Snider, 2000:174.

[62]   Smith, 1997:30.

[63]   Cowe, 1999; Treanor, 1999; Watts and Treanor, 1999.

[64]   Brummer, 1999.

[65]   Brummer, 1999.

[66]   Mokhiber and Weissman, 1999a:131.

[67]   Mokhiber and Weissman, 1999a:131.

[68]   Buckingham and Cowe, 1999, Brummer, 1999.

[69]   Ruigrock and van Tulder, 1995.

[70]   See also Harman, 1996:18-19.

[71]   Chomsky, 1999:66.

[72]   Chomsky, 1999:67-8.

[73]   Mokhiber and Weissman, 1999a:74-6; see also Mokhiber and Weissman, 1999f.

[74]   The OECD includes almost all of the world's largest economies. The comparisons listed here are based upon OECD data for 1999 (OECD, 2000) and the 1999 Fortune Global 500 list (Fortune, 2000).

[75]   Edmonds, 2000.

[76]   U.N. Center of Transnational Corporations, 1984; Knox and Agnew, 1989:192; Hirst and Thompson, 1996:53; Pearce and Tombs, 1998.

[77]   We confine ourselves here to considering processes of economic globalization, even if this is rather an abstraction; on globalization processes more generally, see Albrow, 1996, Waters, 1995, which are also paradigmatic of the analytical looseness of much work in this area. For a brief but searing critique of globalization claims across their general range, see Woodiwiss, 1996.

[78]   Hay, 1999:30.

[79]   Weiss, 1999.

[80]   Lazarus, 1998/99:91.

[81]   Hay, 1999:30.

[82]   Hay, 1999:30; typologies, or attempts to separate out different accounts, of arguments around globalization can be found in Perraton et al., 1997, Weiss, 1998, 1999.

[83]   Pearce and Tombs, 1998:34-70; see also Hirst and Thompson, 1996, for an oft-cited and careful critique of excessive globalization claims around economic globalization.

[84]   See Pearce and Tombs, 1998.

[85]   Jessop, 1982, 1990.

[86]   Lowi, 1993:20-2.

[87]   Hunt, 1993.

88   Miller and Rose, 1990:25.

89   Hazard, 1993:238; Pashukhanis, 1978.

90   Hirst, 1979.

91   Pearce, 1989.

92   Adams and Brock, 1986.

93   Crooks, 1993.

94   Kolko, 1962.

95   Fine, 1990.

96   Powell, 1990.

97   Sayer, 1995:104.

98   Sayer, 1995.

99   Pearce and Tombs, 1998.

100   Gramsci, 1971.

101   Poulantzas, 1973, 1974, 1975.

102   Poulantzas, 1973:191, cited in Mahon, 1979:155.

103   Mahon, 1979:155.

104   Mahon, 1979.

105   Mahon, 1979:157-8.

106   Gill and Law, 1993.

107   Harman, 1996.

108   Hirst and Thompson, 1996:1, 4.

109   Harman, 1996; Hirst and Thompson, 1996; Weiss, 1997.

110   Goldblatt, 1997:140.

111   Weiss, 1997:15.

112   On this point, it is worth noting that recent years have seen the appearance of useful empirical studies in the context of considerations of the regulation of occupational health and safety – which have sought to document through particular case-studies the ways in which, and the effects to which, such discourses of globalization may be used by already powerful companies, not least at moments when they seem most vulnerable to greater state and pro-regulatory scrutiny (Beck and Woolfson, 2000; Whyte, 2000; Whyte and Tombs, 1998).

113   See Pearce and Tombs, 1998; and Tombs, 1996.

114   See below, and Hay, 1999; Hay and Watson, 1998.

115   Cox, 1993:272.

116   Gill, 1990; Cox, 1993, Snider, 2000.

117   Wade, 1996:5.

118   Elliott, 1996.

119   St. Clair, 1999.

120   Cox, 1994; Gill, 1994, 1995; Gowan, 1995; Jackson and Price, 1994; Nelson, 1996; Petras
and Morley, 1990; Pacific Asia Resource Center, 1994; Price, 1994; Tran, 1996; Wade,
1996; Whitfield, 1992; World Bank, 1994.

121   Pauly, 1994; Price, 1994; Young, 1995.

122   Gill and Law, 1993:104, emphasis added; Strange, 1994:215.

123   See Pearce and Tombs, 1998:35-47, 247-279.

124   Pearce and Tombs, 1996.

125   Moran, 1998, Snider, 1990, 2000; and see Pearce and Tombs, 1998:223-246.

126   Hay and Watson, 1998:815, emphases in original.

127   This is clearly illustrated in the European-wide imposition of economic austerity measures as part of the project of convergence towards the single currency. This is the case
even given that social democratic parties currently hold formal political power in the
major EU nations.

128   Cerny, 1996/97.

129   Hirst and Thompson, 1992.

130   Nelson, 1996.

131   Picciotto, 1997.

132   Hobson, 1997:250-251, and passim, Radice, 2000; Weiss, 1998.

133   Hirst and Thompson, 1992:362.

134   Hirst and Thompson, 1992:362.

135   Perraton et al., 1997:259; Weiss, 1998:190-191.

136   Holloway, 1994:38.

137   Holloway, 1994:34-5.

138   Gill and Law, 1993:98; see also Vogel, 1996, and below.

139   See Pearce and Tombs, 1998; Whyte and Tombs, 1998; Hirst and Thompson, 1999;
Pearce and Snider, 1995; Dicken, 1992:131-137.

140   Strange, 1994:215.

141   Mokhiber and Weissman, 1999c:1.

142   Mokhiber and Weissman, 1999c:1.

143   Picciotto, 1994.

144   Mishra, 1999:41-4.

145   Whyte, 1999:140-174, Whyte and Tombs, 1998.

146   Whyte, 1999:167.

147   See Tombs, 1995.

148   Vogel, 1996.

149   Vogel, 1996:18.

150   See also Tombs, 1998.

151   Vogel, 1996:3.

152   Levi, 1995.

153   Calavita and Pontell, 1995.

154   Alvesalo and Tombs, 2000.

155   Yeager, 1991.

156   Barnett, 1995; Block, 1993; Tombs, 1995b.

157   Fine et al., 1999:69.

158   Weiss, 1999:137.

159   Weiss, 1999.

160   Chomsky, 1999:23-4. By contrast, in 1971, 90 percent of such flows were related to the
      real economy, and just 10 percent were speculative (Chomsky, 1999:23-4).

161   Hay and Watson, 1999.

162   Helleiner, 1996:193.

163   Helleiner, 1996.

164   Soros, 1998:175-194, and passim.

165   Wade and Veneroso, 1998.

166   See Michie and Grieve Smith, 1999.

167   MacEwan, 1999:66-98.

168   Moran, 1998.

169   Weiss, 1998:204-8, and passim.

170   Navarro, 1999; Gustafsson and Palmer, 1997; Jannti and Ritakallio, 1997.

171   Pekkarinen, 1997.

172   Andersson, 1996:68.

173   Gustafsson and Uusitalo, 1990; Jannti and Ritakallio, 1997. It should be noted that Fin-
      land experienced a recession in the early part of the 1990s which was more severe than
      that experienced by any other OECD country since the war, and greater than Finland's
      own depression of the 1930s; the effects of this recession, and indeed of the 'recovery'
      from it during the 1990s, have been marked; see Andersson et al., 1993, and Kiander, and
      Vartia, 1996.

174   Esping-Andersen, 1999.

175   Navarro, 1999:48, original emphases; see also, MacGregor, 1998; Therborn, 1986.

176   Pollin, 2000.

177   Sim, forthcoming.

178   *The Observer*, September 5, 1999, cited in Sim, forthcoming.

179   Hay, 1999:145-180.

180   Sim, forthcoming:n14, and passim.

[181] Holden, 1999:532.

[182] Bienefeld, 1996:417.

[183] Froud et al., 1992, Neocleous, 1999.

[184] Cited in Holden, 1999:531.

[185] Blair, speech at the TUC, 1997, cited in Wilson, 2000:156; see also Giddens, 1999; again, for critical treatments of the Labor Governments "signing up" to globalization and all that this entails, see Hay, 1999.

[186] Anderson, 2000:11.

[187] Sim, forthcoming.

[188] Mishra, 1999:71.

[189] Anderson, 2000:11.

[190] Pollin, 2000:17.

[191] Jospin, 1999.

[192] Jeffreys, 1996. As Dave Whyte has pointed out to us in conversation, using his own ongoing research into the activities of multinational oil companies, there is vibrant class-based resistance to the activities of oil companies, particularly in Latin America but also in parts of Africa. In Latin America, revolutionary movements dedicated not simply to resisting the activities of oil companies but more generally to opposing U.S. demands for economic reform have generated a series of important victories during the 1990s (Petras, 1997). Several questions follow, which cannot be addressed here: why are such struggles, when they are brought to popular attention, overwhelmingly cast in terms of environmental protection, the protection of an indigenous way of life or human rights? Why are academic analyses of these revolutionary movements so conspicuous by their absence? Why is so much attention devoted to so-called new social movements at the expense of class-based struggle?

[193] Lazarus, 1998:97.

[194] Gills, 1997:66; cited in Lazarus, 1997:97.

[195] Evans, 1995; Hobson, 1997; Weiss, 1997, 1998, 1999; Weiss and Hobson, 1995.

[196] Blomstrom and Meller, 1991; Borrego et al., 1996; and, Crouch and Streeck, 1997.

[197] Woodiwiss, 1996:809. To point to the need to incorporate class, and also the role of organized labor, is clearly to prioritize these cleavages under capitalism. It is not, however, to deny the significance of other structural divisions, divisions which have, empirically, been central to the emergence of "new" social movements and a variety of activities of resistance.

[198] Moran, 1998:55.

[199] Radice, 2000.

[200] Burnham, 1997:157.

[201] Radice, 2000:11, 13.

[202] Radice, 2000.

[203] Radice, 2000:5.

204   Radice, 2000:13.

205   Radice, 2000:13.

206   Cited in Cohen, 2000:35.

207   Snider, 2000:171.

208   Slapper and Tombs, 1999:85-109; Snider, 2000.

209   Pearce and Tombs, 1990; Snider, 1990.

210   Pearce and Tombs, 1998; Tombs, 1990, 1996.

211   Snider, 2000:172.

212   Mahon, 1979:157-158.

213   Mahon, 1979:160.

214   Mahon, 1979:160.

215   Carson, 1982:12.

216   Carson, 1982:233-234.

217   See also Snider, 1991, who develops a slightly different theoretical framework for addressing such questions.

218   Pearce, 1973; Pearce, 1976; Pearce, 2000; Pearce and Tombs, 1998; Slapper and Tombs, 1999.

219   Hirst, 1972; O'Malley, 1987; Pearce, 1976; and, Pearce and Tombs, 1998.

References

Adams, W. and J.W. Brock (1991). *Antitrust Economics on Trial: A Dialogue on the New Laissez-Faire*. Princeton, NJ: Princeton University Press.

Adams, W. and J.W. Brock (1986). *The Bigness Complex: Industry, Labor and Government in the American Economy*. New York, NY: Pantheon.

Adeola, F. (1994). "Environmental Hazards, Health, and Racial Inequity in Hazardous Waste Distribution." *Environment and Behavior*, 26(1):99-125.

Albrow, M. (1996). *The Global Age: State and Society Beyond Modernity*. Cambridge, UK: Polity.

Alvesalo, A. (forthcoming Ph.D. thesis). "The Control System(s) of White Collar Crime and the Problems of Control" (working title). Faculty of Law, University of Turku.

Alvesalo, A. (1999b). "I Fight the Law: White Collar Crime and Criminalizations." Unpublished paper presented at the American Society of Criminology Conference, November 1999, Toronto.

Alvesalo, A. (1999b). "Ylämäki, Alamäki? Talousrikollisuuden Tutkimus ja Kontrolli Suomessa." (Uphill, Downhill? On the Study and Control of White Collar Crime in Finland." In A. Alvesalo (ed.). *Kirjoituksia Talousrikollisuudesta I* (Essays On Economic Crime), pp. 5-13. Poliisiammattikorkeakoulun tiedotteita 1/1998. Helsinki: Oy Edita Ab.

Alvesalo, A. (1998a). "They Are Not Honest Criminals." In *Organised Crime & Crime Prevention – What Works?* Rapport fra NSfK´s 40. forskeseminar. Espoo, Finland. Copenhagen: Scandinavian Research Council from Criminology.

Alvesalo, A. (1994). "The Phenomenon Called Economic Crime." In A. Alvesalo and A. Laitinen (eds.). *Perspectives of Economic Crime*. Turku: Pallosalama Oy.

Alvesalo, A. and S. Tombs (forthcoming). "Understanding the Limits and Prospects for Regulating Economic Crime: A Comparison with Finland and Britain." Unpublished.

Alvesalo, A. and S. Tombs (2001). "Can Economic Crime Control Be Sustained? The Case of Finland." *Innovation*, 14, 1:35-53.

Alvesalo, A. and S. Tombs (2000). "The Emergence of a "War" on Economic Crime: The Case of Finland." Paper presented at Crimes of the Future: The Future(s) of Criminology, British Criminology Conference, Leicester, 5-7 July.

Amin, S. (1997). *Capitalism in the Age of Globalization*. London, UK: Zed Books.

Amin, S. (1997). *Empire of Chaos*. New York, NY: Monthly Review Press.

Amin, S. (1990). *Maldevelopment: Anatomy of a Global Failure*. Tokyo, Japan: United Nations University Press.

Amy, D.J. (1985). "Potential Political Problems in Wisconsin's 'Consensus Process'." Unpublished paper. Cited by Gedicks. 1993. *The New Resource Wars: Native and Environmental Struggles Against Multinational Corporations.* Boston, MA: South End Press.

Anderson, Martin (1992). *Impostors in the Temple.* New York, NY: Simon and Schuster.

Anderson, P. (2000). "Editorial: Renewals." *New Left Review,* 1(January/February):5-24.

Anderson, P. (1977). "The Antinomies of Antonio Gramsci." *New Left Review,* (January/February):100.

Andersson, J.O. (1996). "Fundamental Values for a Third Left." *New Left Review,* 216(March/April):66-78.

Andersson, J.O., P. Kosonen, and J. Vartiainen (1993). "The Finnish Model of Economic and Social Policy: From Emulation to Crash." *Åbo.*

Anderton, D. (1996). "Methodological Issues in the Spatiotemporal Analysis of Environmental Equity." *Social Science Quarterly,* 77(3):508-515.

Anderton, D., A. Anderson, J. Oakes, and M. Fraser (1994). "Environmental Equity: The Demographics of Dumping." *Demography,* 31(2):229-247.

Anderton, D., A. Anderson, P. Rossi, J. Oakes, M. Fraser, E. Weber, and E. Calabrese (1994). "Hazardous Waste Facilities: Environmental Equity Issues in Metropolitan Areas." *Evaluation Review,* 18(2):123-140.

Anderton, D., J. Oakes, and K. Egan (1997). "Environmental Equity in Superfund: Demographics of the Discovery and Prioritization of Abandoned Toxic Sites." *Evaluation Review,* 21(1):3-26

Andrews, J. (1994). "Health-Care Industry Fraud Eats Up Billions Yearly." *The Christian Science Monitor,* (August 4):3.

Anishinabe N. (n.d.) *Questions and Answers About Exxon's Proposed Crandon/Mole Lake Mine.* Pamphlet.

Appadurai, A. (1999). "Globalization and the Research Imagination." *International Social Science Journal,* 160:230.

Ashworth, G. (1999). "The Silencing of Women." In T. Dunne and N.J. Wheeler (eds.) *Human Rights in Global Politics,* pp. 259-276. Cambridge, UK: Cambridge University Press.

Athens, L. (1987). *The Creation of Dangerous Violent Criminals.* Urbana, IL: University of Illinois Press.

Aulette, J. and R. Michalowski (1993). "Fire in Hamlet: A Case Study of State-Corporate Crime." In K. Tunnell (ed.) *Political Crime in Contemporary America: A Critical Approach,* pp. 171-206. New York, NY: Garland Publishing, Inc.

Bailey, F. and D. Hale (1998). *Popular Culture, Crime & Justice.* Belmont, CA: West/Wadsworth.

Barak, Gregg (ed.) (1991). *Crimes by the Capitalist State.* Albany, New York, NY: State University of New York Press.

Barlett, D. and J. Steele (1998a). "Corporate Welfare." *Time,* (November 9):37-54.

Barlett, D. and J. Steele (1998b). "Fantasy Islands." *Time,* (November 16):79-93.

Barnett, H. (1995). "Can Confrontation, Negotiation, or Socialization Solve the Superfund Enforcement Dilemma?" In F. Pearce and L. Snider (eds.) *Corporate Crime. Contemporary Debates.*

Bauerlin, M. (1991). "Fish Tales: For Multinational Mining Companies, Wisconsin's Spearfishing Wars are a Gold Mine." *City Pages*, 12(542):3.

Beal, D. (1978). "Will New Mining Bring Pollution and Peril the Wolf River's Future?" *The Milwaukee Journal*, 1.

Beck, M. and C. Woolfson (forthcoming). "Piper Alpha and the Hidden Deregulation of Britain's Offshore Oil Industry." In E. Coles, D. Smith, and S. Tombs (eds.) *Risk Management and Society*. Amsterdam: Kluwer-Nijhoff.

Been, V. (1994). "Locally Undesirable Land Uses in Minority Neighborhoods: Disproportionate Siting or Market Dynamics." *Yale Law Journal*, 103(6):1383-1422.

Beirne, P. and J. Messerschmidt (1991). *Criminology*. New York, NY: Harcourt Brace Jovanovich.

Bell, D. (1975). *Cultural Contradictions of Capitalism*. New York, NY: Basic Books.

Benekos, P. (1983). "Sentencing the White-collar Offender: Evaluating the Use of Sanctions." Paper presented at the Academy of Criminal Justice Sciences annual meeting, San Antonio, TX, March.

Benson, M. (1996). "Denying the Guilty Mind: Accounting for Involvement in White-Collar." In E. Goode (ed.) *Crime In Social Deviance*. Boston, MA: Allyn and Bacon.

Benson, M.L. and F.T. Cullen (1998). *Combatting Corporate Crime: Local Prosecutors at Work*. Boston, MA: Northeastern University Press.

Benson, M. L. and E. Moore (1992). "Are White-Collar and Common Offenders the Same? An Empirical and Theoretical Critique of a Recently Proposed General Theory of Crime." *Journal of Research in Crime and Delinquency*, 29:251-272.

Benson, M.L. and E. Walker (1988). "Sentencing the White-Collar Offender." *American Sociological Review*, 53:294-302.

Bienefeld, M. (1996). "Is a Strong National Economy a Utopian Goal at the End of the Twentieth Century?" In R. Boyer and D. Drache (eds.) *States Against Markets. The Limits of Globalization*, pp. 415-440. London, UK: Routledge.

Birnbaum, J. (1992). *The Lobbyists: How Influence Peddlers Get Their Way in Washington*. New York, NY: Times Books.

Blankenship, M. (1993). *Understanding Corporate Criminality*. New York, NY: Garland Publishing, Inc.

Block, A. (1993). "Defending the Mountaintop: A Campaign Against Environmental Crime." In F. Pearce and M. Woodiwiss (eds.) *Global Crime Connections*. London, UK: Macmillan.

Blomstrom, M. and P. Meller (eds.) (1991). *Diverging Paths: Comparing a Century of Scandinavian and Latin American Economic Development*. Washington, DC: Inter-American Development Bank/John Hopkins University Press.

Boer, T., M. Pastor, J. Sadd, and L. Snyder (1997). "Is There Environmental Racism? The Demographics of Hazardous Waste in Los Angeles County." *Social Science Quarterly*, 78(4):793-810.

Bohm, R. (1993). "Social Relationships That Arguably Should Be Criminal Although They Are Not: On the Political Economy of Crime." In K. Tunnell (ed.) *Political Crime in Contemporary America: A Critical Approach*, pp. 3-30. New York, NY: Garland Publishing, Inc.

Bonsignore, J. (1994). *Law and Multinationals*. Englewood Cliffs, NJ: Prentice Hall.

Borrego, J., A. Alvarez, and K.S. Jomo (eds.) (1996). *Capital, the State and Late Industrialization*. Boulder, CO: Westview Press.

Bovard, J. (1995). *Archer Daniels Midland: A Case Study in Corporate Welfare*. Washington, DC: Cato Institute.

Bowen, W., M. Salling, K. Haynes, and E. Cryan (1995). "Toward Environmental Justice: Spatial Equity in Ohio and Cleveland." *Annals of the Association of American Geographers*, 85(4):641-63.

Bowman, S. (1996). *The Modern Corporation and American Political Thought: Law, Power, and Ideology*. University Park, PA: The Pennsylvania State University Press.

Box, S. (1983). *Power, Crime and Mystification*. London, UK: Tavistock.

Bradshaw, J. (2000). "Prospects for Poverty in Britain in the First Twenty-Five Years of the Next Century." *Sociology*, 34(1):53-70.

Bragg, R. (1999). "Politics Hinted in ValuJet-Crash Charges." *The New York Times*, (July 15):A12.

Braithwaite, J. (1984). *Corporate Crime in the Pharmaceutical Industry*. Boston, MA: Routledge & Kegan Paul.

Braithwaite, J. and B. Fisse (1990). "On the Plausibility of Corporate Crime Theory." In W.S. Laufer and F. Adler (eds.) *Advances in Criminological Theory*. New Brunswick, NJ: Transaction.

Brenner, R. (1998). "The Economics of Global Turbulence. A Special Report on the World Economy." 1950-1988. *New Left Review*, 229:1-265.

Bresette, W. (1992). *Remarks From A Watershed Conference on Mining and Treaty Rights*. Tomahawk, WI.

Brewton, P. (1992). *The Mafia, CIA and George Bush*. New York, NY: SPI Books/Shapolsky Publishers.

Browning, F. and J. Gerassi (1980). *The American Way of Crime*. New York, NY: Putnam.

Brummer, A. (1999). "Monster Mania." *The Guardian*, (May 26):17.

Buckingham, L. and R. Cowe (1999). "Merger Mania – Coming to a Company Near You." *The Guardian*, (January 23):7.

Bullard, R. (1994). *Dumping in Dixie: Race, Class, and Environmental Quality*, Second Edition. Boulder, CO: Westview Press.

Bullard, R. (1993). *Confronting Environmental Racism: Voices from the Grassroots*. Boston, MA: South End Press.

Bullard, R. (1983). "Solid Waste Sites in the Black Houston Community." *Sociological Inquiry*, 53(2/3):273-88.

Bunch, C. and N. Reilly (1994). *Demanding Accountability: The Global Campaign and Vienna Tirbunal for Women's Rights*. New Brunswick, NJ: Center for Women's Global Leadership, and New York, NY: UNIFEM.

Bunch, C. (1990). "Women's Rights as Human Rights: Toward a Re-Vision of Human Rights." *Human Rights Quarterly*, 12:486-98.

Burnham, P. (1997). "Globalization: States, Markets and Class Relations." *Historical Materialism*, 1(Autumn):150-160.

Calavita, K. and H.N. Pontell (1995). "Saving the Savings and Loans? U.S. Government Response to Financial Crime." In F. Pearce and L. Snider (eds.) *Corporate Crime: Contemporary Debates*.

Calavita, K. and H. Pontell (1993). "Savings and Loan Fraud As Organized Crime: Toward a Conceptual Typology of Corporate Illegality." *Criminology,* 31(4):519-48.

Calavita, K. and H. Pontell (1990). "Heads I Win, Tails You Lose: Deregulation, Crime and Crisis in the Savings and Loan Industry." *Crime & Delinquency,* 36:309-341.

Calavita, K. and H. Pontell (1990). "Other People's Money Revisited: Collective Embezzlement in the Savings and Loan and Insurance Industries." *Social Problems,* 38:94-112.

Callaghan, J. and S. Tunney (2000). "Prospects for Social Democracy: A Critical Review of the Arguments and Evidence." *Contemporary Politics,* 6(1):55-75.

Callinicos, A. (1999). "Capitalism, Competition and Profits: A Critique of Robert Brenner's Theory of Crisis." *Historical Materialism,* 4(Summer):9-31.

Callinicos, A. (1998). "World Capitalism at the Abyss." *International Socialism,* 81(Winter):3-43.

Cameron, M.O. (1964). *The Booster and the Snitch: Department Store Shoplifting.* New York, NY: Free Press.

Caplow, T. and R.J. McGee (1997). *The Academic Marketplace.* New York, NY: Arno Press.

Carbonell-Catilo, A. (1986). "The Philippines: The Politics of Plunder." *Corruption and Reform,* 1:235-243.

Carlson, K. (1979). *Statement Before the Congressional Committee on Education and Labor, Subcommittee on Compensation, Health and Safety, Hearings on Asbestos-Related Occupational Diseases*, pp. 25-52. 95th Congress, Second Session. Washington, DC: U.S. Government Printing Office.

Carson, R. (1994, 1962). *Silent Spring.* New York, NY: Houghton Mifflin.

Carson, W.G. (1982). *The Other Price of Britain's Oil.* Oxford, UK: Martin Robertson.

Cashmore, E. (1989). *United Kingdom? Class, Race and Gender Since the War.* London, UK: Unwin Hyman.

Caulfield, S.L. and N.A. Wonders (1993). "Personal AND Political: Violence Against Women and the Role of the State." In K.D. Tunnell (ed.) *Political Crime in Contemporary America: A Critical Approach*, pp. 79-100. New York, NY: Garland.

Cavender, G. and A. Mulcahy (1998). "Trial by Fire: Media Constructions of Corporate Deviance." *Justice Quarterly,* 15:697-717.

Center for Policy Alternatives (1994). *Toxic Waste and Race Revisited.* Washington, DC: Center for Policy Alternatives.

Cerny, P.G. (1996/97). "Paradoxes of the Competition State: The Dynamics of Political Globalization." *Government and Opposition,* 32(1):Spring.

Chambliss, W. (1989). "State-Organized Crime." *Criminology,* 27:183-208.

Chambliss, W. (1988). *On the Take,* Second Edition. Bloomington, IN: Indiana University Press.

Chambliss, W. (1982). "Toward a Radical Criminology." In D. Kairys (ed.) (1982). *The Politics of Law: A Progressive Critique.* New York, NY: Pantheon Books.

Chambliss, W. and R. Seidman (1982). *Law, Order, and Power*, Second Edition. Reading, MA: Addison Wesley Publishing Company.

Chomsky, N. (1999). *Profit Over People. Neo-liberalism and Global Order*. New York, NY: Seven Stories Press.

Christie, N. (1986). "Suitable Enemies." In H. Bianchi and R. van Swaaningen (eds.) (1986). *Abolitionism. Towards a Non-Repressive Approach to Crime*. Amsterdam: Free University Press.

Citizens Against Toxic Exposure (1997). "Profiles of Dioxin Treated Communities: Mt. Dioxin." [On-line]. Available: http://www.essential.org/cchw/campaign/Profiles.html

Claubert, J.M. and J.F. Burton, Jr. (1966). *Sherman Act Indictments, 1955-1986*. New York, NY: Federal Legal Publications.

Clifford, M. (1998). *Environmental Crime: Enforcement, Policy, and Social Responsibility*. Gaithersburg, MA: Aspen.

Clinard, M. (1952). *The Black Market*. New York, NY: Rinehart.

Clinard, M. and R. Quinney (1973). "Corporate Criminal Behavior." In M. Clinard and R. Quinney (eds.) *Criminal Behavior Systems: A Typology*, Second Edition, pp. 206-223. New York, NY: Holt, Rinehart & Winston.

Clinard, M. and P. Yeager (1980). *Corporate Crime*. New York, NY: Free Press.

Clinard, M. and P. Yeager (1979). *Illegal Corporate Behavior*. Washington, DC: Law Enforcement Assistance Administration.

Coates, B. (1999). "Time to Shatter 'Free Trade' Myth." *The Observer*, 21(November) Business:6.

Cohen, M.G. (1996). "Women, Democracy and the Future of Nations." In R. Boyer and D. Drache (eds.) *States Against Markets: The Limits of Globalization*, pp. 383-414. London, UK: Routledge.

Cohen, N. (2000). "Without Prejudice." *The Observer*, (June 4):35.

Cohen, S. (1996). "Crime and Politics: Spot the Difference." *British Journal of Sociology*, 47:1-21.

Cohen, W. (1994). *Gaming the Health Care System: Billions of Dollars Lost to Fraud and Abuse Each Year*. U.S. Senate Special Committee on Aging.

Colborn, T., D. Dumanoski, and J. Myers (1997). *Our Stolen Future*. New York, NY: Plume.

Coleman, J. (1994). *The Criminal Elite*, Third Edition. New York, NY: St. Martin's Press.

Coleman, J. (1989). *The Criminal Elite*. New York, NY: St. Martin's Press.

Colmey, J. and D. Liebhold (1999). "It's All in the Family: A Time Investigation into Indonesia's Suharto and His Children Uncovers a $15 Billion Fortune." *Time*, (May 31):68-69.

Colodny, L. and R. Gettlin (1991) *Silent Coup: The Removal of a President*. New York, NY: St. Martin's Press.

Connors, J. (1999). "NGOs and the Human Rights of Women at the United Nations." In P. Willetts (ed.) *'The Conscience of the World': The Influence of Non-governmental Organizations in the UN System*, pp.147-180. Washington, DC: The Brookings Institution.

Cortese, A., E. Kline, and J. Smith (1994) *Second Nature Partnership Training Manual*.

Council of Churches for Britain and Ireland (1997). *Unemployment and the Future of Work. An Enquiry for the Churches*. London, UK: CCBI.

Cowe, R. (1999). "Wal-Mart Fuels European Mergers." *The Guardian*, (June 28):20.

Cowell, A. (1999). "Insurers Agree to Pay on Victims, Pre-Holocaust Policies." *The New York Times*, (May 7):A3.

Cox, E., R. Fellmuth, and J. Schultz (1969). *Nader's Raiders: Report on the Federal Trade Commission*. New York, NY: Grove Press.

Cox, R.W. (1994). "Global Restructuring: Making Sense of the Changing International Political Economy." In R. Stubbs and G.R. Underhill (eds.) *Political Economy and the Changing Global Order*.

Cox, R.W. (1993). "Structural Issues of Global Governance: Implications for Europe." In S. Gill (ed.) *Gramsci, Historical Materialism and International Relations*. Cambridge: Cambridge University Press.

Cray, C. and M. Harden (1998). "Environmental Justice in Louisiana." Environmental Research Foundation: Maryland. [On-line]. Available: http://www.rachel.org/bulletin/bulletin.cfm?Issue_ID=1012&bulletin_ID=48

Cressey, D.R. (1953). *Other People's Money: A Study in the Social Psychology of Embezzlement*. New York, NY: Free Press.

Cressey, D.R. (1988). "The Poverty of Theory in Corporate Crime Research." In F. Adler and W.S. Laufer (eds.) *Advances in Criminological Theory*, pp. 31-56. New Brunswick, NJ: Transaction.

Crooks, H. (1993). *Giants of Garbage*. Toronto, CN: Lorrimer.

Crouch, C. and W. Streeck (eds.) (1997). *Political Economy of Modern Capitalism. Mapping Convergence and Diversity*. London, UK: Sage.

Crown, J. (1980). "Exxon Steps Up Copper, Zinc Prospecting in Wisconsin." *American Metal Market*, 88(96):1.

Cullen, F.T., W. Maakestad, and G. Cavender (1987). *Corporate Crime Under Attack: The Ford Pinto Case and Beyond*. Cincinnati, OH: Anderson Publishing Co.

Currie, E. (1997). "Market, Crime and Community: Toward a Mid-Range Theory of Post-Industrial Violence." *Theoretical Criminology*, (May) 1(2).

Currie, E. (1990). *Heavy with Human Tears: Free Market Policy, Inequality and Social Provision in the United States*. In I. Taylor (ed.) *The Social Effects of Free Market Policies*. Hemel Hempstead: Harvester Wheatsheaf.

Dahrendorf, R. (1990). *Reflections on the Revolution in Europe*. London.

Daly, K. (1989). "Gender and Varieties of White-Collar Crime." *Criminology*, 27:769-793.

Danner, M., L. Fort, and G. Young (1999). "International Data on Women and Gender: Resources, Issues, Critical Use." *Women's Studies International Forum*, 22:249-59.

Danziger, E. (1990). *The Chippewa of Lake Superior*. Norman, OK: Oklahoma Press.

Davies, W. (1982). "Managing Political Vulnerability." *Engineering and Mining Journal*, 183(2):88.

Decision of Principle of the Finnish Government 22.10.1998 on the action plan to combat economic crime and the black economy.

Decision of Principle of the Finnish Government 1.2.1996 on the action plan to combat economic crime and the black economy.

Delaney, J. (1993). "Handcuffing Employee Theft." *Small Business Reports*, (July):29-37.

Denman, B. (2000). "Normandy Park Apartments Site Proposed Plan." USEPA-Region 4: Georgia.

Denny, C. (2000). "Legacy Left Britain with Worst Deprivation in West." *The Guardian*, (January 22):10.

Derber, C. (1992) *Money, Murder, and the American Dream: Wilding from Main Street to Wall Street*. Boston, MA: Farber & Farber.

Detroit Summer Coalition (1992). *Green Net*, 5(3):1-3.

Dicken, P. (1992). *Global Shift. The Internationalization of Economic Activity*. London, UK: Paul Chapman.

Dixon, D. (1997). *Law in Policing: Legal Regulation and Police Practices*. Oxford, UK: Clarendon Press.

Doedler de, E. and A.R. Hartmann (1999). "The Criminal Liability of Private and Public Corporations." *Turku Law Journal*, 1(1):75-92.

Domhoff, G.W. (1990). *The Power Elite and the State.* New York, NY: Aldine de Gruyter.

Domhoff, G.W. (1970). *The Higher Circles: The Governing Class in America*. New York, NY: Vintage.

Domhoff, G.W. (1967). *Who Rules America?* Englewood Cliffs, NJ: Prentice Hall.

Dorgan, M. (1977). "Indians Claim They Own Land Bearing Exxon Ore." *The Capital Times*, pp. 1-2. Madison, WI.

Dowd, D. (1993). *U.S. Capitalist Development Since 1776: Of, By, and For Which People?* New York, NY: M.E. Sharpe.

Dryzek, J. (1993). "From Sciences to Argument." In F. Fischer and J. Forester (eds.) *The Argumentative Turn in Policy Analysis and Planning*, pp. 10-15. Durham, NC: University Press.

Edmonds, J. (2000). "Third World Still Can't See Past Western Self-Interest." *The Guardian*, (April 17):21.

Ehrlich, P. and A. Ehrlich (1996). *Betrayal of Science and Reason: How Anti-Environmental Rhetoric Threatens Our Future*. Washington, DC: Island.

Eismeier, T. and P. Pollock, III (1988). *Business, Money, and the Crime of Corporate PACS in American Elections*. New York, NY: Quorum Books.

Eitzen, D. and M. Zinn (1992). *Social Problems*. Boston, MA: Allyn and Bacon.

Elliott, L. (1999). "Rise and Rise of the Super-Rich." *The Guardian*, (July 14):G2, 2-3.

Elliott, L. (1996). "Putting Trade in Its Place." *The Guardian*, May 27.

Erlanger, S. (1995). "A Corrupt Tide in Russia from State-Business Ties." *The New York Times*, (November 3):Al.

Esping-Anderson, G. (1999). *Social Foundations of Post-Industrial Economies*. Oxford, UK: Oxford University Press.

Evans, P. (1995). *Embedded Autonomy: States and Industrial Transformation*. Princeton, NJ: Princeton University Press.

Evans, T., F. Cullen, and P. Dubeck (1993). "Public Perceptions of Corporate Crime." In M. Blankenship (ed.) *Understanding Corporate Criminality*, pp. 85-114. New York, NY: Garland Publishing, Inc.

Ewall, M. (1998). "Environmental Racism in Chester." Campus Coalition Concerning Chester (C-4): Pennsylvania. [On-line]. Available: http://www.penweb.org/chester/ewall_article. html

Fagin, D. and M. Lavelle (1996). *Toxic Deception: How the Chemical Industry Manipulates Science, Bends the Law, and Endangers Your Health*. Birch Lane.

Faison, S. (1998). "China's Paragon of Corruption." *The New York Times*, (March 6):Cl.

Feminist Majority Foundation (1999). "Gender Apartheid in Afghanistan Fact Sheet." http://www.feminist.org/afghan/facts.html. (Retrieved June 27, 2000.)

Fine, B. (1990). *The Coal Question: Political Economy and Industrial Change from the Nineteenth Century to the Present Day*. London, UK: Routledge.

Fine, B., C. Lapavitsas, and D. Milonakis (1999). "Addressing the World Economy: Two Steps Back." *Capital & Class,* 67(Spring):47-90.

Fine, B. (1990). "Scaling the Commanding Heights of Public Enterprise Economics." *Cambridge Journal of Economics,* 14.

Finkelstein, M.J. (1989). *The American Academic Profession*. Columbus, OH: Ohio State University Press.

Fischer, F. and J. Forester (1993). *The Argumentative Turn in Policy Analysis and Planning*. Durham, NC: Duke University Press.

Fortune (2000). "1999 Fortune Global Five Hundred." http://www.fortune.com/fortune/ global500/index.html

Friedman, D. (1999). *The Lexus and the Olive Tree*. New York, NY: Farrar, Straus, Giroux.

Friedman, L.M. (1993). *Crime and Punishment in American History*. New York, NY: Basic Books.

Friedmann, W. (1967). *Legal Theory*. London, UK: Stevens & Sons.

Friedrichs, D. (ed.) (1998). *State Crime – Volumes I and II*. Aldershot, UK: Ashgate/Dartmouth.

Friedrichs, D. (ed.) (1998). *State Crime* Vol.1, Hants, England: Dartmouth Publishing Company Ltd.

Friedrichs, D. (1997). "The Downsizing of America: A Neglected Dimension of the White Collar Crime Problem." *Crime, Law & Social Change,* 16:351-366.

Friedrichs, D. (1996). *Trusted Criminals*. Belmont, CA: Wadsworth Publishing Company.

Friedrichs, D. (1996a). *Trusted Criminals: White Collar Crime in Contemporary Society*. Belmont, CA: ITP/Wadsworth Publishing Co.

Friedrichs, D. (1996b). "Governmental Crime, Hitler and White Collar Crime: A Problematic Relationship." *Caribbean Journal of Criminology and Social Psychology,* 2:44-63.

Friedrichs, D. (1995). "State Crime or Governmental Crime: Making Sense of the Conceptual Confusion." In J. Ross (ed.) *Controlling State Crime: An Introduction*, pp. 53-79. New York, NY: Garland Publishing, Inc.

Friedrichs, D.O. (1996). *Trusted Criminals: White Collar Crime in Contemporary Society.* Belmont. CA: Wadsworth.

Fritzell, J. (1993). "Income Inequality Trends in the 1980s: A Five Country Comparison." *Acta Sociologica*, 36:47-62.

Froud, J., C. Haslam, S. Johal, A. Leaver, J. Williams, and K. Williams (1999). "The Third Way and the Jammed Economy." *Capital & Class,* 67(Spring):155-166.

Fukuyama, F. (1992). *The End of History and the Last Man.* New York, NY: Avon Books.

Gallagher, A. (1997). "Ending the Marginalization: Strategies for Incorporating Women into the United Nations Human Rights System." *Human Rights Quarterly,* 19:283-333.

Gardiner, K. (1997). "A Survey of Income Inequality Over the Last Twenty Years – How Does the UK Compare?" In P. Gottschalk et al. (eds.) *Changing Patterns in the Distribution of Economic Welfare: An International Perspective*, pp. 36-59.

Gedicks, A. (1993). *The New Resource Wars: Native and Environmental Struggles Against Multinational Corporations.* Boston, MA: South End Press.

Gedicks, A. (1990, November). *Wisconsin's Resource Wars: The Chippewa Battle Kennecott.* Somerville, MA: Economic Affairs.

Gedicks, A. (1982). *Land Grab: The Corporate Theft of Wisconsin's Mineral Resources.* Madison, WI: Center for Alternative Mining Development.

Geis, G. (1991). "Sanctioning the Selfish: The Operation of Portugal's New Bad Samaritan Law." *International Review of Victimology,* 1:297-313.

Geis, G. (1967). "The Heavy Electrical Equipment Antitrust Case of 1961." In M.B. Clinard and R. Quinney (eds.) *Criminal Behavior Systems: A Typology*, pp. 139-150. New York, NY: Holt, Rinehart and Winston.

Geis, G., R.F. Meier, and L. Salinger (1995). "Introduction." In G. Geis, R.F. Meier, and L.M. Salinger (eds.) *White-Collar Crime. Classic and Contemporary Views*, pp. 1-19. New York, NY: The Free Press.

Geis, G. and L. Salinger (1998). "Antitrust and Organizational Deviance." In P.A. Bamberger and W.F. Sonnestuhl (eds.) *Research in the Sociology of Organizations: Deviance in and of Organizations*, pp. 74-110. Stamford, CT: JAI Press.

General Accounting Office (1995). *Hazardous and Nonhazardous Waste: Demographics of People Living Near Waste Facilities.* United States GAO (GAO/RCED-95-84): Washington, DC.

General Accounting Office (1983). *Siting of Hazardous Waste Landfills and Their Correlation with Racial and Economic Status of Surrounding Communities.* United States GAO (GAO/RCED-83-168): Washington, DC.

Gerring, J. (1999). "What Makes a Concept Good? A Criterial Framework for Understanding Concept Formation in the Social Sciences." *Polity,* 31:3.

Gibbs, L. (1995). *Dying from Dioxin.* Boston, MA: South End.

Gibbs, L. (1982). *Love Canal, My Story.* Albany, NY: State University of New York.

Giddens, A. (1999). "Globalization. BBC Reith Lectures 1999." http://news.bbc.c.uk/hi/English/static/events/rieth_99/week1/week1.htm

Gill, S. (1995). "Globalization, Market Civilization and Disciplinary Neoliberalism." *Millennium,* 24(3).

Gill, S. (1994). "Knowledge, Politics and Neo-Liberal Political Economy." In R. Stubbs and G.R.D. Underhill (eds.) *Political Economy and the Changing Global Order*. London, UK: Macmillan.

Gill, S. (1990). *American Hegemony and the Trilateral Commission*. Cambridge: Cambridge University Press.

Gill S. and D. Law (1993). "Global Hegemony and the Structural Power of Capital." In S. Gill (ed.) *Gramsci, Historical Materialism and International Relations*. Cambridge: Cambridge University Press.

Gill, S. and D. Law (1988). *The Global Political Economy*. Baltimore, MD: Johns Hopkins University Press.

Gills, B. (1997). "Whither Democracy?: Globalization and the 'New Hellenism.'" In C. Thomas and P. Wilkin (eds.) *Globalization and the South*. London, UK: Macmillan.

Glass, A. (1997). "The Young and the Feckless." *The New Republic,* (September 15).

Goldblatt, D. (1997). "At the Limits of Political Possibilities: The Cosmopolitan Democratic Project." *New Left Review*, 225(September/October):140-150.

Gottfredson, M. and T. Hirschi (1990). *A General Theory of Crime*. Stanford, CA: Stanford University Press.

Gottschalk, P. (1997). "Policy Changes and Growing Earnings Inequality in the U.S. and Six Other OECD Countries." In P. Gottschalk (eds.) *Changing Patterns in the Distribution of Economic Welfare: An International Perspective*, pp. 12-35.

Gottschalk, P., B. Gustafsson, and E. Palmer (eds.) (1997). *Changing Patterns in the Distribution of Economic Welfare: An International Perspective*. Cambridge: Cambridge University Press.

Gottschalk, P., B. Gustafsson, and E. Palmer (1997). "What's Behind the Increase in Inequality? An Introduction." In P. Gottschalk et al. (eds.) *Changing Patterns in the Distribution of Economic Welfare: An International Perspective*, pp. 1-11.

Gould, J. (1986). *Quality of Life in American Neighborhoods*. Boulder, CO: Westview Press.

Gowan, P. (1995). "Neo-Liberal Theory and Practice for Eastern Europe." *New Left Review,* 213(September/October).

Gramsci, A. (1971). *Selections from the Prison Notebooks of Antonio Gramsci*. Translated by Q. Hoare and G. Nowell Smith. New York, NY: International Publishers.

Gray, J. (1998). *False Dawn: The Delusions of Global Capitalism*. London, UK: Granta.

Great Lakes Indian Fish and Wildlife Commission (1993). *Chippewa Treaty Rights,* pp. 1-2. Odanah, WI.

Green, M., B. Monroe, and B. Wasserstein (1972). *The Closed Enterprise System: Ralph Nader's Study Group Report on Anti-Trust Enforcement*. New York, NY: Grossman.

Greenberg, J. (1997). "The STEAL Motive: Managing the Social Determinants of Employee Theft." In R. Giacalone and J. Greenberg (eds.) *Anti-social Behavior in Organizations*, pp. 85-108. Thousand Oaks, CA: Sage.

Greenberg, M. (1987). "Proving Environmental Inequity in Siting Locally Unwanted Land Uses." *Risk: Issues in Health and Safety*, 4(2):235-252.

Greer, J. and K. Bruno (1996). *Greenwash: The Reality Behind Corporate Environmentalism*. New York, NY: Apex.

Gregor, N. (1998). *Daimler-Benz in the Third Reich*. New Haven, CT: Yale University Press.

Greider, W. (1997). *One World, Ready or Not: The Manic Logic of Global Capitalism*. New York, NY: Simon and Schuster.

Gross, B. (1980). *Friendly Fascism: The New Face of Power in America*. New York, NY: M. Evans and Co.

Gross, E. (1980). "Organization Structure and Organizational Crime." In G. Geis and E. Stotland (eds.) *White-Collar Crime: Theory and Research*, pp. 52-76. Beverly Hills, CA: Sage.

Gustafsson, B. and E. Palmer (1997). "Changes in Swedish Inequality: A Study of Equivalent Income, 1975-1991." In P. Gottschalk et al. (eds.) *Changing Patterns in the Distribution of Economic Welfare: An International Perspective*, pp. 293-325.

Gustafsson, B. and H. Uusitalo (1990). "The Welfare State and Poverty in Finland and Sweden from the Mid-1960s to the Mid-1980s." *Review of Income and Wealth,* 36(3):249-266.

Hagan, F. (1994). *Introduction to Criminology*. Chicago, IL: Nelson-Hall.

Hagan, F. (1986). *Introduction to Criminology: Theories, Methods and Criminal Behavior.* Chicago, IL: Nelson-Hall.

Hagan, J., I. Nagel, and C. Albonetti (1980). "The Differential Sentencing of White-Collar Offenders in Ten Federal District Courts." *American Sociological Review,* 45(September):802-820.

Hagan, J. and P. Parker (1985). "White-Collar Crime and Punishment: The Class Structure and Legal Sanctioning of Securities Violations." *American Sociological Review,* 50:302-316.

Hagan, F. and D.R. Simon (1993). "Crimes of the Bush Era." Presented at the 1993 Meeting of the American Society of Criminology, New Orleans.

Hall, S. (1984). "Authoritarian Populism, Two Nations and Thatcherism." *New Left Review,* 147.

Hamilton, J. (1995). "Testing for Environmental Racism: Prejudice, Profits, Political Power." *Journal of Policy Analysis and Management,* 14(1):107-32.

Harman, C. (1996). "Globalization: A Critique of a New Orthodoxy." *International Socialism*, 73(Winter):3-33.

Hawkesworth, M. (1992). "Epistemology and Policy Analysis." In W. Dunn and R. Kelly (eds.) *Advances in Policy Studies Since 1950,* pp. 295-329). New Brunswick, NJ: Transaction Publishers.

Hay, C. (1999). *The Political Economy of New Labor*. London, UK: Unwin Hyman.

Hay, C. and M. Watson (1998). "The Discourse of Globalization and the Logic of No Alternative: Rendering the Contingent Necessary in the Downsizing of New Labour's Aspirations for Government." In A. Dobson and J. Stanyer (eds.) *Contemporary Political Studies 1998, Volume II*, pp. 812-822. Nottingham: Political Studies Association.

Hayes, P. (1998). "State Policy and Corporate Involvement in the Holocaust." In M. Berenbaum and A.J. Peck (eds.) *The Holocaust and History.* Washington, DC: United States Holocaust Memorial Museum.

Hayes, P. (1987). *Industry and Ideology: IG Farben in the Nazi Era.* New York, NY: Cambridge University Press.

Häyrynen, J. (1998). "Arvopaperien Liikkeeseenlasku ja Rikosoikeudellinen Vastuu." (On the Emission of Securities and Criminal Responsibility) In A. Alvesalo and R. Lahti (eds.) *Kirjoituksia Talousrikollisuudesta II*, (Essays On Economic Crime II), pp. 20-48. Poliisiammattikorkeakoulun tiedotteita 10/1999. Helsinki: Oy Edita Ab.

Hazard, G.C. (1993). "The Role of the Legal System in Responses to Public Risk." In E.J. Burger (ed.) *Risk*. Ann Arbor, MI: University of Michigan Press.

Hedley, R. (1999). "Transnational Corporations and Their Regulation: Issues and Strategies." *International Journal of Comparative Sociology,* 40:215-230.

Heilbroner, R. (1973). *In the Name of Profit: Profiles in Corporate Irresponsibility*. New York, NY: Warner Paperback Library.

Helleiner, E. (1996). "Post-Globalization: Is the Financial Liberalization Trend Likely to Be Reversed?" In R. Boyer and D. Drache (eds.) *States Against Markets. The Limits of Globalization*, pp. 193-210. London, UK: Routledge.

Henry, S. and M. Lanier (1998). "The Prism of Crime: Arguments for an Integrated Definition of Crime." *Justice Quarterly,* 15:612.

Hilberg, R, (1961). *The Destruction of the European Jews*. Chicago, IL: Quadrangle.

Hills, S. (ed.) (1987). *Corporate Violence*. Totowa, NJ: Rowman and Littlefield.

Hills, S. (1971). *Crime, Power, and Morality*. Scranton, PA: Chandler.

Hird, J. (1993). "Environmental Policy and Equity: The Case of Superfund." *Journal of Policy Analysis and Management,* 12(2):323-343.

Hirschhorn, J. (1997). "Two Superfund Environmental Justice Case Studies." Presented at the Air and Waste Management Association's 90th Annual Meeting and Exhibition, Toronto, Ontario, Canada. [On-line]. Available: http: //www.igc.org/envjustice/hirschhorn.html

Hirschi, T. and M. Gottfredson (1987): "Causes of White Collar Crime." *Criminology*, 25(4):949-974.

Hirst, P.Q. (1996). *Globalization In Question: The International Economy And The Possibilities Of Governance*. Cambridge, MA: Blackwell Publishers.

Hirst, P.Q. (1979). *On Law and Ideology*. London, UK: Macmillan.

Hirst, P.Q. (1972). "Marx and Engels on Law, Crime and Morality." *Economy and Society* (1)(February):1.

Hirst, P.Q. and G.F. Thompson (1999). *Globalization in Question: The International Economy and the Possibilities for Governance*, Second Edition. Cambridge, UK: Polity Press.

Hirst, P.Q. and G. Thompson (1996). *Globalization in Question*. Cambridge, UK: Polity Press.

Hirst, P.Q. and G. Thompson (1992). "The Problem of Globalization." *Economy and Society,* (4)(November):21.

Hobson, J.M. (1997). *The Wealth of States: A Comparative Study of International Economic and Political Change*. New York, NY: Cambridge University Press.

Holden, C. (1999). "Globalization: Social Exclusion and Labour's New Work Ethic." *Critical Social Policy*, 19(4):529-538.

Holloway, J. (1994). "Global Capital and the Nation-State." *Capital & Class,* (Spring):52.

Honkonen, R. (1999). *Poliisi ja Opintoviikon Metsästys*. (Police and the Hunting of Credits) Koulutus Pollisimiehen Elämässä. Tampere: Tampereen Yliopistopaino Oy.

HONOR Digest (1994). "Sinsinawa Dominicans Lead Shareholders' Challenge of Crandon Mine." 5(5):10.

Hoogvelt, A. (1996). *Globalization and the Postcolonial World: The New Political Economy of Development*. Houndmills, Basingstoke, Hampshire: Macmillan.

Howard, P. (1994). *The Death of Common Sense: Suffocating America*. New York, NY: Random House.

Hughes, A. (1992). "Big Business, Small Business and the 'Enterprise Culture.'" In Michie (ed.) *The Economic Legacy 1979-1992*. London, UK: The Academic Press.

Human Rights Watch (2000a). "Women's Human Rights." *World Report 2000*. Human Rights Watch (http:www.hrw.org/wr2k/)

Human Rights Watch (2000b). "Corporations and Human Rights." World Report 2000. *Human Rights Watch* (http:www.hrw.org/wr2k/)

Hunt, A. (1993). *Explorations in Law and Society: Towards a Constitutive Theory of Law*. London, UK: Routledge.

Hunt, A. (1986). "The Theory of Critical Legal Studies." *Oxford Journal of Legal Studies*, 6:11-37.

Hunt, A. (1985). "The Ideology of Law: Advances and Problems in Recent Applications of the Concept of Ideology to the Analysis of Law." *Law and Society Review*, 19(1):11-37.

Instructions for the victim in the Internet pages of the Finnish Police.WWW document *http://www.poliisi.fi/english/index.htm*. Read 20.2.2000

International Labor Organization (1997). "Sex Industry Assuming Massive Proportions in Southeast Asia," ILO Press Release, August 19. Geneva: International Labor Organization.

International Women's Tribune Centre (1997). *Rights of Women: A Guide to the Most Important United Nations Treaties on Women's Human Rights*. New York, NY: International Women's Tribune Centre.

Interview of David O. Friedrichs, Professor of Sociology and Criminal Justice, University of Scranton, Scranton, Pennsylvania (1998). *Corporate Crime Reporter,* 12(46): 11-16.

Interview of the Finnish Minister of Interiors, Kari Häkämies 2.2.2000 on the National (Suomen Yleisradio) Radio News.

Jaatinen, H. (1999): "Corporate Criminal Liability and Neo-Classical Criminal Policy." *Turku Law Journal,* 1(1):103-108.

Jachcel, E. (1981). "Towards a Criminological Analysis of the Origins of Capital." Ph.D. Dissertation, University of Sheffield.

Jackson, P.M. and C.M. Price (eds.) (1994). *Privatization and Regulation. A Review of the Issues*. London, UK: Longman.

Jamieson, K.M. (1994). *The Organization of Corporate Crime: Dynamics of Antitrust Violations*. Thousand Oaks, CA: Sage.

Jantti, M. and V.M. Ritakallio (1997). "Income Inequality and Poverty in Finland in the 1980s." In P. Gottschalk et al. (eds.) *Changing Patterns in the Distribution of Economic Welfare: An International Perspective*, 326-350.

Jeffery-Jones, R. (1989). *The CIA and American Democracy*. New Haven, CT: Yale University Press.

Jeffreys, S. (1996). "France 1995: The Backward March of Labor Halted?" *Capital & Class,* 52.

Jesilow, P., H. Pontell, and G. Geis (1985). "Medical Criminals: Physicians and White Collar Offenses." *Justice Quarterly,* 2:149-158.

Jessop, B. (1990). *State Theory: Putting Capitalist States in Their Place*. Cambridge, UK: Polity Press.

Jessop, B. (1982). *The Capitalist State*. Oxford: Martin Robertson.

Jessop, B., K. Bonnett, S. Bromley, and T. Ling (1988). *Thatcherism: A Tale of Two Nations*. Cambridge, UK: Polity Press.

Johnston, M. (1996). "The Search for Definitions: The Vitality of Politics and the Issue of Corruption." *International Social Science Journal,* 149:321-336.

Jones, K. (1982). *Law and Economy: The Legal Regulation of Corporate Capital*. London, UK: Academic Press.

Josephson, M. (1934, 1962). *The Robber Barons: The Great American Capitalist, 1861-1901*. New York, NY: Harcourt, Brace & World.

Jospin, L. (1999). "Only on Our Terms." *The Guardian*, (November 16):17.

Kappeler, V., M. Blumberg, and G.W. Potter (1993) *The Mythology of Crime and Criminal Justice*. Prospect Heights, IL: Waveland Press.

Karliner, J. (1997). *The Corporate Planet: Ecology and Politics in the Age of Globalization*. San Francisco, CA: Sierra Club Books.

Katz, J. (1980). "The Social Movement Against White-Collar Crime." In E. Bittner and S. Messinger (eds.) *Criminology Review Yearbook. Volume 2*, pp. 161-184. Beverly Hills, CA: Sage.

Kauzlarich, D. and R. Kramer (1998). *Crimes of the American Nuclear State: At Home and Abroad*. Boston, MA: Northeastern University Press.

Kauzlarich, D. and R. Kramer (1998). *Crimes of the American Nuclear State*. Boston, MA: Northeastern University Press.

Kearns, R. (1998). "Chester Lawsuit Declared Moot by U.S. Supreme Court: Environmental Justice Still Doable Through Courts Despite Recent Supreme Court Decision." Chester Residents Concerned for Quality Living: Pennsylvania. [On-line]. Available: http://www.penweb.org/chester/moot.html

Kelly, K. (1992). "How Did Sears Blow This Gasket? Some Say the Retailer's Push for Profits Spurred its Auto-Repair Woes." *Business Week*, (June 29):38.

Kelman, M. (1982). "Criminal Law: The Origins of Crime and Criminal Violence." In D. Kairys (ed.) (1982). *The Politics of Law. A Progressive Critique*. New York, NY: Pantheon Books.

Kempadoo, K. and J. Dozema (1997). *Global Sex Workers: Rights, Resistance and Redefinition*. London, UK: Routledge.

Kewley, M. (1990). "Band Opposes Mine on Spiritual Grounds." *Wassau Daily Herald* (July 16):A4.

Kiander, J. and P. Vartia (1996). "The Great Depression of the 1990s in Finland." *Finnish Economic Papers,* 9(1):72-88.

Knox, M. (1993). "Their Mother's Keepers." *Sierra Magazine*, 78(2):50.

Knox, P. and J. Agnew (1989). *The Geography of the World Economy*. London, UK: Edward Arnold.

Kofman, E. and G. Youngs (eds.) *Globalization Theory and Practice*. London, UK: Pinter.

Kolko, G. (1963). *The Triumph of Conservatism*. New York, NY: Free Press.

Kolko, G. (1962). *Wealth and Power in America: An Analysis of Social Class and Income Distribution*. New York, NY: Praeger.

Korander, T. (forthcoming Ph.D. Dissertation): "The Finnish Police Culture." (working title). Department of Social Sciences. University of Kuopio.

Korten, D.C. (1996). *Globalizing Civil Society: Reclaiming Our Right to Power*. New York, NY: Seven Stories Press.

Korten, D.C. (1995). *When Corporations Rule the World*. West Hartford, CT: Kumerian Press.

Korzeniewicz, R.P. and T.P. Moran (1997). "World-Economic Trends in the Distribution of Income." 1965-1992. *American Journal of Sociology*, (January):102(4).

Kramer, R. (1992). "The Space Shuttle Challenger Explosion: A Case Study of State-Corporate Crime." In K. Schiegel and D. Weisburd (eds.) *White-Collar Crime Reconsidered*, pp. 214-243. Boston, MA: Northeastern University Press.

Kramer, R. (1984). "Corporate Criminality: The Development of an Idea." In E. Hochstedler (ed.) *Corporations as Criminals*. Beverly Hills, CA: Sage.

Kramer, R.C. and R.J. Michalowski (1990). "State-Corporate Crime." Paper presented at the Annual Meeting of the American Society of Criminology, Baltimore, November 7-12, 1990.

Kreig, E. (1995). "A Socio-Historical Interpretation of Toxic Waste Sites." *The American Journal of Economics and Sociology*, 54(1):1-14.

Lacey, N. (1995) "Contingency and Criminalisation." In I. Loveland (ed.) *Frontiers of Criminality*. London, UK: Sweet and Maxwell.

LaDuke, W. (1993). "A Society Based on Conquest Cannot Be Sustained." In A. Gedicks (ed.) *The New Resource Wars: Native Struggles Against Multinational Corporations* (forward). Boston, MA: South End Press.

Lahti, R. (1997): "Rikoslain Kokoanaisuudistuksen Ensimmäinen Vaihe: Varallisuus- ja Talousrikossäännökset." (The First Phase of The Total Reform of The Penal Code). In Lahti (ed.): *Nykyajan Rikosoikeus* (Contemporary Criminal Law), pp. 95-190. Rikosoikuden Julkaisuja 4. Helsinki, Herlsingin yliopiston rikos-ja prosessioikeuden sekä oikeuden yleistieteiden laitos.

Laitinen A. and A. Alvesalo (1994): *Talouden Varjopuoli*. (The Dark Side of Economy). Helsinki: Sisäasiainministeriön poliisiosasto. Poliisin oppikirjasarja.

Larzarsfeld, P.F. and W. Thielens, Jr. (1958). *The Academic Mind*. Illinois: The Free Press of Glencoe.

Lavalle, M. and M. Coyle (1992). "Unequal Protection: The Racial Divide in Environmental Law: A Special Edition." *National Law Journal*, (September 21):S1-S12.

Lazarus, N. (1998/99). "Charting Globalization." *Race & Class*, 40(2/3):92-109.

Lee, M.T. and M.D. Ermann (1999). "Pinto 'Madness' as a Flawed Landmark Narrative of Organizational and Network Analysis." *Social Problems,* 46:30-48.

Lee, P. Nan-Shong (1990). "Bureaucratic Corruption During the Den Xiaoping Era." *Corruption and Reform,* 5:29-47.

Levi, M. (1995). "Serious Fraud in Britain: Criminal Justice Versus Regulation." In F. Pearce and L. Snider (ed.) *Corporate Crime: Contemporary Debates.*

Levi, M. and L. Osofsky (1995). "Investigating, Seizing and Confiscating the Proceeds of Crime." *Crime Detection & Prevention Series.* Paper 61. London, UK: Police Research Group.

Lewis, C. (1998). *The Buying of Congress.* New York, NY: Avon Books.

Lewis, L.S. (1975). *Scaling the Ivory Tower.* Baltimore MD: The John Hopkins University Press.

Lloyd, J. (1999). "The Russian Devolution." *The New York Times Magazine,* (August 15):34+.

Lo, T.W. (1993). *Corruption and Politics in Hong Kong and China.* Buckingham, UK: Open University Press.

Lofquist, W. (1998). "Constructing 'Crime': Media Coverage of Individual and Organizational Wrongdoing." *Justice Quarterly,* 14:243-263.

Lohr, S. (1990). "At the End of a Twisted Trail, Piggy Bank for a Favored Few." *The New York Times,* (August 12):Al.

Lorentzen, L.A. and J. Turpin (1996). "Introduction: The Gendered New World Order." In *The Gendered New World Order: Militarism, Development and the Environment*, pp. 1-11. London, UK: Routledge.

Lowi, T.J. (1993). In E.J. Burger (ed.) *Risk*. Ann Arbor, MI: University of Michigan Press.

Lynch, M. and P. Stretesky (1999a). "Criticism and Clarifying the Analysis of Environmental Justice: Further Thoughts on the Critical Analysis of Environmental Justice Issues." *The Critical Criminologist,* 9(3):5-8.

Lynch, M. and P. Stretesky (1999b). "Conspiracy, Deception and Misinformation." *The Critical Criminologist,* 10(1):14-18.

Lyons, K. (1979). "A First Environmental Case." Unpublished paper.

MacEwan, A. (1999). *Neo-Liberalism or Democracy? Economic Strategy, Markets and Alternatives for the 21st Century*. London, UK: Zed Books.

MacGregor, S. (1999). "Welfare, Neo-Liberalism and New Paternalism: Three Ways for Social Policy in Late Capitalist Societies." *Capital & Class,* 67(Spring):47, 91-118.

Madeley, J. (1999). *Big Business, Poor Peoples: The Impact of Transnational Corporations on the World's Poor*. London, UK: Zed Books.

Madison Treaty Rights Support Group (n.d.). *Pamphlet.*

Magdoff, H. (1992) "Globalization – To What End?" In R. Miliband and L. Panitch (eds.) *Socialist Register 1992*. London, UK: The Merlin Press.

Mahon, R. (1979). "Regulatory Agencies: Captive Agents or Hegemonic Apparatuses." *Studies in Political Economy,* 1, (1).

Manchester, W. (1968). *The Arms of Krupp*. Boston, MA: Little Brown.

Mander, J. (1991). *In the Absence of the Sacred: The Failure of Technology and the Survival of the Indian Nations*. San Francisco, CA: Sierra Club Books.

Mander, J. and E. Goldsmith (1996). *The Case Against the Global Economy*. San Francisco, CA: Sierra Club Books.

Marfleet, P. (1998). "Globalization and the Third World." *International Socialism,* 81(Winter):91-130.

Matthews, R. and D. Kauzlarich (1997). "The FAA and ValuJet: A Case Study in State-Facilitated Crime." Paper presented at the Annual Meeting of the American Society of Criminology, San Diego, November.

May, E. and R. Shilling (1977). "Case Study of Environmental Impact–Flambeau Project." *Mining Congress Journal*, p. 39.

Mayer, A.E. (1995). "Cultural Particularism as a Bar to Women's Rights: Reflections on the Middle Eastern Experience." In J. Peters and A. Wolper (eds.) *Women's Rights, Human Rights: International Feminist Perspectives*, pp. 176-188. New York, NY: Routledge.

Mayer, A. and J. Bishop (1976). "Antitrust: Snap, Crackle and Pop." *Newsweek*, (June 14):14.

McCormick, A., Jr. (1977). "Rule Enforcement and Moral Indignation: Some Observations on the Effects of Criminal Antitrust Convictions Upon Societal Reaction Process." *Social Problems*, 25:30-39.

Melossi, D. (1994): "The 'Economy' of Illegalities: Normal Crimes, Elites and Social Control in Comparative Analysis." In E. Nelken (ed.) *The Futures of Criminology*. London, UK: Sage Publications.

Mensman, C. (1999). "Pro Bono Publico: Its History, Development, and Future." Louisiana State University Law Center: Louisiana. [On-line]. Available: http://www.law.lsu.edu/library/ELS.html

Meny, Y. (1996). ""Fin de siecle" Corruption: Change, Crisis, and Shifting Values." *International Social Science Journal*, 149:321-336.

Merton, R.K. (1964). "Anomie, Anomia, and Social Integration: Contexts of Deviant Behavior." In M.B. Clinard (ed.) *Anomie and Deviant Behavior: A Discussion and Critique*, pp. 213-242. New York, NY: Free Press.

Messerschmidt, J. (1986). *Capitalism, Patriarchy, and Crime: Toward a Socialist Feminist Criminology*. Totowa, NJ: Rowman and Littlefield.

Messner, S. and R. Rosenfeld (1994). *Crime and the American Dream*. Monterey, CA: Wadsworth.

Metzger, W.P. (1955). *Academic Freedom in the Age of the University*. New York, NY: Columbia University Press.

Michalowski, R. (1990). "A Critical Model for the Study of Crime." In D. Kelly (ed.) *Criminal behavior: Text and Readings in Criminology,* Second Edition, p. 196. New York, NY: St. Martin's Press.

Michalowski, R.J. and R.C. Kramer (1987). "The Space Between the Laws: The Problem of Corporate Crime in a Transnational Context." *Social Problems,* 34:34-53.

Michie, J. and J. Grieve Smith (eds.) (1999). *Global Instability. The Political Economy of World Governance*. London, UK: Routledge.

Midwest Treaty Network (n.d.). "Wisconsin Treaties: What's the Problem?" *Pamphlet*, p. 3.

Millen, J.V. and T.H. Holtz (2000). "Dying for Growth, Part I: Transnational Corporations and the Health of the Poor." In J. Yong Kim, J.V. Millen, A. Irwin, and J. Gershman (eds.) *Dying for Growth: Global Inequality and the Health of the Poor*, pp. 177-223. Monroe, Maine: Common Courage Press.

Miller, P. and N. Rose (1990). *Governing Economic Life. Economy and Society*. 19(February):1.

Mills, C. (1952). "A Diagnosis of Moral Uneasiness." In I. Horowitz (ed.) *Power, Politics and People*, pp. 330-339. New York, NY: Ballantine.

Mills, C. (1956, 1959). *The Power Elite*. New York, NY: Oxford University Press.

Minda, G. (1995). *Postmodern Legal Movements. Law and Jurisprudence at Century's End*. New York, NY: New York University Press.

Mintz, M. and J. Cohen (1988). *Power, Inc.:Public and Private Rulers and How to Make Them Accountable*. New York, NY: The Viking Press.

Mishra, R. (1999). *Globalization and the Welfare State*. Cheltenham: Edward Elgar.

Mohai, P. and B. Bryant (1992). "Environmental Racism: Reviewing the Evidence." In P. Mohai and B. Bryant (eds.), *Race and the Incidence of Environmental Hazards: A Time for Discourse,* pp. 163-176. Boulder, CO: Westview.

Mokhiber, R. (1988). *Corporate Crime and Violence*. San Francisco, CA: Sierra Club Books.

Mokhiber, R. and R. Weissman (1999a). *Corporate Predators. The Hunt for Mega-Profits and the Attack on Democracy*. Monroe, ME: Common Courage.

Mokhiber, R. and R. Weissman (1999b). "Electronic Ankle Bracelets Anyone?" *Focus on the Corporation*. http://lists.essential.org/focus, September 21: four pages.

Mokhiber, R. and R. Weissman (1999c). "Make Lots of Money and Avoid Paying Taxes." *Focus on the Corporation*. http://lists.essential.org/focus, June 8: three pages.

Mokhiber, R. and R. Weissman (1999d). "The Trouble with Larry." *Focus on the Corporation*. http://lists.essential.org/focus, May 18: three pages.

Mokhiber, R. and R. Weissman (1999e). "A Moment of Silence." *Focus on the Corporation*. http://lists.essential.org/focus, May 4: three pages.

Mokhiber, R. and R. Weissman (1999f). "Banana Republic." *Focus on the Corporation*. http://lists.essential.org/focus, April 7, three pages.

Moran, J. (1998). "The Dynamics of Class Politics and National Economies in Globalization: the Marginalisation of the Unacceptable." *Capital & Class,* 66:53-83.

Moseley, F. (1999a). "The United States at the Turn of the Century: Entering a New Era of Prosperity." *Capital & Class,* 67(Spring):25-45.

Moseley, F. (1999b). "The Decline of the Rate of Profit in the Post-War United States Economy: Due to Increased Competition or Increased Unproductive Labor?" *Historical Materialism,* 4, Summer, 131-148.

Moseley, F. (1997). "The Rate of Profit and Economic Stagnation in the United States Economy." *Historical Materialism,* 1, Autumn, 161-174.

Mueller, G. and F. Adler (1985). *Outlaws of the Ocean*. New York, NY: Hearst Maritime Books.

Multinational Monitor (1997). "Beat the Devil: The Ten Worst Corporations of 1997." (December):18, 12.

Multinational Monitor (1996). "The Ten Worst Corporations of 1996." (December):17, 12.

Multinational Monitor (1995). "Shameless: 1995's 10 Worst Corporations." (December):16, 12.

Nader, R. (1985). "America's Crime Without Criminals." *New York Times*, (May 19):F3.

Nader, R. (1982). "Approaching Strategy for Confronting the Corporate Threat." *Akwesasne Notes*, 14(6):5.

Nader, R. and R. Brownstein (1980). "Beyond Love Canal." *The Progressive*, 44(May):28, 10.

Nader, R., M. Green, and J. Seligman (1976). *Taming the Giant Corporation*. New York, NY: Norton.

Nader, R. and W. Smith (1996). *No Contest: Corporate Lawyers and the Perversion of Justice in America*. New York, NY: Random House.

Nagel, I.H. and W.M. Swenson (1993). "The Federal Sentencing Guidelines for Corporations: Their Development, Theoretical Underpinnings, and Some Thoughts About Their Future." *Washington University Law Quarterly*, 71:205-259.

National Research Council (1995). *Neem, A Tree for Solving Global Problems*. Washington, DC: National Academy.

Navarro, V. (1999). "The Political Economy of The Welfare State in Developed Capitalist Countries." *International Journal of Health Services*, 29(1):1-50.

Nelson, P.J. (1996). "Internationalizing Economic and Environmental Policy: Transnational NGO Networks and the World Bank's Expanding Influence." *Millennium*, 24(3).

Neocleous, M. (1999). "Radical Conservatism, or the Conservatism of Radicals. Giddens, Blair and the Politics of Reaction." *Radical Philosophy*, 93, (January/February):24-34.

New York Times (1990). "Corporate Tax Cheating Seen." (April 18):6.

Nikolic-Ristanovic,V. (1996). "War and Violence Against Women." In J. Turpin and L.A. Lorentzen (eds.) *The Gendered New World Order: Militarism, Development and the Environment*, pp. 195-210. New York, NY: Routledge.

Noonan, J., Jr. (1984). *Bribes*. Berkeley, CA: University of California Press.

Nuutila, A. (1996): *Rikosoikeudellinen Huolimattomuus*. Helsinki: Kauppakaari Oy, Lakimiesliiton Kustannus.

O'Malley, P. (1987). "In Place of Criminology: A Marxist Reformulation." Paper presented to the Annual Meeting of the Canadian Sociology and Anthropology Association, Hamilton, Ontario, 2-5 June.

Oakes, J., D. Anderton, and A. Anderson (1996). "A Longitudinal Analysis of Environmental Equity in Communities with Hazardous Waste Facilities." *Social Science Research*, 25(1):125- 148.

OECD (2000). "OECD Statistics." *Gross Domestic Product*. http://www.oecd.org/std/gdp.htm

Oikeusministeriön lainvalmisteluosaston julkaisu 20/(1988) (Publication of the Ministery of Justice's law drafting department). Oikeushenkilön rangaistusvastuu. Tiivistelmä lausunnoista. (On the liability of a legal person. Summary of statements). Helsinki, 1988.

Oppenheim, C. and L. Harker (1996). *Poverty. The Facts*. London, UK: Child Poverty Action Group.

Otto, D. (1999). "Subalternity and International Law: The Problems of Global Community and the Incommensurability of Difference." In E. Darian-Smith and P. Fitzpatrick (eds.) *Laws of the Postcolonial*, pp. 145-180. Ann Arbor, MI: University of Michigan Press.

Pacific Asia Resource Center (1994). *The People vs Global Capital. The G-7, TNCs, SAPs and Human Rights*. ARENA: Hong Kong.

Pashukhanis, E. (1978). *Law and Marxism*. London, UK: Inklinks.

Passas, N. (1996). "The Genesis of the BCCI Scandal." *Journal of Law and Society,* 23:5-72.

Passas, N. (1993). "Structural Sources of International Crime: Policy Lessons from the BCCI Affair." *Crime, Law and Social Change,* 20:293-309.

Pauly, L.W. (1994). "Promoting a Global Economy: The Normative Role of the International Monetary Fund." In R. Stubbs and G.R. Underhill (eds.) *Political Economy and the Changing Global Order*.

Pearce, F. (2000). "Crime and Capitalist Business Corporations." In N. Shover and P.J. Wright (eds.) *Crimes of Privilege*. New York, NY: Oxford University Press.

Pearce, F. (1989). *The Radical Durkheim*. London, UK: Unwin-Hyman.

Pearce, F. (1976). *Crimes of the Powerful: Marxism, Crime and Deviance*. London, UK: Pluto Press.

Pearce, F. (1973). "Crime, Corporations and the American Social Order." In I. Taylor and L. Taylor (eds.) *Politics and Deviance*. Harmondsworth: Penguin.

Pearce, F. and L. Snider (1995). "Regulating Capitalism." In F. Pearce and L. Snider (eds.) *Corporate Crime: Contemporary Debates*.

Pearce, F. and L. Snider (eds.) (1995). *Corporate Crime: Contemporary Debates*. Toronto, CN: University of Toronto Press.

Pearce, F. and S. Tombs (1998). *Toxic Capitalism: Corporate Crime and the Chemical Industry*. Aldershot: Ashgate.

Pearce, F. and S. Tombs (1996). "Hegemony, Risk and Governance: "Social" Regulation and the U.S. Chemical Industry." *Economy and Society,* (3)(August):25.

Pearce, F. and S. Tombs (1995). "Ideology, Hegemony and Empiricism: Compliance Theories of Regulation." *British Journal of Criminology,* (Autumn):423-443.

Pekkarinen, J. (1997). "Corporatism and Economic Performance in Sweden, Norway and Finland." In J. Pekkarinen, M. Pohjola, and B. Rowthorn (eds.) *Social Corporatism – a Superior Economic System?*, pp. 298-337. Oxford: Clarendon Press.

Peltier, L. (1992). Statement made to *Native Support Network News*, Grassroots publication, (April):3.

Perraton, J., D. Goldblatt, D. Held, and A. McGrew (1997). "The Globalization of Economic Activity." *New Political Economy*, 2(2):257-277.

Peshek, P. and T. Dawson (1981). "The Role of an Attorney in a Wetlands Destruction Case." In A. Gedicks, *The New Resource Wars: Native and Environmental Struggles Against Multinational Corporations*. Boston, MA: South End Press.

Peterson, M. (1989). "An Historical Perspective on the Incidence of Piracy." In E. Ellen (ed.) *Piracy at Sea. Paris*, pp. 41-60. International Maritime Bureau.

Peterson, V.S. and A. Sisson Runyan (1999). *Global Gender Issues*. Boulder, CO: Westview Press.

Petras, J. (1997). "Latin America: The Resurgence of the Left." *New Left Review,* 223(May/June):17-47.

Petras, J. and Morley (1990) *U.S. Hegemony Under Siege: Class, Politics and Development in Latin America*. London, UK: Verso.

Pfohl, S. (1994). *Images of Deviance and Social Control: A Sociological History,* Second Edition. New York, NY: McGraw-Hill.

Picciotto, S. (1997). "Fragmented States and International Rules of Law." *Social & Legal Studies,* 6, (2).

Picciotto, S. (1994). "Transfer Pricing and the Antinomies of Corporate Regulation." In J. McCahery, S. Picciotto, and C. Scott (eds.) *Corporate Control and Accountability. Changing Structures and the Dynamics of Regulation*, pp. 375-405. Oxford: Clarendon.

Picciotto, S. (1991). "The Internationalization of the State." *Capital & Class,* (Spring):43.

Pietilä, H. and J. Vickers (1990). *Making Women Matter: The Role of the United Nations*. London, UK: Zed.

Pizzo, S. et al. (1991). *Inside Job: The Looting Of America's Savings and Loans*. New York, NY: Harper Collins.

Poclad (1988). "Engage Us." *Program on Corporations, Law and Democracy*.

Pollin, R. (2000). "Anatomy of Clintonomics." *New Left Review,* (May/June):17-46.

Pollock, P. and E. Vittas (1995). "Who Bears the Burdens of Environmental Pollution? Race, Ethnicity, and Environmental Equity in Florida." *Social Science Quarterly,* 76(2):294-327.

Pontell, H.N., K. Calavita, and R. Tillman (1994). "Corporate Crime and Criminal Justice System Capacity: Government Response to Financial Institution Fraud." *Justice Quarterly,* 11(3):383-410.

Pontell, H., P. Jesilow, and G. Geis (1982). "Policing Physicians: Practitioner Fraud and Abuse in a Government Medical Program." *Social Problems,* 30:117-135.

Posner, R.A. (1970). "A Statistical Study of Antitrust Enforcement." *Journal of Law and Economics,* 13:365-419.

Potter, G. and V. Kappeler (1998). *Constructing Crime: Perspectives on Making News and Social Problems*. Prospect Heights, IL: Waveland Press, Inc.

Poulantzas, N. (1974). *Fascism and Dictatorship*. London, UK: New Left Books.

Poulantzas, N. (1973). *Classes in Contemporary Capitalism*. London, UK: New Left Books.

Poulantzas, N. (1973). *Political Power and Social Classes*. London, UK: New Left Books.

Prados, J. (1986). *Presidents's Secret Wars: CIA and Pentagon Covert Operations from World War II through Iranscram*. New York, NY: Morrow.

Price, C.M. (1994). "Privatization in Less Developed Countries." In P.M. Jackson and C.M. Price (eds.) *Privatization and Regulation: A Review of the Issues*.

Prügl, E. and M. Meyer (1999). "Gender Politics in Global Governance." In M.K. Meyer and E. Prügl (eds.) *Gender Politics in Global Governance*, pp. 3-16. New York, NY: Rowman and Littlefield.

Radice, H. (2000). "Responses to Globalization: A Critique of Progressive Nationalism." *New Political Economy,* 5(1):5-19.

Ramirez, O. (1992). "The Year of Indigenous Peoples." *Social Justice: A Journal of Crime, Conflict and World Order*, 19(2):78-86.

Rao, A. (1995). "The Politics of Gender and Culture in International Human Rights Discourse." In J. Peters and A. Wolper (eds.) *Women's Rights, Human Rights: International Feminist Perspectives*, pp. 167-175. New York, NY: Routledge.

Reed, G.F. and P.C. Yeager (1996). "Organizational Offending and Neoclassical Criminology: Challenging the Reach of a General Theory of Criminology," *Criminology*, 34:357-382.

Reiman, J. (1997). *The Rich Get Richer and the Poor Get Prison. Ideology, Class and Criminal Justice*. Boston, MA: Allyn and Bacon.

Reiner, R. (1989) "The Politics of Police Research in Britain." In Weatheritt (ed.) *Police Research. Some Future Prospects*. Published in association with The Police Foundation. Avebury: Gower.

Reiss, Jr., A.J. and A. Biderman (1990). *Data Sources on White-Collar Law-Breaking*. Washington, DC: National Institute of Justice, U.S. Department of Justice.

Reschler, N. (1997). *Objectivity, the Obligations of Impartial Reason*. Notre Dame, IN: University of Notre Dame Press.

Rich, F. (1998). "What's Good for General Motors . . ." *The New York Times*, (December 2):A27.

Rifkin, J. (2000). *The Age of Access: The New Culture of Hypercapitalism Where All of Life is a Paid-For Experience*. New York, NY: Jeremy P. Tarcher/Putnam.

Rifkin, J. (1998). *The Biotech Century*. New York, NY: Putnam.

Ringquist, E. (1997). "Equity and the Distribution of Environmental Risk: The Case of TRI Facilities." *Social Science Quarterly*, 78(4):811-29.

Robertson, R. (1992). *Globalization: Social Theory and Practice*. London, UK: Sage.

Robinson, W. (1998/99). "Latin America and Global Capitalism." *Race & Class*, 40, 2/3, 111-131.

Robinson, W. (1996). "Beyond Nation-State Paradigms: Globalization, Sociology, and the Challenge of Transnational Studies." *Sociological Forum*, 13:561-594.

Rodda, A. (1991). *Women and the Environment*. London, UK: Zed Books.

Ross, J.I. (ed.) (1995). *Controlling State Crime*. New York, NY: Garland Publishing, Inc.

Rosset, P. and M. Benjamin (1994). *The Greening of the Revolution: Cuba's Experiment with Organic Agriculture*. Melbourne, Australia: Ocean.

Roy, A.N. (1999) *The Third World in the Age of Globalization. Requiem or New Agenda?* London, UK: Zed Books.

Rudovsky, D. (1982). "The Criminal Justice System and the Role of the Police." In D. Kairys (ed.) (1982). *The Politics of Law: A Progressive Critique*. New York, NY: Pantheon Books.

Ruigrock, W. and R. van Tulder (1995). *The Logic of International Restructuring*. London, UK: Routledge.

Rusk County Citizens Action Group (n.d.). *Pamphlet*.

Sale, K. (1990). *The Conquest of Paradise*. New York, NY: Knopf.

Salminen, M. (1998). *Velallisen Rikos*. (Crime of the Debtor) Porvoo: WSOY.

Sanger, D. (1997). "Swiss Find More Bank Accounts from the War, and Publish List." *The New York Times*, (July 23):A1.

Sargent, N. (1990). "Law, Ideology and Social Change: An Analysis of the Role of Law in the Construction of Corporate Crime." *The Journal of Human Justice*, 1(2):97-116.

Sargent, N. (1989). "Law, Ideology and Corporate Crime: A Critique of Instrumentalism." *Canadian Journal of Law and Society*, 4:39-65.

Sassen, S. (1996). *Globalization and Its Discontents: Essays on the New Mobility of People and Money*. NY: The New Press.

Savelsberg, J.J. (1994). *Constructing White-Collar Crime. Rationalities, Communication, Power*. Philadelphia, PA: University of Pennsylvania Press.

Sawyer, M. (1992). "Industry." In M.J. Artis (ed.) *Prest and Coppock's UK Economy*. London, UK: Weidenfield and Nicolson.

Sayer, A. (1995). *Radical Political Economy. A Critique*. Oxford: Blackwell.

Schlegel, K. and D. Weisburd (eds.) (1992). *White-Collar Crime Reconsidered*. Boston, MA: Northeastern University Press.

Schoepf, B G., C. Schoepf, and J.V. Millen (2000). "Theoretical Therapies, Remote Remedies: SAPs and the Political Ecology of Poverty and Health in Africa." In J. Yong Kim, J.V. Millen, A. Irwin and J. Gershman (eds.) *Dying for Growth: Global Inequality and the Health of the Poor*, pp. 91-125. Monroe, ME: Common Courage Press.

Schraeger, L. and J. Short, Jr. (1978). "Toward a Sociology of Organizational Crime." *Social Problems,* 25:407-419.

Seager, J. (1993). *Earth Follies: Coming to Feminist Terms with the Global Environmental Crisis*. New York, NY: Routledge.

Sears, A. and C. Morera (1994). "The Politics of Hegemony: Democracy, Class Struggle and Social Movements." *Transformations,* I.

Seely, R. (1991). "Northern Officials Give State Poor Grades." *Wisconsin State Journal*, (March 24):13A.

"Senate Permanent Subcommittee on Investigations, Committee on Governmental Affairs." (1983). 98th Congress, First Session, August 3.

Shapiro, S. (1990). "Collaring the Crime, Not the Criminal: Reconsidering the Concept of White-Collar Crime." *American Sociological Review,* 55:346-355.

Shavelson, L. (1988). "Tales of Troubled Waters." *Hippocrates,* (March/April):70-77.

Shenon, P. (1998). "For Asian Nation's First Family, Financial Empire Is in Peril." *The New York Times*, (January 16):Al.

Shiva, V. (1997). *Biopiracy: The Plunder of Nature and Knowledge*. Boston, MA: South End.

Sim, J. (forthcoming). "One Thousand Days of Degradation: New Labor and Old Compromises at the Turn of the Century." *Social Justice*.

Simon, D. (1999). *Elite Deviance*, Sixth Edition. Boston, MA: Allyn and Bacon.

Simon, D.R. (1995). *Social Problems: The Sociological Imagination*. New York, NY: McGraw-Hill.

Simon, D.R. (1993). "Criminology & The Kennedy Assassination," *Quarterly Journal of Ideology,* (Autumn):15-26.

Simon, D.R. (1992). "Watergate and The Nixon Presidency: A Comparative Ideological Analysis." In L. Friedman and W.F. Levantrouser (eds.) *Watergate and Afterward: The Legacy of Richard M. Nixon,* pp. 5-22. Westport, CT: Greenwood Press.

Simon, D.R. and D.S. Eitzen (1990). *Elite Deviance.* Boston, MA: Allyn and Bacon.

Simon, D. and S. Eitzen (1982). *Elite Deviance.* Boston, MA: Allyn and Bacon.

Simpson, S.S. (1986). "The Decomposition of Antitrust: Testing a Multi-Level, Longitudinal Level of Profit Squeeze." *American Sociological Review,* 51:859-875.

Singh, A. (1999). " 'Asian Capitalism' and the Financial Crisis." In J. Michie and J. Grieve Smith (eds.) *Global Instability*, 9-36.

Sivanandan, A. (1998/99). "Globalism and the Left." *Race & Class,* 40(2/3):5-19.

Slapper, G. and S. Tombs (1999). *Corporate Crime.* Dorset: Longman Criminology Series.

Smith, P. (1997). *Millennial Dreams. Contemporary Culture and Capital in the North.* London, UK: Verso.

Snider, L. (2000). "The Sociology of Corporate Crime: An Obituary." (Or: Whose Knowledge Claims Have Legs?). *Theoretical Criminology,* 4(2):169-206.

Snider, L. (1993): *Bad Business: Corporate Crime in Canada.* Toronto, CN: University of Toronto Press.

Snider, L. (1991). "The Regulatory Dance: Understanding Reform Processes in Corporate Crime." *International Journal of the Sociology of Law,* 19:209-236.

Snider, L. (1990). "Co-Operative Models and Corporate Crime: Panacea or Cop-Out?" *Crime & Delinquency,* 36(2):373-90.

Snider, L. (1982). "Traditional and Corporate Theft: A Comparison of Sanctions." In P. Wickman and T. Dailey (eds.) *White-Collar and Economic Crime*, pp. 235-258. Lexington, MA: Lexington.

Soros, G. (1998). *The Crisis of Global Capitalism. Open Society Endangered.* London, UK: Little, Brown and Company.

Spitzer, S. (1975). "Toward a Marxian Theory of Deviance." *Social Problems*, 22: 641-651.

St. Clair, J. (1999). "Seattle Diary: It's a Gas, Gas, Gas." *New Left Review,* 238(November/December):81-96.

Stallbaumer, L.M. (1999). "Big Business and the Persecution of the Jews: The Flick Concern and the 'Aryanization' of Jewish Property Before the War." *Holocaust and Genocide Studies,* 13:1-27.

Stauber, J. and S. Rampton (1995). *Toxic Sludge Is Good for You: Lies, Damn Lies and the Public Relations Industry.* Monroe, ME: Common Courage.

Staudt, K. and K. Timothy (1997). "Strategies for the Future." In K. Staudt (ed.) *Women, International Development, and Politics: The Bureaucratic Mire*, pp. 333-351. Philadelphia, PA: Temple University Press.

Steady, F.C. (1996). "Gender Equality and Ecosystem Balance: Women and Sustainable Development in Developing Countries." *Race, Class and Gender*, 6(1):13-32.

Steffensmeier, D. (1989). "On the Causes of 'White-Collar Crime': An Assessment of Hirschi and Gottfredson's Claims." *Criminology,* 27:345-358.

Steingraber, S. (1998). *Living Downstream: A Scientist's Personal Investigation of Cancer and the Environment.* New York, NY: Vintage.

Stephen, J.F. (1883). *A History of the Criminal Law of England*. London, UK: Macmillan.

Stone, C. (1975). *Where the Law Ends: The Social Control of Corporate Behavior.* New York, NY: Harper Colophon Books.

Stone, R. (1992). "A Biopesticidal Tree Begins to Blossom." *Science*, 28(February):1070.

Strange, S. (1994). "Wake Up, Krasner! The World Has Changed." *Review of International Political Economy*, (2)(Summer):1.

Stretesky, P. (1998). "Testing a Broader Model of Environmental Justice." *Social Pathology*, 4(2):73-86.

Stretesky, P. (1997). "Waste Wars: Hazardous Waste, Environmental Justice and Race: The Case in Florida." Ph.D. Dissertation. Florida State University. Dissertation Abstracts International, 58-07A, 2863.

Stretesky, P. and M. Hogan (1998). "Environmental Justice: An Analysis of Superfund Sites in Florida." *Social Problems*, 45(2):268-287.

Stretesky, P. and M. Lynch (1999). "Environmental Justice and Prediction of Distance to Accidental Chemical Releases in Hillsborough County, Florida." *Social Science Quarterly*, 80(4):830-846.

Sutherland, E. (1949). *White Collar Crime*. New York, NY: Holt, Rinehart and Winston.

Sutherland, E.H. (1956). "Crimes of Corporations." In A. Cohen, A. Lindesmith and K. Schuessler (eds.) *The Sutherland Papers*, pp. 78-96. Bloomington, IN: Indiana University Press.

Sutherland, E.H. (1949). *White Collar Crime*. New York, NY: Dryden.

Sutherland, E.H. (1940). "White-Collar Criminality." *American Sociological Review,* 5:1-12.

Swigert, V. (1984). "Public-Order Crime." In R. Meier (ed.) *Major Forms of Crime*, pp. 95-117. Beverly Hills, CA: Age.

Szyajkowski, E. (1985). "Organizational Illegality: Theoretical Integration and Illustrative Application." *Academy of Management Review,* 10:558-567.

Talvela, T. (1998). "Joitakin havaintoja Taloudellisen Rikollisuuden kontrollin ongelmista."(Some Discoveries on the Problems of Controlling Economic Crime). In A. Alvesalo (ed.) *Kirjoituksia talousrikollisuudesta I.* (Esseys on Economic Crime I), pp. 133-152. Poliisiammattikorkeakoulun tiedotteita 1/1998, Helsinki, Edita.

Tang, S. (1996). "Official Corruption in a Developing Economy: The Case of The People's Republic of China." *Humanity ~ Society,* 20: 58-71.

Taylor, I., P. Walton, and J. Young (1973). *The New Criminology: For A Social Theory of Deviance*. New York, NY: Harper, Colphon.

Theobald, R. (1990). *Corruption, Development and Underdevelopment*. Durham, NC: Duke University Press.

Therborn, G. (1986). *Why Some Peoples Are More Unemployed Than Others*. London, UK: Verso.

Thompson, Bankole (1999). *The Criminal Law of Sierra Leone*. Lanham, MD: University Press of America Inc.

Tillman, R. and H. Pontell (1995). "Organization and Fraud in the Savings and Loan Industry." *Social Forces,* 73:1439-1463.

Tomasevski, K. (1993). *Women and Human Rights*. London, UK: Zed.

Tombs, S. (1998). "Tony Prosser: Law and the Regulators; Julie Black: Rules and Regulators." *Journal of Law and Society,* 25(3)(September):452-460.

Tombs, S. (1990). "Industrial Injuries in British Manufacturing." *Sociological Review*, 38, 2(May):324-343.

Tombs, S. (1996). "Injury, Death and the Deregulation Fetish: The Politics of Occupational Safety Regulation in UK Manufacturing." *International Journal of Health Services,* 26(2).

Tombs, S. (1995). "Law, Resistance and Reform: "Regulating" Safety Crimes in the UK." *Social & Legal Studies,* 4(3).

Tonry, M. and A. Reiss, Jr. (1993). *Beyond the Law: Crime in Complex Organizations*. Chicago, IL: The University of Chicago Press.

Tran, M. (1996). "UNCTAD Changes Corporate Tune." *The Guardian*, May 20.

Träskman, P.O. (1987). *Taloudellinen Rikollisuus Tutkimuksen Kohteena*. (Economic Crime as an Object of Research) Oikeus, 2:122-133.

Treanor, J. (1999). "Making a Fortune out of Scraps." *The Guardian*, (August 19):23.

Truell, P. and L. Gurwin (1992). *False Profits: The Inside Story of BCCI, the World's Most Corrupt Financial Empire*. New York, NY: Houghton Mifflin.

Turner, H. (1969). "Big Business and the Rise of Hitler." *American Historical Review,* 75:56-70.

U.W. Greens Northwoods Taskforce (n.d.). *Rio Tinto Zinc in Ladysmith and Prospects for Plunder in the Northwoods*. Pamphlet.

U.S. News & World Report (1982). "Corporate Crime: The Untold Story." (September 6):25.

United Church of Christ, Commission for Racial Justice (1987). *Toxic Wastes and Race in the United States: A National Report on the Racial and Socioeconomic Characteristics of Communities with Hazardous Waste Sites*. New York, NY: United Church of Christ.

United Nations Development Programme (1998). *Human Development Report 1998*, http:www.undp.org/ undp/hdro/e98over.htm

United Nations Development Programme (1996). *Human Development Report*, 1996. New York, NY: Oxford University Press.

Valaskakis, K. (1999). "Globalization as Theatre." *International Social Science Journal,* 160:153.

Vaughan, D. (1996). "The Challenger Launch Decision: Risky Technology, Culture and Deviance at the NASA." Chicago, IL: University of Chicago Press.

Vaughan, D. (1996). *The Challenger Launch Decision: Risky Technology, Culture, and Deviance at NASA*. Chicago, IL: University of Chicago Press.

Vogel, S. (1996). *Freer Markets, More Rules: Regulatory Reform in Advanced Industrial Countries*. Ithaca, NY: Cornell University Press.

Wade, R. (1996). "Japan, the World Bank, and the Art of Paradigm Maintenance: The East Asian Miracle in Political Perspective." *New Left Review,* 217 (May/June).

Wade, R. and F. Veneroso (1998). "The Asian Crisis: The High Debt Model Versus the Wall Street-Treasury-IMF Complex." *New Left Review,* 228, (March/April):3-23.

Wade, R. and F. Veneroso (1998). "The Gathering World Slump and the Battle Over Capital Controls." *New Left Review,* 231(September/October):13-42.

Wald, M. (1999). "Murder Charges Filed by Florida in ValuJet Crash." *The New York Times*, (July 14):A1.

Wallach, L. and M. Sforza (1999). *The WTO: Five Reasons to Resist Corporate Globalization.* New York, NY: Seven Stories Press.

Ward, P. (ed.) (1987). *Corruption, Development and Inequality.* London, UK: Routledge.

Wardynski, J. (1999). "Environmental Justice Case Study: Shintech PVC Plant in Convent, Louisiana." [On-line]. Available: http://www.umich.edu/~snre492/shin.html

Waring, M. (1988). *If Women Counted: A New Feminist Perspective.* New York, NY: Harper Collins.

Waters, M. (1995). *Globalization.* London, UK: Routledge.

Watts, J. and J. Treanor (1999). "Merger Mania Hits Japan." *The Guardian*, (August 21):28.

Weinberg, S. (1990) "The Mob, the CIA, and the S&L Scandal: Does Pete Brewton's Story Check Out?" *Columbia Journalism Review*, (November/December):33-36.

Weinstein, J. (1968). *The Corporate Ideal in the Liberal State: 1900-1918.* Boston, MA: Beacon Press.

Weisburd, D., E. Waring, and E. Chayet (1995). "Specific Deterrence in a Sample of Offenders Convicted of White-Collar Crime." *Criminology,* 33:587-607.

Weisburd, D., S. Wheeler, E. Waring, and N. Bode (1991). *Crimes of the Middle Class: White-Collar Offending in the Federal Courts.* New Haven, CT: Yale University Press.

Weiss, L. and J.M. Hobson (1995). *States and Economic Development.* Cambridge, UK: Polity.

Weiss, L. (1999). "Managed Openness: Beyond Neoliberal Globalism." *New Left Review,* 238(November/December):126-140.

Weiss, L. (1998). *The Myth of the Powerless State.* Cambridge, UK: Polity.

Weiss, L. (1997). "Globalization and the Myth of the Powerless State." *New Left Review,* 225(September/October):3-27.

Wellford, H. (1972). *Sowing the Wind: A Report from Ralph Nader's Center for Study of Responsive Law.* New York, NY: Grossman.

Wheeler, S. (1993). "The Prospects for Large-Scale Collaborative Research: Reviewing the Yale White-Collar Crime Research Program." *Law and Social Inquiry,* 18:101-113.

Wheeler, S., D. Weisburd, and N. Bode (1982). "Sentencing the White-Collar Offender: Rhetoric and Reality." *American Sociological Review,* 47:641-659.

Whitfield, D. (1992). *The Welfare State.* London, UK: Pluto Press.

Whyte, D. (forthcoming). "Learning the Lessons of Piper Alpha? Offshore workers' Perceptions of Changing Levels of Risk." In E. Coles, D. Smith, and S. Tombs (eds.) *Risk Management and Society.* Amsterdam: Kluwer-Nijhoff.

Whyte, D. (1999). "Power, Ideology and the Regulation of Safety in the Post-Piper Offshore Oil Industry." Unpublished Ph.D. Dissertation. Liverpool John Moores University.

Whyte, D. and S. Tombs (1998). "Capital Fights Back: Risk, Regulation and Profit in the UK Offshore Oil Industry." *Studies in Political Economy,* 57(September):73-101.

Wickman, P. and P. Whitten (1980). *Criminology: Perspectives on Crime and Criminality*. Lexington, MA: D.C. Heath.

Williams, H.E. (1997). *Investigating White Collar Crime. Embezzlement and Financial Fraud*. Illinois: Charles C Thomas Publisher Ltd.

Williams, R. (1987). *Political Corruption in Africa*. Aldershot, UK: Gower Publishing Co.

Wilson, G. (2000). "Business, State and Community: "Responsible Risk Takers," New Labor, and the Governance of Corporate Business." *Journal of Law and Society,* 27(1):151-77.

Wilson, W.J. (1992). "Another Look at the Truly Disadvantaged." *Political Science Quarterly,* 106.

Wilson, J.Q. and R.R. Herrnstein (1985). *Crime and Human Nature*. New York, NY: Simon and Schuster.

Wilson, J.Q. (1975). *Thinking About Crime*. New York, NY: Basic Books.

Winslow, A. (1995). *Women, Politics, and the United Nations*. Westport, CT: Greenwood Press.

Wonders, N. and R.J. Michalowski (1999). "Bodies, Borders, and Sex Tourism in a Globalized World: A Tale of Two Global Cities – Amsterdam and Havana." Paper presented at the annual meeting of the American Sociological Association, Chicago, Illinois.

Woodiwiss, A. (1996). "Searching for Signs of Globalization." *Sociology,* 30(4):799-810.

World Bank (1994). *Averting the Age Old Crisis. Policies to Protect the Old and Promote Growth*. Oxford, UK: Oxford University Press.

Wright, J., F. Cullen, and M. Blankenship (1995). "The Social Construction of Corporate Violence: Media Coverage of the Imperial Food Products Fire." *Crime & Delinquency,* 41:20-36.

Yandle, T. and D. Burton (1996). "Reexamining Environmental Justice: A Statistical Analysis of Historical Hazardous Waste Landfill Siting Patterns in Metropolitan Texas." *Social Science Quarterly,* 77(3):477-492.

Yeager, P. (1991). *The Limits of the Law: The Public Regulation of Private Pollution*. Cambridge: Cambridge University Press.

Young, T. (1995). "'A Project to Be Realised': Global Liberalism and Contemporary Africa." *Millennium,* 24(3).

Young, G., L. Fort, and M. Danner (1994). "Moving from 'The Status of Women' to 'Gender Inequality': Conceptualization, Social Indicators and an Empirical Application." *International Sociology,* 9:55-85.

Zeitlin, M. (1989). *The Large Corporation and Contemporary Classes*. New Brunswick, NJ: Rutgers University Press.

Ziegler, J. (1977). *The Swiss, the Gold, and the Dead: How Swiss Bankers Helped Finance the Nazi War Machine*. New York, NY: Harcourt Brace & Co.

Zimmerman, R. (1993). "Social Equity and Environmental Risk." *Risk Analysis,* 13(4):649-666.

Index

A

Abandoned waste sites, 125-126
Abbott Laboratories, 8
Abedi, Hasan Agha, 61
Academic deviance, 73
  analysis and conclusion, 81-83
  nature and scope of, 76
  normative framework of academia, 76-81
  problems, kinds of, 74-75
  when it occurs, 78
Academic freedom, 78
Accident Release Information, 118
Accidental chemical releases (ACRs), 118,
  126-127
Acton, Lord, 39
Adolph Coors Company, 20
AEG-Telefunken, 58
Aerojet-General Corporation, 27
Afghanistan, 180
"Age of access," 167
"Agency capture," 62
Agenda 21, 178-179
Agent Orange, 138
Agnew, Spiro, 39
Agribusiness, 174
Al-Nahyan, Sheik, 61
Alamo, Tony, Televangelist, 13
ALCOA, 21
Allende, Salvadore, 60
Allied Clinical Laboratories, 16
Alumax Entrusions Inc., 115
Alvesalo, Anne, 149-164
American Cynamid, 21
American presidents lying about the CIA,
  139
American Steel, 6
Ames, Oakes, 58
Amoco Minerals, 92
Anglo-Saxon political economies, 206
Anomie theory, 43

Anthropomorphic conception of justice,
  77-78
Antitrust. *See* Trust and antitrust
Aramony, William, 13
Archer Daniels Midland (ADM), 14, 26
ArcView, 118
Arizona Chemical Company, 19
Army Chemical Corps, 139
Arousal of fear, 4-9
"Aryanization" process, 58-59
Asbestos industry, 6-7
Asian tigers, 188
Autobiography of a White Collar Worker,
  42
Autonomy, professional, 78-79
Avocational crime, 54

B

Banca Lavoro (BNL) Affair, 142-144
Bank for International Resettlement, 200
Bank fraud, 15-16
Bank of Credit and Commerce
  International, 15
Bartell, Angela, Judge, 100
Bateson, William, 94
Baxter International, 11
Bayer AG, 14
BCCI (Bank of Commerce and Credit Inter-
  national), 15-16, 61, 144
Bebe, Herman, 144
Beech-Nut Nutrition Corporation, 7
Bell, Daniel, 43-44
Bethlehem Steel, 20
Bethship-Sabine Yard, 20
BHP-Utah, 92
Biennial Reporting System (BRS), 114-115
Blair, Tony, Prime Minister, 187, 200-201,
  207, 208
Blue Cross/Blue Shield of Illinois, 16
Blue Shield of California, 16

253